D0923234

INTERNAL REFLECTION SPECTROSCOPY

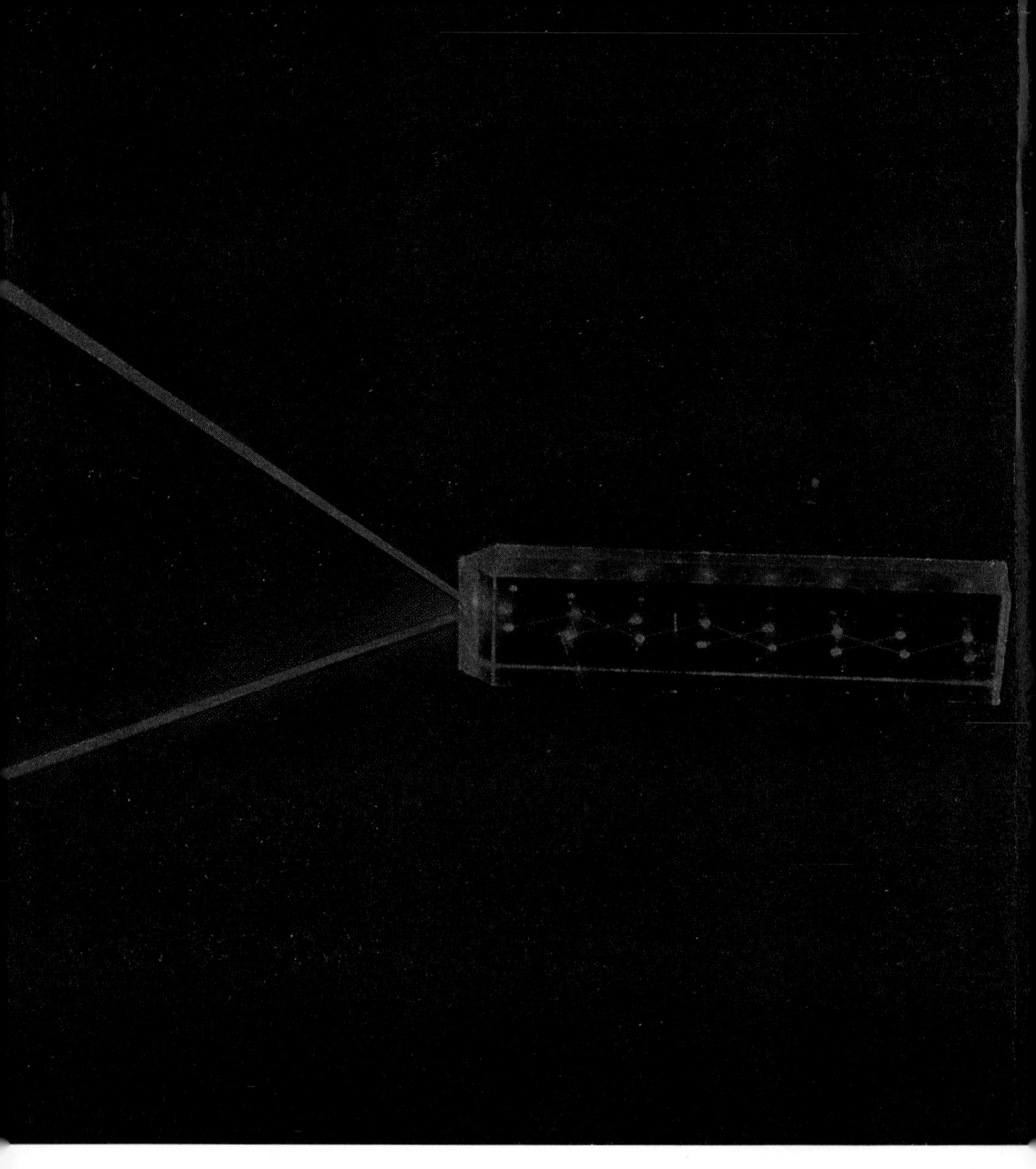

A laser beam path inside and outside an internal reflection element, photographed by the author. Used as a cover illustration for *Applied Optics,* January 1966 and reproduced by permission.

INTERNAL REFLECTION SPECTROSCOPY

N. J. Harrick
Philips Laboratories,
Briarcliff Manor, New York

Interscience Publishers
a division of John Wiley & Sons
New York • London • Sydney

Library of Congress Catalog Number 67-13944
Printed in the United States of America

PREFACE

In his studies of the total reflection of light at the interface between two media of different refractive indices Newton discovered, more than 250 years ago, that an evanescent wave extends in the rarer medium beyond the reflecting interface. This phenomenon has been subsequently studied in great detail and has found many applications. Since 1959 still another application was developed when it was pointed out that optical absorption spectra could conveniently be obtained by a measure of the interaction of the evanescent wave with the external medium. Furthermore, this method could be employed in some cases in which conventional techniques either required extensive sample preparation or failed. Examples of these are the recording of spectra of powdered materials and of monomolecular films, respectively. This method of obtaining spectra has found numerous applications and has developed into a distinct branch of spectroscopy called Internal Reflection Spectroscopy.

The purposes of this book are to systematically describe and discuss theory, instrumentation, and applications of internal reflection spectroscopy and to provide the necessary background for the practical spectroscopist to enable him to apply the method to his own problems. The information presented here was selected from both previously published and unpublished data. The fundamentals of general optical spectroscopy, which are well treated in a number of books on this subject and listed in the bibliography, are not covered.

Chapter I provides a brief historical introduction which describes the development of internal reflection spectroscopy.

An attempt has been made to treat the fundamentals in Chapter II from a point of view which would give the practical spectroscopist physical insight into the nature of the interaction mechanisms for both non-absorbing and absorbing media rather than to provide a rigorous treatment which can be found in published books and papers. For instance, the standing electromagnetic fields developed near the totally reflecting interface are calculated for non-absorbing media. The interaction of this evanescent field with weakly absorbing media can then be described in terms of an "effective thickness" which is the sample thickness that would be required in transmission spectroscopy to yield spectra of comparable contrast. The dependence of this effective thickness on angle of incidence and refractive indices is shown by simple equations which are valid for many applications. This understanding enables the spectroscopist to optimize the technique for each application by enabling him to judge beforehand what polarization, refractive index, and angle of incidence to choose for the internal reflection element without having to rely on laborious calculations. This knowledge also enables him to judge where this technique should *not* be employed. We have found this "low absorption approximation" extremely helpful in these respects.

Chapter III considers the effect of the dispersion in the refractive index near an absorption band on the nature of the spectra for bulk materials and thin films. An understanding of this is helpful in the interpretation of the change in the character of the spectra with change in angle of incidence, although it is not essential in the application of internal reflection spectroscopy.

Chapter IV is devoted to a treatment of "internal reflection elements," i.e., the transparent optical elements used for establishing the conditions necessary to obtain internal reflection spectra of materials. The design of the internal reflection element determines the ease with which internal reflection techniques can be effectively employed. The requirements on length, thickness, aperture, surface preparation, and materials are discussed. A number of the geometrical requirements mentioned may appear obvious; however, neglect of these in some instances has led to poor performance. Various types of internal reflection elements are discussed and suggested applications, e.g., to solids, to liquids, to thin films, and to the detection of minute quantities, are given.

In Chapter V it is shown that enhanced absorptions can be obtained with certain more complicated internal reflection elements. In these "optical cavities," consisting of thin film resonant structures, intense electromagnetic fields can be obtained and enhancement of absorption over that obtainable via a single reflection by an order of magnitude or more can be realized.

A number of optical layouts for use with internal reflection elements as well as special instrumentation and techniques are described in Chapter VI.

The final chapter deals with applications of internal reflection spectroscopy. The examples given for some areas represent the present "state-of-the-art" and other examples will be available in the future. The infrared spectral region is emphasized although some examples are given on the application to the potentially equally important ultraviolet and visible regions. Unique applications resulting from the ease of sample handling and from the ability to record the spectra of monomolecular films are described. The spectra of fibers and powders, for example, can be recorded with no sample preparation. The applicability to monomolecular films is indicated in areas such as the study of electrode reactions, catalysis, adsorbed species, and medical and biological problems and should be of considerable interest in the future. Another area of fundamental interest where internal reflection was found to have advantages over conventional techniques is the measurement of optical constants.

The bibliography provides about 450 references, some of which were taken from a list kindly provided by Dr. T. Hirschfeld of Falcultad De Quimica, Montevideo, Uruguay. An attempt was made to include all the literature on internal reflection spectroscopy available at the time the manuscript was delivered to the printer.

The results of many workers who have contributed to the field of internal reflection spectroscopy are discussed in this book. I was fortunate to have the cooperation of a number of these workers in supplying me with unpublished data as acknowledged in the text. The bulk of the material, however, is the result of some of the author's work at Philips Laboratories during the last ten years, parts of which have not been previously published. I wish to express my gratitude to Dr. J. A. Hipple, Director of Philips Laboratories, for encouragement during the course of this work and for permission to publish this book. Throughout this entire period the assistance of many people at Philips Laboratories has been invaluable; of these, Dr. F. K. du Pré has been especially helpful. He has generously found the time to discuss new ideas and results and has been particularly helpful with mathematical computations. Thanks are also due to Mr. J. L. Teekle for the cooperative and competent assistance in carrying out many of the experiments and to Miss H. P. Goodman for help with many of the illustrations. The burden of the task was made lighter by the conscientious and cheerful assistance of Mrs. E. E. Martinson with the typing, organization of illustrations and references, and attention to numerous other details.

During the preparation of this book I have benefited from the comments and advice of a number of colleagues and friends who graciously consented to read early versions of the manuscript. These include Dr. R. W. Hannah of Perkin-Elmer Corp., Norwalk, Connecticut, Prof. E. R. Lippincott of the University of Maryland, College Park, Maryland, and Dr. F. K. du Pré and Dr. R. S. Levitt, both of Philips Laboratories. The latter two reviewers, in fact, critically read the manuscript at two stages of completion.

N. J. Harrick

Briarcliff Manor
New York
February 1967

CONTENTS

CHAPTER ONE

INTRODUCTION

> The Rays of Light in going out of Glass into a Vacuum, are bent towards the Glass; and if they fall too obliquely on the Vacuum, they are bent backwards into the Glass, and totally reflected; and this Reflexion cannot be ascribed to the Resistance of an absolute Vacuum, but must be caused by the Power of the Glass attracting the Rays at their going out of it into the Vacuum, and bringing them back. For if the farther Surface of the Glass be moisten'd with Water or clear Oil, or liquid and clear Honey, the Rays which would otherwise be reflected will go into the Water, Oil, or Honey; and therefore are not reflected before they arrive at the farther Surface of the Glass, and begin to go out of it. If they go out of it into the Water, Oil, or Honey, they go on, because the Attraction of the Glass is almost balanced and rendered ineffectual by the contrary Attraction of the Liquor. But if they go out of it into a Vacuum which has no Attraction to balance that of the Glass, the Attraction of the Glass either bends and refracts them, or brings them back and reflects them. And this is still more evident by laying together two Prisms of Glass, or two Object-glasses of very long Telescopes, the one plane, the other a little convex, and so compressing them that they do not fully touch, nor are too far asunder. For the Light which falls upon the farther Surface of the first Glass where the Interval between the Glasses is not above the ten hundred thousandth Part of an Inch, will go through that Surface, and through the Air or Vacuum between the Glasses, and enter into the second Glass, as was explain'd in the first, fourth, and eighth Observations of the first Part of the second Book. But, if the second Glass be taken away, the Light which goes out of the second Surface of the first Glass into the Air or Vacuum, will not go on forwards, but turns back into the first Glass, and is reflected; and therefore it is drawn back by the Power of the first glass, there being nothing else to turn it back.
>
> —NEWTON, *Opticks*.*

Total internal reflection (TIR) is a familiar phenomenon. It can be observed with a glass of water, for example. If the side of the glass below the water level is viewed obliquely through the water surface, it appears to be completely silvered and one can no longer see objects behind it. The reason for this is that light striking the glass surface is totally reflected and therefore does not pass through the surface to illuminate these objects. Newton (N4) observed that total reflection can be destroyed; i.e., reflection is made less

* 2nd (English) ed., 1717, book III, part 1, query 29.

than total, not only when a suitable object is brought into contact with the reflecting surface, but also when the object is brought sufficiently close to this reflecting surface. This is also easily demonstrated with the aid of the glass of water; for if one looks at one's fingers touching the glass, the skin patterns are clearly evident which indicates that total reflection has been destroyed where contact is made, viz., at the ridges of the skin but not at the valleys of the skin where no contact is made. This clarity is explained by the penetration of the electromagnetic field into the rarer medium a fraction of a wavelength beyond the reflecting surface and that when a suitable object is brought near enough to the surface to interact with this penetrating field, total reflection is destroyed. Although electromagnetic theory and total internal reflection have been studied in great detail since the time of Newton, as recently as 1947 a new phenomenon (G13,G14) associated with total internal reflection was discovered. Goos and Hänchen showed that there is a slight displacement of a light beam upon reflection. The path of the light in the vicinity of the reflecting interface may thus conveniently be represented by a penetration and displacement as shown in Fig. 1. It is interesting to note that Newton's ideas included such a displacement, since he suggested (N4) that the path of the ray was a "parabola with the vertex in the rarer medium."

A very common reaction to the penetration of the light into the rarer medium and to the picture shown in Fig. 1 is: "Why does the light return if it has escaped the denser medium?" Newton's explanation was that the light is attracted back by the denser medium. We now know that this explanation

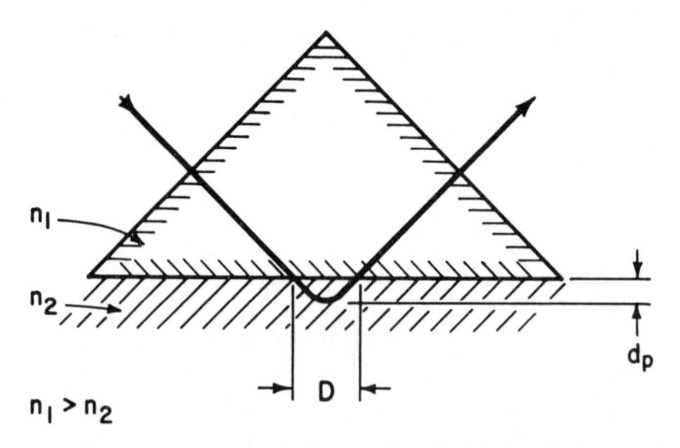

Fig. 1. Schematic representation of path of a ray of light for total internal reflection. The ray penetrates a fraction of a wavelength (d_p) beyond the reflecting surface into the rarer medium of refractive index n_2 and there is a certain displacement (D) upon reflection.

and picture, although convenient, are incorrect since the light is not propagated in the manner shown. There is, in fact, no propagation perpendicular to the surface except very near the edges of the beam. Instead, a standing wave (H30) normal to the reflecting surface is established in the denser medium and there is an evanescent, nonpropagating field in the rarer medium whose electric-field amplitude decays exponentially with distance from the surface.

Many elegant experiments have been performed to demonstrate the presence of the evanescent wave. Newton observed its presence since, as described in the introductory quotation, he points out that the lens need not make actual contact with the prism for the light to pass through. The presence of this evanescent wave can also be demonstrated by totally reflecting light from an interface between glass and water containing fluorescein (S12,W12). It will be seen that if light is directed through the glass towards this interface and is totally reflected, only a thin sheet of the liquid adjacent to the prism fluoresces, whereas the rest of the liquid remains dark. If a razor blade is brought near a totally reflecting surface, the edge of the blade will become illuminated before contact is made. More experiments of this nature will be described in the next chapter, in which the characteristics of total internal reflection will be discussed in detail.

The unusual characteristics associated with total internal reflection can be utilized with advantage in many areas. These applications include precision measurements of angles (L5) and refractive indices (T1,T2,T3,J2,J3,L5b); the construction of beam splitters (H25), optical filters (L4,T5,T6,B19,B20,B21, P18,G3), laser cavities (S30), light modulators (A7,A18), light deflectors (C5), cold mirrors (P15); and the measurement of film thicknesses and surface reliefs (Y1,Y2,H24,H27,M12,M14). How total internal reflection can be employed for these purposes will be explained in the next chapter. As a specific example, the application of total internal reflection to fingerprinting (H27), i.e., the measurement of surface reliefs, will be briefly described.

There is little point in taking a direct photograph of one's finger to record the fingerprint because, as can be seen by looking at a finger, there is little contrast between the hills and the valleys. It was already pointed out that if one looks at one's finger in contact with a glass of water, a high contrast image of the skin pattern can be seen. The reason for this is (as was previously stated) that the reflection is destroyed at the points of contact (ridges of the skin) but not at the valleys. A very simple instrument, consisting of a light source, prism, and camera (such as that shown in Fig. 2), can be constructed to record high contrast images of surface reliefs such as fingerprints. A fingerprint recorded in this way is shown in Fig. 3. The clarity of the

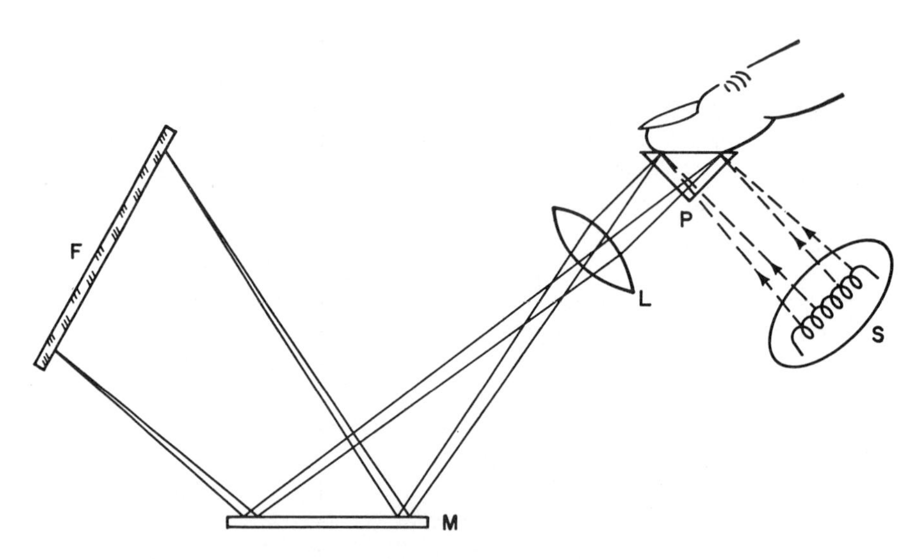

Fig. 2. Schematic diagram of inkless fingerprint recording instrument. The finger is pressed against the hypotenuse of the prism (*P*) illuminated by the light source (*S*) and imaged onto the screen or photofilm (*F*) by the lens (*L*) and mirror (*M*). Total reflection is destroyed only where contact is made between the skin and the prism, i.e., at the ridges but not at the valleys, and thus a high contrast image of surface reliefs is obtained.

details is remarkable. The minutiae are clearly evident; the dots in the figure are pores in the ridges of the skin. This technique has recently been successfully employed to record prints of newborn infants in cases in which the age-old ink techniques could not be used because of poor resolution and smudging, with the resulting loss of detail. The nature of skin pattern in human beings is apparently affected by chromosome abnormalities (P5), which in turn are responsible for mongolism, Turner's syndrome, etc. Viral attacks during early stages of pregnancy (e.g., German measles) also affect skin patterns (A4,A4a). From a study of the handprints, such as that of the abnormal infant's print, using the new technique (shown in Fig. 4), it may be possible to diagnose these conditions.

There are thus many general and specific applications of total internal reflection. This book, however, is concerned mainly with still another application of internal reflection, viz., to optical spectroscopy. This application of internal reflection to optical spectroscopy is a new technique which is called internal reflection spectroscopy (IRS).

Conventional optical spectroscopy, particularly in the infrared region—the so-called "fingerprint" region because the vibrational and rotational bands

Fig. 3. Typical adult fingerprint which was recorded using the instrument shown in Fig. 2. The dark lines are the ridges in the skin pattern and the dots are the pores in the ridges.

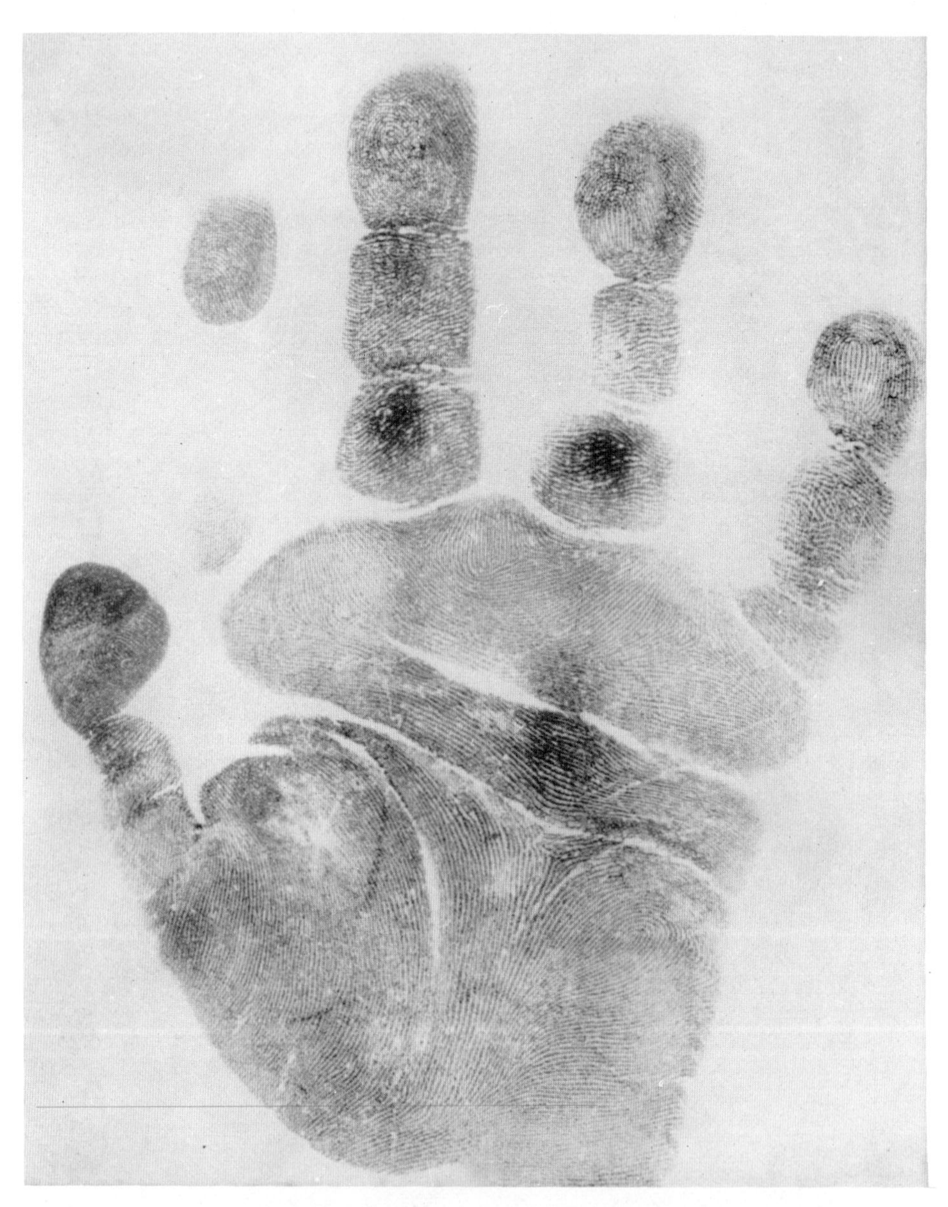

Fig. 4. Inkless handprint of abnormal infant. A simian line and high triradius are clearly evident. The same details as those appearing in Fig. 3 are visible when greater magnification is used. Prints such as these were used by Dr. R. Achs et al. (A4,A4a) to establish that dermatoglyphic irregularities can be caused by viral attacks during early stages of pregnancy. (Courtesy of Dr. Ruth Achs, Downstate Medical Center, Brooklyn, New York.)

are found there—is one of the powerful analytical tools in use today (B13, B35,C8,P22,R5). In the usual technique, shown in Fig. 5a, a light beam is passed through a certain thickness of sample material, and the transmission is measured as a function of wavelength which yields characteristic spectra of the type shown in Fig. 5c. Such spectra have become very useful for identification purposes principally because of the general knowledge in this field. It will become evident in Chapter Three that these spectra do not closely resemble either of the optical constants of the material, the index of refraction, or the attenuation index, but instead are some complicated composite. This is not a serious disadvantage because the spectra are quite reproducible and entire libraries of spectra are available for comparison purposes. Furthermore, workers in the field have considerable experience in interpretation and identification of such spectra.

Internal reflection spectroscopy is the technique of recording the optical spectrum of a sample material that is in contact with an optically denser but transparent medium and then measuring the wavelength dependence of the *reflectivity* of this interface by introducing light into the denser medium, as shown in Fig. 5b. In this technique the reflectivity is a measure of the interaction of the evanescent wave with the sample material and the resulting spectrum is also a characteristic of the sample material. For most angles of incidence above the critical angle, the reflection spectra resemble transmission spectra fairly closely; however, for angles of incidence just below the critical angle the spectra may resemble the mirror image of the dispersion in the index of refraction. Compared to transmission, there is another parameter in these measurements, viz., angle of incidence, which controls the nature of the spectrum and which can be a powerful weapon if used properly. Since this technique complements conventional optical absorption techniques and can be used in some instances wherein conventional techniques cannot readily be applied, the areas of application of optical spectroscopy are thus extended. The technique was initially proposed and developed simultaneously and independently at the Dutch Shell Laboratories by Fahrenfort and at Philips Laboratories in New York by Harrick for different purposes, but the principles involved are substantially the same.

Fahrenfort (F1,F2) proposed and developed internal reflection spectroscopy utilizing a single reflection for measuring the spectra of bulk materials which could not easily be prepared for conventional measurements. His ideas were inspired by the theoretical calculations of Simon (S22) on a two-angle method of evaluating optical constants. These calculations showed that strong absorptions could be obtained at certain angles of incidence when the refractive index of the sample material was less than unity. Fahrenfort

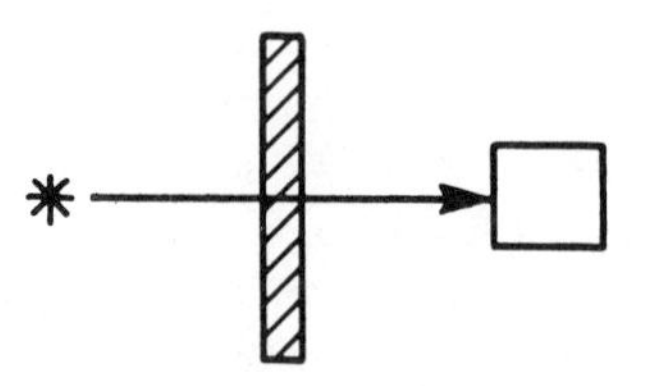

a. TRANSMISSION

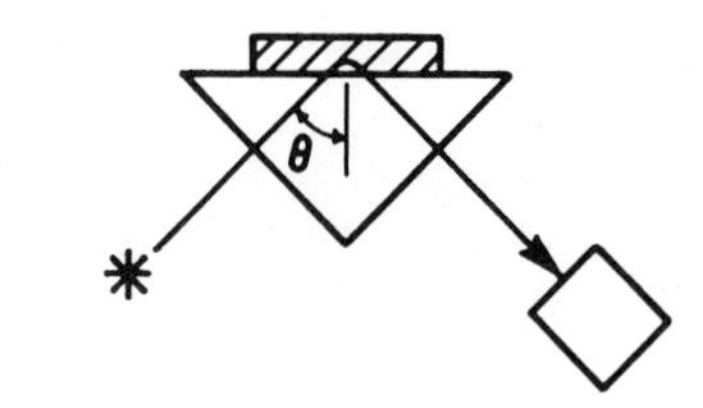

b. INTERNAL REFLECTION

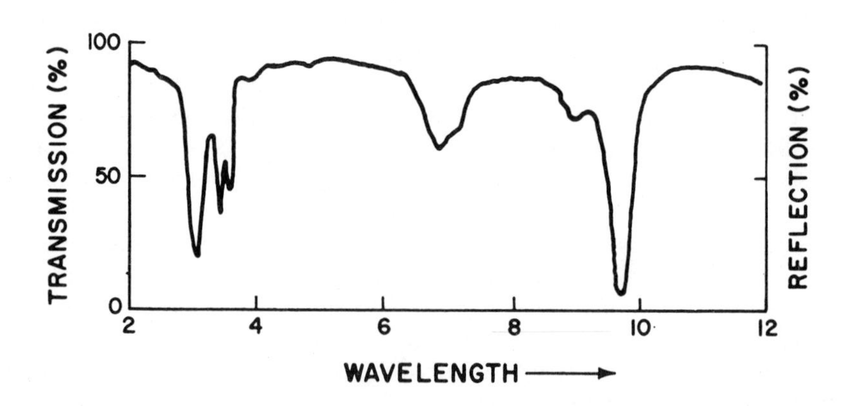

c. OPTICAL SPECTRUM

Fig. 5. Comparison of conventional transmission and internal reflection spectroscopy. In the latter technique, the sample material absorbs energy via interaction with the evanescent wave. Spectra characteristic of the material are obtained via both techniques.

realized that this condition could be achieved for most materials by placing the sample material in contact with an optically transparent material of higher refractive index and working above the critical angle. He then demonstrated that high contrast spectra, i.e., strong absorption bands, could indeed be obtained for certain materials with a single reflection (sampling) and that optical constants could be directly determined using this technique. He later employed this technique using from three to five reflections. [His name for the technique was "Attenuated Total Reflection" (ATR). The term ATR has been redefined by The American Society for Testing and Materials (ASTM) (A19) and given a more restricted usage to describe the effect of a coupling mechanism (see Chapter Two).]

Harrick (H20,H21,H22) proposed and developed internal reflection spectroscopy techniques utilizing multiple reflections, for studying surfaces and thin films. These techniques were the natural outgrowth of his use of multiple internal reflection techniques for the study of contacts (H12,H13, H14,H15,H16,H18) and of the properties of free carriers in semiconductor space charge regions (H15), where multiple reflections were employed to amplify weak absorptions. In some of the earlier work, the evanescent field was a nuisance since it contributed to the reduction in sensitivity of the measurements on semiconductor space charge regions when the semiconductors were placed in contact with metals (H16). This, however, led to a better understanding of the nature of total internal reflection and to the proposal (H20) that the evanescent field might be employed to record spectra of adsorbed molecules. In surface work on adsorbed molecules, over 500 internal reflections have been used in a single analysis and the spectra of monolayer films have been measured. [This technique was called "Frustrated Total Reflection" (FTR) as an extension of FTR already proposed in 1947 by Leurgans and Turner (L4) when they developed the FTR filter. The term FTR is also now being restricted to a description of a coupling mechanism (see Chapter Two) in accordance with the ASTM definitions (A19).]

Internal reflection spectroscopy has been further developed by research groups and instrument companies. Applications to the study of thin films and chemisorbed molecules have been made independently by a number of workers. There are many areas in which monolayer films play an important role, e.g., catalysis, oxidation, electrode reactions, and numerous medical and biological phenomena where internal reflection spectroscopy should be useful. Another important application of internal reflection spectroscopy is to the measurement of optical constants of dielectrics and metals. In recent experiments other possible applications have been demonstrated, such as the possibility of recording the spectra of one-tenth microgram quantities and the

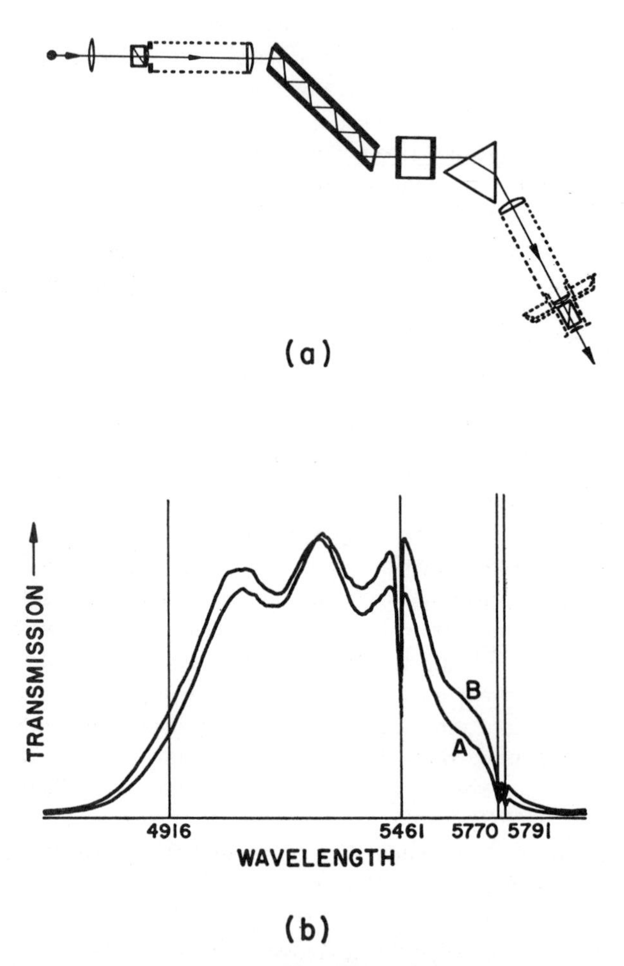

Fig. 6. Two illustrations reproduced from papers on "Studies in Refractive Index" published in the *Journal of the Optical Society of America* in 1933 by A. M. Taylor and coworkers. (a) Experimental arrangement where a ray of light is multiply reflected in a rhombus surrounded by liquid under study. (b) Some experimental results. Curve *A* represents the transmission spectrum of potassium permanganate and curve *B* the reflection spectrum at an angle just greater than the critical angle. The slight displacement and distortion of curve *B* relative to curve *A* is characteristic of internal reflection spectra recorded just above the critical angle. The technique employed in these measurements is similar to that employed in internal reflection spectroscopy.

spectra of powdered samples with no scattering of light. Applications of internal reflection spectroscopy will be covered in detail in Chapter Seven.

Although numerous papers dealing with internal reflection were published prior to 1960, many of which might have triggered off the idea for internal reflection spectroscopy, it was not until the advantages of total reflection for optical spectroscopy were specifically mentioned a few years ago that this technique attracted the attention of other workers and came into general usage. Prior to this, either the time was not ripe for internal reflection spectroscopy, or its advantages and/or applications were not fully appreciated. Perhaps the earliest work that came closest to internal reflection spectroscopy is critical angle refractometry. The same equations are involved in both techniques and similar results are obtained when measuring optical constants. An example of this similarity is demonstrated by the publications of Taylor and co-workers (T1,T2,T3). Figure 6 shows two illustrations published in 1933 in their papers entitled "Studies in Refractive Index." Figure 6a shows the technique employed by them. The similarity in this technique to that employed in internal reflection spectroscopy will become evident in the following chapters. Figure 6b shows the spectra of bulk potassium permanganate recorded by them both via transmission (curve A) and internal reflection (curve B). There is a close resemblance between the two; however, some typical features of internal reflection spectra of bulk materials recorded at angles of incidence just above the critical angle are seen in the slight displacement of the absorption bands to longer wavelengths and the broadening of the bands on the long wavelength side relative to transmission spectra. At larger angles of incidence the internal reflection spectra resemble transmission spectra more closely; although, in general, the bands at longer wavelengths tend to be relatively stronger. All of these and other features of internal reflection spectra can be understood from a consideration of the interaction mechanism of the evanescent wave with the absorbing rarer medium, which will be discussed in the next two chapters.

CHAPTER TWO

PRINCIPLES OF INTERNAL REFLECTION SPECTROSCOPY

A. Introduction

The principles of internal reflection spectroscopy are described in this chapter, first in terms of the classical reflection equations of Fresnel and of Snell's law, however, the same results can be obtained by starting with Maxwell's equations which clearly show the essential presence of the evanescent wave. From this mathematical treatment the dependence of reflection on angle of incidence and polarization is obtained for non-absorbing and absorbing media. The reflection phenomenon is then treated from a physical viewpoint which is valid for low absorptions. This later treatment gives a clear insight into the interaction mechanisms of the evanescent wave with the absorbing rarer medium for bulk materials and thin films. It is found convenient to define an effective thickness for this interaction which gives a measure of the strength of coupling to the absorbing medium and can be used to compare internal reflection to transmission measurements. Experimental evidence is presented which verifies all of the factors that control the effective thickness equations.

B. Reflection Formulas of Fresnel

1. Non-Absorbing Media

Light striking an interface between two *transparent* semiinfinite media of different refractive indices will be partially reflected and partially transmitted. The transmitted beam is refracted as shown in Fig. 1*b* according to Snell's law

$$n_1 \sin \theta = n_2 \sin \varphi. \tag{1}$$

It is often convenient to write Snell's law in terms of the refractive index ratio $n_{12} = n_1/n_2$ or $n_{21} = n_2/n_1$. For the reflected beam the angle of reflection is equal to the angle of incidence. The reflected amplitudes for unit incoming amplitudes and for perpendicular polarization and parallel polarization wherein the electric field vector vibrates in the plane perpendicular to the plane of incidence and parallel to it, respectively, are given by Fresnel's equations, viz.,

$$r_{\perp} = -\frac{\sin(\varphi - \theta)}{\sin(\varphi + \theta)} \tag{2}$$

and

$$r_{\parallel} = \frac{\tan(\varphi - \theta)}{\tan(\varphi + \theta)} \tag{3}$$

[Perpendicular polarization is also known as TE (transverse electric) or s (senkrecht) waves. Parallel polarization is also known as TM (transverse magnetic) or p (parallel) waves.] Near normal incidence, where $\varphi \sim n_{12}\,\theta$, the reflectivity, which represents the percentage of reflected power, given by the square of the amplitude $R = r^2$, is identical for both components and has the same value whether the light strikes the interface from the rarer or denser medium and is given by

$$R = \frac{(n_{12} - 1)^2}{(n_{12} + 1)^2}. \tag{4}$$

For external reflection (Fig. 1a), i.e., when the light strikes the interface from the rarer medium, the reflectivity versus the angle of incidence is calculated from equations (2) and (3) and is shown by the solid curves of Fig. 2. For perpendicular polarization, the reflectivity, $R_{\perp}$, rises monotonically from a value given by equation (4) at normal incidence to 100% at grazing incidence. For parallel polarization, the reflectivity, $R_{\parallel}$, decreases at first as the angle of incidence increases and becomes zero at Brewster's angle which is given by

$$\theta_B = \tan^{-1} n_{12}. \tag{5}$$

This is the well-known polarizing angle. It should be noted that θ_B and φ_B are complementary angles and therefore $R_{\parallel}$ must be zero, since $\tan(\theta_B + \varphi_B) = \tan 90° = \infty$. That $R_{\parallel}$ must be zero at θ_B can be understood from a simple physical argument. It should be recalled that for propagating waves, the electric field vector vibrates perpendicular to the direction of propagation. The electric field vector lies parallel to the plane of incidence for parallel polarization. Since the refracted and reflected beams are 90° apart, the electric field oscillates in the direction of $R_{\parallel}$ for the refracted beam and therefore there can be no propagation in the reflected beam. All of the power is therefore transmitted into medium *1*. For angles greater than θ_B, $R_{\parallel}$ rises sharply and becomes 100% at grazing incidence.

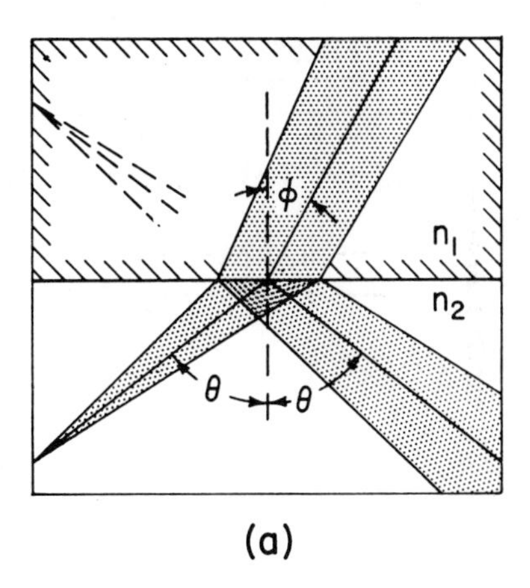

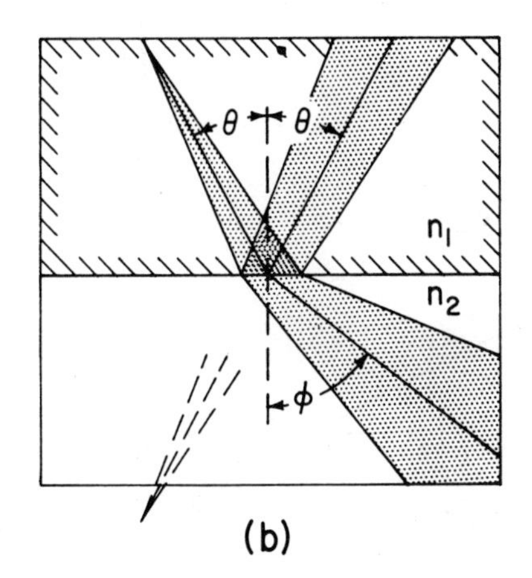

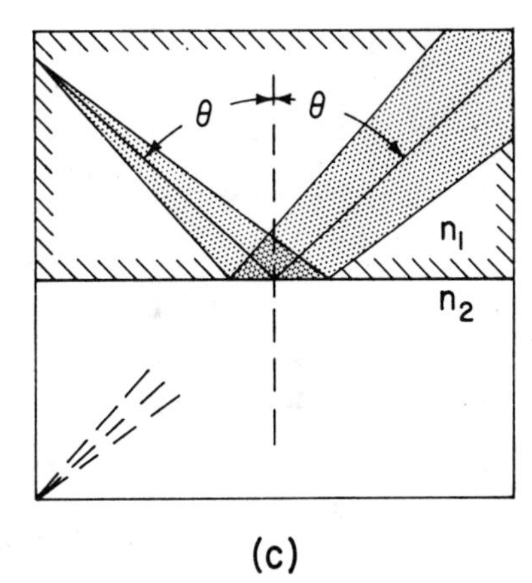

Fig. 1. Reflection and refraction of a ray of light. (a) External reflection, (b) Internal reflection, $\theta < \theta_c$. (c) Total internal reflection, $\theta > \theta_c$. θ_c is the critical angle.

For internal reflection (Figs. 1b and 1c), i.e., when the light approaches the interface from the denser medium, the reflectivities are again calculated from equations (2) and (3). Curves are obtained similar to those for external reflection for a much smaller range of angles of incidence, as shown by the dashed curves in Fig. 2. Both $R_\perp$ and $R_\parallel$ become 100% at the critical angle $\theta = \theta_c$, given by

$$\theta_c = \sin^{-1} n_{21}. \tag{6}$$

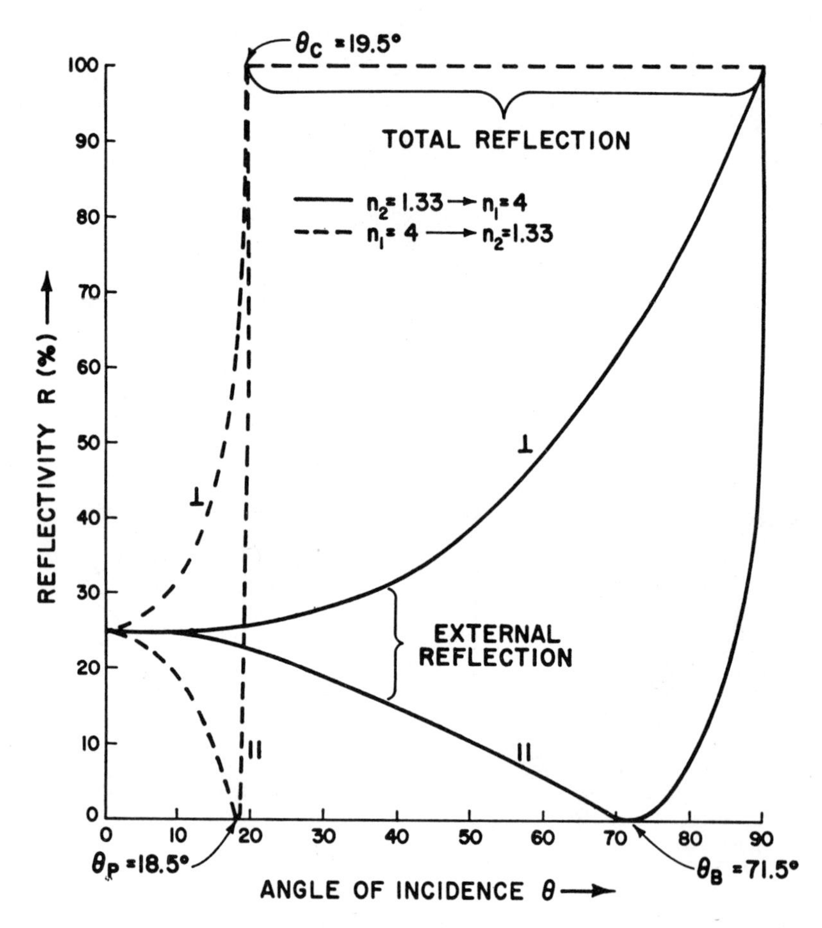

Fig. 2. Reflectivity versus angle of incidence for an interface between media with indices, $n_1 = 4$ and $n_2 = 1.33$, for light polarized perpendicular, $R_\perp$, and parallel, $R_\parallel$, to plane of incidence for external reflection (solid lines) and internal reflection (dashed lines). θ_c, θ_B, and θ_p are the critical, Brewster's, and principal angles, respectively.

There is an internal polarizing angle, θ_p, called the principal angle, which is equal to the refracted angle φ_B. θ_p is the complement of θ_B and is given by

$$\theta_p = \tan^{-1} n_{21}. \tag{7}$$

When n_{12} is large, $R_\parallel$ increases very abruptly for internal reflection between the angles θ_p and θ_c. For the case shown in Fig. 2, $R_\parallel$ changes from 5% to 100% for a change in θ of only $\frac{1}{2}°$. The abrupt change in $R_\parallel$ between θ_p and

θ_c is accompanied by an abrupt change in the refracted angle. For θ changing from 18.5° to 19.5°, φ changes from 71.5° to 90°—a magnification of 18.5. Advantage can be taken of these abrupt changes in $R_\parallel$ and $R_\perp$ to measure index of refraction, for angle sensing, light modulation, and light deflection.

As θ approaches the critical angle, the slopes for $R_\perp$ and $R_\parallel$ become infinitely large. $R_\perp$ and $R_\parallel$ reach 100% exactly when $\theta = \theta_c$ (i.e., θ_c is mathematically sharp) and $\varphi = \pi/2$. For angles larger than θ_c, φ becomes imaginary. This is evident from equation (1), where $\sin^2 \theta > n_{21}^2$ and the refracted angle may be obtained from

$$\cos \varphi = (1 - \sin^2 \varphi)^{1/2} = i \frac{(\sin^2 \theta - n_{21}^2)^{1/2}}{n_{21}}. \tag{8}$$

Using equations (1) and (8), φ can be eliminated from (2) and (3) and the Fresnel reflection equations become

$$r_\perp = \frac{\cos \theta - i(\sin^2 \theta - n_{21}^2)^{1/2}}{\cos \theta + i(\sin^2 \theta - n_{21}^2)^{1/2}} \tag{9}$$

and

$$r_\parallel = \frac{n_{21}^2 \cos \theta - i(\sin^2 \theta - n_{21}^2)^{1/2}}{n_{21}^2 \cos \theta + i(\sin^2 \theta - n_{21}^2)^{1/2}}. \tag{10}$$

It is evident that $|r_\perp| = |r_\parallel| = 1$, indicating that the reflection is total when n_{21} is real. The interpretation, due to Fresnel, of this imaginary angle is that no energy is transmitted into medium *2* and all of the power is reflected; i.e., total internal reflection occurs for θ between the critical angle and grazing incidence. A totally reflecting surface represents a perfect mirror and this can be achieved for external reflection only when the refractive index is purely imaginary. Its high reflectivity can be appreciated when compared to a metal mirror, for example, whose reflectivity may be 95%. After ten reflections from this metal mirror, the fraction of power left in the light beam is

$$P = R^{10} = (0.95)^{10} = 0.60.$$

For total internal reflection, on the other hand, hundreds and even tens of thousands of reflections have been successfully employed in fiber optics (K8,K9). This indicates that the reflectivity associated with total reflection is indeed very high. In many cases, the largest attenuation comes from absorption losses in the bulk rather than reflection losses. It is sometimes the very small reflection loss that is of interest, however. By employing many reflections this reflection loss can be amplified and measured.

It is informative to note the dependence of the reflectivity on the change in refractive index of medium *2* for non-absorbing media. This dependency can be calculated from equations (1), (2), and (3) or, more conveniently, from a reformulation of Fresnel's equations by Stern (S31). Calculations for $n_1 = 2$ and $\theta = 30°$ have been plotted in Fig. 3. [Any small change in n_2 can also be related to a change in angle of incidence through equation (1).] For values of n_2 less than the critical index, $n_2 = n_1 \sin \theta_c$; the reflectivity is unchanged and remains 100% for both polarizations. (For the parameters chosen in Fig. 3, TIR occurs only when $n_2 < 1$.) For larger values of n_2, $R_\perp$ and $R_\parallel$ both drop sharply, become zero when the refractive indices are

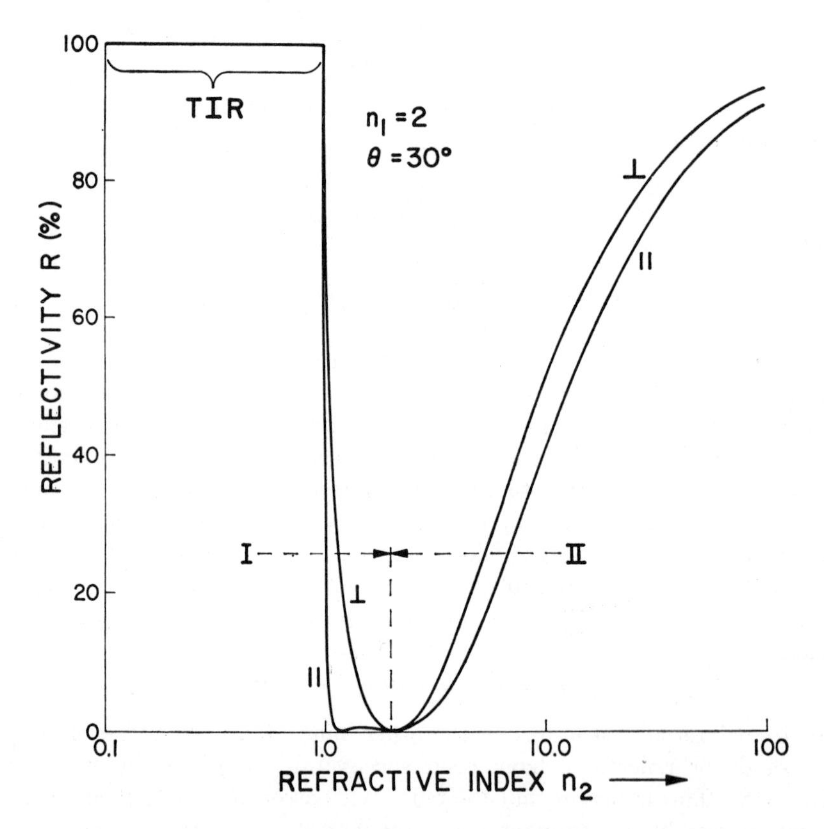

Fig. 3. The dependence of the reflectivity on change in the refractive index of medium *2*. Regions I and II represent internal and external reflection, respectively. Note the sharp drop in the reflectivity for an increase of n_2 above the critical index, $n_2 = n_1 \sin \theta_c$. The reflectivity is zero when $n_1 = n_2$ and then increases for further in increase in n_2.

matched (i.e., when $n_2 = n_1$), and then rise again as n_2 becomes greater than unity. The region marked I represents internal reflection since $n_{21} < 1$ whereas the region marked II represents external reflection since $n_{21} > 1$. These curves also show that internal reflection is more sensitive to refractive index changes than is external reflection. It is interesting to note that for the parameters chosen, $R_\parallel$ is zero for *two* values of n_2, viz., (1) when the indices are matched, $n_2 = n_1$, and (2) when n_2 equals the principal index given by $n_2 = n_1 \tan \theta_p$. These two minima coincide when $\theta = 45°$.

2. Absorbing Rarer Medium

The discussion thus far has been concerned with non-absorbing media. If the rarer medium is absorbing, the reflectivity can still be calculated from equations (9) and (10) by replacing n_2 by the complex refractive index, i.e.,

$$\hat{n}_2 = n_2(1 - i\kappa_2). \tag{11}$$

In general, the attenuation index, κ, is related to the absorption coefficient, α, via

$$n\kappa = \alpha c/4\pi\nu. \tag{12}$$

The Fresnel equations which were at first very simple [equations (2) and (3)] have now become very complicated and calculations become very tedious without an electronic computer. An example of the dependence of the internal reflectivity on the angle of incidence when the rarer medium is a fairly strong absorber is shown in Fig. 4 by the dashed curves, where $\alpha = 10^4$. Some significant conclusions can be drawn by comparing these curves to the ones for the non-absorbing interface. It can be seen that internal reflection for $\theta = 0$ up to $\theta \approx \theta_p$ is rather insensitive to changes in absorption coefficient. The region around $\theta \approx 0$ is more or less equivalent to external reflection and it should be noted that the reflectivity for the absorbing medium does not deviate noticeably from that for the non-absorbing medium; in fact, this deviation is only about 1 part in 10^3 for the curves where $\alpha_2 = 10^4$ shown in Fig. 4. This becomes evident from an examination of the reflectivity equation for normal incidence when the second medium is absorbing. The reflectivity is then given by

$$R = \frac{(n_2 - n_1)^2 + n_2^2\kappa_2^2}{(n_2 + n_1)^2 + n_2^2\kappa_2^2}. \tag{13}$$

At a wavelength of 3 μ, for example, $n_2\kappa_2 = 2.5 \times 10^{-5}\alpha_2$. Thus it is evident that for external reflection κ_2 contributes little to the reflectivity except for strongly absorbing materials (e.g., metals).

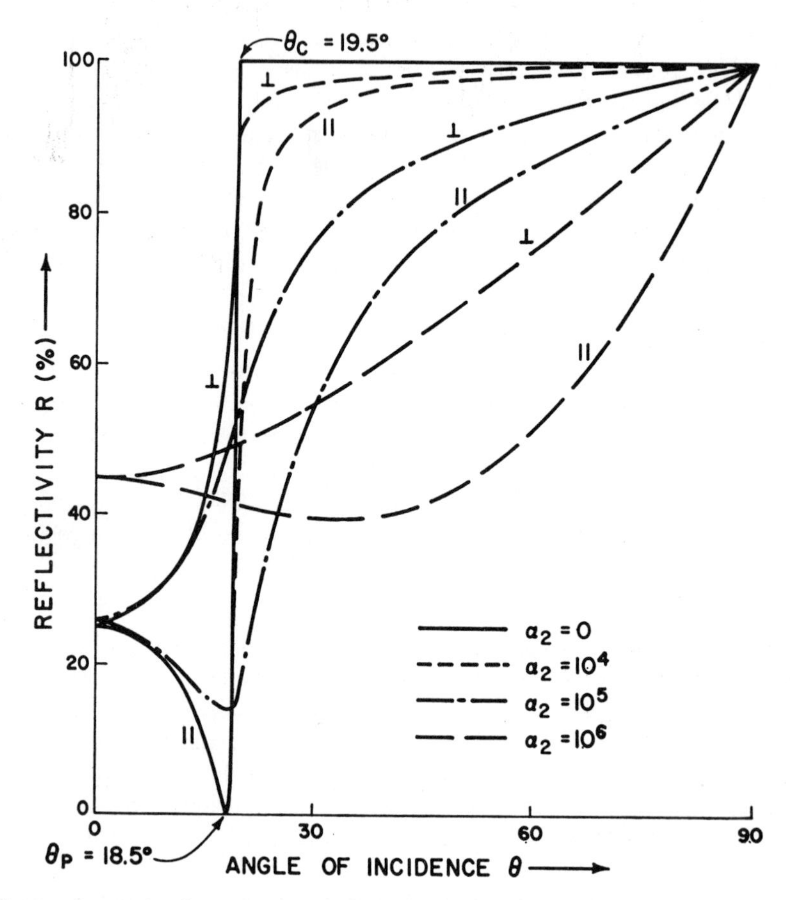

Fig. 4. Internal reflectivity of an interface versus angle of incidence at $\lambda = 0.4\ \mu$ for $n_{21} = 0.333$ and various values of absorption coefficient α_2. Note that the curves tend to resemble those for external reflection when α_2 becomes high.

An absorbing medium may, however, strongly affect the reflectivity for internal reflection, particularly so, in the vicinity of the critical angle. It should be noted that when the rarer medium is absorbing, the critical angle loses its significance; i.e., there is no longer a sharp critical angle for the absorbing case as there was for the non-absorbing one and the reflectivity curves become less steep in this region. The absorption loss is quite large near the critical angle, is greater for parallel polarization than it is for perpendicular polarization, and decreases with increasing angle of incidence for both polarizations. The physical reasons for this behavior will be given later.

An important conclusion that can be drawn from Fig. 4 is that internal reflection measurements, particularly in the vicinity of the critical angle, may be extremely sensitive to changes in absorption coefficient and thus offer a convenient way of measuring absorption coefficients.

As the absorption coefficient of the second medium increases, the reflectivity curves begin to lose all resemblance to those for total internal reflection from non-absorbing media, as shown in Fig. 4 by the curves where $\alpha_2 = 10^5$ and where $\alpha_2 = 10^6$. In fact, when the absorption coefficient is very high ($\alpha_2 = 10^6$) the reflection becomes metallic and the curves begin to resemble more nearly those shown in Fig. 2 for external reflection from non-absorbing media. It is interesting to note that by choosing the parameters appropriately, the curves for internal reflection may resemble those for external reflection very closely. Figure 5, for example, shows the reflectivity curves for a Ge–Hg interface at $\lambda = 3\ \mu$ where the light is propagating inside the germanium. The close resemblance to the curves for external reflection is clearly evident. Also by comparing the curves of Fig. 5 ($\lambda = 3\ \mu$) to the curves of Fig. 4 ($\lambda = 0.4\ \mu$) where $\alpha_2 = 10^6$, it is evident that the minimum for $R_\parallel$ becomes deeper and shifts to a larger angle as the wavelength is increased.

It is interesting to note the dependence of the reflectivity on absorption coefficient for internal reflection at angles exceeding the critical angle. This has been calculated from equations (9) and (10) for both polarizations and for two selected angles. It should first be recalled that transmission, neglecting reflection losses, follows an exponential law, viz.,

$$I/I_0 = e^{-\alpha d}. \tag{14}$$

Here α is the absorption coefficient and d, the sample thickness. Internal reflectivity has a much more complicated dependence on absorption coefficient, as can be noted from Fig. 6. The absorption parameter, a, shown in Fig. 6, is defined as the reflection loss per reflection, i.e.,

$$a = (100 - R)\%. \tag{15}$$

It should be noted that, as concluded from Fig. 4, the absorption parameter is greater near the critical angle than it is for larger angles and is also greater for $\parallel$-polarization than it is for $\perp$-polarization. The absorption parameter rises from zero for non-absorbing media, reaches a maximum value, and then decreases again to zero when the absorption coefficient becomes very high

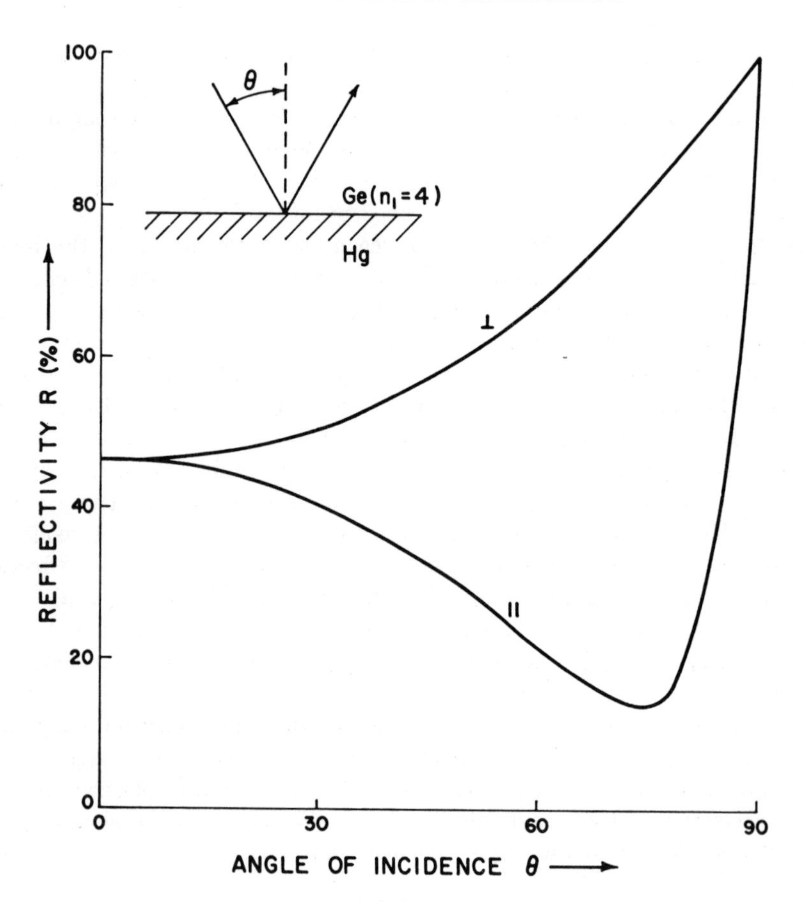

Fig. 5. The reflectivity of a Ge–Hg interface at $\lambda = 3\ \mu$ for light approaching the interface through the germanium—an example of the reflectivity of a dielectric–metallic interface. These curves closely resemble those for external reflection of Fig. 2.

and the absorbing medium exhibits metallic characteristics. Although very high reflection losses (in excess of 50%) can be attained, complete absorption for a single reflection cannot be achieved, regardless of the value of the absorption coefficient. Whereas there is no reason to doubt the validity of these calculations, they give little physical insight into the interaction mechanisms involved.

The change in the internal reflection with change in absorption for bulk materials (semiinfinite media) can easily be measured by varying the concentration of an absorbing component in solution. Numerous attempts (F2,

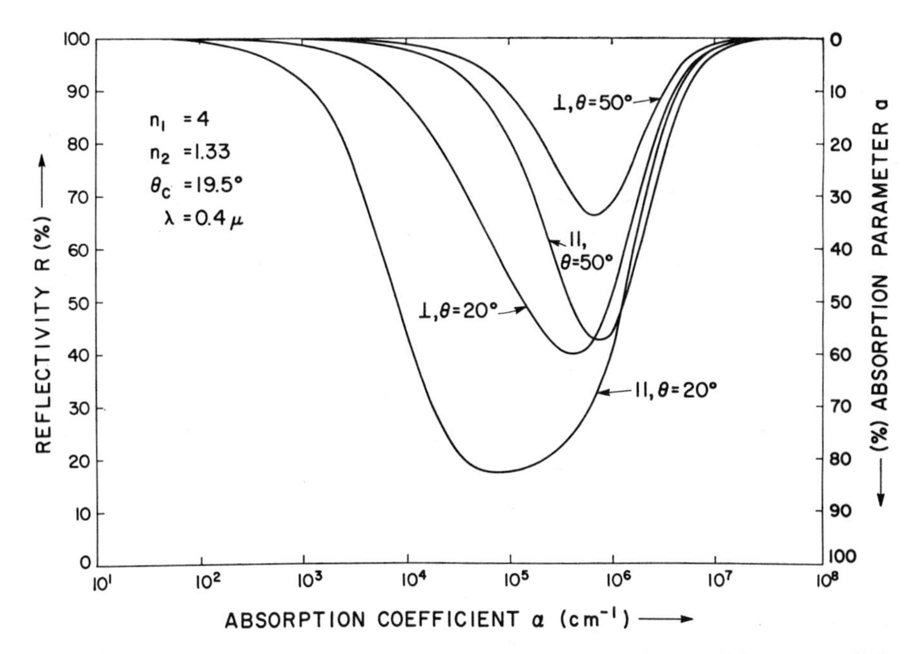

Fig. 6. The dependence of the reflectivity on absorption coefficient of the rarer medium for ⊥- and ∥-polarization at two selected angles of incidence; $\lambda = 0.4\ \mu$, $n_{21} = 0.333$. The reflectivity decreases, reaches a minimum, and increases as the absorption coefficient of the rarer medium increases. The reflection loss is greater for ∥-polarization than it is for ⊥-polarization.

K17,H7,M4) have been made to show that the reflection follows Beer's law. It is basically incorrect to assume a logarithmic dependence for this data, as shown in Fig. 6, where the reflectivity at first decreases then reaches a minimum and finally increases as the absorption coefficient increases. The data used here follows a linear law up to approximately 10% absorption and an exponential law up to about 30% absorption; then the law becomes very complicated as the absorption further increases.

The foregoing discussions were concerned with semiinfinite media in which the absorption of the rarer medium was changed by changing the concentration of the absorbing phase. Another method of changing the absorption is to place absorbing films of various thicknesses on the reflecting surface. Flournoy and Huntsberger (F10a) checked the theory for internal reflection by measuring absorption losses resulting from films on a germanium plate. They placed films of nitrocellulose ($n_2 = 1.4$) of various thicknesses on a germanium plate and monitored the strength of the absorption band at

6.03 μ as a function of thickness. (The films of various thicknesses were cast on the germanium surfaces from successively more dilute solutions, as described by Huntsberger (H53), and the thickness was measured interferometrically where monolayer variations could be detected.) Their data are shown in Fig. 7. The agreement between experiment and theory is considered excellent in view of the experimental difficulties involved. Saturation in absorption with increasing film thickness, similar to that shown in Fig. 7, has also been measured by Harrick (H21) and Reichert (R9).

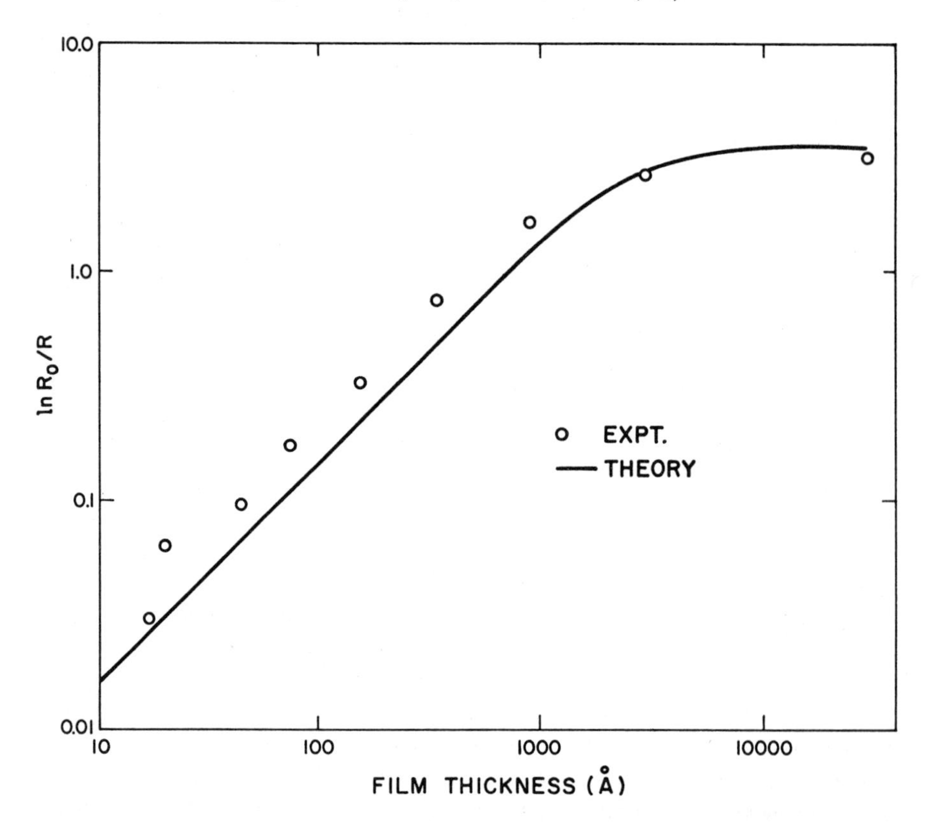

Fig. 7. Reflectivity versus film thickness deduced by monitoring a nitrocellulose band at 6.03 μ using a Ge plate, $\theta = 45$, $N = 19$. The saturation in the reflectivity is due to the limited depth of penetration of the electromagnetic field in the rarer medium. As the angle of incidence is decreased, the saturation point occurs at a greater thickness. (Courtesy of P. A. Flournoy and J. R. Huntsberger, E. I. du Pont de Nemours and Co., Wilmington, Delaware.)

Calculations from the reflectivity equations of Fresnel have shown that by choosing the angle of incidence carefully, internal reflection measurements can be made very sensitive to changes in the absorption coefficient or to changes in the refractive index. As was pointed out already, these calculations, although correct, give little physical insight into the nature of the interaction mechanisms since there has been no mention of the evanescent wave. Another approach will now be taken which will give a clearer picture of the electromagnetic wave pattern near a surface for total internal reflection. This wave pattern is helpful in understanding the interaction mechanisms.

C. Electromagnetic Wave Pattern Near a Reflecting Interface

The results discussed in the previous section, including Fresnel's equations, can be obtained from a more fundamental approach with the aid of Maxwell's equations. This approach can serve to give physical insight into the interaction mechanisms at a reflecting surface. In particular, it can be shown from Maxwell's equations (B27) that standing waves are established normal to a totally reflecting surface because of the superposition of the incoming and reflected waves (H30,K2), i.e.,

$$E = 2 \cos\left(\frac{2\pi z}{\lambda_e} + \varphi\right). \tag{16}$$

A right-handed rectangular-coordinate system wherein the reflecting interface is the xy plane and the y axis is normal to the direction of propagation, will be used throughout this book.

1. Reflection from a Metal Mirror

Standing-wave patterns for light reflected from a metal mirror were demonstrated many years ago (1890) in an elegant experiment by O. Wiener (W7). He placed a thin photographic emulsion at a small angle with respect to a metal mirror and reflected light through it, as shown in Fig. 8. After developing the emulsion he found that it was not uniformly darkened but that darkening did occur at periodic distances equal to an odd number of quarter wavelengths from the surface. This is explained by the existence of a standing-wave pattern established normal to the reflecting surface and by the location of the nodes of the electric field of this standing-wave pattern relative to the surface. Darkening of the emulsion occurs only near the antinodes (loops) of the standing-wave pattern but not at the nodes. (In fact, it was the purpose of Wiener's experiment to demonstrate that the interaction of the

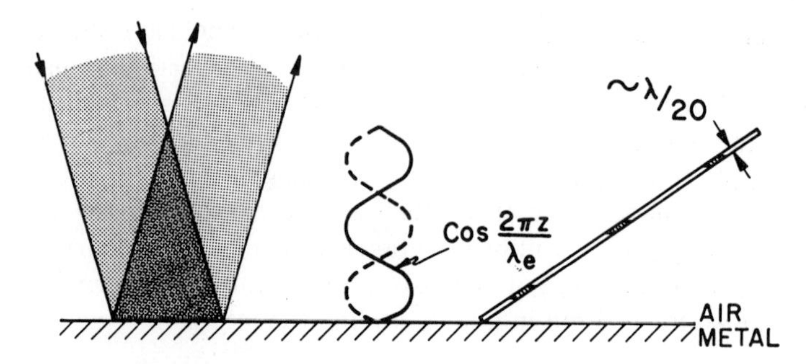

Fig. 8. Experiment of O. Wiener (1890). The superposition of the incoming waves with those reflected from the metal mirror establish the standing-wave pattern shown in the center. A thin photographic emulsion placed in this field will show interaction (darkened areas) only near the maximum electric fields (loops) of the standing waves. Because of the high conductivity of the metal, there is a node near the surface. The angle of the emulsion relative to the metal surface is highly exaggerated.

light with the emulsion occurs via the electric field rather than via the magnetic field.) When light is reflected from a metal, there is a propagating, but highly damped, wave in the metal with a depth of penetration (skin depth) of less than 100 Å. For the superposition of the incoming and reflected light, which is responsible for the standing-wave pattern, there must be a node ($E = 0$) very near the surface because of the high conductivity ($\sigma \sim \infty$) of the metal. Thus there can be no strong interaction with an absorber on the surface whose thickness is much less than a quarter wavelength. This phenomenon has also been discussed by Hass (H40) in connection with protective coatings for front surface mirrors. He points out that an absorbing material may be used as the coating material without introducing large reflection losses.

A number of attempts have been made to record spectra of very thin films by placing them on metal mirrors (F14,H2,G19) and reflecting the light from the mirrors many times to amplify the small absorption. With a node at the surface, this would appear to be the best place to hide a thin film absorber to escape detection. This indeed is the case for perpendicular polarizations at all angles of incidence and for parallel polarization at normal incidence. For oblique incidence and parallel polarization, the phase change upon reflection is such that there results a finite value of the electric field at the surface and thus interaction with an absorbing film is possible. The interaction with the substrate, however, also increases and the reflectivity therefore decreases making it possible to use only a limited number of reflections. Spectra of three monolayer films of fatty acids have been recorded in this way (F14,H2).

It should be possible to enhance the absorption of a thin film on a metal surface by placing a quarter-wave dielectric spacer between the film and metal surface in order to locate the film at the loop where the electric field is a maximum. Structures of this type have been proposed to enhance the photoemission in photocathodes (D15).

2. Total Internal Reflection

a. Electric Field Amplitudes

For total internal reflection the situation is quite different from what it is for metals where, due to the high conductivity ($\sigma \sim \infty$) and the boundary conditions, the electric field amplitude at the surface is nearly zero. For total internal reflection, there is still a sinusoidal variation (H30) of the electric field amplitude with distance from the surface in the denser medium; however, by selecting the angle of incidence, it is possible to obtain large electric field amplitudes and even to locate the electric field maximum (antinode) at the surface. The electric field amplitude near the reflecting surface for total internal reflection is shown in Fig. 9. This field has been calculated for total internal reflection at a non-absorbing interface (H30). For unit incoming amplitude for the $\perp$-polarization mode and for unit incoming amplitude for the $\|$-polarization mode (following the coordinate system shown in Fig. 10 where the y axis points outwards), the electric field amplitudes at the interface, but in the rarer medium, are

$$E_{y0} = \frac{2\cos\theta}{(1 - n_{21}{}^2)^{1/2}}, \tag{17}$$

$$E_{x0} = 2\frac{(\sin^2\theta - n_{21}{}^2)^{1/2}\cos\theta}{(1 - n_{21}{}^2)^{1/2}[(1 + n_{21}{}^2)\sin^2\theta - n_{21}{}^2]^{1/2}}, \tag{18}$$

and

$$E_{z0} = \frac{2\sin\theta\cos\theta}{(1 - n_{21}{}^2)^{1/2}[(1 + n_{21}{}^2)\sin^2\theta - n_{21}{}^2]^{1/2}}, \tag{19}$$

where $n_{21} = n_2/n_1$ is the ratio of the refractive index of the rarer medium to that of the denser medium. The curves in Fig. 10 give the magnitude of the E fields and their variation with angle of incidence for the silicon($n_1 = 3.5$)–air interface. E_{y0} represents the electric field amplitude for perpendicular polarization. For parallel polarization it is more convenient to calculate the x and z components separately. The total electric field amplitude is given by

$$E_{\|} = (|E_{x0}|^2 + |E_{z0}|^2)^{1/2}. \tag{20}$$

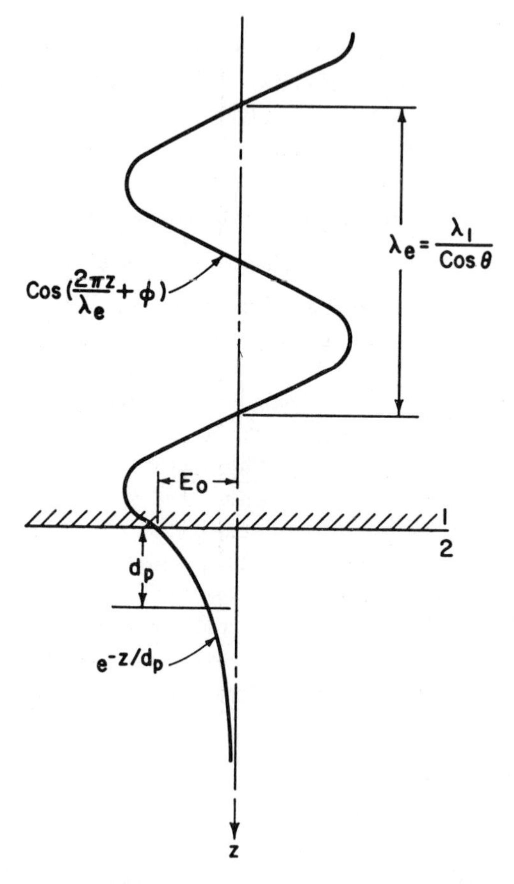

Fig. 9. Standing-wave amplitudes established near a totally reflecting interface: There is a sinusoidal dependence of the electric field amplitude on the distance from the surface in the denser medium *1* and an exponentially decreasing amplitude in the rarer medium *2*. The E field may have a large value at the surface.

The boundary conditions state that the tangential components of the electric fields are continuous; hence E_{x0} and E_{y0} have identical values in the rarer and denser media. At the critical angle where $\cos \theta_c = (1 - n_{21}^2)^{1/2}$, $E_{y0} = 2$. This factor of 2 arises from the superposition of the incoming and reflected amplitudes. For larger angles, E_{y0} decreases according to a cosine law and becomes zero at grazing incidence. E_{x0} is zero at the critical angle, rises abruptly as θ increases, reaches a maximum nearly equal to E_{y0}, and then decreases to zero as θ approaches $\pi/2$.

The normal component, E_{z0}, is discontinuous at the interface, having a

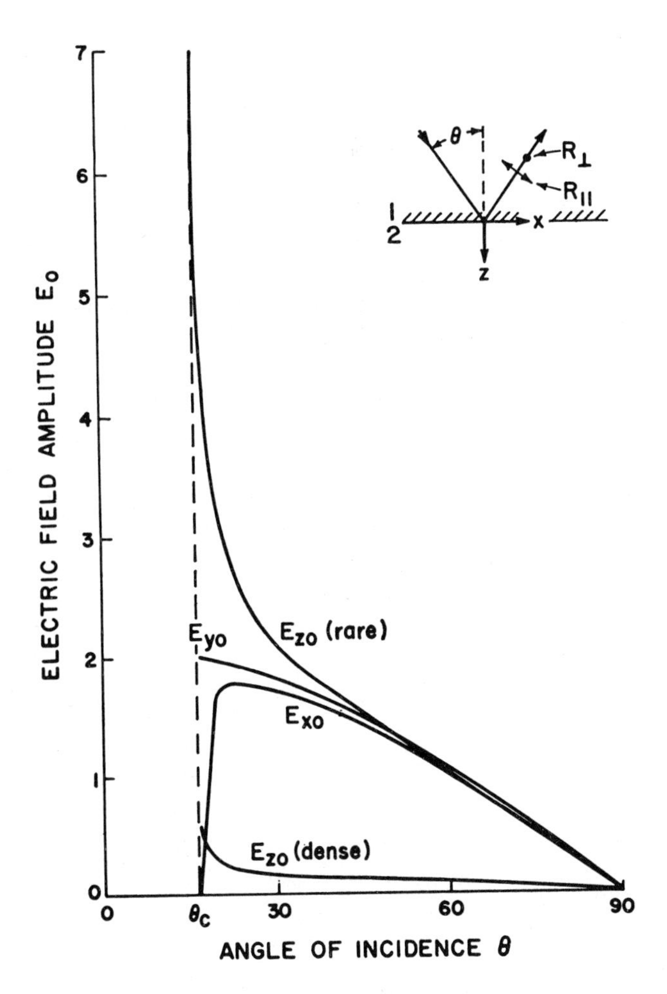

Fig. 10. Calculated electric field amplitudes for unit incident amplitude for perpendicular polarization and unit incident amplitude for parallel polarization versus angle of incidence at a totally reflecting interface for $n_{21} = 0.285$. Two values of E_{z0}, differing by n_{12}^2, are shown; the larger refers to the rarer medium *2*. E_y is the field for ⊥-polarization whereas E_x and E_z are the components of the field for ||-polarization.

value smaller, by a factor n_{21}^2, in the denser medium. The reason for this is that the displacement, D_z, must be continuous across the interface. At the critical angle, $E_{z0} = 2n_{21}$ in the denser medium and $E_{z0} = 2n_{12}$ in the rarer medium. Rather intense fields normal to the surface can thus be obtained with materials having high refractive indices. In the rarer medium the electric field amplitude reaches a maximum for both polarizations at the critical angle.

It is important to note that E fields exist in all spatial directions at the reflecting interfaces. This is different from the situation for a single propagating wave wherein Maxwell's equations dictate that the E fields can exist only normal to the direction of propagation. This is one reason for a difference between internal reflection and transmission spectra; i.e., dipoles will absorb energy in internal reflection regardless of their orientation, whereas for transmission, dipoles oriented parallel to the direction of propagation cannot absorb energy. It should further be noted that the E fields in general have different values for the different spatial directions. Therefore the intensity of an absorption band will depend on the orientation of the dipole for internal reflection whereas for transmission, provided that the dipole is oriented perpendicular to the direction of propagation, the band intensity is independent of orientation. A further implication of this is that for quantitative measurements, the degree of polarization of the light in a spectrometer must be known for internal reflection measurements even on isotropic materials. It will become evident later that for internal reflection, the dependence of absorption on polarization is in general different for thin films than for bulk materials.

b. Penetration

Newton's experiments showed, and it follows from Maxwell's equations (B27), that an electromagnetic disturbance exists in the rarer medium beyond the reflecting interface for total internal reflection. This disturbance is unusual since it exhibits the frequency of the incoming wave, but it is an evanescent wave whose electric field amplitude falls off exponentially with distance from the surface, i.e.,

$$E = E_0 e^{-z/d_p} . \tag{21}$$

This penetrating field joins onto the sinusoidal field, as was shown in Fig. 9, at the surface where the boundary conditions must be satisfied. (Tangential electric field amplitudes and normal displacement are continuous.) There is no net flow of energy into the non-absorbing rarer medium, since the time average of Poynting's vector is zero.

The depth of penetration, defined as the distance required for the electric field amplitude to fall to e^{-1} of its value at the surface, is given by

$$d_p = \frac{\lambda_1}{2\pi(\sin^2\theta - n_{21}^2)^{1/2}} , \tag{22}$$

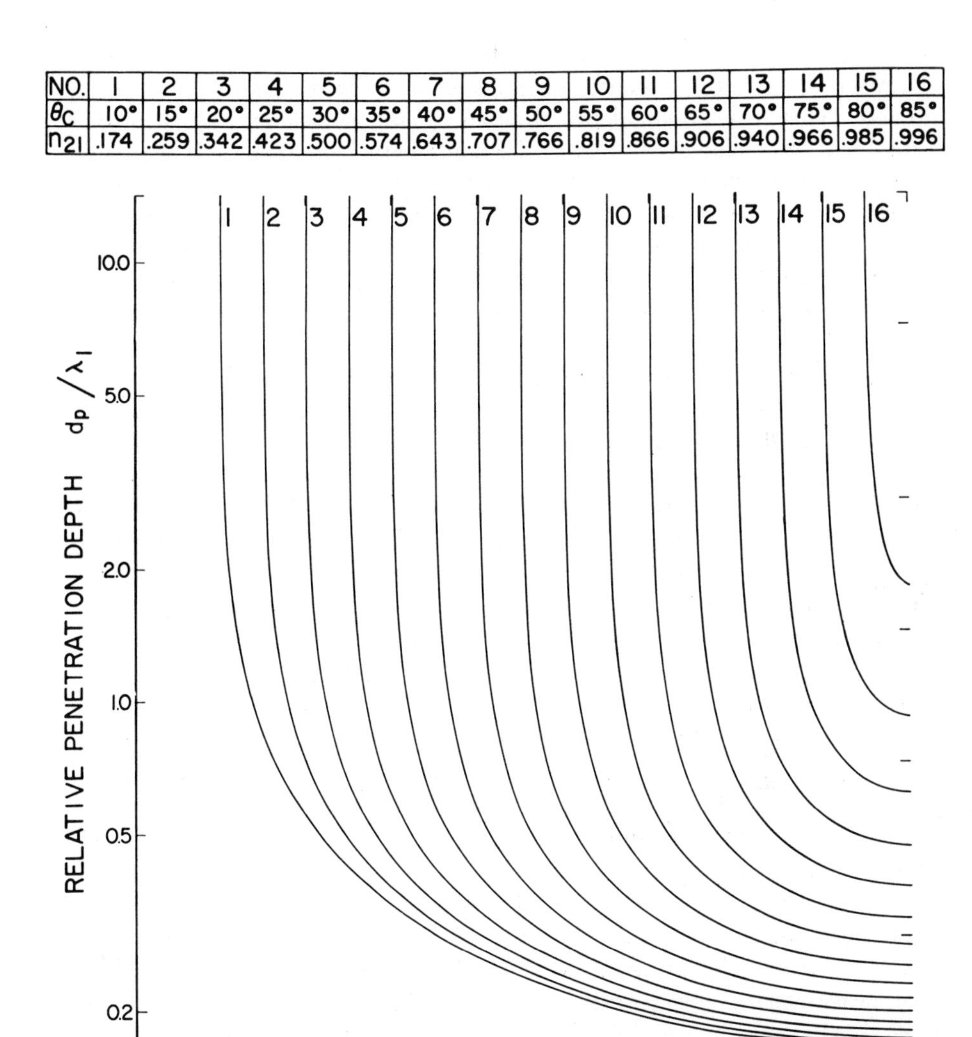

NO.	1	2	3	4	5	6	7	8	9	10	11	12	13	14	15	16
θ_c	10°	15°	20°	25°	30°	35°	40°	45°	50°	55°	60°	65°	70°	75°	80°	85°
n_{21}	.174	.259	.342	.423	.500	.574	.643	.707	.766	.819	.866	.906	.940	.966	.985	.996

Fig. 11. Fractional penetration depth of electromagnetic field in rarer bulk medium for total internal reflection versus angle of incidence for a number of interfaces. The penetration depth is infinitely large at the critical angle and is about one-tenth the wavelength at grazing incidence for relatively high index media. $\lambda_1 = \lambda/n_1$ is the wavelength in the denser medium.

where $\lambda_1 = \lambda/n_1$ is the wavelength in the denser medium and $n_{21} = n_2/n_1$ is the ratio of the refractive index of the rarer medium divided by that of the denser. This penetration depth divided by the wavelength λ_1 is plotted versus angle of incidence, in Fig. 11, for a number of interfaces. It should be noted that the penetration is about one-tenth the wavelength in the denser medium near grazing incidence ($\theta \sim 90°$) for high index materials, but becomes indefinitely large as θ approaches θ_c. At a fixed angle, the penetration depth is larger for better index matching (i.e., as $n_{21} \rightarrow 1$). The penetration depth is also proportional to wavelength and hence is greater at longer wavelengths.

Some of the numerous ingenious experiments that have been performed to demonstrate the existence of the evanescent wave have been described briefly in the introduction and others will be described later in the section on coupling mechanisms. One experiment, resulting from Newton and Hall (N4,H1), which demonstrates all of the features of the penetration depth equation, is shown in Fig. 12. Light incident on the prism at angles exceeding the critical angle will be totally reflected. If a lens of large radius of curvature is placed in contact with the prism, the light will pass on through at the point of contact. If the area of the spot is measured, however, it is found to be larger than the actual contact area, indicating that light is transmitted through the system even where no contact is made. If the angle of incidence is increased, the size of the spot decreases in accordance with equation (22). With white incident light the edge of the transmitted spot is found to be red whereas the edge of the hole in the reflected beam is found to be blue. This verifies the wavelength dependence of the penetration—the longer "red" waves are transmitted whereas the shorter "blue" waves are reflected.

To demonstrate the existence of this evanescent wave and to measure its depth of penetration, it is necessary to disturb it either by absorbing some of its energy or by redirecting it. Care must be exercised in making quantitative measurements of penetration depth in this way because the results are related to penetration depth in a complicated way. In one experiment, for example, the penetration depth was determined by placing a thin film absorber on a reflecting surface and then increasing its thickness until no further decrease in the reflectivity could be detected (H21). It will become evident later that what is measured in this way is the "effective thickness" and not the penetration depth. Fortuitously for the particular interface studied ($n_{21} = 0.25$ and $\theta = 45°$), the penetration depth was almost identical to the effective thickness.

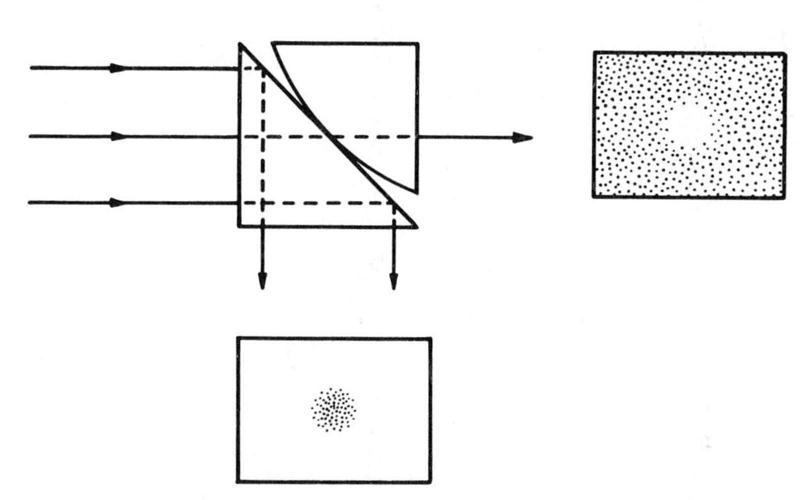

Fig. 12. An experiment which demonstrates penetration into the rarer medium and its dependence on wavelength and angle of incidence. A lens of large radius of curvature is placed in contact with a totally reflecting prism. The following points can be observed: The size of the spot is larger than the area of contact; the edge of the transmitted spot is red while the edge of the reflected spot is blue; the size of the spot is reduced in area when the angle of incidence is increased.

c. Displacement

In spite of the fact that electromagnetic theory, and total internal reflection, in particular, was studied in great detail, particularly around the turn of the century, a new phenomenon associated with total internal reflection was discovered as recently as 1947. Goos and Hänchen (G13,G14) showed in a remarkable experiment that a beam totally internally reflected is displaced upon reflection. The displacement is equal to a fraction of a wavelength, is proportional to the penetration depth, and is greater for parallel polarization than it is for perpendicular polarization.

The experiment of Goos and Hänchen, shown schematically in Fig. 13a, consisted of illuminating the edge of a plate of glass with a narrow beam of light, propagating the light via multiple internal reflection down the length of the plate, and making a photographic record of the exit beam. The center strip of the plate along its length was metallized, thus the output beam consisted of three parts. The two outer parts were propagated via total internal reflection whereas the center portion was propagated via metallic reflection. In spite of low intensity in the central portion because of attenuation resulting from multiple metallic reflections, Goos and Hänchen were able to measure

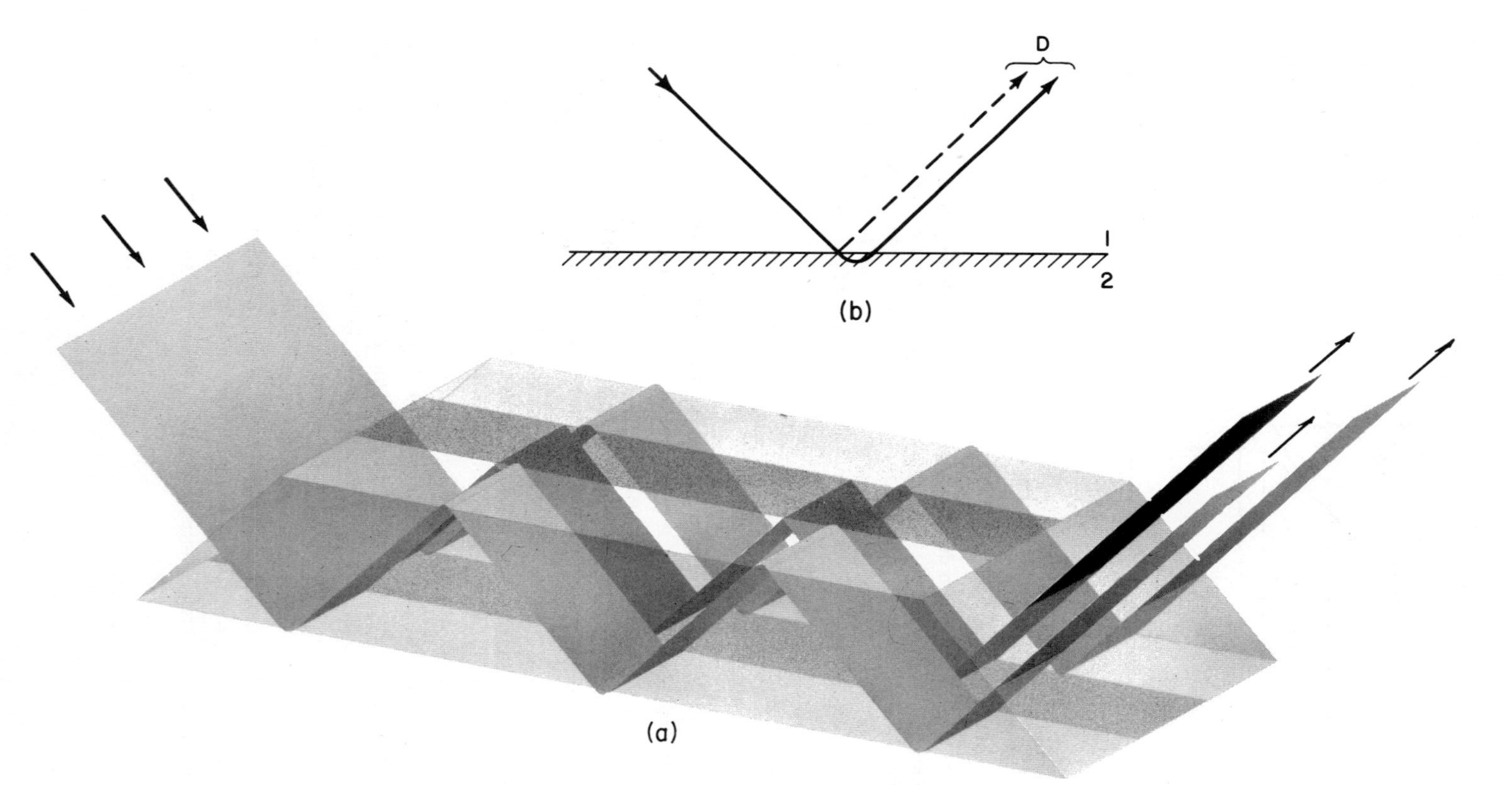

Fig. 13. The Goos and Hänchen displacement. (a) Experimental setup used by Goos and Hänchen to demonstrate displacement of light upon total reflection. The shaded area on the glass plate indicates the metallized portion of the glass. The totally reflected beam emerges displaced with respect to the beam which suffered metallic reflection. (b) Schematic representation for path of light for metallic (dashed line) and total internal reflection (solid line). Note the displacement upon reflection for TIR.

a displacement of the outer beams relative to the central one. Since for metallic reflection there is little or no penetration into the metal, they concluded that the rays reflected from the metal emanate from the point of incidence, as shown by the dashed line in Fig. 13b, whereas for total internal reflection there is a displacement, as shown by the solid line. With penetration and displacement it is convenient to represent the path of the light ray as shown by the solid line. As was discussed already, however, this picture, although convenient, is incorrect since apart from the very edges of the beam there is no propagation normal to the reflecting interface in the rarer medium.

This displacement is, of course, meaningless for a plane wave of infinite extent. Narrow beams, on the other hand, are difficult to treat theoretically because of diffraction effects. Artmann (A9), Fragstein (F12), and Picht (P12) have considered all of these complications and have shown theoretically that a displacement as measured by Goos and Hänchen is predicted by theory and that it is dependent on angle of incidence and polarization. Recently the theory of the Goos-Hänchen displacement was reconsidered by Renard (R10). Theory indicates that the displacement arises from a transfer of the energy in the light beam from one side to the other. This results in a flow of energy along the surface parallel to the plane of incidence; however, total reflection still occurs. It is emphasized again that the standing waves discussed earlier are *normal* to the reflecting surface. Hora (H50) has shown theoretically that such a displacement should also occur for particle waves reflected from a potential barrier.

By using the highly collimated laser beams available at the present time, it should be possible to make rather precise measurements of the displacement. This phenomenon is discussed, not because it is utilized in internal reflection spectroscopy, but because it sheds some light on the nature of the reflection process.

As a final hint that there is still something to be learned about reflection phenomena, attention is drawn to experiments (A5,O1,O2) which showed that light escaping a medium very near the critical angle may be coupled back into this medium and reappear at a distance along the surface, considerably removed from the point of escape. This phenomenon is not yet understood.

D. Coupling to the Evanescent Wave

There are two distinctly different methods of coupling to the evanescent wave and extracting energy from it and thereby making the reflection less than total. In one coupling mechanism some or all of the energy is redirected and there is no energy loss, whereas in the other, energy is absorbed and there is a loss. These coupling mechanisms give rise to frustrated total reflection (FTR) and attenuated total reflection (ATR), respectively (both previously mentioned in Chapter One). FTR is concerned with a change in refractive index whereas ATR is concerned with a change in absorption coefficient. Although a change in absorption coefficient is accompanied by a change in refractive index, the two coupling mechanisms, frustrated and attenuated, can be demonstrated independently, as will be shown. Intimate contact is not required to frustrate or to attenuate the reflection.

1. Lossless Coupling—Frustrated Total Reflection (FTR)

Frustrated total reflection is due to a non-absorbing coupling mechanism whereby the reflectivity for total internal reflection can be made less than 100% and can be continuously adjusted between zero and 100% by placing another suitable optically transparent medium near the reflecting surface or by choosing an appropriate angle of incidence and changing the index of refraction of one of the media (A19) or by taking advantage of the wavelength dispersion of the refractive index. Power is then propagated through the interface without loss at the reflecting interface, and $T + R = 100\%$. The transmitted beam exhibits all of the properties of the incoming beam (e.g., coherence). When the reflection is made less than total in this way, the reflection is said to be frustrated. This term is well known in optics and was coined by Leurgans and Turner (L4) when they invented the FTR filter (described in Chapter Five). There are three methods of frustrating the reflection.

The classical method of frustrating the reflection is shown in Fig. 14a. Here light is initially totally reflected from the first prism. If another prism of the same index is brought to within a fraction of a wavelength from the reflecting surface of the first prism, part of the beam is transmitted on through the second prism. There is no energy loss; i.e., $T + R = 100\%$. The curves in Fig. 14b show that the transmitted and reflected powers can be adjusted continuously between 0 and 100% by adjusting the separation between the two prisms. When the prisms are in contact, all the light is transmitted as if there were no interface; when the prisms are far apart, the evanescent wave is unaware of the presence of the second prism and all of the light is reflected. If the prisms have different refractive indices, 10%0 transmission will not be obtained when the prisms are brought into contact. As has been pointed out already, frustrated total reflection was first demonstrated by Newton (N4) with a prism and lens and studied by Hall (H1) in

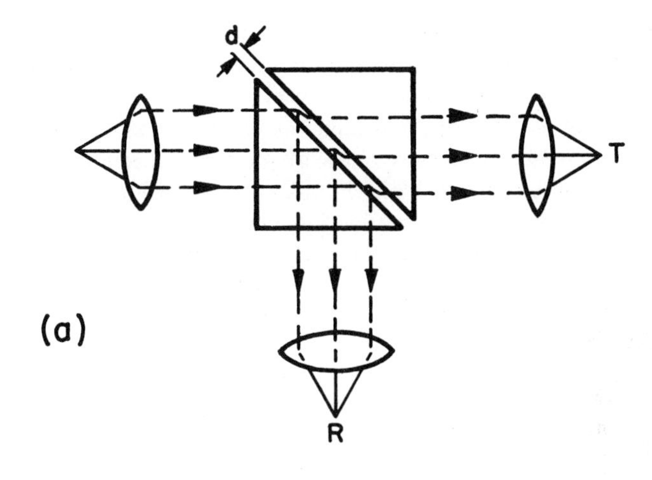

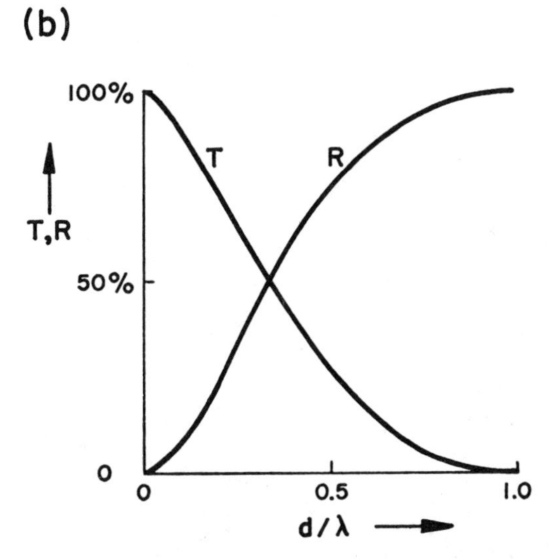

Fig. 14. The experiment of Schaefer and Gross demonstrating controlled coupling to the penetrating field. (a) The double-prism assembly used to obtain controlled coupling to penetrating field. Note that there is a transverse displacement of the light beam as it passes the intervening space between the two prisms. (b) Results showing that the transmission decreases and reflection increases continuously as the distance separating the prism is increased. The coupling is lossless; i.e., $T + R = 100\%$.

great detail. An experimental arrangement similar to that shown in Fig. 14a using paraffin prisms and electromagnetic energy of 15-cm wavelength was also used by Schaefer and Gross (S3) to check the theory carefully. The degree of coupling is dependent on angle of incidence and polarization, as is shown in Fig. 15 by the curves for a given set of parameters (C10). It should be noted that because of the increase in penetration depth with wavelength and the decrease in angle of incidence, the coupling increases accordingly. It should also be noted that the coupling is generally greater

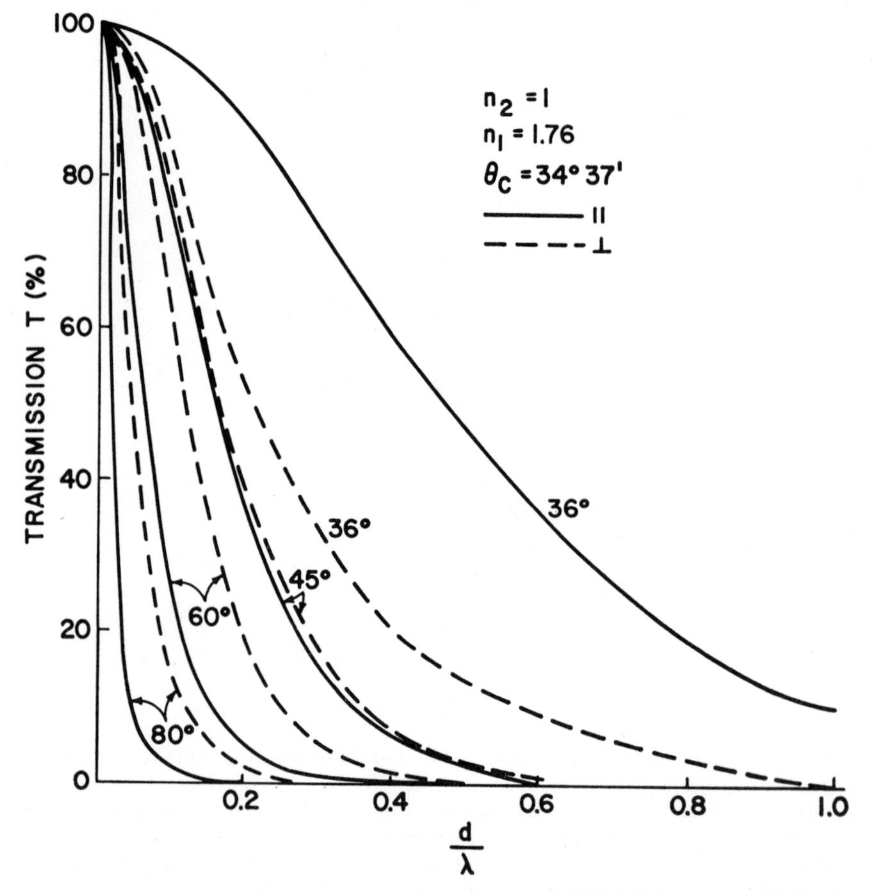

Fig. 15. Calculated transmission of the double-prism arrangement of Fig. 14 versus the separation of the two identical prisms for several angles of incidence. The transmission is higher for ||-polarization (solid curves) than it is for ⊥-polarization (dashed curves) for large angles of incidence whereas near the critical angle, the opposite is true (C10).

(i.e., the transmission is higher), for ||-polarization than it is for ⊥-polarization; however, near the critical angle, the reverse is true.

The transmission and reflection are smooth functions of the wavelength and the distance that separates the prisms. The important conclusion from this is that there is no interference phenomenon associated with frustrated total reflection. The hypotenuses of both prisms thus act as a single reflecting surface. As will become evident, the absence of interference fringes is a significant advantage of internal reflection over transmission in recording spectra.

It should be noted in Fig. 14a that the transmitted beam is shown displaced with respect to the incident beam. Mundel and Zucker (M19) have shown that the propagating component, T, is apparently "refracted" in the intervening space, d, because the transmitted beam was not axial with the incoming beam but was displaced. This displacement, which was found to increase with an increase of the spacing d, has important implications in the FTR filter since it leads to a deterioration of its performance.

Another method of frustrating the reflection is to change the index of refraction of medium *1* or medium *2*. It was already shown in Fig. 3 that if the angle of incidence is set near the critical angle, an increase in n_2 results in a sharp decrease in the reflectivity and part of the incident beam becomes a propagating beam in the second medium. The degree of refraction of the transmitted beam will depend on the magnitude of the change in the refractive index. In principle, this phenomenon could be employed as a means of deflecting the light beam. The refractive index changes can be achieved in a number of ways including the use of electric fields (Kerr effect), pressure, temperature, flow-birefringence, and strain. Perhaps the best method of frustrating the reflection by refractive index changes is to use a structure such as that shown in Fig. 14a, or a similar one employing multiple reflections, and to fill the space d with a polarizable liquid. If the prisms are made from conducting materials (semiconductors) the refractive index of the liquid can be changed by applying an electric field between the prisms.

The reflection can also be frustrated by the wavelength dispersion of the refractive index. If the angle of incidence is chosen near the critical angle, preferably just below, the reflectivity will be strongly wavelength dependent if there is dispersion in the refractive index. This is a very important phenomenon in internal reflection spectroscopy especially in the measurement of optical constants and will be discussed in the next chapter.

Frustrated total reflection is a very important phenomenon because of its wide range of applications. By controlling the spacing d in Fig. 14a or, for a fixed spacing, by changing the angle of incidence by rotating the two-prism assembly (H25), a continuously variable beam splitter is obtained. The same structure serves as a cold mirror because it can be used to separate heat waves from the shorter wavelength light waves. By modulating the distance *d* mechanically by means of a loudspeaker coil, magnetostrictively (A7), piezoelectrically (A18), or ultrasonically, light modulators can be constructed. Changing the refractive index of one of the media can also be employed to modulate light. Frustrated total reflection is also employed to couple energy out of laser cavities employing total internal reflection (S30). Frustrated total reflection is also used with advantage to measure refractive indices (J2,J3,L5b,T1,T2,T3) and may also be employed for angle sensing (L5).

2. Lossy Coupling—Attenuated Total Reflection (ATR)

Attenuated total reflection is due to an absorbing coupling mechanism whereby the reflectivity for total internal reflection can be continuously adjusted between some value greater than 0 (e.g., 40%) and 100% by placing an absorbing medium in contact with the reflecting surface (A19). The resulting reflection is said to be attenuated; the energy is absorbed and is not transmitted but may, for example, be converted to heat. In special cases, by using fluorescent materials (S12,H47), for example, the energy may be absorbed and reemitted.

The possibility of attenuating the reflection was clearly shown by Figs. 4 and 6 where reflectivity changes are achieved by changing the absorption. It was pointed out previously that zero reflectivity cannot be obtained by adjusting the absorption coefficient and that the attenuation is greater for parallel polarization than it is for perpendicular polarization. Attenuated total reflection is observed when the angle of incidence is set and remains above the critical angle and the wavelength is swept through an absorption band. It is possible to modulate the attenuation in some cases. For example, in semiconductors with very sharp absorption edges, the band gap can be noticeably changed with the aid of an electric field (F15,K19,K20, B25,W10) and the absorption edge is shifted. (This is called field-assisted absorption or the Franz-Keldyš effect.) A light beam having a wavelength just above the absorption edge is transmitted by the semiconductor in the absence of the field. When the field is applied, however, the absorption edge is shifted and the light is then absorbed. Thus it is possible to modulate the attenuation by the Franz-Keldyš effect.

It is also possible to modulate the attenuation by changing the distance between the absorbing and reflecting media. This was demonstrated in an experiment in which an absorbing ferrite was moved via magnetostriction in and out of the region of the evanescent wave (A7). Calculations (D23) show that the absorption decreases (reflection increases) for both polarizations as the absorbing medium is moved away from the reflecting surface. For special cases, it can be shown that the absorption for parallel polarization can actually increase until it reaches a maximum and then decrease as the absorber is moved away from the reflecting surface (Y2). (This maximum in absorption can be utilized to measure film thickness.)

E. Effective Thickness of Bulk Materials and Thin Films

The interaction of the evanescent wave for total internal reflection with the absorbing rarer medium is expressed exactly by Fresnel's equations using a complex refractive index or can be calculated directly from Maxwell's equations. The reflection loss due to this interaction does not follow a simple law and can best be determined with the aid of an electronic computer. Such calculations, although rigorous, do not yield any physical insight into the absorption mechanism or into the interaction of the penetrating field with the absorbing medium.

It was found useful and informative to consider the low absorption approximation (when the absorption loss does not exceed 10%) for the interaction of the evanescent field with bulk materials and thin films. The strength of interaction can then be conveniently expressed in terms of an effective thickness, for which simple expressions can be found.

It should be recalled that for conventional transmission sample thickness is important. If reflection losses are neglected, the transmission follows a simple exponential law $I/I_0 = e^{-\alpha d}$. For low absorptions, i.e., $\alpha d < 0.1$, $I/I_0 \approx 1 - \alpha d$, where d is the film thickness and α is the absorption coefficient.

For internal reflection, the reflectivity for bulk materials or thin films can be written as

$$R = 1 - \alpha d_e, \tag{23}$$

where d_e is defined as an effective thickness and is related to the absorption parameter of equation (15) via $d_e = a/\alpha$ for a single reflection. For multiple reflections the reflected power is given by

$$R^N = (1 - \alpha d_e)^N, \tag{24}$$

where N is the number of reflections. For $\alpha d_e \ll 1$,

$$R^N \simeq 1 - N\alpha d_e;$$

i.e., the reflection loss is increased by the factor N. The effective thickness is a measure of the strength of coupling to the sample and is useful in comparing internal reflection spectra to transmission spectra. By comparing the low absorption approximation expressions for transmission and reflection, where it should be noted that the same absorption coefficient is involved, this effective thickness represents the actual thickness of film that would be required to obtain the same absorption in a transmission measurement as that obtained in a reflection measurement using a semiinfinite bulk sample (F7,H7,H30,H37).

For low absorptions in bulk materials or for very thin films, d_e is not dependent on α and simple expressions can be derived for the effective thickness. (In general, d_e is very complicated, especially for large α's.) The expressions as presented in the following sections are found to be extremely useful since they are sufficiently accurate for many applications. Furthermore, they serve to give insight into the nature of the interaction for internal reflection measurements, which is helpful in choosing the angle of incidence and refractive index of the internal reflection element for optimum absorption.

These effective thicknesses can be determined from the first term of the series expansion of Fresnel's equations (F6,H7) with respect to α or from a consideration of the perturbation of the electric field amplitudes in the zero-absorption case (H37). The derivation will not be given here since, although straightforward, it is rather lengthy. Effective thicknesses will be considered separately for bulk materials and thin films.

1. Bulk Materials

For bulk materials in which the thickness of the rarer medium is much greater than the penetration depth (equation 22) of the evanescent field, the low absorption approximation for the effective thickness is calculated from the electric fields for zero absorption in the following way:

$$\begin{aligned} d_e &= \frac{n_{21}}{\cos\theta}\int_0^\infty E^2 dz, \\ &= \frac{n_{21}\, E_0^2 d_p}{2\cos\theta}. \end{aligned} \tag{25}$$

Here $E = E_0\, e^{-z/dp}$ is the electric field amplitude in the rarer medium assuming that the incident wave in the denser medium has unit electric field amplitude. This equation shows that there are four factors which determine the magnitude or strength of coupling of the evanescent wave to the absorbing rarer medium.

The net effect of all of these factors is to give a decrease of the strength of coupling with increasing θ. The following four factors are involved:

a. Depth of Penetration

The best known of these factors is the depth of penetration, equal to d_p (defined in equation 22), which decreases with increasing θ. The depth of penetration is the same for both polarizations and it decreases with increasing θ, as was shown in Fig. 11 for a number of interfaces.

b. Electric Field Strength

Another factor which controls the strength of coupling is the electric field intensity of the standing wave at the reflecting interface (E_0^2), which also decreases with increasing θ. Here E_0 is the electric field amplitude in the rarer medium at the interface for unit incoming amplitude in the denser medium and is greater for $\|$-polarization than it is for $\perp$-polarization. The calculated decrease of E_0 with θ was shown in Fig. 10 for a non-absorbing interface, and E_0 is assumed to be unchanged for a weakly absorbing interface.

c. Sampling Area

The third factor is the sampling area which is proportional to $1/\cos\theta$ and which increases with increasing θ. This factor is obvious in transmission measurements in which the sample thickness increases as $1/\cos\theta$ for oblique incidence.

d. Index Matching

The last factor is the matching of the refractive index of the denser medium to that of the rarer medium, given by n_{21}. Index matching controls the strength of coupling. This term is independent of θ. It predicts an increase of coupling with better matching (i.e., as $n_{21} \rightarrow 1$).

Because the electric field amplitudes in the rarer medium are different for equal incident amplitudes of perpendicular and parallel polarization, the effective thicknesses are different for the two polarizations—the one for parallel polarization is always greater. On inserting appropriate expressions for E_0^2, the *relative* effective thicknesses for isotropic media for perpendicular and parallel polarization are, respectively,

$$\frac{d_{e\perp}}{\lambda_1} = \frac{n_{21}\cos\theta}{\pi(1 - n_{21}^2)(\sin^2\theta - n_{21}^2)^{1/2}} \tag{26}$$

and

$$\frac{d_{e\|}}{\lambda_1} = \frac{n_{21}\cos\theta\,(2\sin^2\theta - n_{21}^2)}{\pi(1 - n_{21}^2)\,[(1 - n_{21}^2)\sin^2\theta - n_{21}^2]\,(\sin^2\theta - n_{21}^2)^{1/2}}\,. \tag{27}$$

It is emphasized that these are the quantities that control the strength of interaction of the evanescent field with the rarer medium, rather than the depth of penetration of the evanescent field which, as was pointed out, is only one of the four factors governing the effective thicknesses. The effective thickness is thus measured in terms of λ_1, the wavelength of light in the denser medium, and has a finite value, except at the critical angle, even though the sample thickness may be infinite. In Fig. 16 the effective thickness and the depth of penetration have been plotted versus angle of incidence for the interface, $n_{21} = 0.423$, which corresponds to $\theta_c = 25°$. It should be noted that for $\theta = 45°$, $d_{e\perp} = \frac{1}{2}d_{e\parallel}$ (generally true at 45°) and the average effective thickness [i.e., $(d_{e\perp} + d_{e\parallel})/2$] is about equal to the depth of penetration. For smaller angles of incidence, the effective thicknesses are larger than the penetration depth and may be equal to many wavelengths for those angles wherein the penetration depth is the major controlling factor. For larger angles, however, the effective thicknesses are smaller than the penetration depth and, because of the rapid decrease of the E fields with θ, approach zero as θ approaches grazing incidence. Because the penetration depth is proportional to the wavelength, the effective thickness also increases with wavelength. This is the reason that for internal reflection spectra of bulk materials, the absorption bands at the longer wavelengths are relatively stronger in intensity; i.e., two bands which record equal in strength in transmission spectra will have unequal intensities in internal reflection spectra—the longer wavelength bands appear relatively stronger. This wavelength dependence also results in greater absorption on the longer wavelength side of a single absorption band, contributing to band distortion.

Relative effective thicknesses for perpendicular and parallel polarization for a number of interfaces are plotted in Figs. 17 and 18, respectively. These curves are useful in selecting the angle of incidence and the index of refraction for internal reflection elements (IRE's). The desired effective thickness for either polarization and for any IRE can be obtained by selecting the angle of incidence or, for a fixed angle of incidence, by selecting the refractive index of the IRE. It is possible, for example, with the aid of these curves, to match the effective thicknesses for two IRE's, i.e., to insure that the contrasts of the spectra are the same for both IRE's. Suppose that for $n_{21} = 0.375$, a spectrum is recorded at $\theta = 23°$. The point a of Fig. 17 shows that this corresponds to a relative effective thickness, $d_{e\perp}/\lambda_1$, of about 0.7. The same relative effective thickness and hence a spectrum with the same contrast should, according to point b of Fig. 17, be obtained for $\perp$-polarization at $\theta = 45°$ for $n_{21} = 0.625$, i.e., by using an internal reflection element whose index is lower by a factor of 1.6. (According to Fig. 18, spectra of equal contrast are obtained for $n_{21} = 0.375$, $\theta = 25°$; and $n_{21} = 0.625$, $\theta = 45°$.)

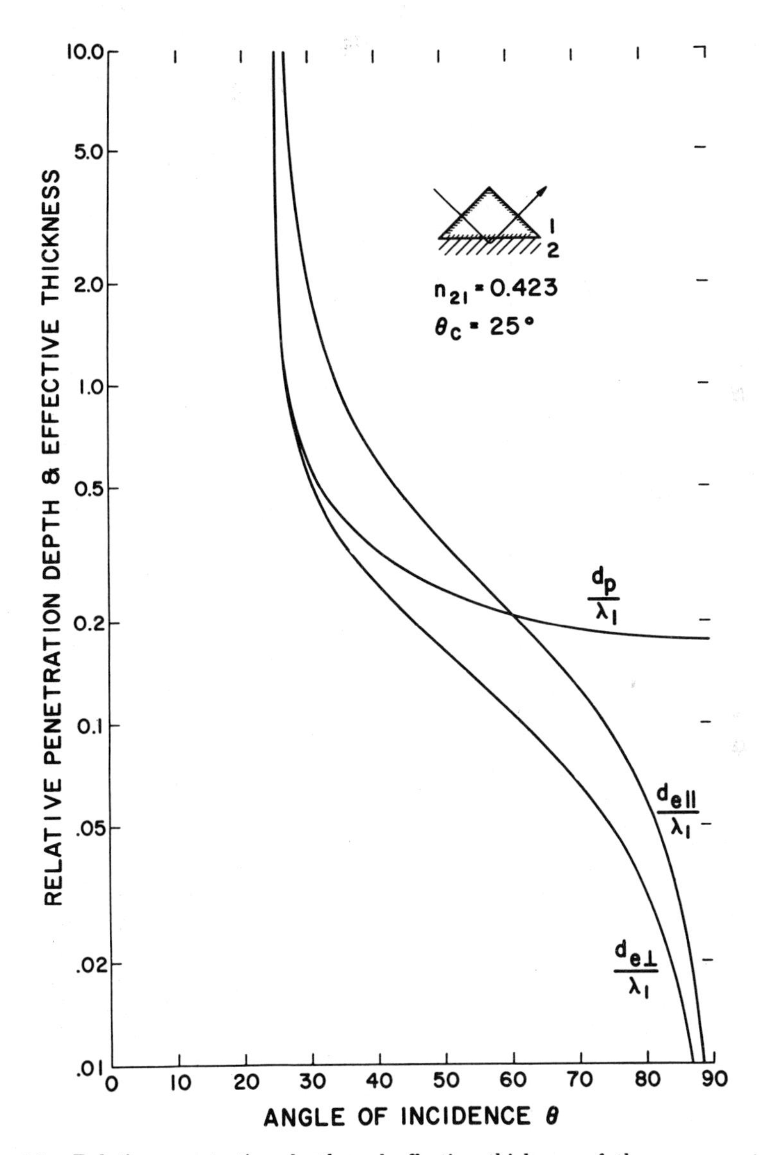

Fig. 16. Relative penetration depth and effective thickness of the evanescent wave versus the angle of incidence for an interface whose refractive index ratio is $n_{21} = 0.423$. Near the critical angle, the effective thicknesses for both polarizations are greater than the penetration depth and at large angles, they are less.

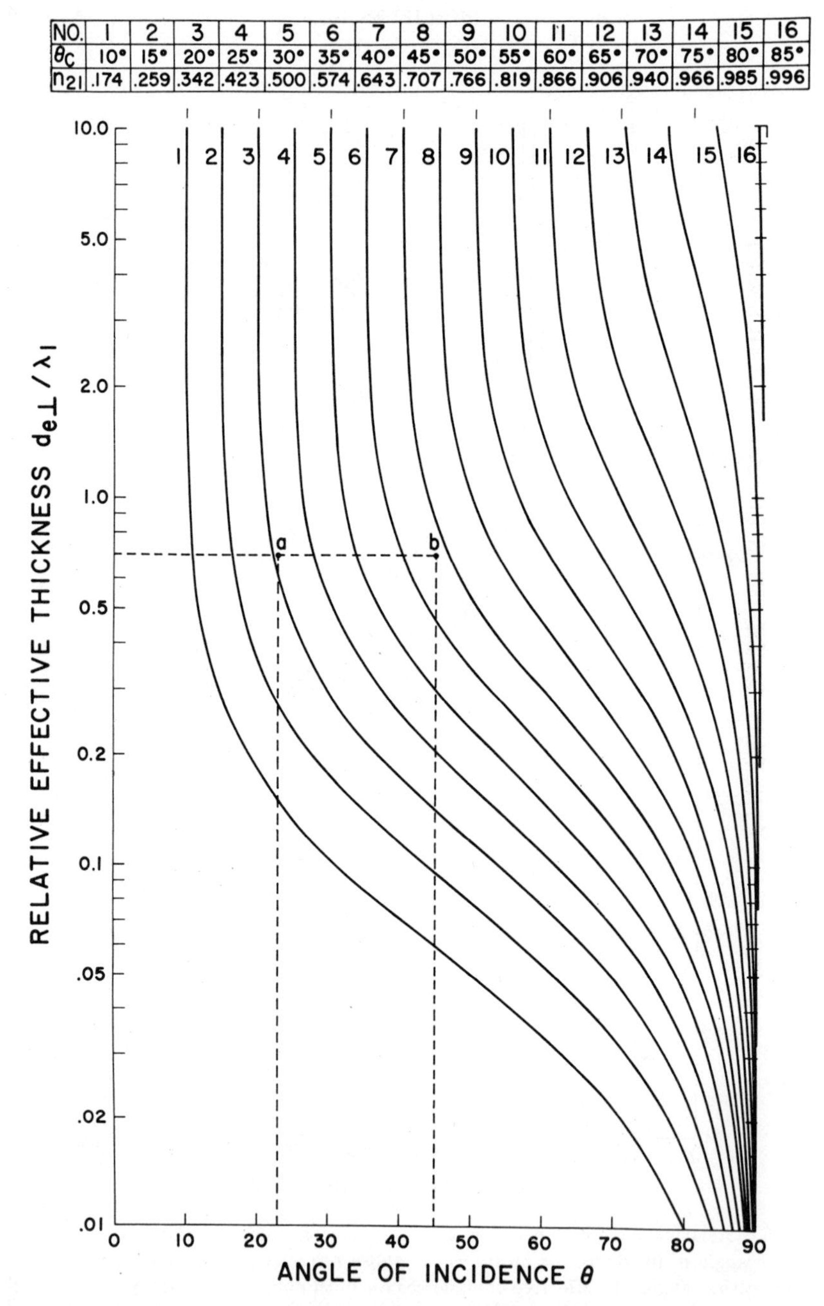

NO.	1	2	3	4	5	6	7	8	9	10	11	12	13	14	15	16
θ_c	10°	15°	20°	25°	30°	35°	40°	45°	50°	55°	60°	65°	70°	75°	80°	85°
n_{21}	.174	.259	.342	.423	.500	.574	.643	.707	.766	.819	.866	.906	.940	.966	.985	.996

Fig. 17. Working curves for relative effective thickness of bulk materials for $\perp$-polarization versus angle of incidence for a number of interfaces. $\lambda_1 = \lambda/n_1$ is the wavelength in the denser medium. Points *a* and *b* illustrate matching of effective thickness for $n_{21} = 0.375$, $\theta = 23°$ and $n_{21} = 0.625$, $\theta = 45°$.

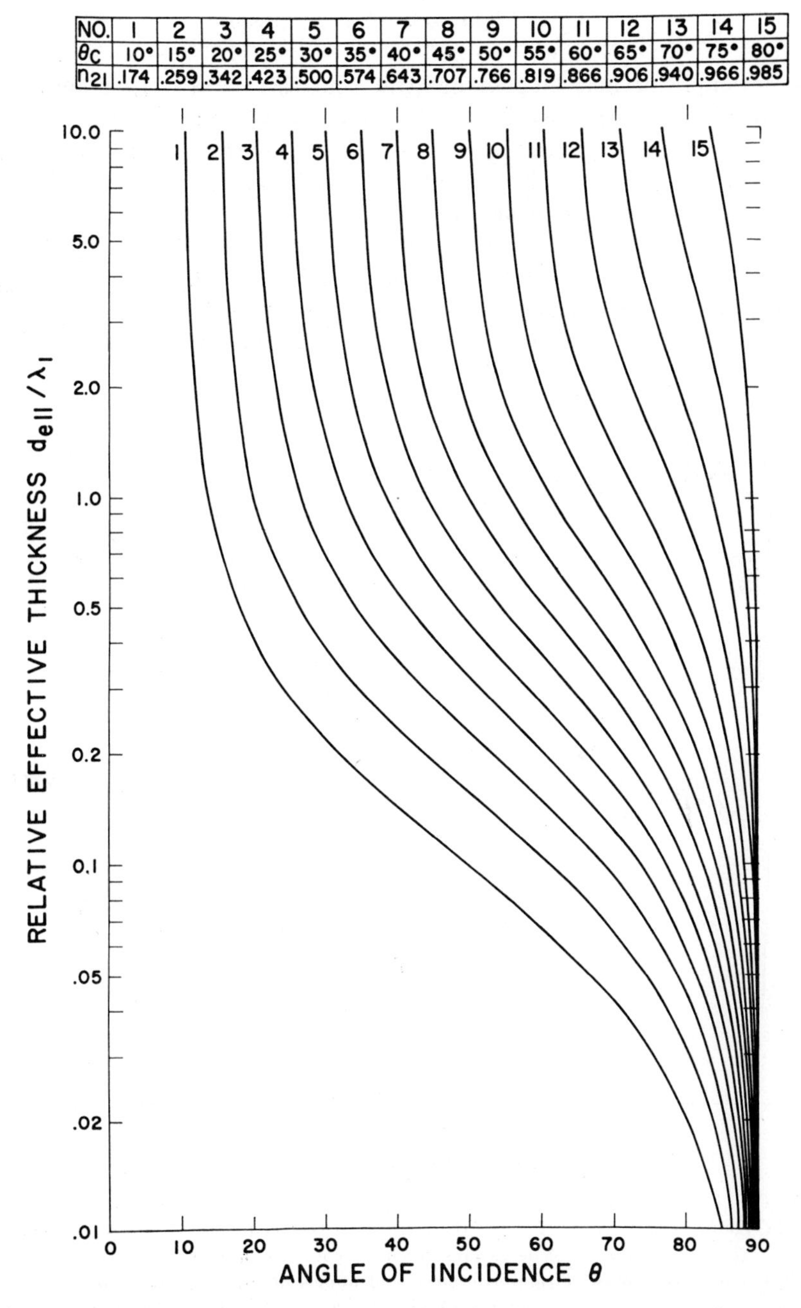

NO.	1	2	3	4	5	6	7	8	9	10	11	12	13	14	15
θ_C	10°	15°	20°	25°	30°	35°	40°	45°	50°	55°	60°	65°	70°	75°	80°
n_{21}	.174	.259	.342	.423	.500	.574	.643	.707	.766	.819	.866	.906	.940	.966	.985

Fig. 18. Working curves for relative effective thickness of bulk materials for ‖-polarization versus angle of incidence for a number of interfaces.

An example of matching of spectral contrasts by selecting angles for different IRE's, as was just discussed, is shown in Fig. 19. Figure 19a is the spectrum of polypropylene ($n_2 \sim 1.5$) using a Ge ($n_1 = 4.0$) IRE; hence $n_{21} = 0.375$, at $\theta = 23°$. Figure 19b is the spectrum of polypropylene using a KRS-5 ($n_1 = 2.4$) IRE; hence $n_{21} = 0.625$, at $\theta = 45°$.

Examples showing typical ranges of effective thicknesses obtainable are given in Table I for $n_{21} = 0.457$ (e.g., $n_1 = 3.5$, $n_2 = 1.6$, where $\theta_c = 27\frac{1}{2}°$) and for three selected angles. It should be noted that the effective thickness may be anywhere from a fraction of a wavelength to many wavelengths and

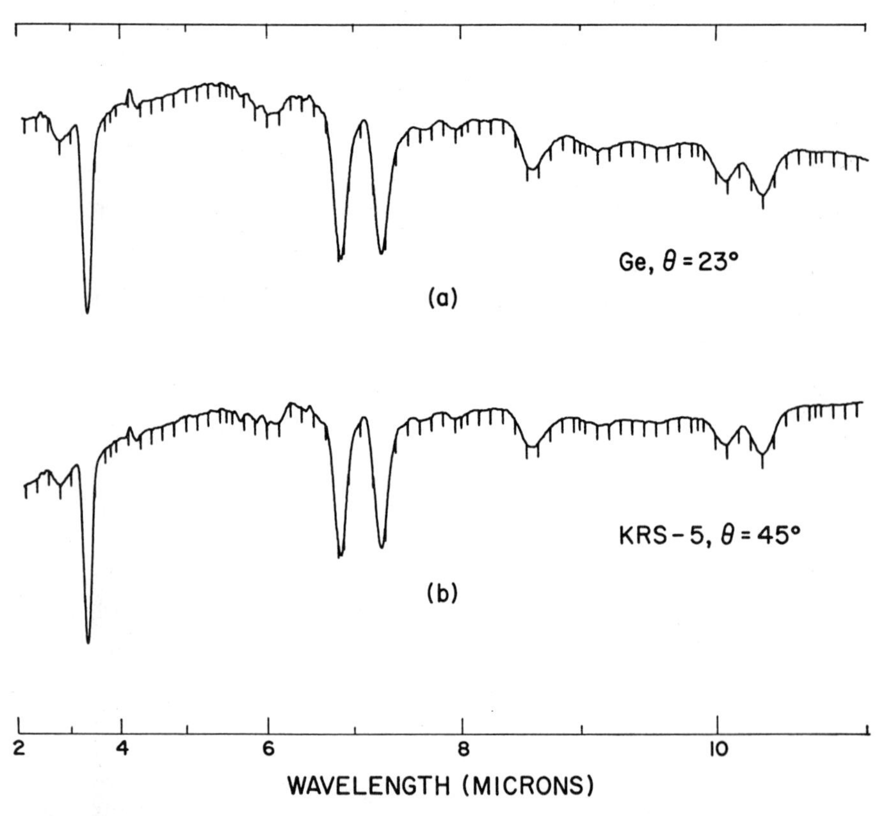

Fig. 19. Comparison of the spectra of polypropylene ($n_2 = 1.5$) for a single reflection using (a) Ge ($n_1 = 4.0$) at $\theta = 23°$ and (b) KRS-5 ($n_1 = 2.4$) at $\theta = 45°$. The two spectra, taken at the same ordinate scale expansion, have comparable contrast. Equal contrast for these combinations of refractive indices and angles of incidence is predicted by the effective thickness equation and points *a* and *b* of Fig. 17. The C—H band at 3.4 μ represents about 30% absorption.

that $d_{e\parallel}$ is greater than $d_{e\perp}$. Where multiple reflections are employed, d_e is increased by the factor N, the number of reflections.

TABLE I

Relative Effective Thickness, d_e/λ_1, for Various Angles of Incidence for $n_{21} = 0.457$

θ	28°	30°	45°
$d_{e\perp}/\lambda_1$	5.17	0.8	0.24
$d_{e\parallel}/\lambda_1$	22.5	2.5	0.36

As was shown earlier, the depth of penetration is only one of the factors which determines the degree of absorption for internal reflection. Choosing a reflection plate whose index is closer to that of the sample material (i.e., $n_{21} \rightarrow 1$) contributes to an increase in coupling in three ways for a fixed angle of incidence. The three factors are changes of penetration depth, E field, and matching and are given, respectively, by $(\sin^2 \theta - n_{21}^2)^{-1/2}$, $(1 - n_{21}^2)^{-1}$, and n_{21}. (This change in E field applies in the case of perpendicular polarization which was chosen for simplicity.) It is interesting to compare the relative increases in the three factors involved. This is done in Table II for two selected angles of incidence where a Ge ($n_1 = 4$) reflector plate is replaced by a KRS-5 ($n_1 = 2.4$) plate when measuring the spectrum of a material whose index is 1.6.

TABLE II

Increase in the Various Factors Controlling the Effective Thickness, $d_{e\perp}$, with Replacement of a Ge ($n_1 = 4$) IRE by a KRS-5 ($n_1 = 2.4$) IRE

θ	42°	45°
d_p	5.6	2.0
E	1.5	1.5
n_{21}	1.67	1.67
Net increase in $d_{e\perp}$	14.3	5

Although all of the factors are about equal for $\theta = 45°$, the effect of the penetration depth strongly predominates when the angle of incidence approaches the critical angle. The variation of the penetration depth with change in angle of incidence has been adequately demonstrated in numerous earlier experiments. The effect of the change in coupling due to change in the E field or matching can be demonstrated by eliminating the larger effect due to change in penetration depth. This can be done by making measurements on films which are thin compared to the penetration depth. (This represents the other limiting case for effective thickness.)

The simple equations for effective thickness are valid over a surprisingly wide range of absorption coefficients, as shown in Fig. 20, where exact computer calculations are compared to values predicted by the approximate equations. They are exact for very low absorption and deviate from exact calculations by only 10% for a reflection loss of 10% per reflection. For strong absorptions these equations can still be used by employing large angles of incidence where the absorption loss per reflection is low. Multiple reflections should be employed to enhance the total absorption.

2. Thin Films

Another case of interest that can be treated in a straightforward manner is that of very thin films (H37). When the films are much thinner than a pene-

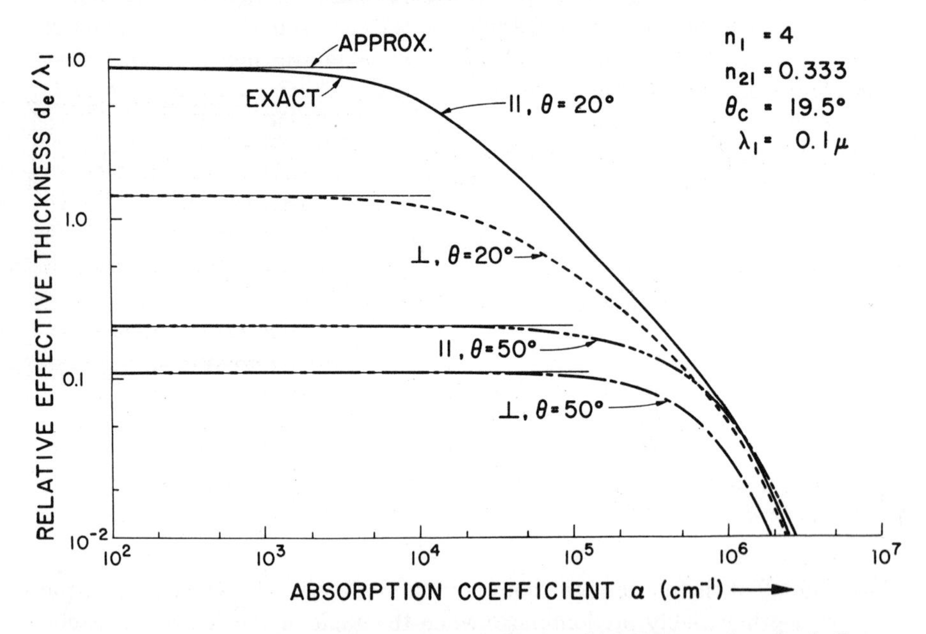

Fig. 20. Range of validity of approximate effective thickness equations for bulk materials with variation in absorption coefficient. The exact computer curves become asymptotic to the approximate values, determined from the equations for the low absorption approximation, at lower values of the absorption coefficient. The approximate values become more valid as the angle of incidence is increased (and the effective thickness decreases).

tration depth, i.e., $d \ll d_p$, the electric field can be assumed to be constant over the film thickness and the effective thickness is then given by

$$d_e = \frac{n_{21} E_0^2 d}{\cos \theta}. \tag{28}$$

The electric field amplitudes in the film are given by

$$E_\perp = 2 \cos \theta / (1 - n_{31}^2)^{1/2} \tag{29}$$

and

$$E_\parallel = \frac{2 \cos \theta \, [(1 + n_{32}^4) \sin^2 \theta - n_{31}^2]^{1/2}}{(1 - n_{31}^2)^{1/2} \, [(1 + n_{31}^2) \sin^2 \theta - n_{31}^2]^{1/2}}. \tag{30}$$

There are now three media, as shown in Fig. 21, and it should be noted that the fields are controlled more nearly by media *1* and *3* rather than by media *1* and *2*. (Attention is drawn to an error in a publication (H30) that describes the measurements of the angular dependence of the fields in which it was assumed that the fields were controlled by medium *2*. This correction, however, does not affect the conclusions in that paper.) On inserting these E fields in equation (28), the effective thicknesses for perpendicular and parallel polarization are, respectively,

$$d_{e\perp} = \frac{4 \, n_{21} \, d \cos \theta}{(1 - n_{31}^2)} \tag{31}$$

and

$$d_{e\parallel} = \frac{4 \, n_{21} \, d \cos \theta [(1 + n_{32}^4) \sin^2 \theta - n_{31}^2]}{(1 - n_{31}^2) \, [(1 + n_{31}^2) \sin^2 \theta - n_{31}^2]}. \tag{32}$$

These equations are quite practical, since they are good to a few percent when $2\pi d/\lambda_1 < 0.1$ and $\kappa_2 < 0.1$.

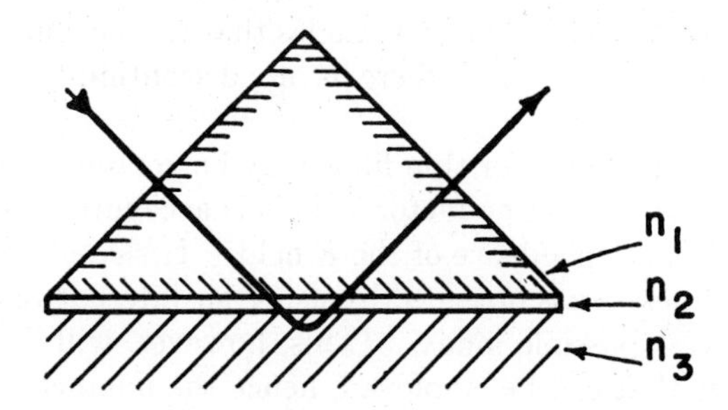

Fig. 21. Measurements on thin films via internal reflection spectroscopy. Note that three media are involved.

The same factors that control the effective thickness for bulk materials also control the effective thickness for thin films, except for penetration depth. In place of penetration depth, the effective thickness for thin films is proportional to the actual film thickness, d. The important consequences of this are the following:

1. The effective thickness does not become indefinitely large as the angle of incidence approaches the critical angle $\sin^{-1} n_{31} = \theta_{ca}$.

2. The spectra do not become distorted and displaced for measurements made near this critical angle.

3. The absorption bands at longer wavelengths are no longer relatively stronger as they were for bulk material, nor does an absorption band become broadened on the long wavelength side. The internal reflection spectra of thin films should thus resemble those obtained via transmission more closely than do internal reflection spectra of bulk materials.

A series of calculations of the dependence of effective thickness for films of various refractive indices on internal reflection elements of various indices is shown by the curves of Figs. 22, 23, and 24. In Fig. 22 it is assumed that the refractive index, n_2, of the film equals 1.6 and that it is placed in turn on internal reflection elements with n_1 equal to 1.6, 2.4, and 4. In Figs. 23 and 24 films with indices $n_2 = 2.4$ and 4.0 are placed in turn on these same internal reflection elements. It should be noted that the effective thicknesses terminate at a finite value, unlike the case for bulk materials wherein they become infinitely large at $\theta = \theta_c$. These figures can be used as guidelines in determining the optimum conditions required for the study of any particular film via internal reflection spectroscopy. The following points should be noted:

1. Measurements on thin films can be made over a wider range of angles of incidence than for bulk materials. The critical angle for measurements on thin films is determined by n_{31} and not by n_{21}; i.e., the refractive index of the thin film does not dictate the range of angles that can be employed. When θ passes through $\theta_{cs} = \sin^{-1} n_{21}$, there is no discontinuity in the effective thickness.

2. The effective thickness for thin films may be greater or smaller than the actual film thickness by a large factor. This is accounted for by the magnitude and the angular dependence of the E field. It should be noted that the largest effective thickness is obtained by using an internal reflection element (IRE) of the lowest possible index. (This, however, will limit the smallest angle of incidence that can be employed, hence the number of reflections.)

3. The effective thickness for $\|$-polarization may be greater or smaller than that for $\perp$-polarization depending on whether n_{32}^4/n_{31}^2 is greater or smaller

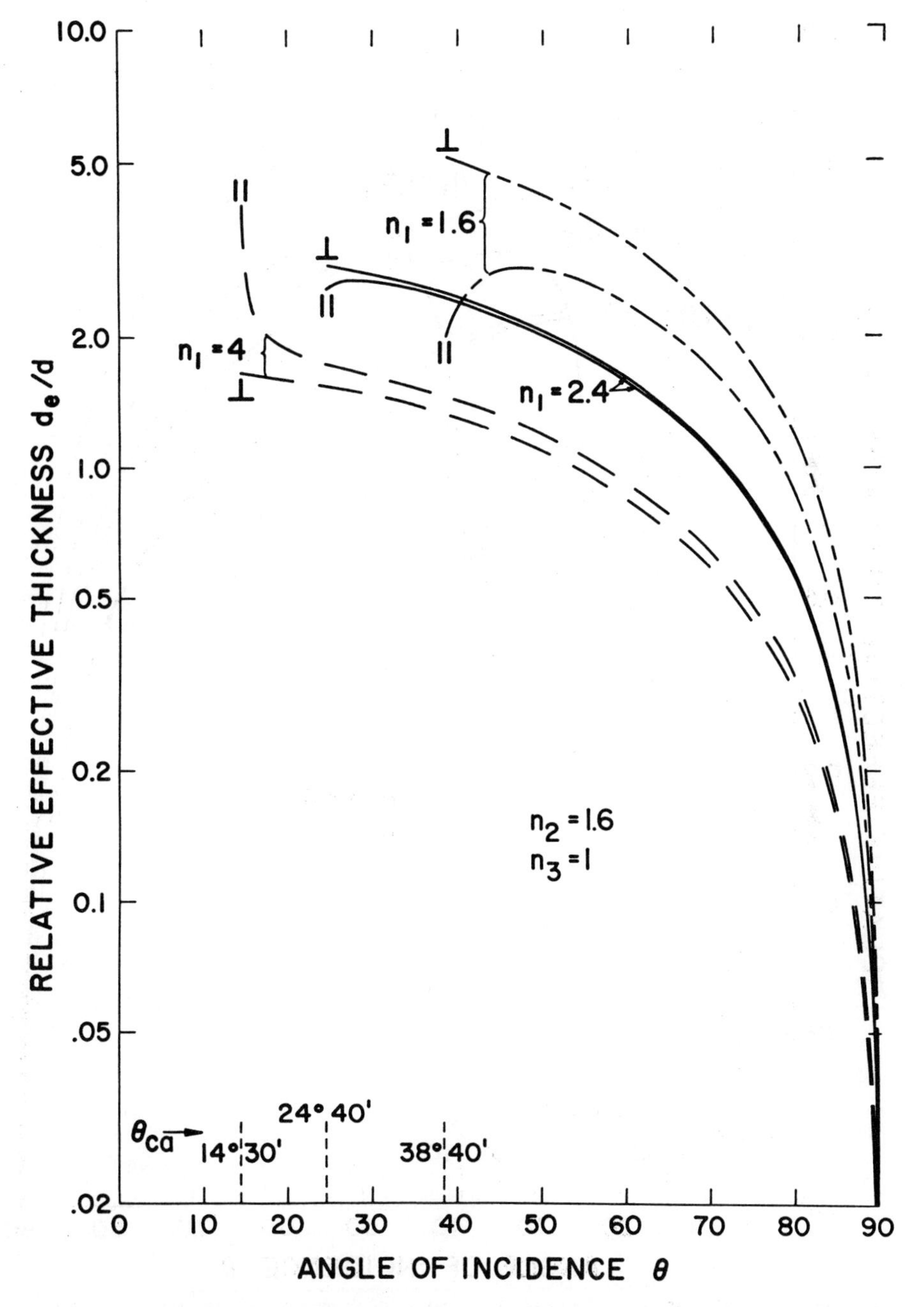

Fig. 22. Relative effective thickness for a thin film of refractive index, $n_2 = 1.6$, on internal reflection elements (IRE's) of various refractive indices, n_1. Here θ_{ca} is the critical angle of the crystal–air interface.

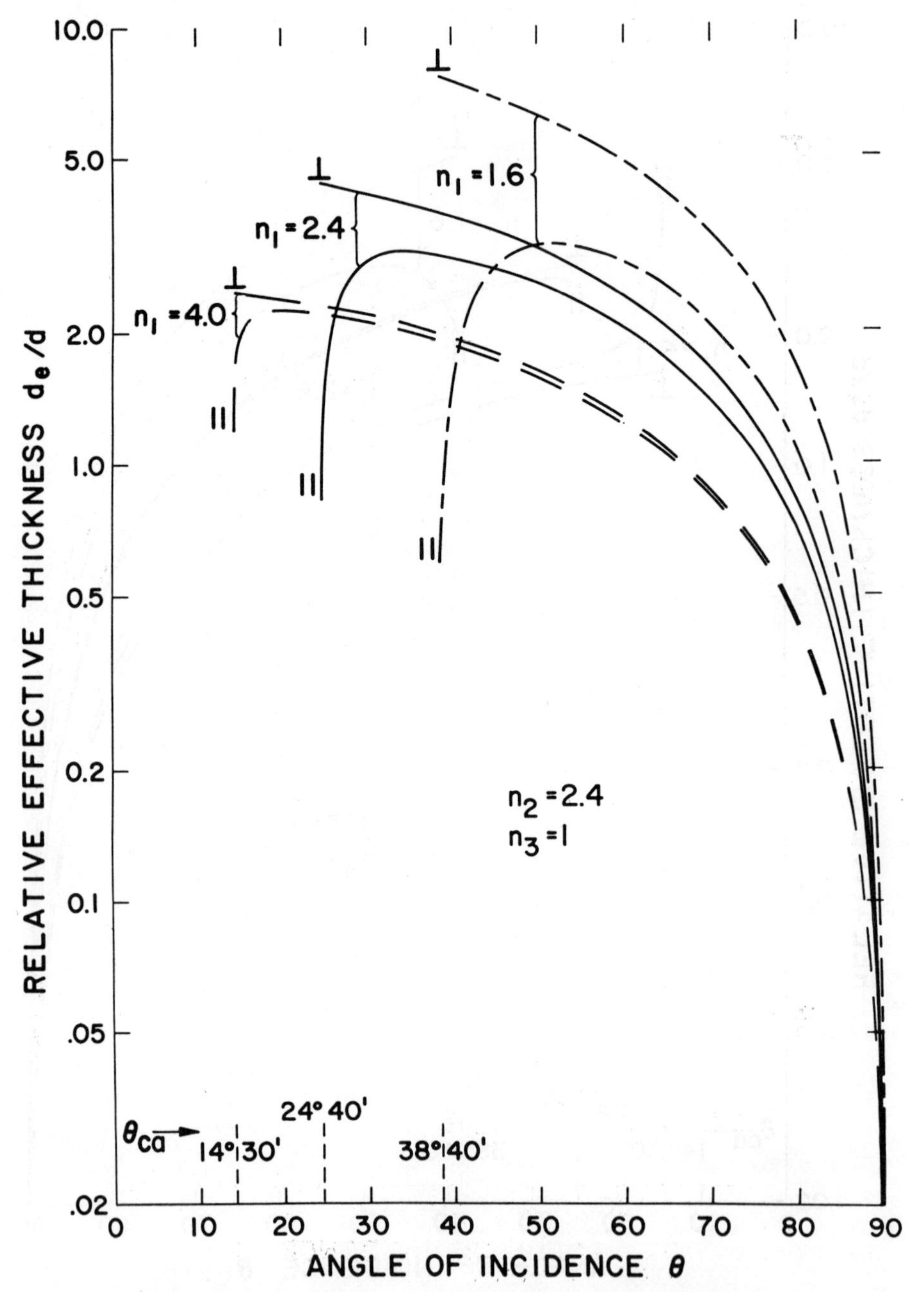

Fig. 23. Relative effective thickness for a thin film of refractive index, $n_2 = 2.4$, on IRE's of various refractive indices, n_1. θ_{ca} is the critical angle of the crystal–air interface.

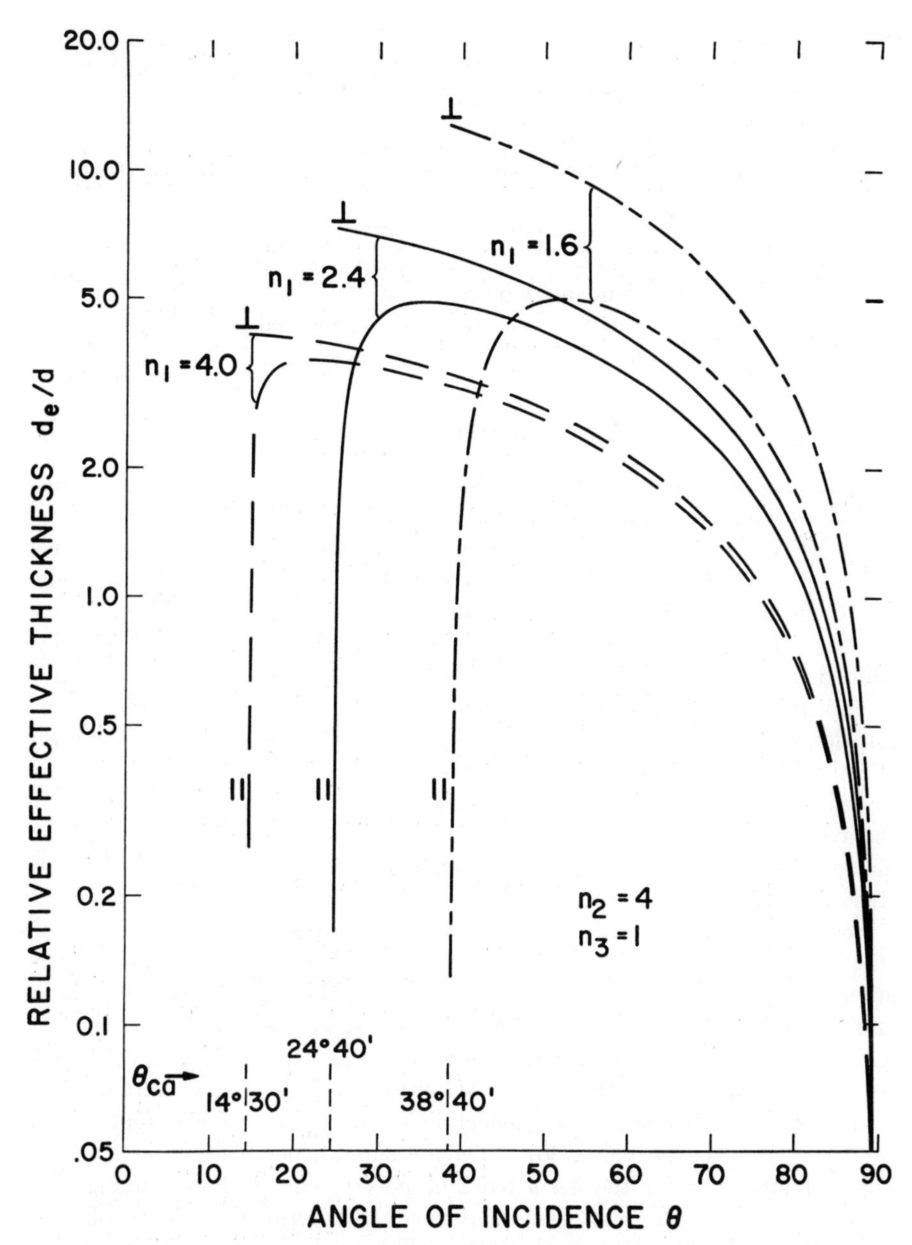

Fig. 24. Relative effective thickness for a thin film of refractive index, $n_2 = 4$ on IRE's of various refractive indices, n_1. θ_{ca} is the critical angle of the crystal–air interface.

than unity, respectively. This is determined by whether or not $E_{\parallel}$ is greater or smaller than $E_{\perp}$. It should be recalled that for bulk materials $E_{\parallel}$ is always greater than $E_{\perp}$ in the rarer medium.

4. Measurements can be made on films which have a higher index than that of the IRE provided the angle of incidence at the IRE–film interface exceeds $\theta_{ca} = \sin^{-1} n_{31}$.

5. With decreasing θ, in the vicinity of the critical angle, $d_{e\parallel}$ may increase or decrease depending on whether n_{32}^4/n_{31}^2 is greater or less than unity, respectively. All of these dependencies on polarization for both bulk material and thin films serve to emphasize the need of using polarized light or of knowing the state of polarization of the light beam for quantitative measurements.

3. Experimental Verification

Almost all of the factors affecting the coupling mechanisms, hence effective thicknesses, for bulk material and thin films have been verified.

The presence of the evanescent field has been demonstrated in many experiments as was discussed previously. The depth of penetration, which strongly affects the effective thickness for bulk materials, however, cannot be measured directly. In the experiment of Schaefer and Gross (S3) in which they studied the coupling between two prisms, the depth of penetration enters in a complicated way. In other experiments which measure the degree of absorption versus absorbing film thickness, the penetration depth enters via the effective thickness. In one particular experiment good agreement was obtained because, fortuitously, the penetration depth was almost identical to the average effective thickness (H21) for the index ratio and for the angle of incidence employed. (Similar measurements have recently been made by Reichert (R9).)

Because the depth of penetration does not appear in the equations of effective thickness for very thin films, these equations can be employed with advantage to measure the angular dependence of the electric field amplitude and sampling area from a measurement of αd_e versus angle of incidence. This was done for the absorption of polystyrene at a wavelength of 3.4 μ and for the poly(methyl methacrylate) (Lucite) band at 5.75 μ employing a variable-angle multiple internal reflection silicon plate. It was found that $d_{e\parallel} > d_{e\perp}$ as was expected (H30). The measured dependence of $\alpha d_{e\perp}$ versus angle of incidence for the 3.4 μ band of polystyrene is shown in Fig. 25. Good agreement with theory is evident since the experimental points follow a cosine law as required by equation (31). This curve also shows that there is no discontinuity as θ passes through $\theta_{cs} = \sin^{-1} n_{21}$ ($27\frac{1}{4}°$).

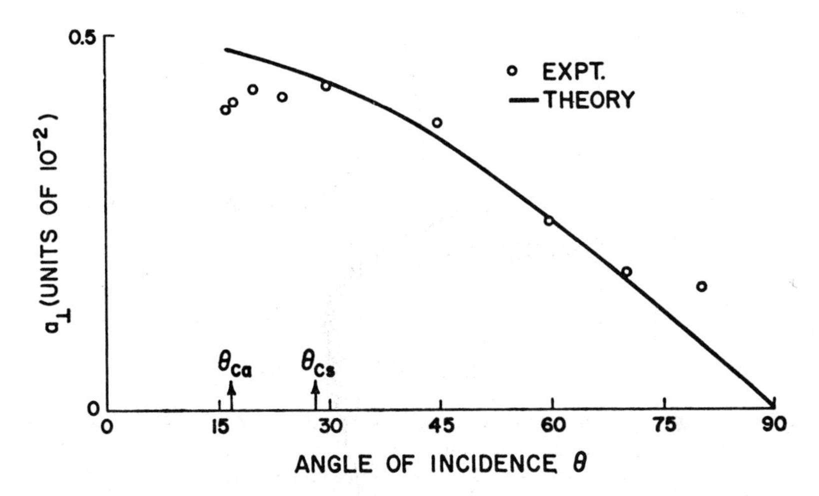

Fig. 25. Absorption parameter, $a_{\perp}$, per reflection versus angle of incidence for a polystyrene film on a silicon internal reflection plate ($n_1 = 3.5$) at a wavelength of 3.4 μ. The solid line represents theoretical curve and the points represent experimental measurements. $a_{\perp}$ decreases as θ increases and there is no discontinuity at θ_{cs}.

Thin films can also be employed to demonstrate the increase in the effective thickness with better matching (i.e., $n_{21} \rightarrow 1$). This can be done by placing an identical amount of thin film absorber on two IRE's of different refractive indices and recording the strength of absorption at the same angle of incidence. Two internal reflection plates made from Ge and KRS-5 were placed in a balanced double-beam system (at $\theta = 45°$). A thin film of poly(methyl methacrylate) (Lucite) (approx. 10^{-5} g) was placed on the surface of the Ge plate and the absorption band showing a maximum at 5.75 μ (upper curve in Fig. 26) was recorded. This represents 25–30% absorption. An identical quantity of Lucite was then placed on the surface of the KRS-5 plate in the reference beam. If the absorption of the reference beam would have been the same, it would have had the effect of exactly canceling the absorption in the sample beam and restoring a flat base line. This effect was not the case, however, since the lower curve of Fig. 26, which represents the resultant tracing, shows a minimum. This finding indicates that the absorption by the same quantity of Lucite on the KRS-5 more than compensates for the absorption by the Lucite on the Ge surface. The signal from the Lucite on the KRS-5 represents 50–60% absorption. The relative absorption parameter for KRS-5 to that of Ge was determined to be approximately 2. Because the material was in thin film form, the effect of penetration depth is eliminated,

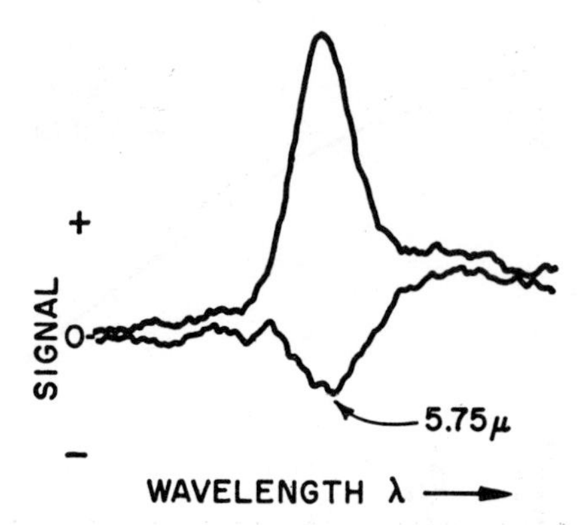

Fig. 26. Experimental results showing increased coupling to evanescent wave resulting from better matching. Results were obtained by placing 10^{-5} g of thin film of Lucite on similar Ge and KRS-5 plates at $\theta = 45°$ in reference and sample beams of a double-beam instrument. Positive deflection represents absorption band when the sample is placed on Ge plate. Negative deflection results when identical quantity is placed on KRS-5 plate without removing sample from the Ge plate. The negative deflection means greater absorption (stronger coupling) for sample on KRS-5 plate than for sample on Ge plate.

and the only contributions to the change in absorption parameter are change in matching and change in E field. Their respective magnitudes are

$$\frac{n_{\mathrm{Ge}}}{n_{\mathrm{KRS\text{-}5}}} = \frac{4}{2.4} = 1.65$$

and

$$\frac{E^2_{\mathrm{KRS\text{-}5}}}{E^2_{\mathrm{Ge}}} = \frac{(1 - n_{31}^{\;2})_{\mathrm{Ge}}}{(1 - n_{31}^{\;2})_{\mathrm{KRS\text{-}5}}} = \frac{1 - (1/4.0)^2}{1 - (1/2.4)^2} = \frac{0.94}{0.83} = 1.15.$$

The net expected gain in absorption parameter from using KRS-5 in place of Ge is thus $1.65 \times 1.15 = 1.9$, which falls within the range of the measured gain. The results shown in Fig. 26 are thus taken as experimental proof of the enhanced absorption coming from better matching.

Other experimental results supporting a number of the conclusions reached regarding the behavior of effective thickness equations for thin films are shown in Figs. 28 and 29. In all of these measurements more than 100 reflections were employed.

It should be recalled that for bulk materials, the lower limit of the working angle is roughly governed by the critical angle of the IRE–specimen interface, $\theta_{cs} = \sin^{-1} n_{21}$. For smaller angles of incidence the reflected beam does not depend as strongly on the absorption coefficient. Furthermore, multiple

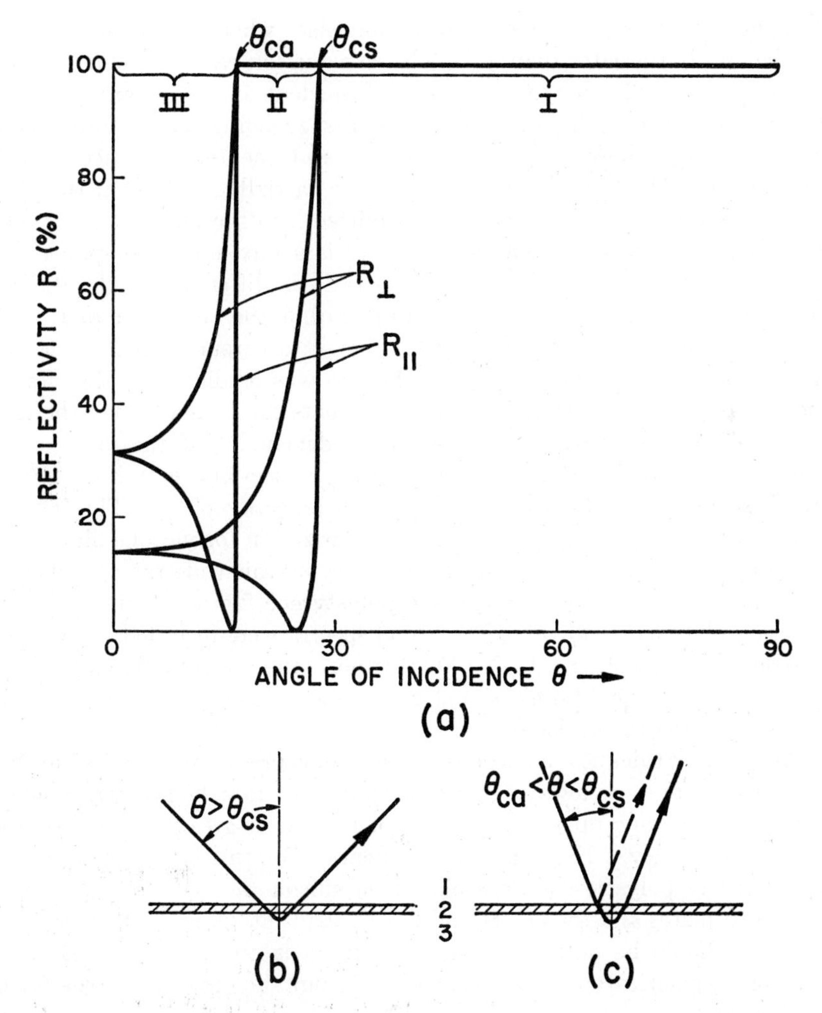

Fig. 27. Internal reflection versus angle of incidence when thin film is present on the surface. There are two critical angles. θ_{cs} is determined by media *1* and *2* while θ_{ca} is determined by media *1* and *3*. Total reflection occurs for all angles greater than θ_{ca}.

reflections cannot be employed because with the lower value of the reflectivity, the energy in the beam is quickly dissipated. For thin films, on the other hand, the lower limit of the working angle is independent of the index of the specimen and is determined only by the critical angle of the IRE–air interface measured in medium *1*, $\theta_{ca} = \sin^{-1} n_{31}$. The reason for this is that the light cannot escape from the reflection plate when the incident angle is less than θ_{cs} but greater than θ_{ca}. This explanation can be understood with reference to Fig. 27 where three ranges of incident angles, separated by two critical angles, can be distinguished. The first region (I) is the normal range from θ_{cs} to 90° where total reflection occurs at the *1–2* interface. In the second region (II), from θ_{ca} to θ_{cs}, the light is partially reflected at the plate–specimen interface, the rest being transmitted into the film but reflected at the film–air interface. Even though there is a mixture or components reflected from the two interfaces and the ratio is different for the different polarizations, all of the light is trapped within the reflection plate. For angles below θ_{ca} (region III), the light is quickly lost from the plate because of the low values of the reflectivities. Thus, as was predicted by the effective thickness equations for thin films, measurements can be made over the range of angles from θ_{ca} to grazing incidence, independent of the index of the surface film, provided that the outer surface of the film is uniform and its outside surface is parallel to the surface of the reflection plate. This has been shown to be the case for both $\perp$- and $\|$-polarization for various films on Ge and Si reflection plates. Measurements showing this wide range of working angles are shown in Fig. 28 for a thin polystyrene film on a silicon internal reflection plate where $\theta_{cs} = 27\frac{1}{4}°$. Good spectra were recorded for angles of incidence as low as $\theta_{ca} = 16.5°$. Furthermore, there was no discontinuity in the effective thickness for either polarization as θ passed through $\theta_{cs} = 27\frac{1}{4}°$, as was predicted theoretically.

The effective thickness equations for thin films predict that, unlike for bulk materials where $d_{e\|}$ is always greater than $d_{e\perp}$, $d_{e\|}$ may be greater or smaller than $d_{e\perp}$, depending upon whether or not n_{32}^4/n_{31}^2 is greater or smaller than unity, respectively. Experimental verification for this is shown in Fig. 29. Thin films of polystyrene were placed on silicon ($n_1 = 3.5$) and sapphire ($n_1 = 1.6$) plates and the O—H and C—H bands at 2.9 and 3.4 μ were measured. It should be noted that the absorption is greater for $\|$-polarization than for $\perp$-polarization for the silicon plate but the opposite is true for the sapphire plate.

In the discussion of the effective thickness equations, it was pointed out that because the depth of penetration does not enter in the equations for effective thickness of thin films, there should be a closer resemblance between the internal reflection spectra for thin films and transmission spectra than between internal reflection spectra of bulk material and transmission spectra. The close resemblance between transmission and internal reflection spectra of thin films is shown in Fig. 30 for the C—H band of polystyrene at 3.4 μ. The close resemblance between internal reflection spectra of thin films and

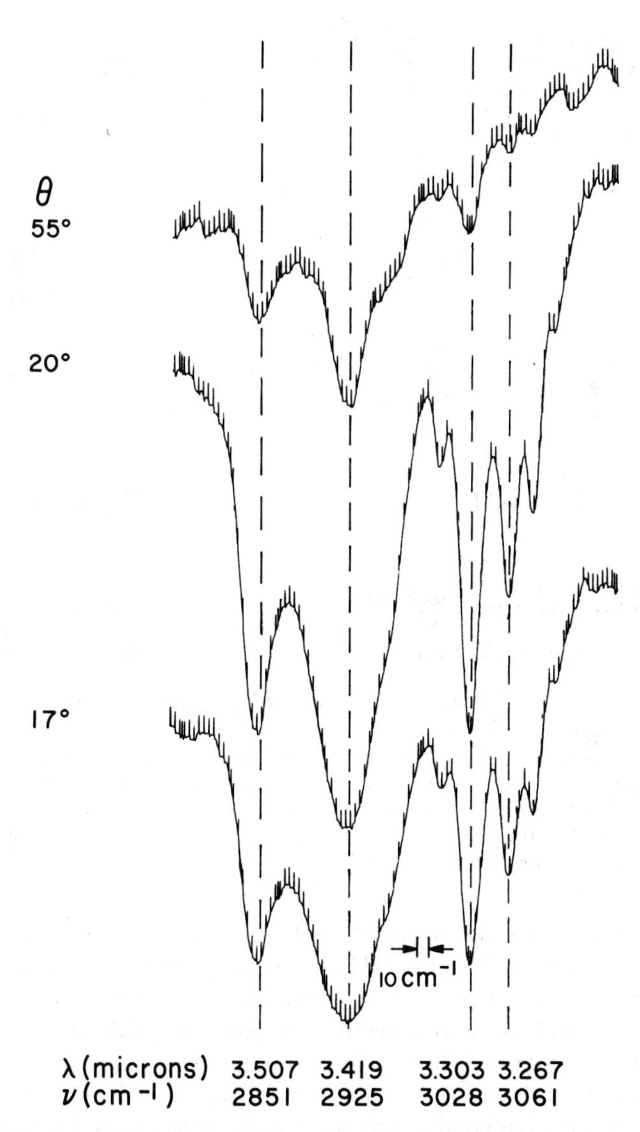

Fig. 28. Comparison of multiple internal reflection spectra, recorded using various angles of incidence, of a thin film of polystyrene on a silicon internal reflection plate for unpolarized light. Note the lack of displacement of the minima over wide range of angles of incidence.

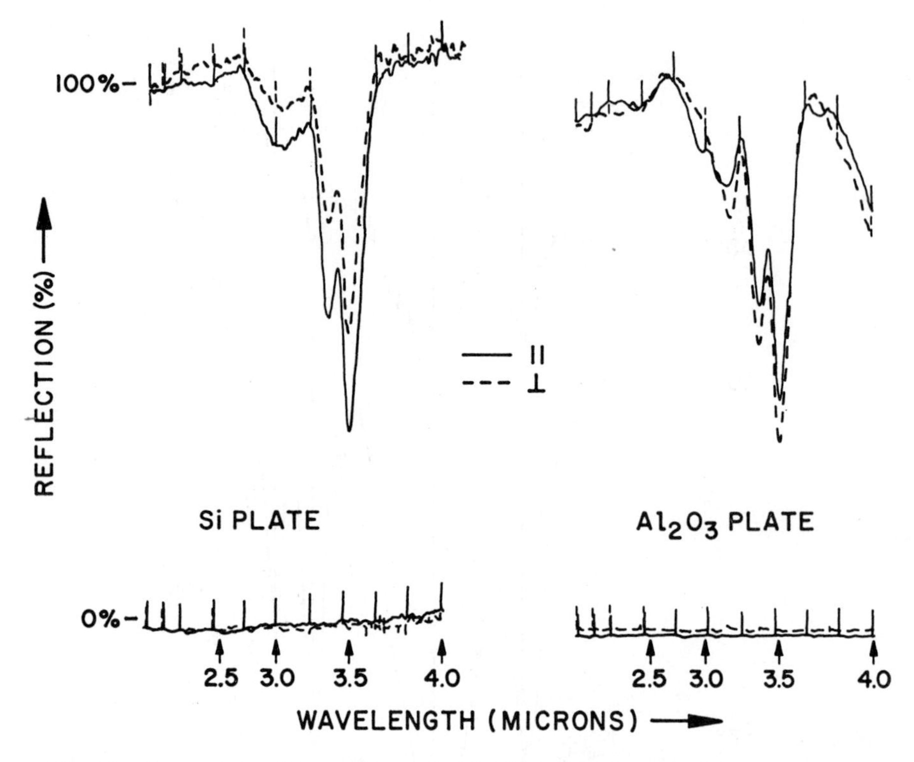

Fig. 29. Comparison of the spectra of the C—H band at 3.4 μ of a thin polystyrene film on a Si plate and on an Al_2O_3 plate for $\perp$- and $\|$-polarization. The O—H band at 3.0 μ is due to adsorbed water on the surfaces of the plates. The contrast of the spectrum is higher for $\|$-polarization than it is for $\perp$-polarization for the Si plate whereas the opposite is true for the Al_2O_3 plate, as predicted by theory.

transmission spectra is also demonstrated by some results of Hermann (H43). Some measurements of Hannah (H4) on silicone lubricant, shown in Fig. 31, in which he compares transmission (curve *a*) to internal reflection on thin films (curve *b*) and internal reflection on bulk materials (curve *c*), clearly demonstrate a number of these points as well. The similarity between the transmission and internal reflection on thin films is evident. It should be noted that the relative band intensities are about the same for these curves. For internal reflection on bulk material, on the other hand, the bands are displaced to longer wavelengths and the bands at the longer wavelengths are relatively stronger due to the increase of the penetration depth of the evanescent wave with increasing wavelength. Numerous other examples comparing

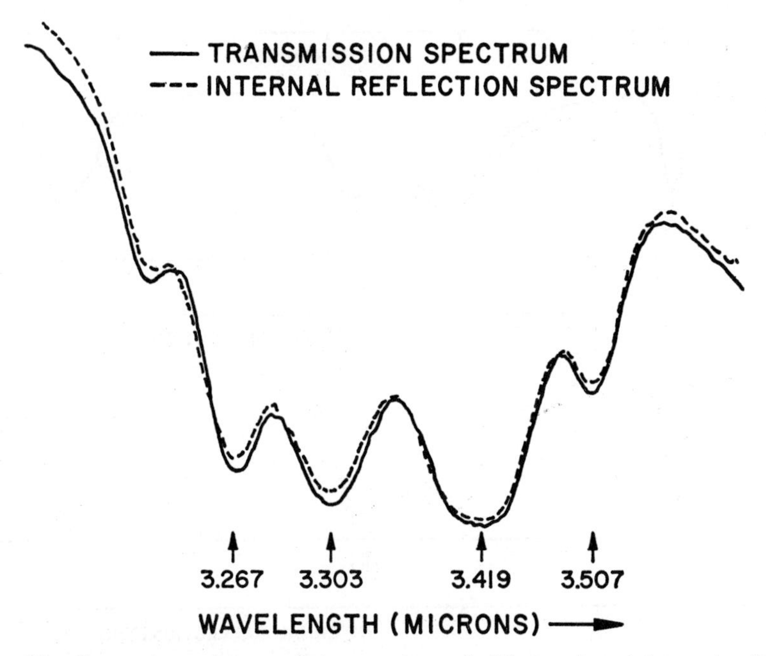

Fig. 30. Comparison of transmission spectrum (solid curve) and internal reflection spectrum (dashed curve) of the band at 3.4 μ of a thin polystyrene film. The close similarity of the two spectra is apparent.

transmission and internal reflection spectra of bulk materials are given in Chapter Seven.

The equations for effective thickness are very useful. They are helpful in understanding the nature of the interaction mechanisms of the evanescent wave with an absorbing medium. They can also be used for quantitative measurements providing the absorptions are low. Their range of usefulness can be extended by employing large angles of incidence (to keep the absorption per reflection small) and then employing multiple reflections to increase the contrast of the spectra.

4. Relative Band Intensities and Profiles

Spectroscopists analyze spectra by noting not only the location of absorption bands but also their relative intensities and profiles or shapes. Since the relative band intensities and profiles may be different for internal reflection compared to transmission and since there are several factors which affect them, a few comments are in order.

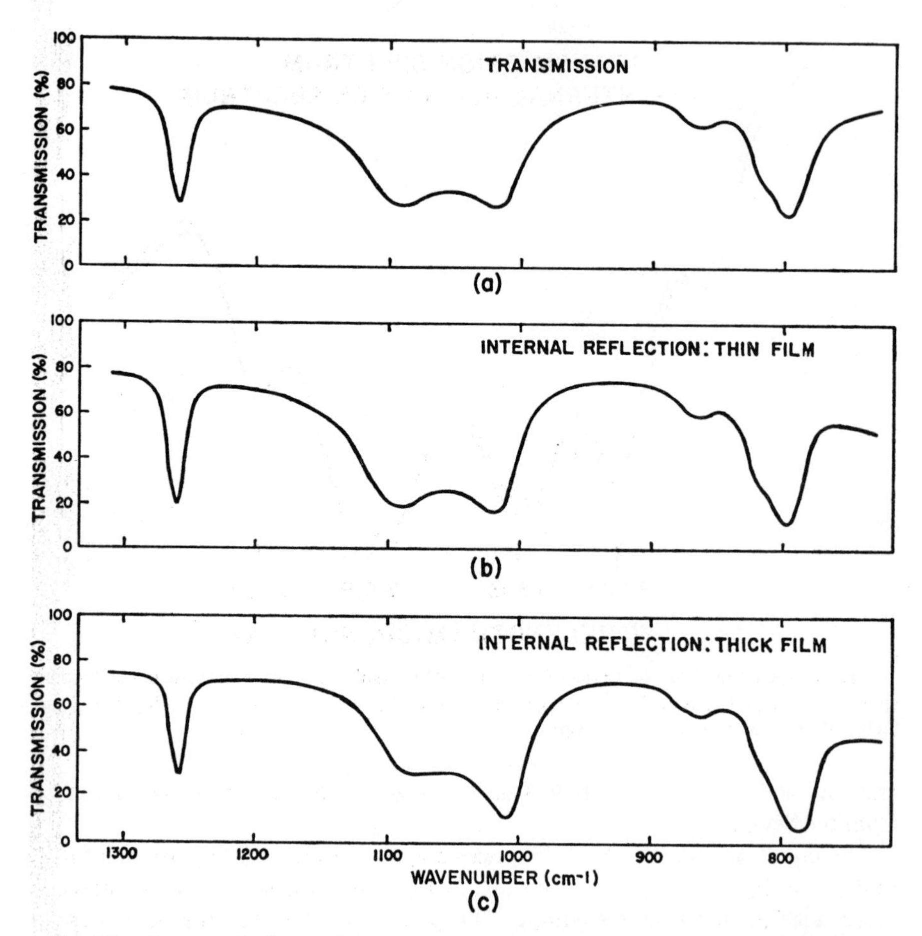

Fig. 31. Spectra of silicone lubricant. (a) Transmission. (b) Internal reflection on thin film, KRS-5 IRE, $\theta = 60°$. (c) Internal reflection on thick film, KRS-5 IRE, $\theta = 60°$. Note the similarity of spectra for transmission and internal reflection for thin film. Also note for thick film displacement of bands to longer λ and greater relative band intensity at longer λ. (Courtesy of R. W. Hannah, Perkin-Elmer Corp., Norwalk, Conn.)

For thin films the effective thickness is independent of wavelength as was shown by equations (31) and (32). Figures 30 and 31 indicate that the relative intensities of the absorption bands of the spectra of thin films recorded via internal reflection are very close to those observed in transmission. The absence of penetration depth and wavelength in the effective thickness equations for thin films also implies that the band profiles will not be sensitive to change in angle of incidence. A careful comparison of band profiles for transmission and internal reflection on thin films has not yet been made; however, since the relative band intensities compare favorably, it is expected that the band profiles will also be not much different.

For bulk materials wherein the absorptions are small, equations (26) and (27) show that the effective thickness is directly proportional to wavelength. For low absorptions approximate comparison of band intensities recorded via internal reflection to those observed in transmission can be made if the intensities of the bands of internal reflection spectra are divided by the wavelength. For strong absorptions, on the other hand, where the absorption law is much more complicated, no simple rule can be given for comparing the intensity of bands recorded via internal reflection to those observed in transmission. This is evident from Figs. 5 and 20. The dependence of the penetration depth on wavelength and on index of refraction can lead to considerable broadening of the band on the long wavelength side as will be discussed in more detail in Chapter Three. Therefore, the profiles of bands recorded via IRS will be different from those recorded via transmission.

The presence of a film between the sample and the IRE or non-uniform contact will result in a much stronger dependence of the band intensity on wavelength than predicted by equations (26) and (27) for low absorptions. This is obvious from the experiments described in connection with Figs. 12, 14, and 15 whereby it was shown that the effect of the FTR layer decreases sharply with wavelength. When good physical contact between the IRE and the sample is not obtained, for comparison to transmission, the necessary correction of the band intensities recorded via internal reflection is a $(\lambda - C)^{-1}$ law (D23) rather than the simple λ^{-1} law which is adequate for good contact. The constant C is rather complicated and is dependent on the thickness of the film separating the sample and the IRE or an average thickness if the contact is non-uniform.

Thus, except for thin films and for low absorptions in bulk material where there is good contact between the sample and the IRE, band intensities and profiles recorded via internal reflection cannot readily be compared to those observed in transmission. This does not, however, detract from the general use of internal reflection spectroscopy as a qualitative tool.

The next chapter will be devoted to a discussion of how these effective thicknesses change due to the dispersion in the index of refraction in the vicinity of absorption bands and how these changes affect the character of the spectra.

CHAPTER THREE

EFFECT OF DISPERSION IN THE REFRACTIVE INDEX ON ABSORPTION AND REFLECTION

A. Introduction

Optical spectra in general represent neither a true measurement of the absorption coefficient nor of the index of refraction. A qualitative discussion of what is recorded via transmission, external reflection, and internal reflection and of how the dispersion in index of refraction affects the spectra is given in this chapter. For internal reflection, the change in the spectrum with change in angle of incidence is correlated with the change in effective thicknesses with angle of incidence.

B. Transmission and External Reflection

Although the optical constants n and κ of absorption bands are fundamental parameters, they are generally not used for identification purposes, principally because they cannot be determined easily. As a result, simple reflection or transmission spectra are often recorded for this purpose; but these spectra are related to the optical constants in a complicated way. It should be recalled that there is a dispersion in the refractive index in the vicinity of an absorption band and this dispersion may be very large for sharp bands. This change in refractive index causes changes in reflectivity losses which are generally not taken into consideration when simple transmission spectra are recorded. These spectra are still useful since the condition for measurement, and hence the spectra, are readily reproduced; entire libraries of characteristic transmission spectra are available which are extremely valuable for analytical purposes. In some cases, the character of the spectrum is dependent on the nature of the sample. In diffuse reflectance measurements (W4), for example, the particle size influences the nature of the spectrum. The interpretation of these spectra is quite complex since the analysis involves transmission, as well as reflection, both of which are dependent on particle size. Conventional transmission and reflection spectra thus represent neither a single physical parameter nor a simple combination of two parameters. The manner in which the dispersion in the refractive index controls the character of the spectrum will be described qualitatively in a later section.

C. Internal Reflection

Internal reflection spectra also do not represent a single optical constant but are related to both the refractive index and absorption coefficients. Just as in transmission measurements, the dispersion in the refractive index affects the spectra for internal reflection. Furthermore, the effect of this dispersion is dependent on the angle of incidence near the critical angle for measurements on bulk materials. For measurements made at angles greater than a few degrees above the critical angle, the character of the spectra does not change much with change in angle of incidence, except for contrast, and the internal reflection spectra can be readily compared to transmission spectra. For measurements made near the critical angle, on the other hand, the bands become broadened on the long wavelength side and shifted to longer wavelengths, both effects increasing as the angle of incidence is decreased. Advantage is taken of this phenomenon in the determination of optical constants (F4,H9,H10,C7,G8,G9).

Since optical spectra are used most widely for analytical purposes, a few simple rules of thumb can be given which are useful as guidelines for recording internal reflection spectra. In general, it is advantageous to use an internal reflection element of low refractive index and an angle near the critical angle because a higher contrast spectrum is obtained in this way. However, the spectra are then more likely to be distorted and shifted. For the special cases of thin films and bulk materials the following remarks can be made.

1. Thin Films

For very thin films, the location of the bands and their shapes are independent of angle of incidence and they usually resemble those recorded via transmission very closely. For such thin films the absorption per reflection is generally very small and the low absorption equations for thin films, (31) and (32) of Chapter Two, are quite valid. In these equations, as already discussed, the change in the penetration depth (d_p) does not affect the effective thickness, since d_p is absent in the equations and the electric field is not controlled by the index of the film (H37) (except slightly for $d_{e\parallel}$). The index of the film enters only via the index matching term, n_{21}, and this is independent of angle of incidence. Therefore, it is understandable that there should be no relative distortion or shift of the absorption bands over the entire range of angles of incidence which is from $\theta_{ca} = \sin^{-1} n_{31}$ to 90°. This has been experimentally verified for the 3.4 μ band of polystyrene using a silicon variable-angle multiple internal reflection plate over angles of incidence ranging from 75° to 16.5°. Some selected spectra from these measurements were shown in Fig. 28

of Chapter Two. Similar measurements were obtained for the absorption band of Lucite at 5.75 μ but using polarized light. No significant shift or distortion with change in angle of incidence was detected for either $\perp$- or $\|$-polarization for measurements at different angles of incidence.

[If there is a very strong dispersion in n_2, it is clearly evident from equations (30) and (31) and Figs. 22, 23, and 24 of Chapter Two that because of the different dependency of the effective thickness on n_2, the absorption maxima for $\perp$- and $\|$-polarization may not occur at the same wavelength. Such a relative shift has been demonstrated (L5a) for the 9.2 μ band of SiO (where n_2 changes from 0 to 7 across the width of the band) on a Ge IRE where the band for $\perp$-polarization was displaced to a longer λ relative to the band for $\|$-polarization with a crossover at $n_2 = 2$, as predicted by equations (31) and (32) of Chapter Two. Furthermore, for such strong dispersion in n_2, displacement of the bands recorded via internal reflection relative to those recorded via transmission should also be expected, as will become evident.]

The close resemblance of internal reflection spectra of very thin films and transmission spectra were shown also in Fig. 30 of Chapter Two for a case where the dispersion in n_2 was presumably not large. In some measurements on thin films a very slight shift (a fraction of a wavelength) to shorter wavelengths relative to transmission spectra was detected. There is no simple explanation for this since transmission spectra depend on n_2 in a complicated way. The equations for effective thickness of thin films show that the internal reflection spectra follow $n_2\alpha_2$ fairly closely. Other examples of internal reflection spectra of thin films which show close resemblance to transmission spectra are measurements of Hermann (H43) and some careful measurements of Hannah (H4), which were shown in Fig. 31 of Chapter Two. Figure 31 demonstrated many of the points discussed in comparing internal reflection spectra of thin films to transmission spectra. In these measurements a very slight shift of internal reflection spectra for thin films to shorter wavelengths relative to transmission spectra was also observed. Good agreement was found between the relative intensity of bands at different wavelengths for internal reflection spectra of thin films and those observed for transmission spectra.

2. Bulk Material (Thick Films)

For bulk materials, the penetration depth, hence the effective thickness, increases with wavelength. Therefore the bands at the longer wavelengths tend to be relatively stronger and, for broad bands, there is a noticeable broadening on the long wavelength side and a shift to longer wavelengths relative to transmission measurements. This was predicted by the equations of Chapter Two and has nothing to do with the dispersion in the refractive index and is easily recognized. Examples of this effect are shown clearly in Fig. 31 of Chapter Two and in numerous illustrations in Chapter Seven. There is another effect, due to dispersion, which contributes to band broadening, which will now be discussed.

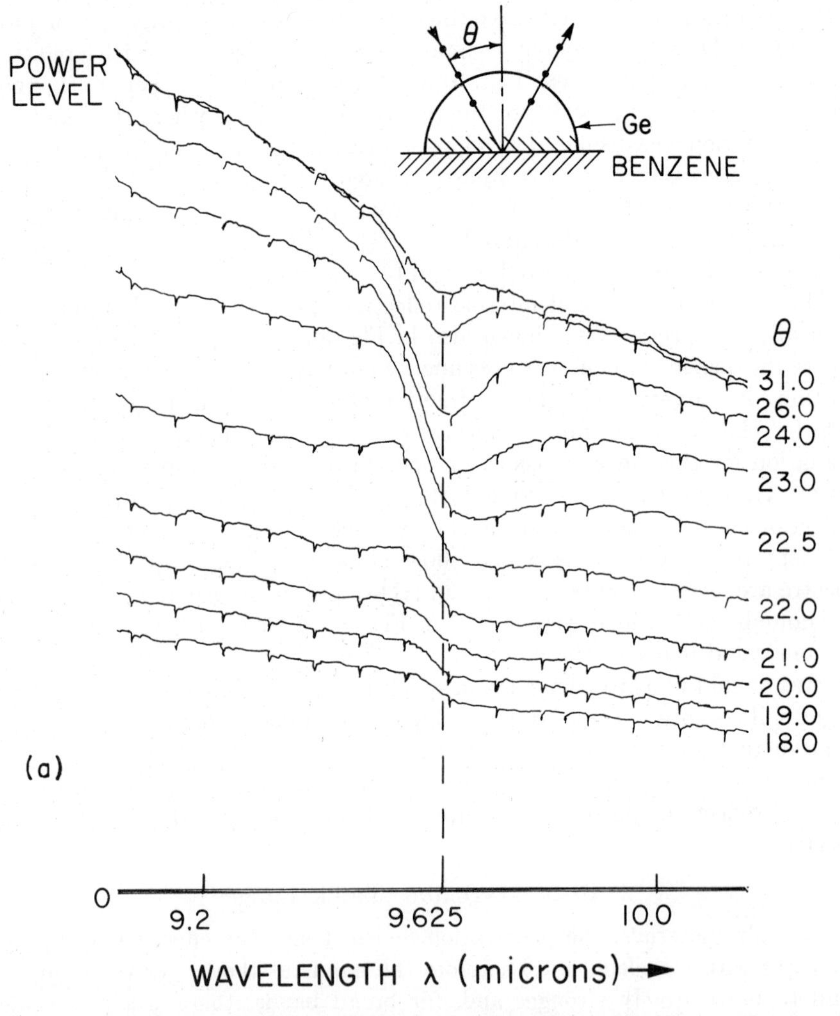

Fig. 1a. Comparison of the spectra of the 9.625 μ absorption band in benzene (n_2 = 1.46) at various angles of incidence for perpendicular polarization using a single reflection [Ge (n_1 = 4.0)] IRE. The change in character with change in angle of incidence is quite evident. See the end of chapter for explanation of results.

The effect of dispersion on the nature of the internal reflection spectrum can be demonstrated by measurements made near the critical angle. Examples of such measurements are shown in Figs. 1a, 1b, and 2a. (These spectra will be explained in more detail later in this chapter.) It will be noted that the

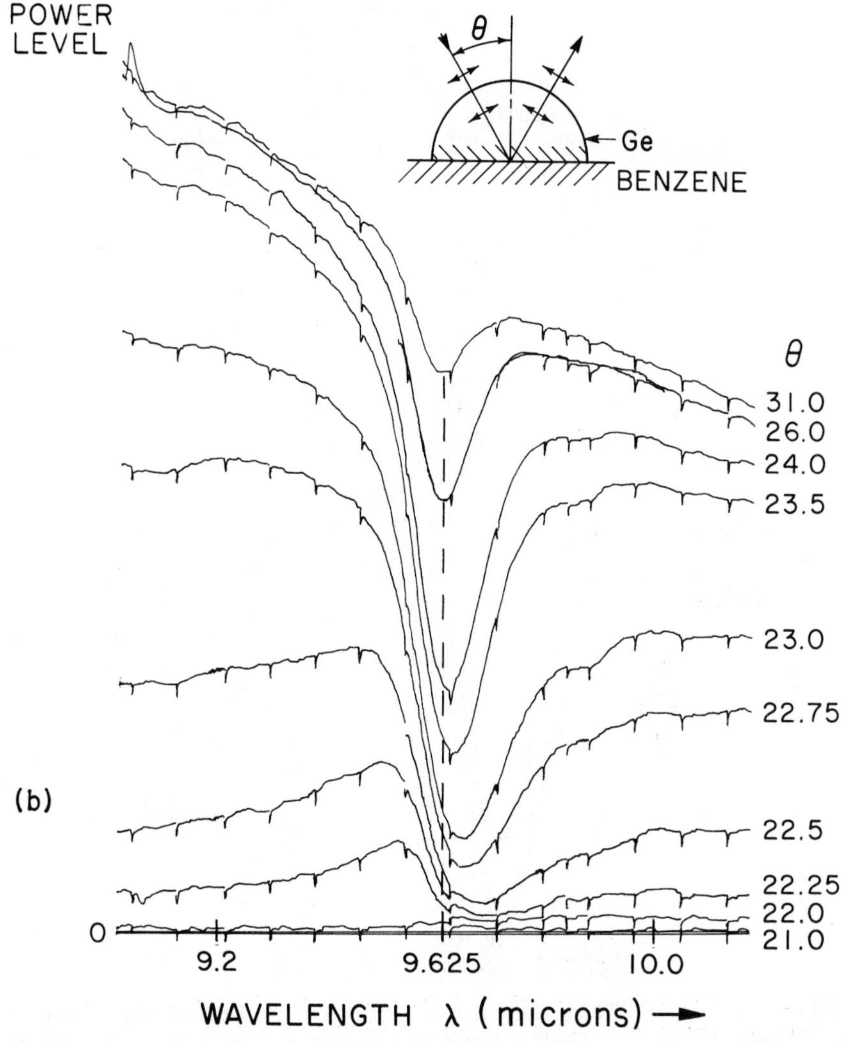

Fig. 1b. Comparison of the spectra of the 9.625 μ absorption band in benzene (n_2 = 1.46) at various angles of incidence for parallel polarization using single reflection Ge (n_1 = 4.0) IRE. The spectral contrast is increased over that observed for ⊥-polarization. Note that $R_\parallel = 0$ at the principal angle.

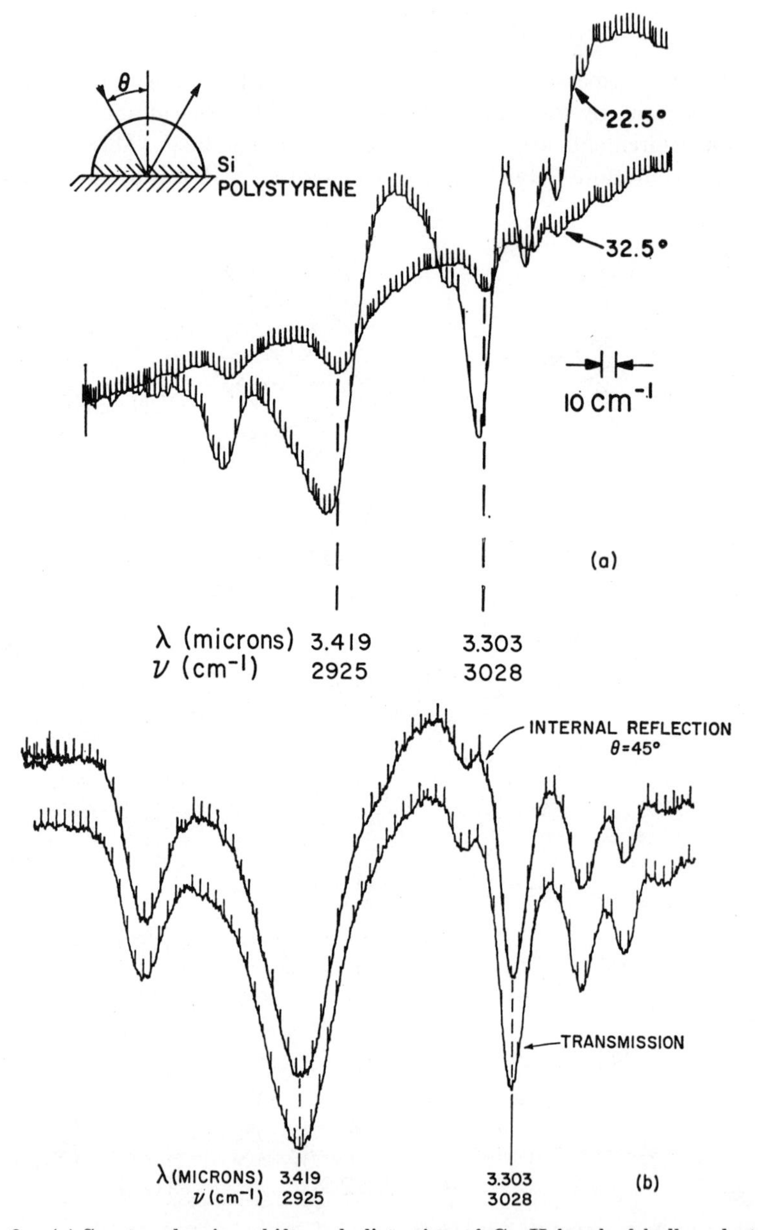

Fig. 2. (a) Spectra showing shift and distortion of C—H band of bulk polystyrene ($n_2 = 1.6$) for a Si ($n_1 = 3.5$) IRE when θ is changed from 32.5° to 22.5°. (b) Comparison of the internal reflection spectrum of the C—H band of bulk polystyrene ($n_2 = 1.6$) for a Si ($n_1 = 3.5$) IRE at $\theta = 45°$ ($\theta_c = 27\frac{1}{4}°$) with the transmission spectrum. These curves show the similarity of the transmission and internal reflection spectra for measurements made well above the critical angle.

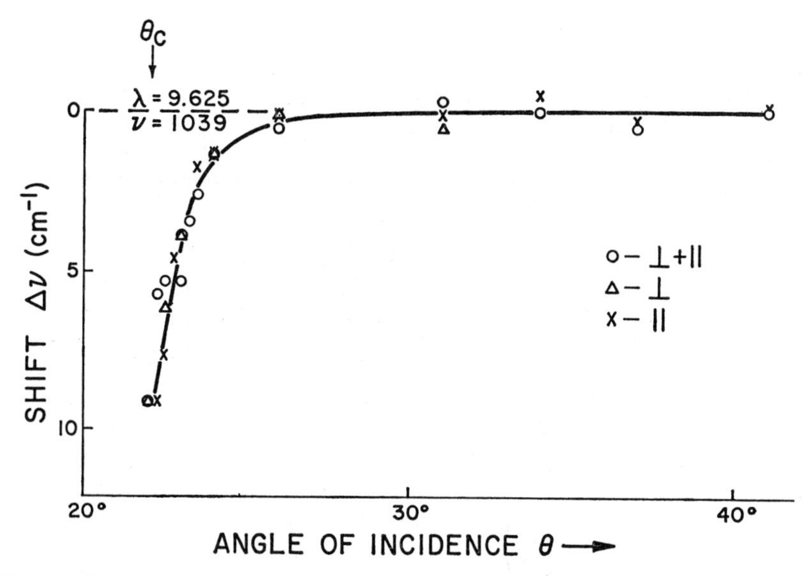

Fig. 3. Shift versus angle of incidence of the absorption band of benzene at 9.625 μ using a Ge hemicylinder. The shift is independent of polarization and is large only near the critical angle. θ_c indicates the approximate location of critical angle.

bands become distorted and shifted to longer wavelengths as θ approaches θ_c. (θ_c equals about $21\frac{1}{2}°$ and $27\frac{1}{4}°$ for Ge-benzene and Si-polystyrene, respectively.) For θ less than θ_c, a dispersion-type curve, qualitatively resembling the mirror image of the dispersion in n_2, is observed. Figure 2b, on the other hand, shows the close resemblance between transmission and internal reflection spectra, when θ is well above the critical angle. The measured shift versus angle of incidence for the 9.625 μ band of benzene using a Ge hemicylinder is shown in Fig. 3 for polarized and unpolarized light. Figure 4 shows the shift versus angle of incidence for one of the polystyrene bands using Si and KRS-5 plates. (This shift is difficult to measure accurately for a single sample because of the large change in the signal, which may be as large as a factor of 100, as the angle of incidence is changed between the critical angle and 75°). Similar shifts have been discussed by Zolotarev and Kislovskii (Z3). Figures 3 and 4 show that the shift is small when the angle of incidence is greater than a few degrees above the critical angle. For the practical application of internal reflection spectroscopy as an analytical technique, one simple rule can be followed to eliminate or to avoid the distortion and shift due to the dispersion in the refractive index: *Stay well above the critical angle.* If the angle of incidence cannot easily be changed, dis-

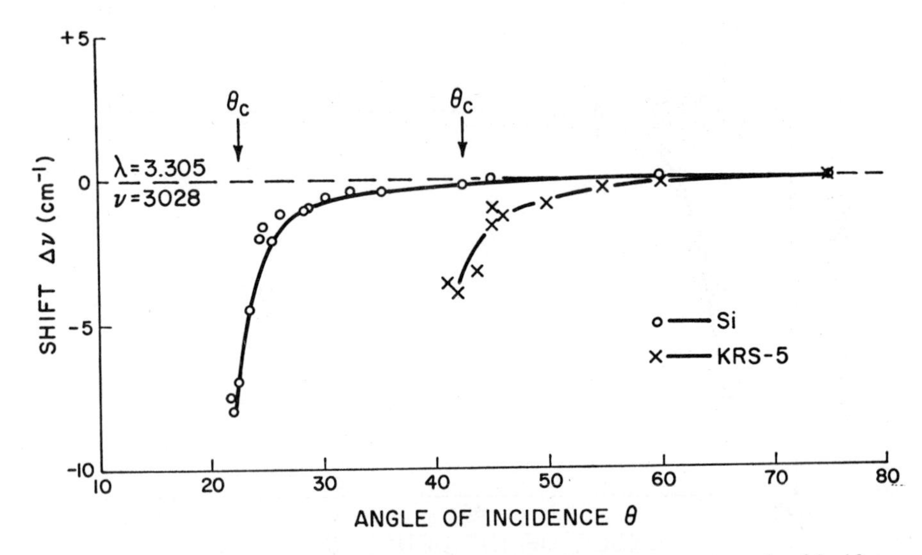

Fig. 4. Shifts of the 3.305 μ absorption band of polystyrene versus angle of incidence for Ge and KRS-5 IRE's. The shift becomes very large near the critical angle. θ_c indicates the approximate location of the appropriate critical angle.

tortion can be eliminated by keeping the angle of incidence fixed but employing an internal reflection element of higher refractive index. The latter course is essential when a sample of high refractive index is being investigated. Both methods of correcting for distortion are shown in Fig. 5. Figure 5a shows the internal reflection spectrum of polypropylene, which is clearly distorted, taken with a KRS-5 IRE at $\theta = 38°$ ($\theta_c \sim 38\frac{1}{2}°$). By increasing the angle of incidence to $42\frac{1}{2}°$, an undistorted spectrum is obtained, as shown in Fig. 5b. The elimination of the distortion, even at a low angle of incidence, by replacing the KRS-5 with a high index IRE is shown in Fig. 5c taken with a Ge IRE at $\theta = 23°$ ($\theta_c \sim 22°$).

The distorted spectra due to dispersion in the refractive index are actually very valuable. It will be discussed in Chapter Seven how advantage is taken of these distorted spectra to determine optical constants of materials. This change in character of the spectrum with change in angle of incidence for measurements made near the critical angle can be readily understood in a qualitative way. The explanation, which involves the dispersion in the refractive index near absorption bands, will be given in the following sections of this chapter and the main features of the distorted spectra shown in Figs. 1 and 2 will be explained. *A knowledge of these details is not essential for the practical application of internal reflection spectroscopy.*

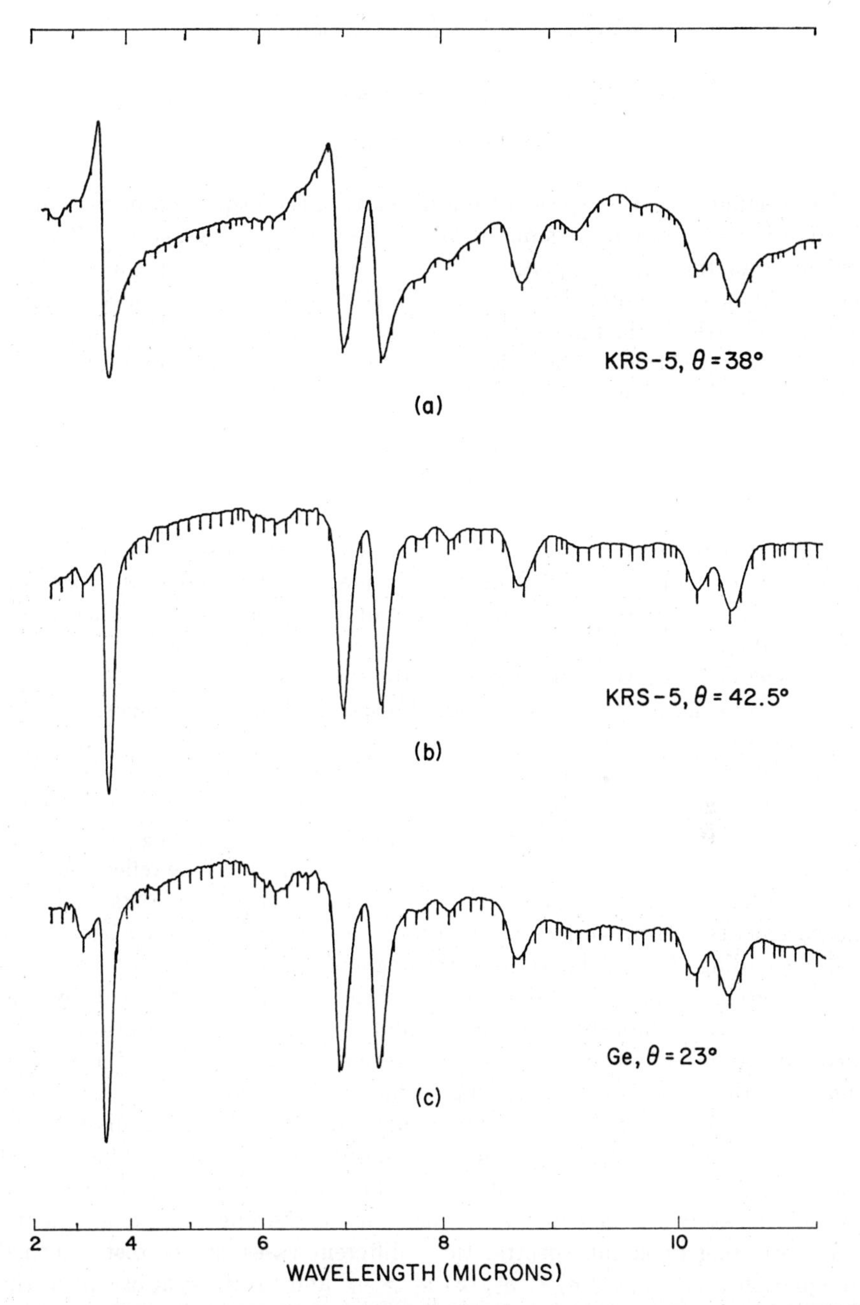

Fig. 5. Distorted spectrum of polypropylene (curve a) obtained by use of KRS-5 IRE at $\theta = 38°$ is corrected either by use of higher angle of incidence (curve b, taken with KRS-5 IRE at $\theta = 42.5°$) or higher index IRE (curve c, Ge IRE at $\theta = 23°$).

D. Qualitative Explanation of Effect of Dispersion in n_2

1. Reflection Spectra

For specular reflection spectra from dielectrics, the dispersion in the index of refraction generally plays a major role in the nature of the spectra. This is evident from the simple equation for the reflectivity, R, near normal incidence, where, in Chapter Two, it was shown that the absorption coefficient contributes little to the reflectivity and that the reflectivity is dominated by the index of refraction. The reflectivity of an interface of two materials for normal incidence is thus approximately

$$R = \frac{(n_2 - n_1)^2}{(n_2 + n_1)^2}. \tag{1}$$

It is informative to consider the consequences of the dispersion in the refractive index as determined from this simple equation and it will become evident that very different spectra are obtained depending upon whether or not n_2 is greater or less than n_1. [Schaefer (S2) has discussed similar effects for the visible and ultraviolet regions of the spectrum.]

Before considering these cases it should be recalled that when measuring the reflection spectra of thin films, it is necessary to distinguish between front-surface and back-surface reflection. Front-surface reflection represents the power reflected in the single component I_{R1} of Fig. 6. The power reflected from the back surface is composed of the multiple components I_{R2}, I_{R3}, etc. in Fig. 6. of which I_{R2} is by far the strongest. The back-surface reflection will, for thin films, qualitatively resemble the spectrum recorded via transmission measurements. However, its contrast may be greater, by as much as a factor of 4, depending on the polarizations, the angle of incidence, and that nature of the reflecting surface (metallic or dielectric). This is explained by the standing waves established within the film due to the superposition of the incoming and the reflected waves and their change of character with a change in the nature of the reflecting surface. It should be emphasized that back-surface reflection for thin films is not simply double transmission. In this book reflection means specular front-surface reflection. The desired component, I_{R1}, can be isolated by employing non-normal incidence and suitably locating the detector or by masking off the unwanted components.

In recording reflection spectra, three different cases can be distinguished in equation (1); viz., (*1*) $n_1 < n_2$; (*2*) $n_1 > n_2$; and (*3*) $n_1 = n_2$ except in the vicinity of the absorption band. It is assumed that the dispersion always occurs in n_2.

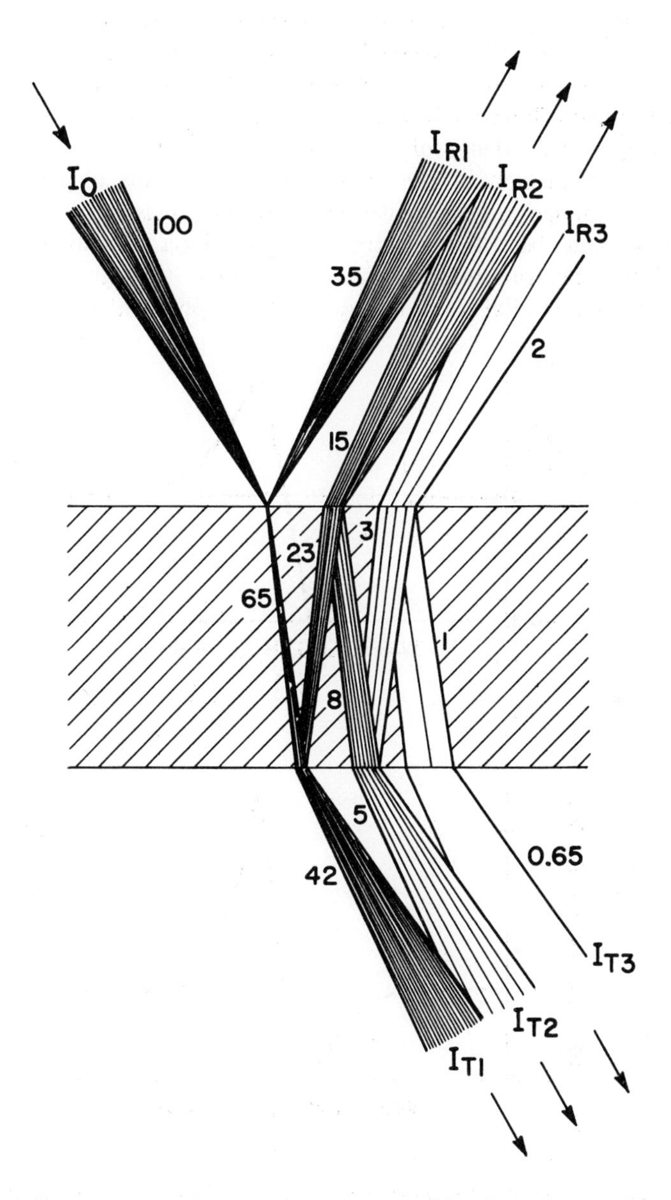

Fig. 6. Reflected and transmitted components resulting from front and back surface reflection in a Ge film. The numbers indicate percentage intensity in each component for reflection near normal incidence.

1. The first case is the one used in recording conventional (external) reflection spectra. For the assumed dispersion in the index of refraction shown in Fig. 7a, the calculated reflectivity from this interface is shown in Fig. 7b, where absorbing medium *2* is more dense optically than medium *1*. The wavelength dependence of the dispersion in reflectivity qualitatively resembles the dispersion in the refractive index. This dispersion in the reflectivity or change in reflectivity with wavelength is generally *not* taken into account when absorption spectra are recorded via transmission measurements. Thus, spectra obtained via transmission through thin films are really a complicated mixture of n and κ and are complicated still further by

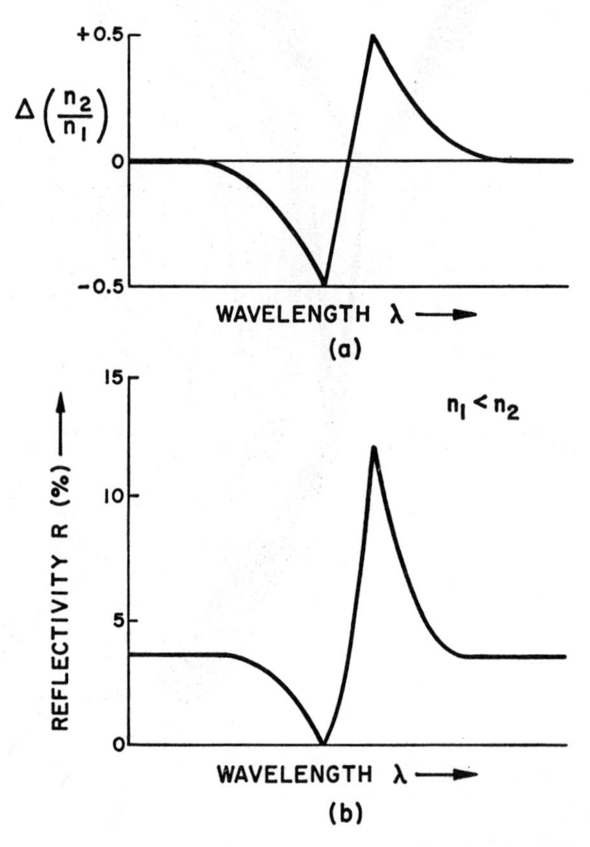

Fig. 7. Dispersion in refractive index near absorption band and resulting dispersion in reflectivity for external reflection. (a) Dispersion in the index of refraction n_2 for the case that initially $n_2/n_1 = 1.5$. (b) Calculated dispersion in reflectivity when light is incident from *rarer to denser* medium. It should be noted that R qualitatively resembles the dispersion in n_2.

the interference phenomenon associated with thin films. The measured dispersion in the reflectivity for this case shows a dip, a sharp rise, and then a return to the original value with increasing wavelength, as calculated and shown in Fig. 7b. Figure 8 shows a measurement demonstrating this behavior for the absorption band in Mylar at a wavelength of 5.75 μ. It should be recalled that this represents the front surface reflection when the electromagnetic radiation is proceeding from a less dense (air) toward a more dense (Mylar) medium. For some materials with undamped oscillations, very large changes in the reflectivity may occur due to the dispersion

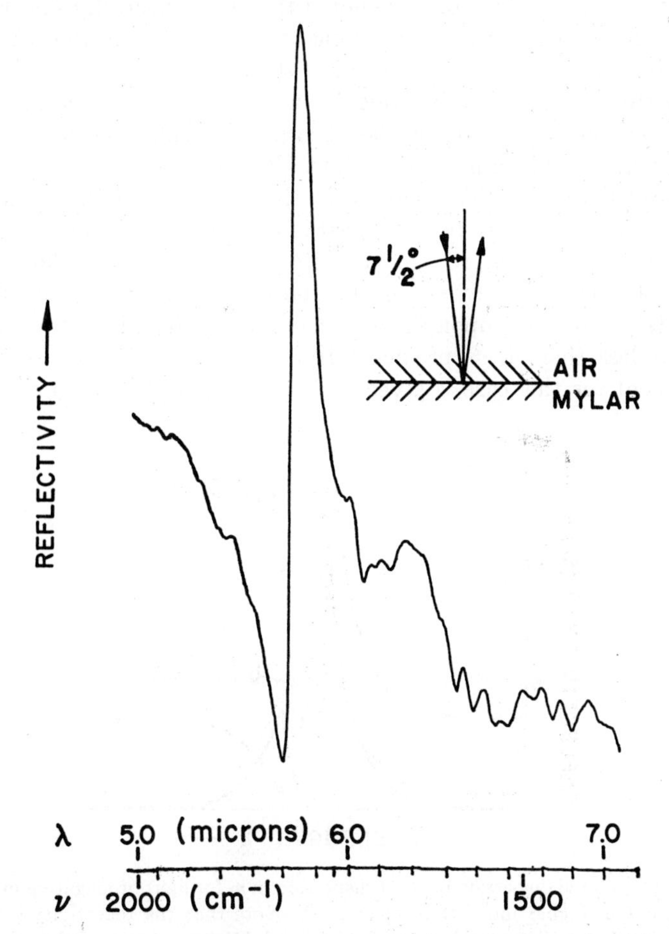

Fig. 8. Reflection from air–Mylar interface near absorption band in Mylar at 5.75 μ. Note that the dispersion in R qualitatively resembles the dispersion in n_2 and the calculated dispersion in R, shown in Fig. 7.

in n_2. In quartz (S28), for example, where n_2 changes from 0 to above 7 R changes from 0 to 75% because of a change in n_2 alone.

2. The second case is one in which the reflectivity is recorded when the refractive index of medium *1* is greater than that of absorbing medium *2*. The reflectivity will still show a dispersion but will now qualitatively resemble the *mirror* image of the dispersion in the refractive index. This is again predicted by equation (1) and shown by the calculated curve *a* in Fig. 9a for the dispersion assumed in Fig. 7a. This case is also demonstrated for Mylar (Fig. 10), but now in contact with silicon ($n_1 = 3.5$) whose index is higher than that of Mylar. It should be noted that the reflectivity first rises, then falls with increasing wavelength. Thus, the dispersion in the reflectivity is reversed by simply inverting the value of the ratio n_1/n_2.

3. The third case is an interesting one wherein the indices of media *1* and *2* are matched on either side of the absorption band. When $n_1 = n_2$, the interface will, of course, not reflect light ($R = 0$). But, it will reflect when n_2 deviates from n_1 and this occurs when there is a mismatch near absorption bands. Hence, two sharp peaks appear in the reflectivity, one on each side of the maximum absorption, as calculated from equation (1) and shown by curve *b* in Fig. 9. The peak at either the shorter or longer wavelength can be accentuated, depending upon the degree of mismatch and whether or not n_1 is greater or less than n_2 as predicted from equation (1). An example of a measurement for this case is given in Fig. 11, again for the 5.75 μ band of

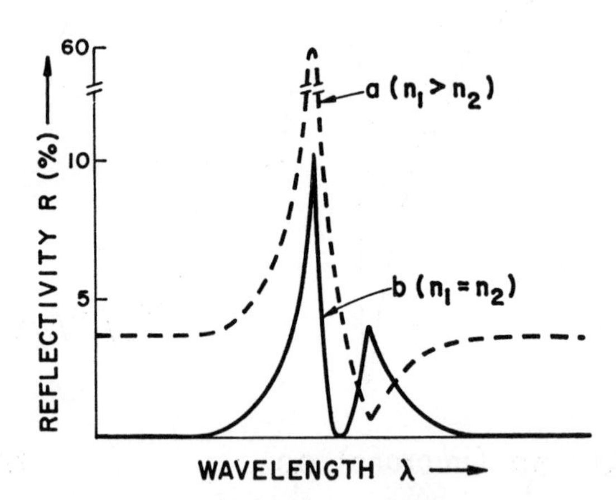

Fig. 9. Calculated dispersion in R for dispersion in n_2 for light propagating in medium *1*. (a) Medium *1* of higher index than medium *2*. Note that the reflectivity resembles the mirror image of the dispersion in n_2 of Fig. 7. (b) Medium *1* same index as medium *2*. Note two reflection peaks.

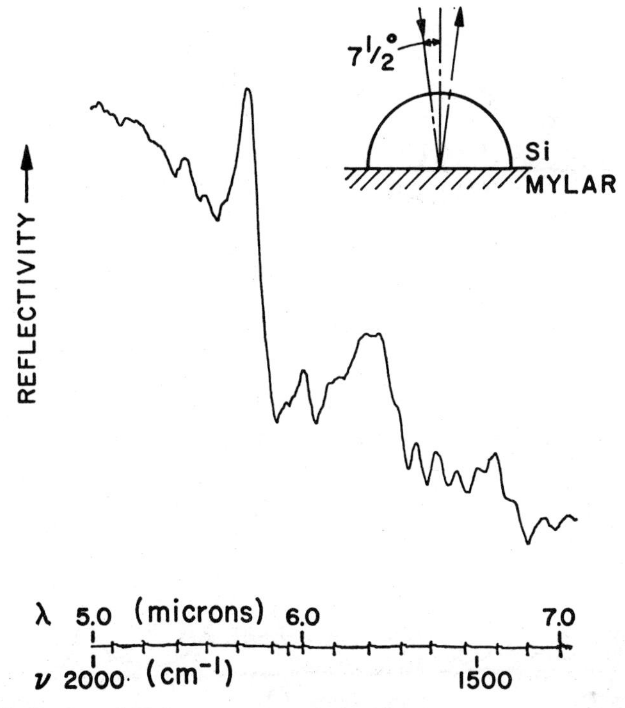

Fig. 10. Reflection of Mylar in contact with higher index silicon exhibiting dispersion as calculated and shown in Fig. 9a. Note that dispersion in R is mirror image of that in n_2.

Mylar where the Mylar ($n_2 = 1.64$) was placed in contact with NaCl ($n_1 = 1.51$). As was expected, the peak at the longer wavelength is accentuated while the weaker band at a shorter wavelength is lost in the noise. (This type of interface offers the possibility of constructing a simple, narrow band filter.)

These examples show that the nature of the reflection spectrum is very sensitive to the value of the ratio of the refractive index of an interface and is predicted directly by the simple equation for reflectivity. A knowledge of these possible variations is helpful for interpretation of spectra and is particularly helpful in understanding the difference in the nature of the spectra as observed in internal reflection spectroscopy and external reflection.

2. Transmission Spectra

For a qualitative discussion of the effect of dispersion on transmission spectra, the low absorption approximation of the equation for transmission

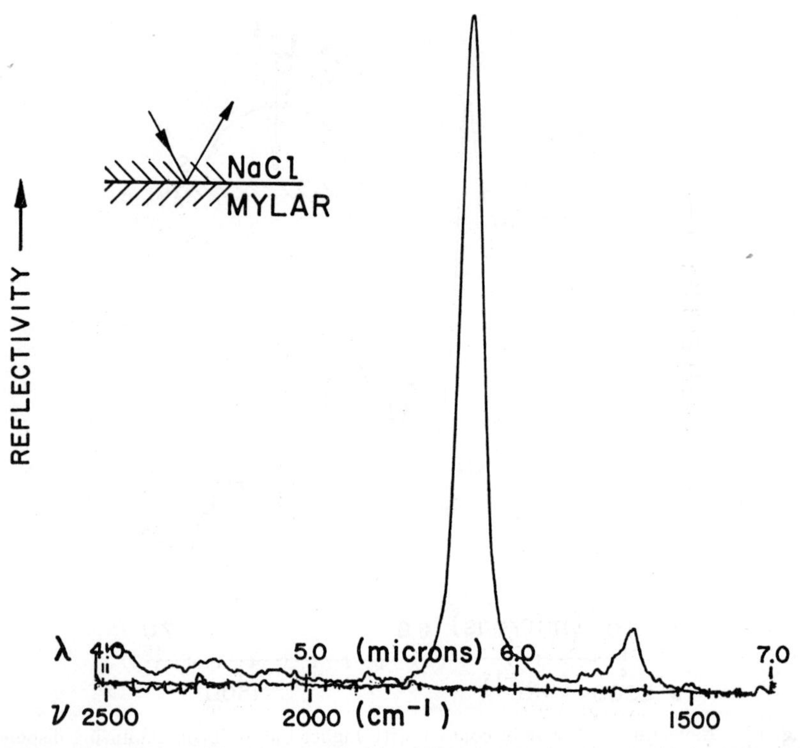

Fig. 11. Example of reflectivity of an interface where refractive indices are substantially matched except near absorption band. Note that reflection is zero except at absorption band as calculated and shown in Fig. 9b. The peak at longer wavelength is enhanced and the weaker peak at the shorter wavelength is obscured in the noise. The peak at 6.5 μ is due to interference from atmospheric water.

through a film of thickness d is considered where only the first two surface reflection losses are included. The transmitted intensity may be written as

$$I/I_0 = (1 - R)^2 (1 - \alpha d)$$
$$= \left(\frac{4n_2}{(n_2 + 1)^2}\right)^2 (1 - \alpha d) \tag{2}$$

when the transparent phase is air ($n_1 = 1$). The recorded spectrum thus does not resemble α_2 (or κ_2) but is modified by the change in reflection loss due to dispersion in the refractive index. This change in reflection loss is qualitatively similar to that shown in Fig. 7b and results in an apparent reduced absorption on the short wavelength side and an enhanced absorption on the long wavelength side.

It can also be concluded from equation (2) that transmission spectra will qualitatively resemble internal reflection spectra of thin films, which follow $n_2\alpha_2$, but the observed close similarity between the two is not readily explained from equation (2) and is evidently due to the small dispersion in n_2. Such close similarity is not expected if the dispersion in n_2 is very large.

3. Internal Reflection Spectra

As was demonstrated in the previous section, the dispersion in the index of refraction in the vicinity of molecular absorption bands affects the nature of the optical spectrum for transmission and reflection. For internal reflection spectroscopy where the range of angles of incidence employed may be from a value somewhat below the critical angle to grazing incidence the dispersion in the refractive index also plays an important role in the nature of the spectrum of bulk materials but the degree of its influence depends on the angle of incidence. For thin films, on the other hand, the effect of the dispersion in the refractive index appears to be qualitatively similar to that observed in transmission since internal reflection spectra and transmission spectra appear quite similar in the cases studied where the dispersion in n_2 was evidently not large, as has already been pointed out. Qualitative reasons for similarity or lack of similarity between internal reflection spectra of bulk materials and transmission spectra will be discussed in the following sections.

It is well known that internal reflection spectra of bulk materials measured a few degrees above from the critical angle tend to resemble those obtained in transmission measurements, except for the increased contrast for the bands at longer wavelengths, while spectra measured near the critical angle tend to resemble the mirror image of the dispersion in the refractive index; i.e., the reflectivity increases, and then decreases, with increasing wavelength. There is a continuous transition from one type of spectrum to the other as the angle of incidence is decreased from above to below the critical angle. The reflectivity versus angle of incidence is precisely expressed by the well-known Fresnel equations, with no complications arising from interference effects (since they are absent). As a result, the optical constants of materials can be precisely determined by combining measurements made at different angles of incidence. Physical insight into the nature of the spectrum can be obtained from a consideration of the absorption parameter equations as the refractive index in the rarer medium changes due to the dispersion near molecular resonances. A number of different cases are considered in the following discussion.

The optical constants, n_2 and $n_2\kappa_2$, near an absorption band, plotted versus increasing wavelength, are shown qualitatively in Fig. 12a. Because of the change in the index of refraction as the wavelength is increased and traverses an absorption band, the critical angle decreases, returns to its original value, increases, and again returns to its original value, as shown in Fig. 12b. If the absorption is neglected, the reflectivity curves versus angle of incidence at the mean (average), minimum, and maximum values of the index of refraction are those shown in Fig. 12c and identified via the critical angles $\theta_{c\ av}$, $\theta_{c\ min}$, and $\theta_{c\ max}$, respectively. It should be recalled that both the depth of penetration into the rarer medium and the electric field strength decrease with increasing angle of incidence or, equivalently, as the separation between the angle of incidence and the critical angle, $\theta - \theta_c$, increases. Any change in the refractive index in the rarer medium changes the separation between the angle of incidence (for a fixed incident angle) and the critical angle, $\theta - \theta_c$, by altering the location of the critical angle. Therefore, both the depth of penetration and electric field amplitude change as the wavelength traverses an absorption band. Furthermore, the index matching at the interface also changes. All of these three factors, which control the coupling to the penetrating electromagnetic field, have larger values on the long wavelength side of an absorption band and smaller values on the short wavelength side. The net effect is to increase the effective thickness on the long wavelength side and decrease it on the short wavelength side. This serves to increase the absorption on the long wavelength side and to decrease it on the short wavelength side. Although, as already pointed out, this distortion occurs to some extent in transmission measurements, for internal reflection spectra of bulk materials this distortion is magnified due to the rapid change in penetration depth with refractive index changes for angles of incidence near the critical angle.

The effect of the dispersion in refractive index on the spectra and the extent to which it affects the spectra via the change in the critical angle, as shown in Fig. 12b, is dependent on the angle of incidence. Any change in the spectra due to the change in critical angle occurs via changes in penetration depth and electric field strength only, since, as was pointed out in Chapter Two, any change in index matching is independent of the angle of incidence. For a predetermined n_1, greater than the maximum value of n_2, three ranges of angles of incidence are distinguished here for which the effect of the dispersion in the refractive index n_2 is discussed. (Arguments similar to the following

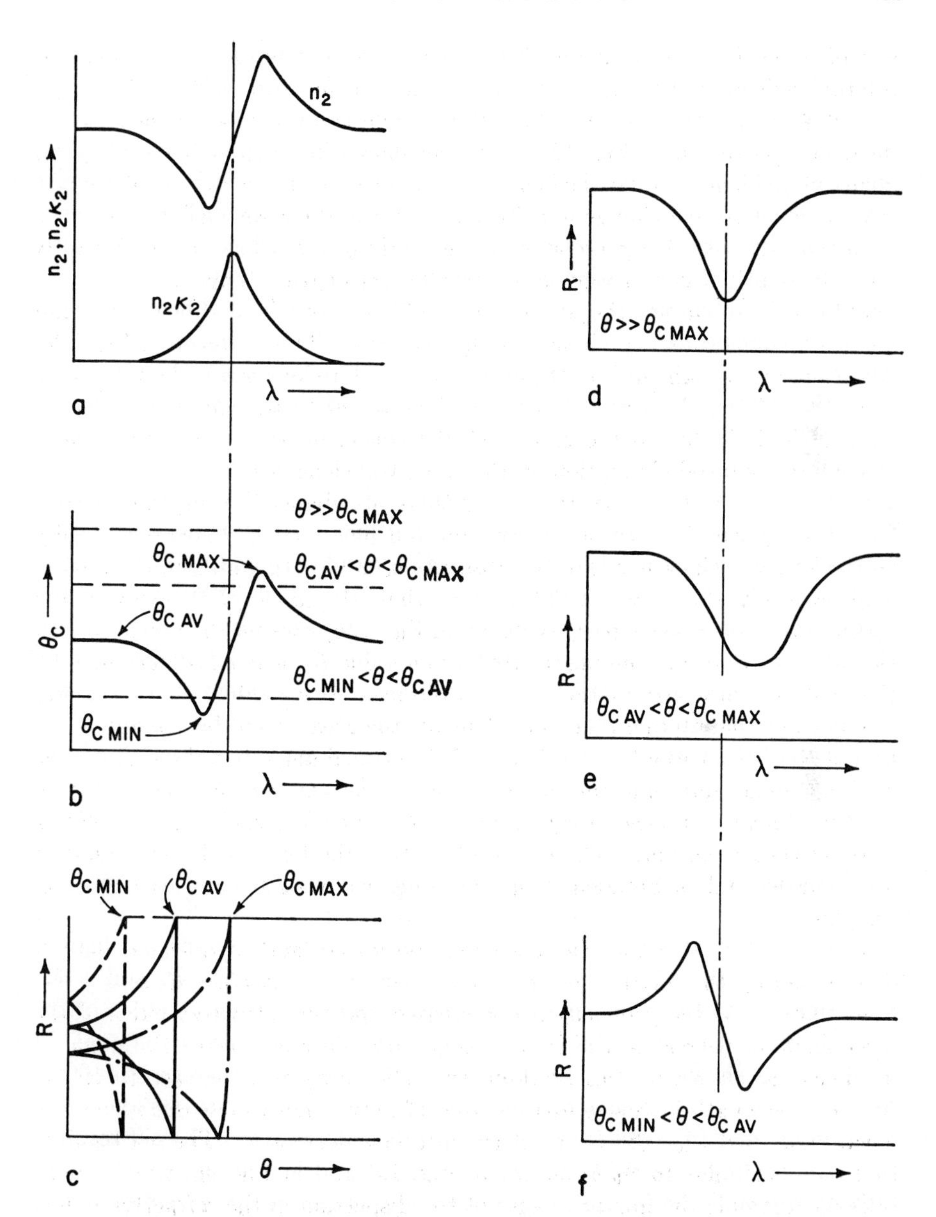

Fig. 12. Effect of the dispersion in the refractive index on the dispersion in the reflectivity, change in the critical angle, and change in character of the spectrum at different angles of incidence. See text for detailed explanation.

can be given for a fixed angle of incidence when the refractive index of the internal reflection element is changed to increase or decrease $\theta_c - \theta$.)

1. $\theta \gg \theta_{c\ av}$. In this case, the critical angle is always below the angle of incidence, as shown in Fig. 12b. As was shown in Chapter Two, for large angles of incidence neither the penetration depth nor the electric field strength is very sensitive to a change in refractive index in the rarer medium; hence, a change in the critical angle relative to the working angle does not significantly alter the depth of penetration or electric field strength. Thus, the spectrum qualitatively resembles the absorption coefficient but is modified somewhat by index changes as has already been observed. This is shown in Fig. 12d. There may be a slight shift of the absorption peak to longer wavelengths and a distortion of the absorption band when compared to transmission measurements. This is due to the enhanced absorption on the longer wavelength side and to reduced absorption on the short wavelength side.

2. $\theta_{c\ av} < \theta < \theta_{max}$. In this range there is enhanced absorption, arising from the increased depth of penetration and increased E values—especially on the long wavelength side of the absorption band. In addition, the critical angle actually shifts to a value greater than the angle of incidence for a certain range of wavelengths, as shown in Fig. 12b, causing the reflectivity of the interface to drop from nearly 100% to a value R_0, which is determined by the relative index of refraction of the interface. It is evident that the lower the index of the internal reflection element, the greater will be the amplification of the "absorption" due to the shift in critical angle to values above the working angle and thus the greater will be the contrast of the spectrum. This amplification is larger for $R_\parallel$ than for $R_\perp$, since $R_\parallel$ can change from 100% to 0 between θ_c and θ_p. The net result is that the band is shifted to longer wavelengths and is broadened on the long wavelength side, as shown in Fig. 12e.

3. $\theta_{c\ min} < \theta < \theta_{c\ av}$. In this case, the initial level of reflected light is determined by the relative index of refraction of the interface R_0 and is less than 100%. As the wavelength is increased and the refractive index of the rarer medium decreases, the critical angle may decrease below the angle of incidence, as shown in Fig. 12c, and the reflectivity will increase to 100%. As the wavelength increases further, the refractive index increases above the mean value and the reflectivity of the interface decreases. The net result is that curves similar to those shown in Fig. 12f and in Fig. 9a, which qualitatively resemble the mirror images of the dispersion in the refractive index, are observed. These curves also qualitatively resemble that shown in Fig. 10 for reflection of the silicon–Mylar interface near normal incidence when light is propagating from a more dense to a less dense medium. It would be expected that the contrast of this spectrum should be enhanced due to the sharp increase in the reflectivity in the vicinity of the critical angle, especially for $R_{\parallel}$. This is indeed the case, as shown in Fig. 13, for measurements made just below the critical angle for the silicon–Mylar interface (compare with Fig. 10).

This discussion describing the effect of the dispersion in the refractive index in the vicinity of absorption bands and the change in character of the spectrum as the angle of incidence is changed is strictly qualitative. However, it serves to give insight into the nature of the spectrum and serves as a guide in choosing the working angle of incidence.

A number of the features illustrated in the earlier figures can now be explained. For example, there was shown in Figs. 1a and 1b the change in strength and character of the absorption band of benzene at 9.625 μ, with decreasing angle of incidence using polarized light. The change in the spectrum from an absorption- to a dispersion-type curve should be noted. As explained above, the expected effects are much more dramatic for parallel

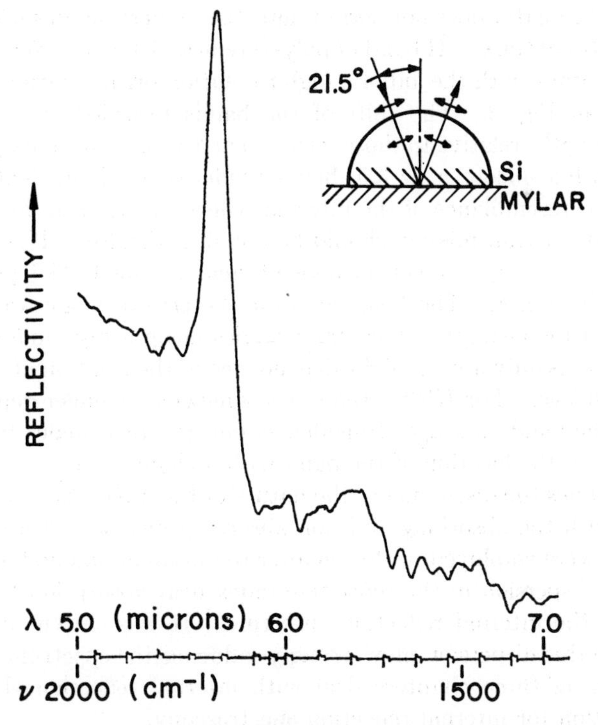

Fig. 13. Reflectivity versus wavelength for the Si–Mylar interface just below the critical angle for ‖-polarization. The contrast is noticeably increased when compared to the measurement made near normal incidence (Fig. 10).

polarization (Fig. 1b) than for perpendicular polarization (Fig. 1a). It should be noted that near the critical angle for ||-polarization, drastic changes in the spectra were obtained for changes in θ of as little as $\frac{1}{4}°$. The actual changes may be even more abrupt than those shown because the observed results may have been limited by the lack of collimation of the light, hence well-defined angle of incidence, at the reflecting interface. As is expected, and shown in Fig. 1b, the power level falls to zero near the principal angle for parallel polarization. Figure 3 shows the measurements made, using a Ge hemicylinder, of the shift of this absorption band versus the angle of incidence for both polarized and unpolarized light. The use of polarized light showed the expected difference in contrast but there was no measurable difference in the shift of the band. There was generally a large shift of the location of the absorption minima to longer wavelengths near the critical angle; however, a few degrees beyond the critical angle there was no detectable change in location of the band as the angle of incidence was changed. This is a rather broad band and the lack of resolution of the single-pass rock salt prism monochromator does not permit detection of very small shifts.

Some spectra of the C—H band of polystyrene at 3.4 μ for different angles of incidence recorded with the aid of a high resolution prism–grating instrument were shown in Fig. 2. The shift of the bands recorded at $\theta = 22.5°$ to longer wavelengths relative to those recorded at $\theta = 32.5°$ for bulk polystyrene in contact with a silicon ($n_1 = 3.5$) hemicylinder is clearly evident in Fig. 2a. Also, the close resemblance of the internal reflection spectrum for $\theta = 45°$ to that recorded via transmission should be noted in Fig. 2b. The shift of one of the bands of polystyrene versus angle of incidence for KRS-5 and Si IRE's were shown in Fig. 4. The behavior near the critical angle was similar to that observed for benzene. For larger angles using a high index (Si) IRE, however, there is only a very slight dependence of the location of the band on angle of incidence. For KRS-5 there is a somewhat stronger dependence on location of the band on angle of incidence, but at larger angles there is little or no change in the location of the band with a change in θ.

This concludes the discussion of the nature of the interaction of the evanescent wave with the absorbing and non-absorbing media. These interaction mechanisms were employed in this chapter to obtain an understanding of the effect of the dispersion in the refractive index near absorption bands on the character of the internal reflection spectrum. It was shown that near the critical angle this dispersion may strongly influence the spectrum.

The following three chapters deal with internal reflection elements and instrumentation for internal reflection spectroscopy.

CHAPTER FOUR

INTERNAL REFLECTION ELEMENTS

A. Introduction

The internal reflection element (IRE) is the transparent optical element used in internal reflection spectroscopy for establishing the conditions necessary to obtain internal reflection spectra of materials (H6,H28,P16). Radiation is propagated through it by means of total internal reflection. The sample material is placed in contact with the reflecting surface or in some cases it may be the reflecting surface itself. The ease of obtaining an internal reflection spectrum and the information obtained from the spectrum are determined by a number of characteristics of the IRE. A choice must be made in the working angle or range of angles of incidence, number of reflections, aperture, number of passes, surface preparation, and material from which it is made. These can be determined with some knowledge of the sample to be studied, the interaction mechanisms discussed in earlier chapters and a few simple considerations regarding the reflection element.

For internal reflection spectroscopy the information obtained is deduced from the deviation of the reflectivity from unity, viz., from

$$R = 1 - a. \tag{1}$$

As was discussed in Chapter Two, the effective thickness of the sample material is defined as $d_e = a/\alpha$ and is determined by the refractive index, n_1, of the IRE (assuming we have no control over the index of the sample material, n_2) and the angle of incidence. Here a is the absorption parameter and α is the absorption coefficient. The contrast of the spectrum increases as d_e increases. Largest effective thicknesses are obtained by selecting the lowest possible refractive index for the IRE and working at the smallest angle of incidence, θ, on the sampling surface. Because of distortion of spectra and other practical considerations, and particularly for thin films, there is an upper limit to d_e. The contrast of the spectrum can then be enhanced by employing multiple reflections when

$$R = (1 - a)^N, \tag{2}$$

where N is the number of reflections. For small a, R can be written as

$$R \simeq 1 - Na. \tag{3}$$

After n_1, θ, and N have been determined, the geometry of the IRE is selected. Because the character of the spectrum depends on the angle of incidence and because of other practical considerations, the IRE should have plane reflecting surfaces. The internal angle of incidence is then easily determined and can be controlled. The IRE should thus not be in the form of a wedge, ring, cylinder, or even a rod, except possibly for special applications. These unusual geometries have associated complications which will be discussed later. Unless otherwise specified, the angle of incidence, θ, refers to the internal angle of incidence on the sampling surface as shown in Fig. 1. This angle is the same as the angle of the apex of the bevel for normal incidence on the aperture. Because of the angular beam spread in most instruments, the angle of incidence, θ, has a certain spread within the IRE (roughly equal to the angular beam spread due to the instrument divided by the index of refraction of the IRE, n_1) unless an attempt has been made to collimate the beam, as will be discussed later.

B. Aperture and Number of Reflections

1. Aperture (A)

The index of refraction of any material changes with wavelength. Therefore, the degree of refraction at the entrance face of the IRE, hence the internal angle of incidence, θ, on the sampling surface is wavelength dependent for oblique incidence. Since it is desirable to maintain the same angle of incidence over the entire wavelength range under investigation,

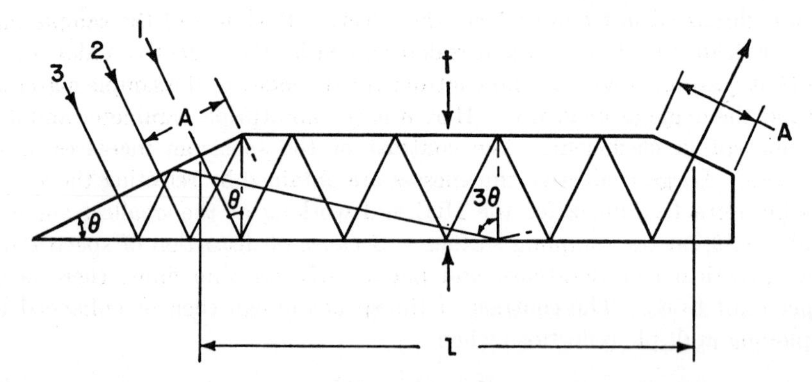

Fig. 1. Single-pass internal reflection element showing path of light, defining aperture A, length l, and thickness t of IRE. For normal incidence on the aperture, the wedge angle is the same as the angle of incidence θ. Light striking the portion of the bevel which is not the aperture will have an internal angle of incidence different from θ, as shown by ray 3.

refraction should be eliminated. This is the case when the light enters and leaves the IRE via the aperture at normal incidence. Normal incidence on the apertures also eliminates changes of polarization of the light beam by the IRE. The entrance and exit faces of the IRE are thus specially shaped or beveled, for example, as shown in Fig. 1. The entire area of the entrance and exit faces does not always serve as "useful" aperture. This is clearly demonstrated by ray *3* which is reflected internally from the beveled face before it enters the plate proper. The internal angle of incidence for this ray on the sampling surface for the second reflection is increased by 2θ, making it 3θ inside the IRE instead of θ as desired.

The aperture of the IRE is thus defined as that portion of the beveled area which can be utilized to conduct the light into the IRE at the desired angle of incidence θ. The aperture is equal to the total area of the beveled face for angles of incidence of 45° or greater and is given by

$$A = t \csc \theta. \tag{4}$$

(See Fig. 1 for definition of terms.) For angles less than 45° only part of the bevel contributes to the useful aperture and this is given by

$$A = 2t \sin \theta. \tag{5}$$

For these angles, in order to eliminate complications such as those depicted by ray *3* of Fig. 1, the IRE should be truncated, as shown for the exit face of the IRE in Fig. 1. Alternatively, the tip of the bevel may be masked.

Aperture is plotted versus angle of incidence in Fig. 2a. It rises from zero at normal incidence to a maximum at 45° where it has a value of 1.414 times the plate thickness, t, and then decreases to a value equal to the plate thickness at grazing incidence.

For $\theta \leq 45°$ the entire area of the broad surfaces is sampled when the total aperture, as defined by equation (5), is illuminated. For $\theta > 45°$, however, the distance between consecutive reflections along the broad surface, i.e., "skip distance," is greater than the projection of the aperture on the broad surface (i.e., beam width on broad surface) and hence the entire area of the broad surfaces is not sampled. For $\theta > 45°$ the aperture can be increased from that given by equation (4) to that given by equation (5) by "trumpeting" the ends of the plate, and then the entire area of the broad surface is sampled when the total aperture is illuminated. Hansen and Horton (H6) have obtained this increase in aperture by placing prisms in contact with the ends of the plate just as is done in the Lummer-Gehrcke interferometer (B27). Hirschfeld (H49c), on the other hand, has shown that when the hypotenuse of a suitable 90° prism is placed in contact with a broad face, the aperture, which equals the length of the bevel from the tip of the plate to the 90° corner of the prism, is given by equation (5). (Unless otherwise stated, the term aperture in this book will refer to that of a simple bevel as defined by equations (4) and (5).)

It will be evident in later sections that for certain structures the exit aperture must be precisely located on the IRE; otherwise the beam may partially or completely miss the aperture and be lost.

2. Number of Reflections (N)

The number of reflections is calculated from simple geometrical considerations. The beam advances a distance ("skip distance") of $t \tan \theta$ for each reflection. If the plate length is l, the total number of reflections for a single pass in the plate is given by

$$N = (l/t) \cot \theta. \tag{6}$$

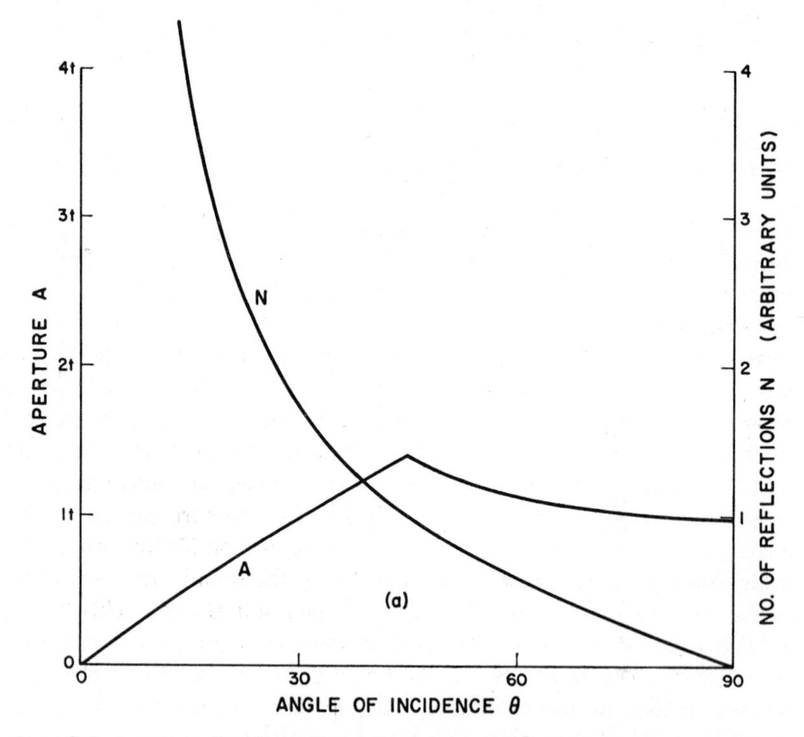

Fig. 2a. Calculated angular dependence of aperture and number of reflections for internal reflection plates of the type shown in Fig. 1.

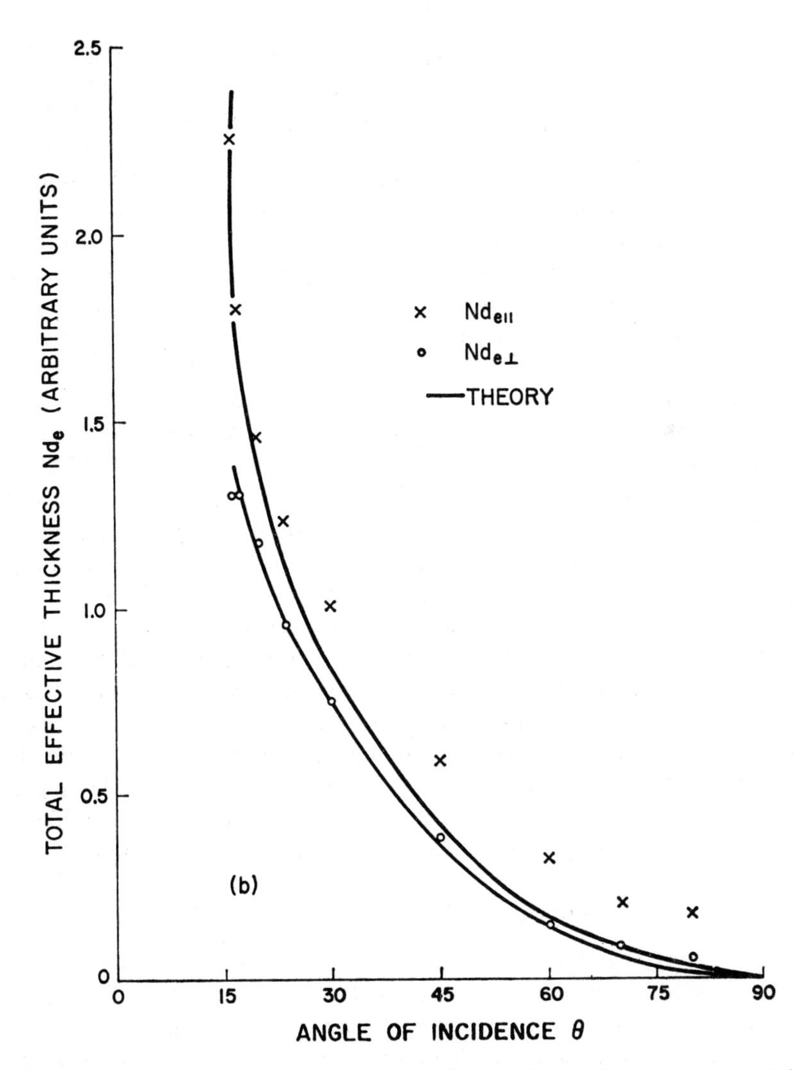

Fig. 2b. Total effective thickness versus angle of incidence for polystyrene stain on silicon surface. The sharp drop with angle of incidence is largely, although not entirely, due to decrease of N with θ. Points represent experimental measurements and solid curves are theoretical calculations.

It should be noted (see Fig. 1) that for single-pass plates l is measured from the center of the entrance aperture to the center of the exit aperture. A curve showing the dependence of N upon θ also appears in Fig. 2a. N is zero for grazing incidence, increases for decreasing θ, and rises sharply for small angles as θ decreases further. N also increases as the plates are made longer and thinner. Because of the practical considerations there are limitations on both l and t. Furthermore, θ must be greater than the critical angle (for Ge, a material of very high refractive index, $\theta_c = 14\frac{1}{2}°$). Another consideration is that a decrease of either θ or t reduces the aperture and this limits the usable light beam width, hence power, that can be employed. For these reasons, N cannot be made indefinitely large. Figure 2b shows measurements exhibiting a decrease in Nd_e, or, equivalently a decrease in spectral contrast, with increase in angle of incidence for the 3.4 μ band of a thin film of polystyrene on a silicon plate. This decrease in sensitivity is principally due to the decrease of N as θ increases, as shown in Fig. 2a. The other factor contributing to the decrease in spectral contrast is the decrease of d_e with increasing θ, as was discussed in Chapter Two. The solid curves for Nd_e in Fig. 2b represent theoretical calculations showing the expected decrease due to both of these factors. The agreement between theory and experiment is excellent for $\perp$-polarization. For $Nd_{e\|}$ there is qualitative agreement between experiment and theory; but at the larger angles the contrast does not drop off as fast as predicted by theory. This deviation is attributed to some unexplained scattering of light for $\|$-polarization observed at the larger angles. The scattering would tend to make N much larger than simple geometrical considerations would predict. Better agreement at these angles was obtained in some other measurements at longer wavelengths where scattering effects were reduced. It should also be noted that the total effective thickness, $Nd_{e\|}$, changes by a factor of 100 for $\|$-polarization over the angles of incidence ranging from the critical angle to 75°. This makes it difficult to make precise measurements over the entire range using one sample.

C. Internal Reflection Elements (IRE's)

A large variety of IRE's have been developed. The geometry of the reflection element determines the ease with which internal reflection spectroscopy techniques can be employed. Some have been designed to simplify instrumentation whereas others have been designed with the nature of the sample in mind, e.g., whether the sample is liquid, powder, thin film, or submicrogram quantity. The IRE's are listed in Table I and will be discussed in their order of complexity. Their uses and limitations will be mentioned. Where possible, each IRE is identified by its shape.

1. Single-Reflection Internal Reflection Elements

Single-reflection IRE's can be used to record spectra of bulk materials in which the absorption is sufficiently strong and in which adequate contact to the sample material can easily be made, e.g., liquids, pliable solids, and samples with smooth surfaces.

a. Fixed-Angle IRE's—Prisms

The simplest of all internal reflection elements is the prism (shown in Fig. 3a). If the light beam is to enter and leave at normal incidence this IRE must be operated at a fixed angle. Prisms can, of course, be prepared for any angle of incidence or facets may be provided on a single prism so that

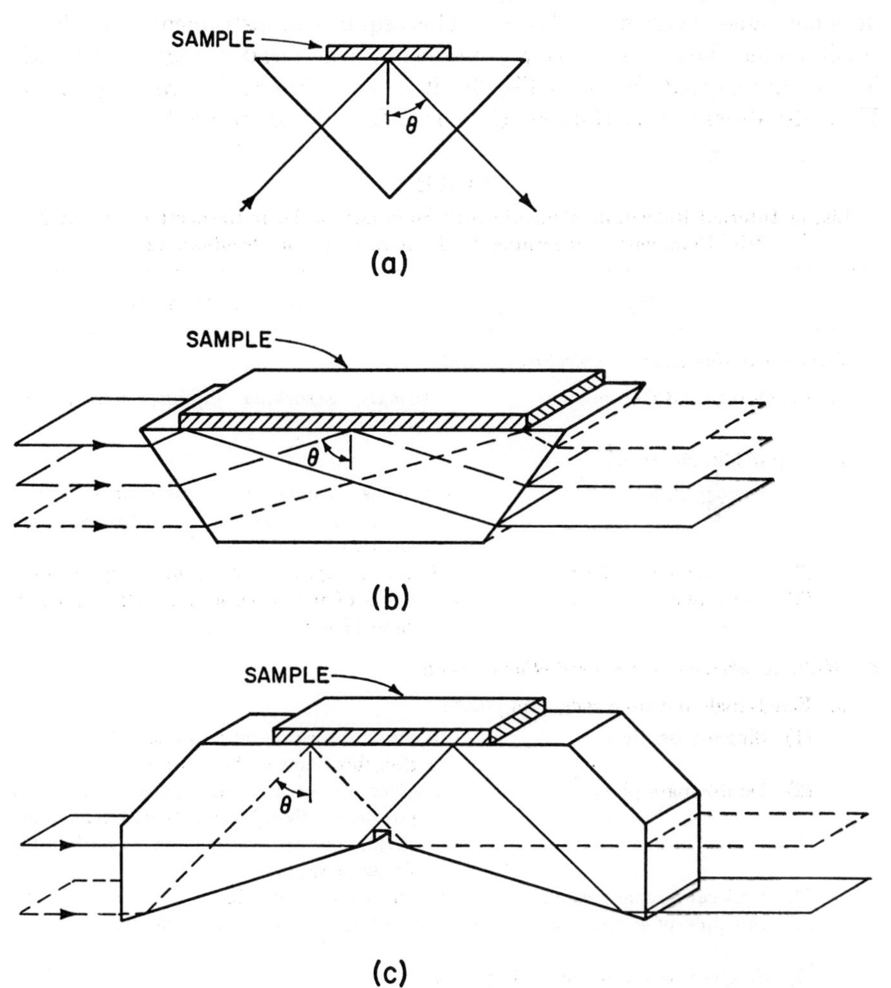

Fig. 3. Fixed-angle, single internal reflection elements. (a) Simple prism. (b) Dove prism. (c) Achromatic prism (H6).

it might be operated at a few selected angles. The sample material is placed in contact with the reflecting surface. For liquids a suitable cell may be built to hold the liquids in contact with the surface. Transfer optics are generally required in order to incorporate such a prism in an unmodified spectrometer.

A Dove prism, shown in Fig. 3b and discussed by Hansen (H6) for use as an IRE, can be used without additional optics in an unmodified spectrometer, providing the defocusing of the light beam due to the introduction of the IRE does not cause severe power losses. This requires an instrument which has a small angular beam spread (low *f* number). One disadvantage of this IRE is that, unlike that shown in Fig. 3a, it is not achromatic. An achromatic IRE, also discussed by Hansen (H6) for IRS, is shown in Fig. 3c.

TABLE I

List of Internal Reflection Elements with Summary of Their Respective Uses and Brief Comments Concerning Their Advantages or Disadvantages

Type	Uses and comments
1. *Single reflection internal reflection elements*	
a. Fixed-angle IRE's—prisms	Strongly absorbing liquids, solids, and pastes.
b. Variable-angle IRE's	
(1) Hemicylinder	Same as prisms—in addition, optical constants, also useful to control spectral contrast.
(2) Microhemicylinder (3) Hemisphere	Small samples and minute quantities. Angle of incidence is not well defined in these IRE's.
2. *Multiple reflection internal reflection elements*	
a. Fixed-angle multiple reflection plates	
(1) Single-pass plate	Weakly absorbing bulk and thin films; very thin films and surface studies.
(2) Double-pass plate	Surface studies, vacuum studies, liquids and powders. Simplifies instrumentation but output power level may be lower than for single-pass plates.
(3) Vertical double-pass plate	Liquids and powders.
(4) Multiple-pass internal reflection plate	Folded system for many reflections.
(5) Single-pass, double-sampling plate (6) Double-pass, double-sampling plate	Has twice the sensitivity of other plates.

(*continued*)

b. Variable-Angle IRE's

(1) **Hemicylinder.** The hemicylinder, shown in Fig. 4a and first used by Fahrenfort (F2) as an IRE, provides the simplest variable-angle IRE. The hemicylinder must be carefully aligned so that its axis is parallel to the monochromator slit. By bringing the light beam to a focus at a distance

$$d = \frac{r}{n_1 - 1} \tag{7}$$

in front of the curved surface, the light beam is, in the first approximation, collimated within the hemicylinder parallel to the slit but not perpendicular to it. The light beam is refocused at the same distance from the surface when it leaves the IRE. Here r is the radius of the hemicylinder and n_1 the

TABLE I (*continued*)

Type	Uses and comments
b. Variable-angle multiple reflection plates	
(1) Single-pass plate (2) Double-pass plate (3) Vertical double-pass plate	All single, double, and multiple-pass plates can be converted into variable-angle plates by providing quarter rounds at entrance and exit apertures. In addition to the uses of the fixed-angle plates, these can be used for measuring optical constants and study of interaction mechanisms at reflecting surfaces. These are complicated structures and should be used only when necessary.
c. Unipoint multiple internal reflection elements	
(1) Optical cavity	Useful for very weak absorbers and very minute quantities. It is a fixed wavelength IRE.
(2) Rosette	Minute quantities—a complex structure and requires precision alignment.
d. Other geometries	
(1) Modified hemicylinder	Same as hemicylinder but employs a few reflections (3 to 5). Can be used over only limited angular range.
(2) V-shaped IRE	Liquids and solids. This IRE can be placed in sampling space and requires no additional instrumentation.
(3) Cylindrical rods and fibers	Simple to make but complicates optics.

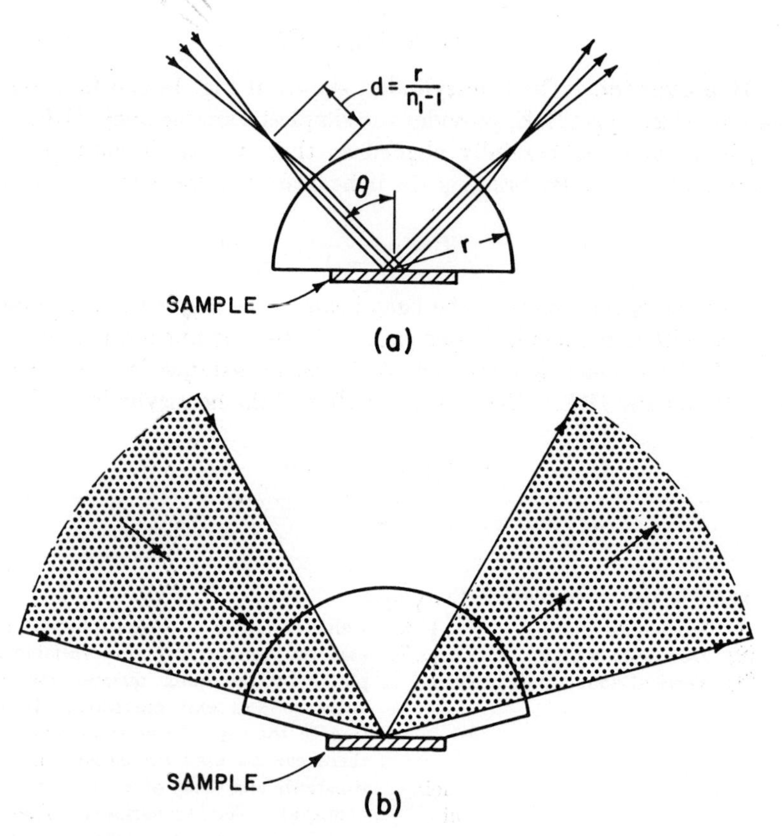

Fig. 4. Variable-angle, single internal reflection elements. (a) Hemicylinder (F2). (b) Hemisphere (F5). To achieve collimated rays inside the IRE an image of the source should be placed a distance d from the surface of the IRE.

refractive index of the hemicylinder material. For Ge ($n_1 = 4$) hemicylinder of radius, $r = 7.5$ mm, $d = 2.5$ mm. It is not a simple matter to adjust this distance accurately unless a screen is placed at this position on which to focus. Workers at the University of Minnesota (G8) have found it convenient to replace the hemicylinder by a cylinder whose radius is equal to

$$r + \frac{r}{n_1 - 1} = \frac{n_1 r}{n_1 - 1},$$

focus on the cylinder and then put the hemicylinder back in place. Collimation within the IRE has the advantage that the angle of incidence is well defined. This is very important for the measurement of optical constants. For good collimation either a very narrow slit image or a hemicylinder of a large radius must be employed. The use of a large radius improves the validity of the foregoing equation for collimating the internal beam but unfortunately increases the width of the beam at the reflecting surface.

The hemicylinder is useful for measuring optical constants where a carefully selected angle of incidence is essential. The possibility of changing the angle of incidence is also useful in controlling the contrast of the spectrum.

(2) **Microhemicylinder.** For small samples, minute quantities, and solid samples where contact to the reflecting surface is not easily achieved, it is desirable to condense the beam size at the reflecting surface. This can be done by condensing the beam and bringing it to a focus at the reflecting surface of the hemicylinder. Collimation of the beam, however, is then not obtained. The beam can be condensed to some extent and collimation can be partially preserved by employing a hemicylinder of small radius. It is evident from equation (7) that the distance d will be reduced and the beam width at the reflecting surface will therefore also be reduced. Collimation of the beam within the hemicylinder, however, degenerates because of the finite width of the slit image and large angular spread of the light beam.

(3) **Hemisphere.** In an attempt to investigate microcrystals, Fahrenfort (F5) employed a hemisphere in the manner shown in Fig. 4b. The bottom section is cone-shaped to facilitate contacting the sample material to the sampling surface. No attempt was made at collimation—in fact the beam was focused down in both dimensions to an area of 1×0.2 mm. The use of a hemisphere in this way resembles most closely the condensing systems as used in conventional transmission. The use of a hemisphere with a strongly converging beam definitely enhances the sensitivity for examining minute quantities. The gain in sensitivity however does not increase as rapidly as the beam area is reduced. The reason for this is that in order to produce a small spot size a highly converging beam is required which, in turn, means that a large range of angles of incidence must be employed. The smallest angle of incidence is determined by the distortion which can be tolerated in the spectrum and the largest angle will be greater by the amount of the angular beam spread. For example, employing a silver chloride hemisphere to investigate a polymer, the minimum angle that should be employed might be 60° and the largest will, of course, be 90°. The average effective thickness for a light beam with this angular spread is $d_{e\perp} = 0.48\lambda_1$, while the same light beam collimated at $\theta = 60°$ has an effective thickness $d_{e\perp} = 0.92\lambda_1$—a gain of almost a factor of 2.

2. Multiple Reflection Internal Reflection Elements

For many bulk materials, thin films, and particularly monomolecular layers, spectra of sufficient contrast cannot be obtained using a single reflection and thus multiple reflections must be employed to enhance the contrast. A variety of IRE's have been developed for this purpose and some geometries are particularly suited for certain applications. Because of simplicity of construction and ease of determining and maintaining a given angle of incidence it is desirable to reflect the light internally from plane, parallel surfaces.

a. Fixed-Angle Multiple Reflection Plates

(1) **Single-Pass Plate.** The simplest and most commonly used multiple internal reflection element is the single-pass plate shown in Fig. 5a. It may be in the form of either a trapezoid or parallelepiped as shown in Fig. 5a or 5b, respectively. Here the light is introduced into the plate via the entrance aperture, is propagated down the length of the plate via multiple internal reflections from the opposing flat surfaces, and leaves via the exit aperture. As was pointed out earlier, the number of reflections is directly proportional to the length of the plate and the cotangent of the angle of incidence and inversely proportional to its thickness. As many as five hundred reflections have been employed. It is impractical to make the plates longer than, say, 10 cm and thinner than 0.25 mm. This places a rough upper limit of 10^3 reflections for this type of IRE.

For single-pass plates a distinction is made between thin and thick plates. For thin plates the light is focused upon the entrance aperture and will entirely fill it. The light is then contained within the plate by the two large flat areas and will illuminate the entire exit aperture and leave the plate with the same beam spread. Both the entrance and exit apertures act as focal points and there is no change in the width of the source image regardless of the length of the plate. The light rays will be completely mixed within the plate if it is sufficiently long. The light rays need not be traced through the plate, it is only necessary to focus the light source on the entrance aperture and focus the exit aperture on the spectrometer slit when the IRE is placed in the sampling space of commercial spectrometers. Equivalently, when the IRE is placed in the monochromatic beam after the exit slit, it is necessary to focus the spectrometer slit image on the entrance aperture of the IRE and focus the exit aperture on the detector element. It should be realized that for $\theta > 45°$, because the skip distance exceeds the projected beam area on the broad surface, the light does not initially fill the entire plate even when the total aperture is illuminated as shown in Fig. 5c. For a divergent beam,

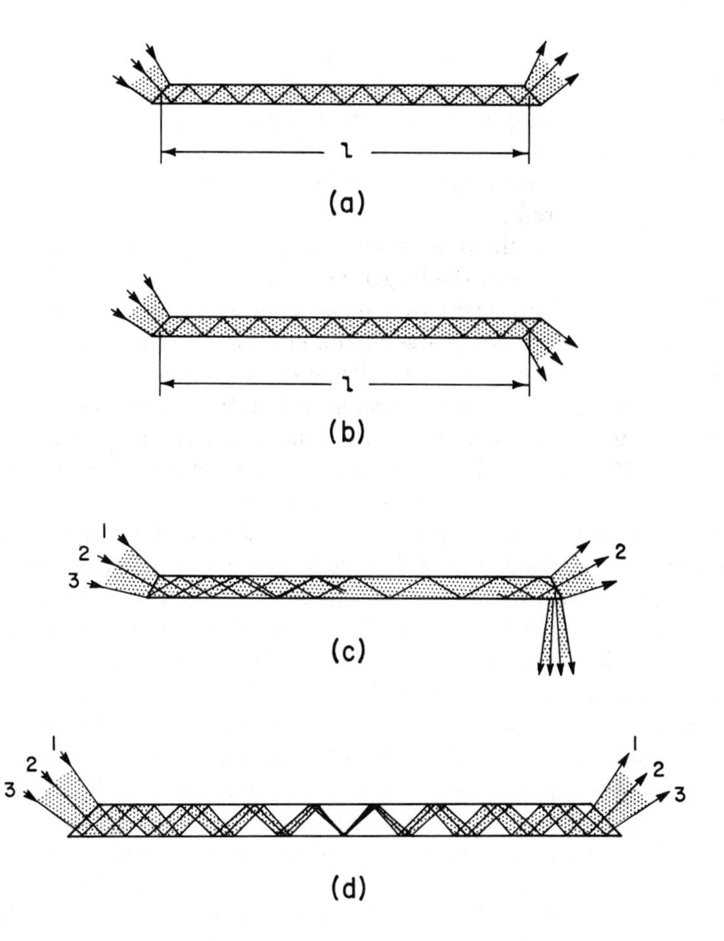

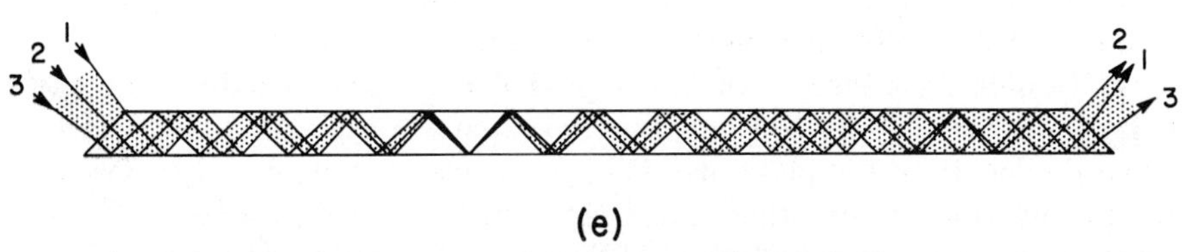

Fig. 5. Fixed-angle, single-pass, multiple internal reflection plates: (a) and (b) Thin trapezoid and parallelogram plates where $\theta < 45°$ and the light beam fills the entire plate; (c) thin plate, $\theta > 45°$—note that entire surface area is not sampled and that some energy is lost through a broad surface; (d) thick plate where light beam is focused near the middle of the plate; (e) intermediate thickness (or long length)—note mixing of light rays.

however, the light will tend to fill the entire plate as it traverses the length of the plate. Therefore some of the light will approach the exit aperture from the wrong direction and be totally reflected by this aperture and be lost even when the exit aperture is placed at the correct location for the central ray, as shown in Fig. 5c. (This energy loss for $\theta > 45°$ can be avoided by "trumpeting" the exit aperture.)

For thick plates, on the other hand, the path of the light beam should be geometrically traced down the length of the plate as shown in Fig. 5d. The light beam should be brought to a focus somewhere near the middle of the plate and the length and thickness should be chosen so that there is no mixing of the light rays. In this case the width of the source image is still maintained but there is an upper limit on the maximum length of the plate. This length, determined by the beam spread within the plate, is that length where the light beam just fills the entire entrance and exit apertures when the focal point is maintained at the center as shown in Fig. 5d.

For a thick plate whose dimensions do not agree with the above rule—i.e., one of the same thickness but of greater length than that shown in Fig. 5d or of the same length but smaller thickness—to avoid vignetting of the light beam the focus cannot be kept at the center of the plate but must be positioned nearer the entrance aperture as shown in Fig. 5e. When this is done, however, there is mixing of the light rays as shown in Fig. 5e and it is no longer possible to reproduce a true image of the source. The width of the source image is increased although the same angular beam spread is maintained. This mixing thus results in a lateral "extension of the source" which is undesirable because it is no longer possible to focus the source image to the same small dimension at the detector and this in turn results in power loss.

Figure 6 is a photograph showing the actual path of a light beam from a laser inside and outside the single-pass plate. The ability to produce intense and highly collimated light beams with lasers makes them ideal for illustrations of this sort since, as may be seen in the photograph, the width of the beam is substantially unchanged over the entire path length.

(2) **Double-Pass Plate.** In double-pass plates (H28) the light beam enters via an aperture at one end and is propagated via multiple total reflection down the length of the plate just as in the single-pass plate. However, it is totally reflected at the other end, from a surface perpendicular to the two large flat areas, at the complement of the angle of incidence on the broad faces and returns via a similar path to exit from the plate through an aperture adjacent to the entrance aperture as shown in Fig. 7. Double-pass plates simplify optical alignment since the entrance and exit beams have a common focal point while single-pass plates have two focal points. For a given

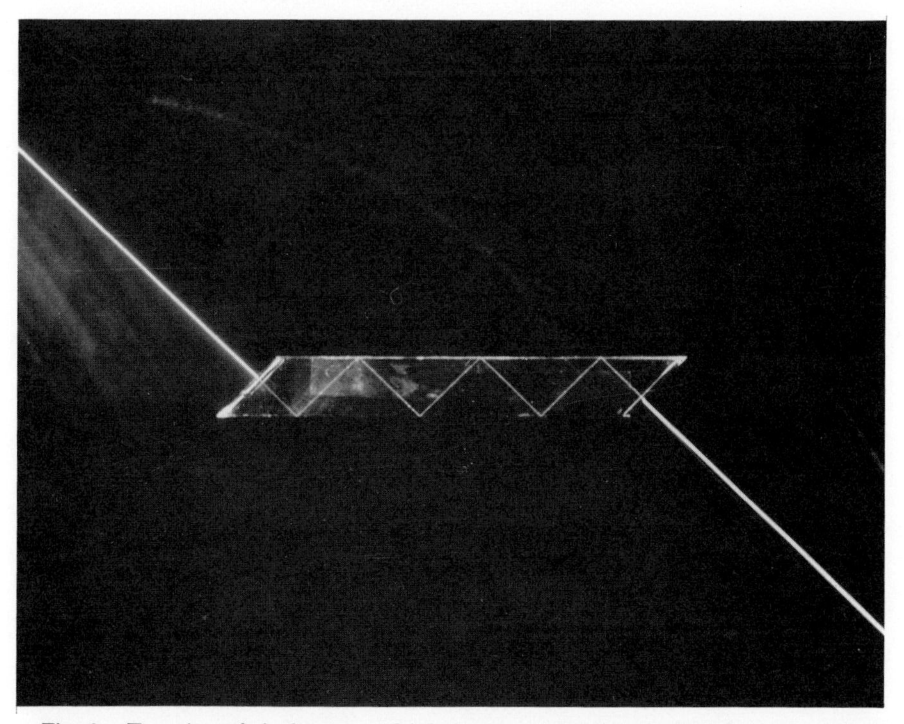

Fig. 6. Top view of single-pass multiple internal reflection plate showing actual light path outside and inside of the plate. In this and in some of the following illustrations, a He–Ne gas laser beam is used for convenience to depict the optical path.

length of plate the number of reflections is increased by a factor of 2 over the single-pass plate; thus, it represents a folded system. The total aperture however (entrance plus exit) is constant and therefore each aperture has been reduced by a factor of two compared to the single-pass plate, when the exit and entrance apertures are of the same area. An important advantage of the double-pass plates is that one end of the plate is free and it can be dipped into a liquid or powder to measure its spectrum, as shown in Fig. 8. The prisms are used to rotate the slit image because the aperture of the IRE is in a horizontal position while the spectrometer slits are vertical. Another important application of the double-pass plates is their use in evacuated systems since only one optical window is now required to bring the beam in and out of a vacuum system. Because the reflection at the end surface occurs at the complement of the angle of incidence on the broad faces, this plate can be used only for angles ranging from θ_c to $(90° - \theta_c)$ rather than from θ_c to 90°.

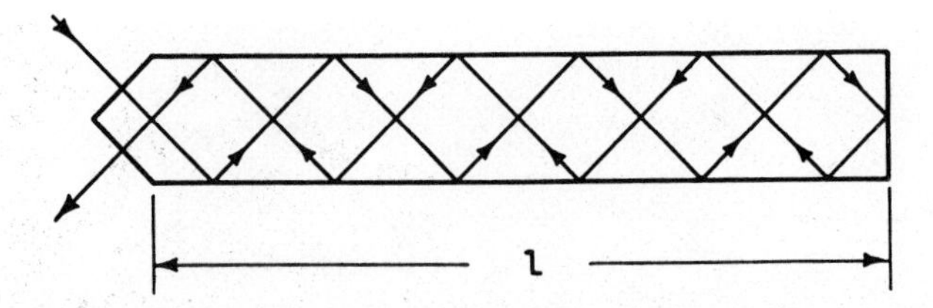

Fig. 7. Double-pass multiple internal reflection plate (H28). The light beam traverses the length of the plate twice, entering and leaving via the same end, hence doubling the number of reflections.

This is not a serious limitation, especially for high index materials, since measurements at grazing incidence are generally of no interest because of the small effective thickness at these angles.

For thin plates where, due to beam divergence, the light fills the entire plate, the emerging energy will leave the plate via the entrance and exit apertures in equal amounts. There is thus a 50% loss in power compared to the single-pass plate and for this reason the double-pass plate should not be employed where its advantages cannot be fully exploited. When external optics are employed and the slit image can be focused to small dimensions this loss can be reduced by making the entrance aperture much smaller than the exit aperture. Photographs showing the path of a laser beam outside and

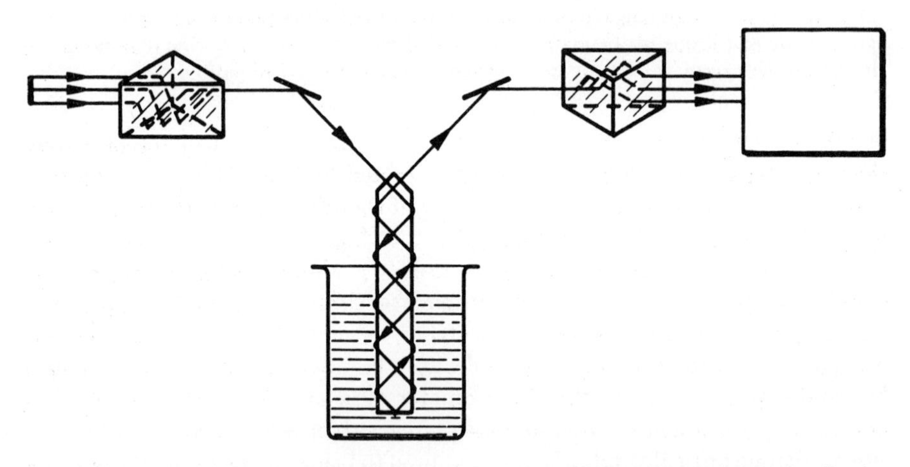

Fig. 8. Schematic diagram showing the use of horizontal double-pass internal reflection plate to measure the spectrum of a liquid or powder. Prisms, tilted at 45°, are required to reorient the spectrometer slit image from the vertical to the horizontal plane and mirrors are required to redirect the light beam (H34).

inside a double-pass plate are reproduced in Figs. 9a and 9b. In the latter figure, the spots on the surface show the actual points of reflection.

A variation of the double-pass plate is one with a single bevel at one end and a cocked end-reflecting surface, as shown in Fig. 10a. In this case the same aperture is employed for both the entrance and exit beams. If the light beam strikes the entrance aperture at normal incidence it is propagated down the length in the usual manner. After it strikes the end surface its angle of incidence on the broad faces for the return path is changed by twice the angle of the tilt, viz., δ (plus or minus depending on the direction of the tilt). The beam will return and strike the entrance aperture at non-normal incidence, and therefore the exit beam will be refracted away from the entrance beam by approximately $n_1 \delta$ degrees, as shown in Fig. 10a. This IRE should not be constructed from crystal materials which have a strong dispersion in refractive index because the direction of the exit beam will then be wavelength dependent. It should be noted from Fig. 10b that in general there will be two return beams with internal angles of incidence $\theta + \delta$ and $\theta - \delta$ and hence two exit beams at $\theta \pm n_1\delta$. The reason for this is that the beam approaches the end-reflecting surface from both the top and bottom reflecting surfaces, and in one case twice the tilt angle will be added to θ and in the other it will be subtracted from θ. The intensity in the two return beams is equally divided for $\theta \leq 45°$ if the entire aperture is employed because the projected area of the end reflecting surface is equal to one-half the useful aperture. For $\theta > 45°$ more power may be found in one return beam than in the other; e.g., for $\theta = 60°$, 75% of the power may be found in one of the return beams if the length of the plate is chosen correctly. (Requirements on length will be discussed in more detail in Section D.)

(3) **Vertical Double-Pass Plate.** It was shown in Fig. 8 that the double-pass plates, with the aid of the necessary additional optical components to reorient the slit images, could be placed in a vertical position and then easily dipped into liquids and powders to record their spectra. This horizontal double-pass plate can be converted into a vertical one (H34), thereby eliminating the need of the additional optical components, by making a 45° diagonal cut and beveling the long edge as shown in Fig. 11a. If the appropriate surfaces are polished, light entering one face of the beveled edge will be propagated horizontally by internal reflection until it strikes the diagonal surface. It is then deflected downwards, where it is propagated by means of multiple internal reflection, from the two opposing broad surfaces, until it strikes the bottom surfaces. Here it is totally reflected, returns via a similar path and is reoriented to a horizontal path after striking the diagonal cut, is propagated horizontally via internal reflection, and exits from the other

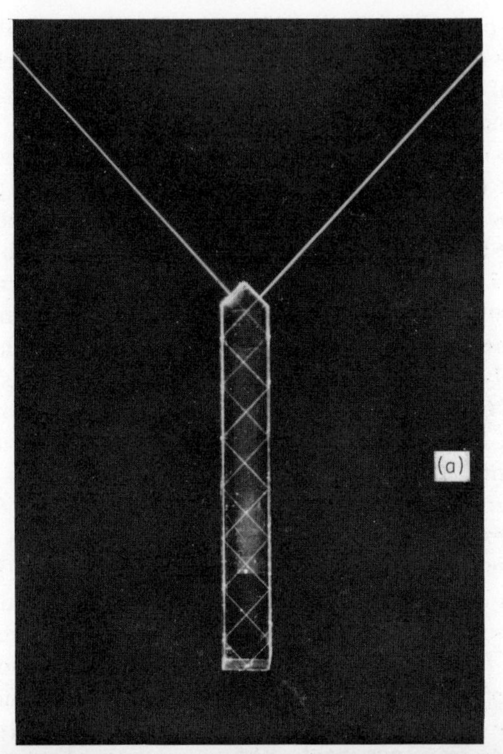

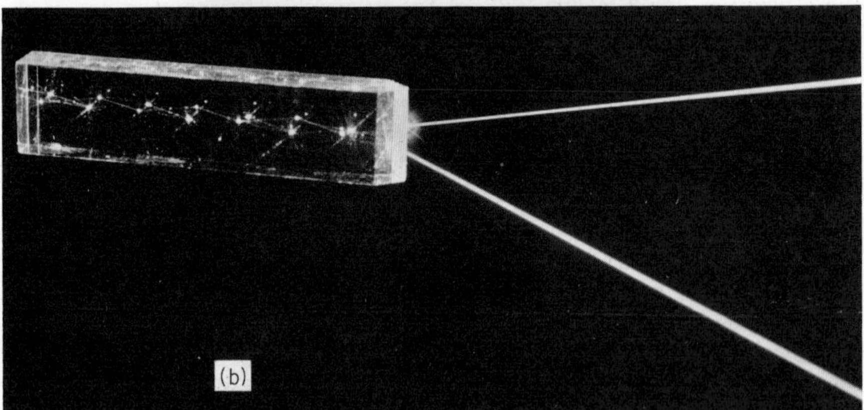

Fig. 9. (a) Top view of double-pass multiple internal reflection plate showing actual light path outside and inside the plate. (b) Oblique view of double-pass multiple internal reflection plate showing actual light path outside and inside the plate. The spots on the sides are points of reflection.

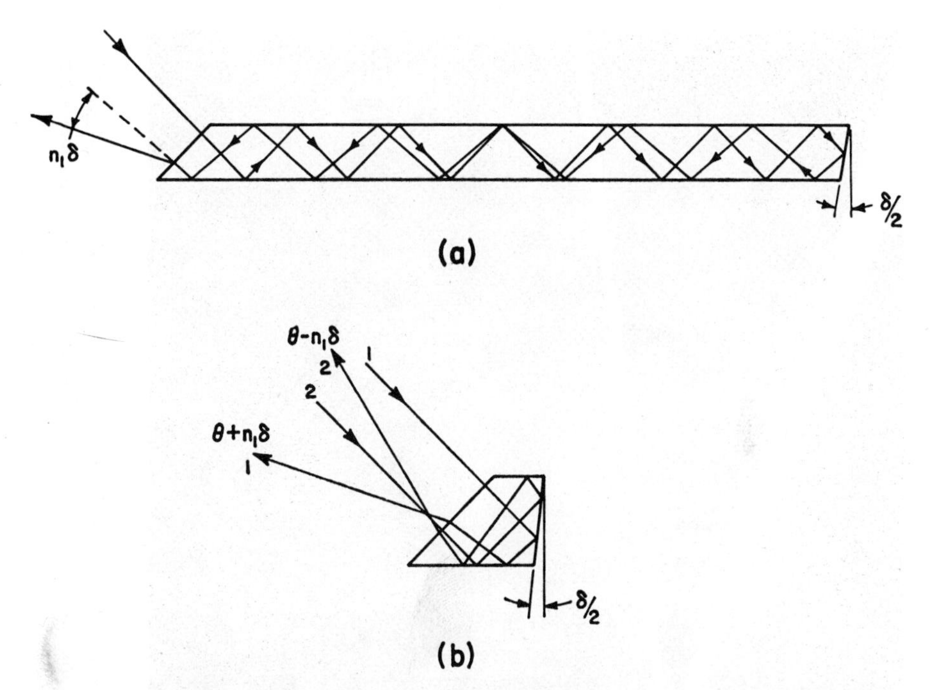

Fig. 10. Double-pass plate with single aperture and cocked end. (a) Separation of exit beam from entrance beam accomplished by changing angle of incidence, via cocked end-reflecting surface, for return beam with resulting refraction at exit aperture. (b) Decomposition of single incoming beam into two exit beams by cocking end-reflecting surface—the angle of incidence for one of the return beams is increased by δ and for the other it is decreased by δ due to the cocked end-reflecting surface.

beveled edge. A photograph showing the actual path of a laser beam through such a vertical double-pass plate is shown in Fig. 11b. The spots on the surface indicate the points where the reflection occurs and the light lines indicate the actual path of the beam within the plate. The vertical double-pass plate is useful for liquids and powders.

The vertical double-pass plate is not restricted to an angle of incidence of 45° but, provided the 45° diagonal plane is maintained, the range of angles of incidence that can be employed is the same as for the horizontal double-pass plate, viz., from the critical angle θ_c to $(90° - \theta_c)$. Thus it is possible to use it at other angles of incidence or to construct a variable angle, vertical double-pass internal reflection element by providing a cylindrical entrance aperture. This can be proved mathematically and is also evident from the geometrical construction shown in Fig. 12. A horizontal beam with arbitrary angle of

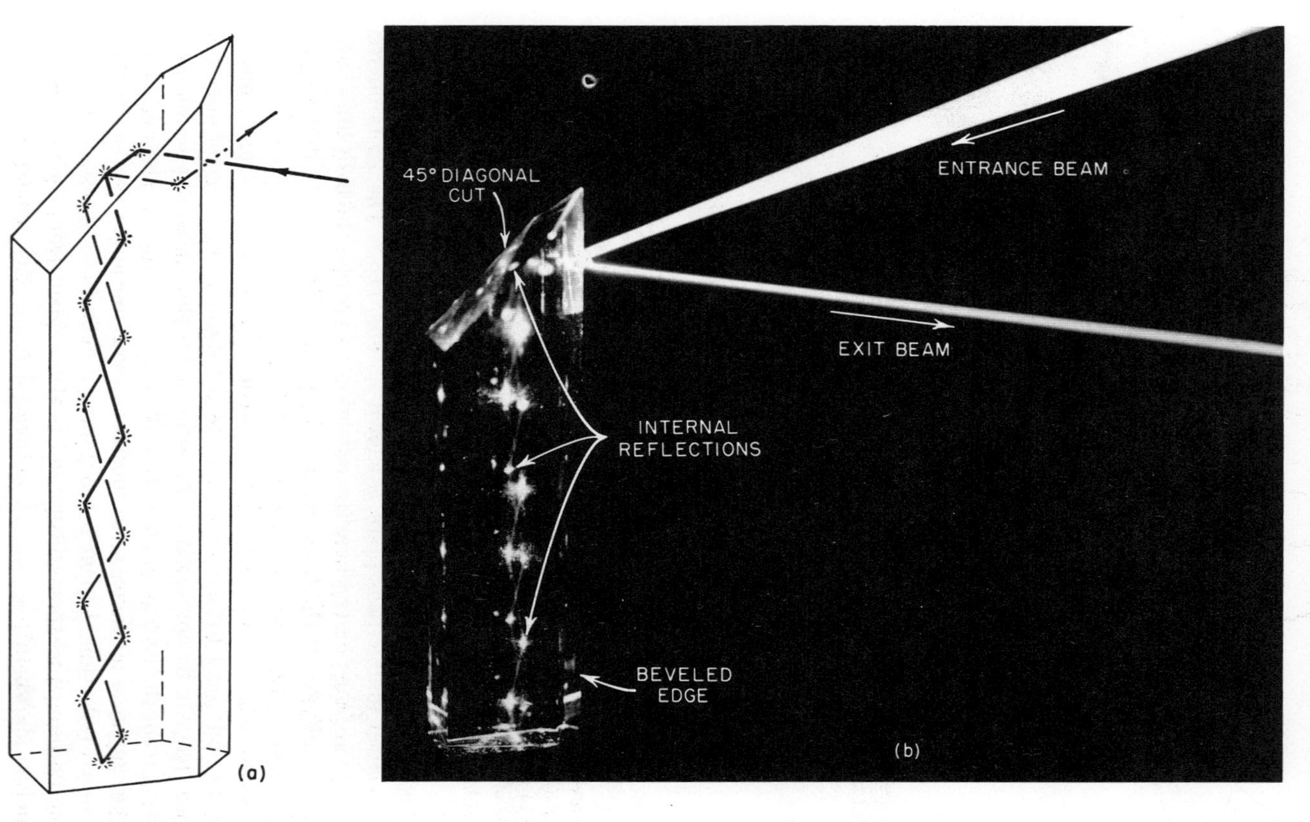

Fig. 11. (a) Schematic diagram of light path in the vertical double-pass multiple internal reflection plate. The light beam enters horizontally, is deflected vertically due to 45° diagonal plane, and returns via a similar path. (b) Photograph showing path of laser beam inside and outside of vertical double-pass plate (H34).

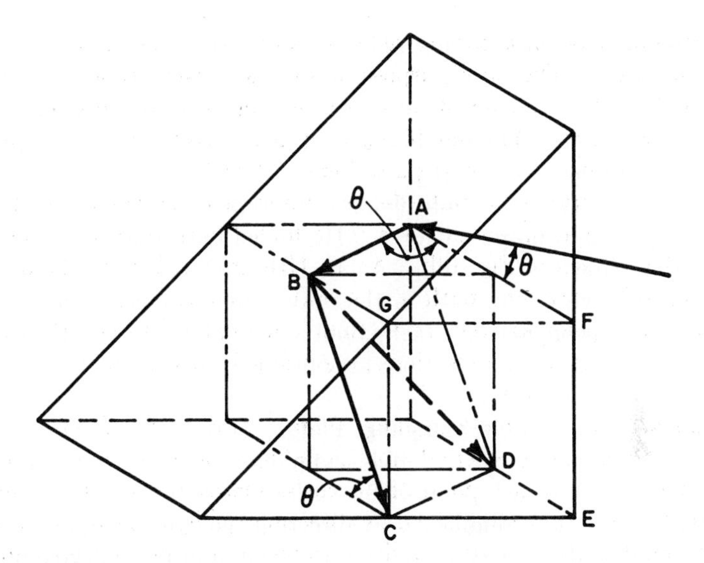

Fig. 12. Geometrical construction of vertical double-pass plate showing reorientation of light beam after reflection from 45° diagonal plane (see text).

incidence θ is reflected at A from a vertical plane and then at B from a 45° plane as shown. This results in a beam BC located in a vertical plane which is perpendicular to the first plane as will now be proved. In Fig. 12 two identical rectangular parallelepipeds have been constructed. Each one has four surfaces which are identical rectangles, defined by diagonal AB and angle θ, and two surfaces which are squares, e.g., $CEFG$. It is only necessary to show that BC, constructed as shown, represents the reflected beam. $ABCD$ is a rhombus since each side is the diagonal of identical rectangles. Note that BD as the diagonal of a square is normal to the 45° plane. Since BD is also a diagonal of the rhombus $ABCD$, it bisects the angle between AB and BC. Therefore, AB, BC, and the normal BD fulfill the condition of reflection; viz., the angle of incidence equals the angle of reflection. Therefore, BC gives the correct position of the reflected beam. Since AB and BC are diagonals of identical rectangles, the angle of incidence of the vertical beam BC is identical to the angle of incidence θ of the incoming horizontal beam.

(4) **Multiple-Pass Internal Reflection Plates.** An extension of the double-pass plate to a multiple-pass plate can obviously be made by providing entrance and exit apertures at one corner of a plate and orienting the entrance beam so that on its return path it misses the exit aperture and propagates back and forth, as shown in Fig. 13a until it reaches the top of the plate. At

the top, the light beam is totally reflected and returns via a similar path to the exit aperture. The only purpose of such a construction is to multiply fold the light path. Thus instead of contending with an internal reflection element of, say, 1 cm wide and 16 cm long, it is possible to obtain the same number of reflections in a square plate 4 cm × 4 cm.

Another geometry for a multiple-pass internal reflection element, which had been previously proposed for a TIR folded-path optical maser cavity (D11), is that shown in Fig. 13b. As an IRE it suffers from the disadvantage that a relatively long path in the optical material is required for each reflection. This geometry is in fact a double-pass plate of twice the thickness where only two additional reflections are obtained—one at the top and one at the end-reflecting surfaces.

(5) **Single-Pass, Double-Sampling Plate.** Hirschfeld (H49b) has proposed a single-pass plate where double-sampling is achieved; i.e., a portion of the light beam strikes each point of the surface twice if the entire aperture is illuminated. This is accomplished by directing the light beam into the plate at a compound angle so that in addition to being multiply reflected down the length, it zigzags across the width as shown in Fig. 14. All the surfaces including the long edges of this plate must be polished. This plate may be constructed in the form of a trapezoid or a parallelepiped. To achieve double sampling for $\theta > 45°$ it is necessary to increase the aperture by trumpeting the ends of the plate as discussed near the beginning of this chapter in Section B-1.

The structure shown in Fig. 14 is similar to the multiple-pass internal reflection plate shown in Fig. 13a in that it is a similar folded system. It should be noted, however, that double-sampling is not achieved in Fig. 13a since, as discussed earlier, the total aperture is reduced by a factor of two in a double-pass type of structure and the entire width of the plate cannot be illuminated. Double-sampling can be achieved in the structure shown in Fig. 13a if the rooftop bevel is replaced by a simple bevel and an exit aperture is provided at the opposite corner.

(6) **Double-Pass, Double-Sampling Plate.** Another method of obtaining double-sampling (Dreyfus (D17) and Harrick), which has the advantage that compound angles are eliminated, is to prepare a single-pass plate where one of the apertures has been slightly cocked and metallized. When the beam strikes this metallized surface internally, it is returned toward the entrance aperture in an almost identical path striking each point of the surface a second time but at a slightly different angle of incidence. The beam will leave the plate at a refracted angle as discussed in connection with the structure having a "cocked end-reflecting" surface, shown in Fig. 13. In the

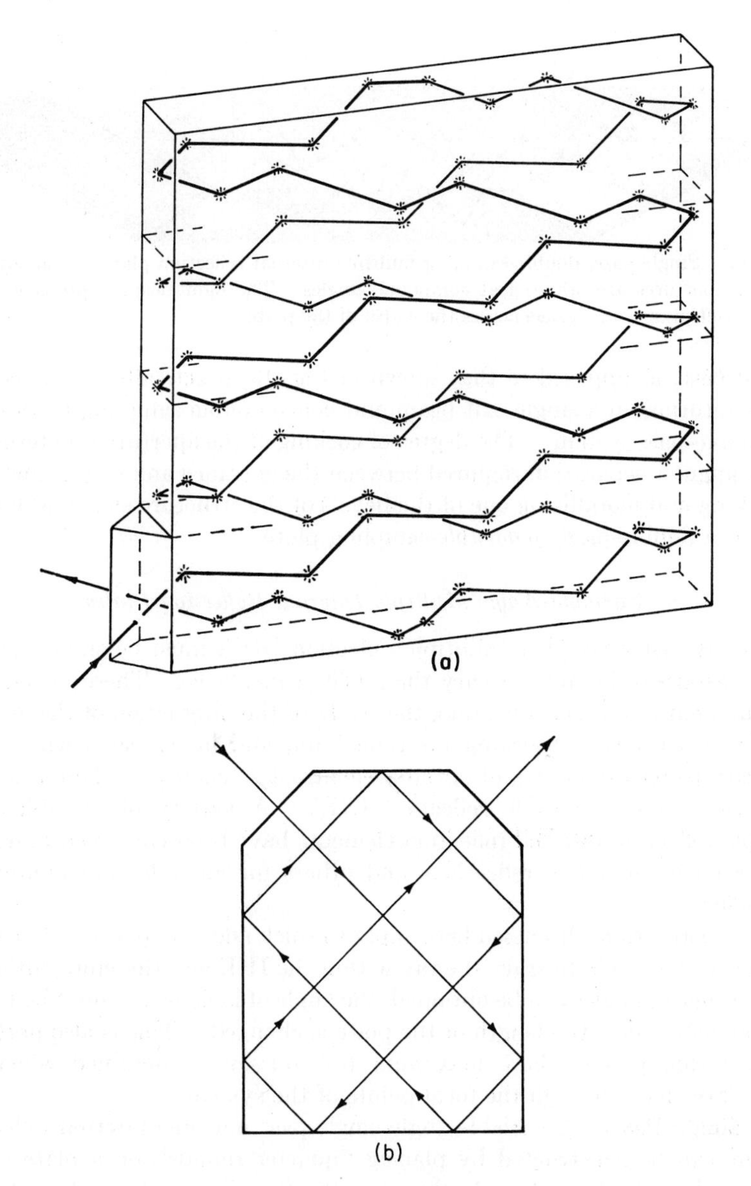

Fig. 13. Folded path multiple-pass internal reflection plates. (a) Corner injection. (b) Thick double-pass plate.

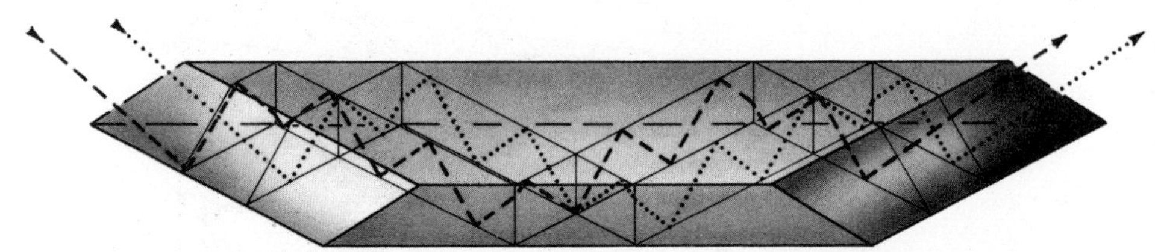

Fig. 14. Single-pass, double-sampling multiple internal reflection plate. The entrance and exit apertures are oriented at compound angles. The light beam is propagated by multiple reflection and zigzags across the width of the plate.

present case, as opposed to that shown in Fig. 13, practically all the energy can be returned in a single exit beam and hence double sampling is achieved in a double-pass system. The degree of cocking of the aperture is determined by the angular separation required between the entrance and exit beams.

Cocking and metallizing one of the bevels of the structure shown in Fig. 14 leads to a double-pass, *quadruple*-sampling plate.

b. Variable-Angle Multiple Internal Reflection Plates

In many instances where multiple reflection IRE's must be employed it is still necessary to be able to vary the angle of incidence. These include the measurement of optical constants, the study of the interaction of the evanescent wave with the absorbing rarer medium, and many cases where it is necessary to record spectra of optimum contrast. Therefore, there is a need for variable-angle multiple reflection IRE's. A variety of variable-angle multiple reflection internal reflection elements have been employed to date—one designed for a few reflections and others for an indefinite number of reflections.

The constructions discussed here apply to thick and thin plates. For thick plates it is necessary to trace the ray within the IRE and therefore, although a wide range of angles can be obtained, the angle of incidence cannot be varied continuously unless the length of the plate is changed. This is also partially true for thin plates where maximum transmission is obtained when the central rays pass through the focal points of the system.

(1) **Single-Pass.** A variable-angle single-pass multiple internal reflection element can be constructed by placing "quarter rounds" on a plate (H28, H30), as shown in Fig. 15a. In this case, the quarter round may be optically contacted to the plate or the entire structure may be molded from a suitable material. The "quarter round" must be cut in such a way that the center of curvature is located at a point midway in the plate. Thus the dimension b is

roughly equal to $(a - t/2)$. The focusing condition for collimation within the IRE discussed earlier can be applied here. The quarter round for the exit beam may be located anywhere along the length of the plate, depending on the number of reflections required. Furthermore, it may be located on the same side of the plate or the opposite side. A photograph of such a structure made from silicon is shown in Fig. 16a.

(2) **Double-Pass.** A double-pass (H28) multiple IRE can obviously be constructed in the same manner as the single-pass one. In this case, however, the "quarter rounds" are placed opposite each other at the same end of the plate. In addition to the possibility of varying the angle of incidence continuously, all of the advantages of the double-pass plate apply to this structure. A schematic diagram and photograph, respectively, of a variable-angle, double-pass plate are shown in Figs. 15b and 16b.

(3) **Vertical Double-Pass.** It was pointed out earlier that the fixed-angle, vertical double-pass plate can be employed for any angle of incidence between θ_c and $(90 - \theta_c)$. A variable-angle, vertical double-pass plate can therefore be constructed by replacing the entrance and exit aperture with suitable quarter rounds.

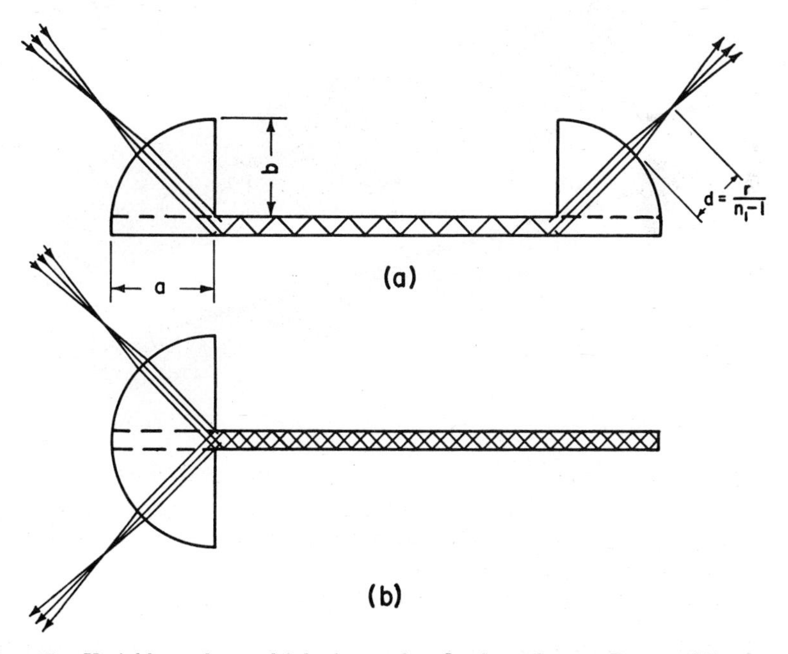

Fig. 15. Variable-angle, multiple internal reflection plates. By providing quarter rounds at the entrance and exit apertures the angle of incidence can be varied continuously. (a) Single-pass. (b) Double-pass.

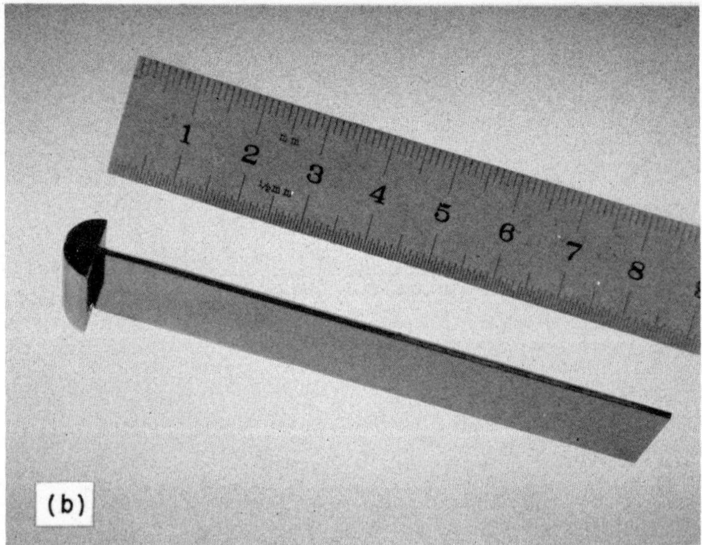

Fig. 16. Photographs of silicon variable-angle multiple reflection plates. (a) Single-pass. (b) Double-pass.

c. Unipoint Multiple Internal Reflection Elements

A unipoint multiple internal reflection element is one in which the light beam interacts with the same point of the sample material many times. This does not occur in any of the internal reflection elements already described. In the double-pass plate, for example, a given light ray is propagated down the length of the plate via multiple reflection at certain points on the surface and returns via a similar path but for the returning beam the reflection points are displaced and it should be noted that even for a thin plate (i.e., one filled with light) each point on the surface is sampled only once. (This is not exactly true because of the angular spread in the beam.) Obviously, the end-reflecting surfaces can be so arranged that the light beam returns via an identical path but then there is a problem of separating the exit beam from the incoming beam.

Multiple reflection from one point can be achieved in certain structures and it is still possible to maintain a clear separation between the entrance and exit beams.

(1) **Optical Cavity.** The optical cavity (H35,B18,H38a) is a structure which employs dielectric films a fraction of a wavelength thick. Such structures make it possible to couple electromagnetic energy into these thin films where multiple reflections occur and very intense electromagnetic fields are developed. Waveguide effects are achieved at optical frequencies. Thus the optical cavity is analogous to the microwave cavity. Because high sensitivity is obtained only when "resonance" condition exists, the cavities must be operated at a fixed wavelength. Tuning over a limited wavelength range can be obtained by changing the angle of incidence. At resonance very high sensitivities are potentially attainable. This type of approach may make it possible to record spectra of nanogram quantities. (The optical cavity will be discussed in more detail in the following chapter.)

(2) **Rosette.** The rosette is a unipoint multiple internal reflection element where the light beam is temporarily trapped and directed to strike a given point on the sampling surface numerous times (H36). Figures 17a and 17b are top and trimetric views, respectively, of such a structure. The beam enters the rosette, travels downwards and strikes the sampling surface at the predetermined angle of incidence, and then rises until it strikes the total internal reflection mirror *1*. This latter mirror is so oriented that it deflects the beam to a horizontal path where it strikes a second mirror, called a coacting mirror, which directs the beam back to the sampling surface at the same angle of incidence. This reflection process is repeated many times wherein it is evident that every third reflection takes place from the sampling surface and the plane of incidence precesses about the axis of the rosette. After the desired number of reflections have been obtained the beam leaves the internal reflection element via an exit aperture. Although only four passes are shown in Fig. 17, it would not be unreasonable to construct one where 10 or perhaps many more can be achieved. For long path lengths within the rosette it is necessary to either collimate the beam or to shape the

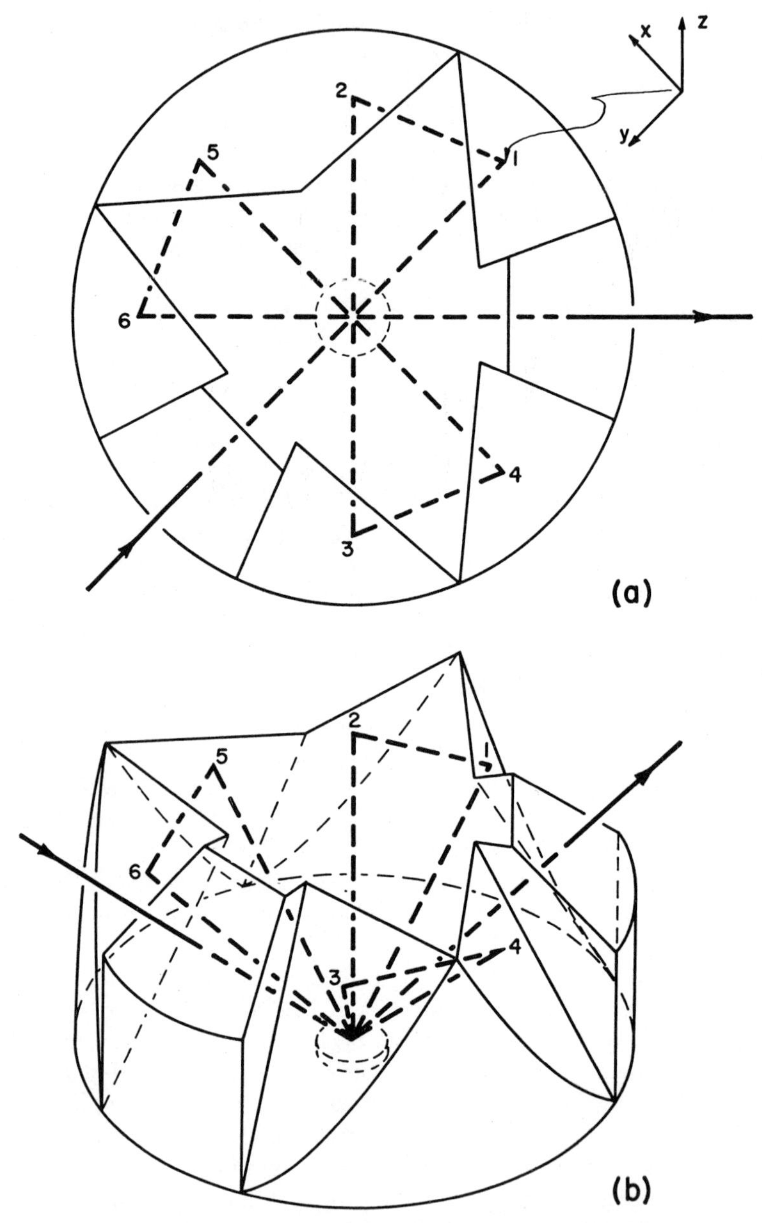

Fig. 17. The rosette—a unipoint multiple internal reflection element. (a) Top view. (b) Trimetric view (H36). The light beam is trapped within the IRE and strikes a point on the sampling surface many times (four times for this unit).

total reflection mirrors with sufficient power to prevent excessive defocusing of the light beam. Because the plane of incidence is rotated on successive reflections, a well-defined polarization cannot be maintained at the sampling surface. Just as for the hemisphere, the bottom section may be cone-shaped to facilitate contacting the sample material to the sampling surface.

A model for four reflections from the sampling surface was constructed and the path of a light beam from a laser through it is clearly shown in Fig. 18. Four (slightly, purposely displaced) reflections on the sampling surface are clearly seen. For axes whose origin is located at the reflection point for the principal ray of mirror *1*, as shown in Fig. 17a, where the yz plane is the plane of incidence, where the y axis is parallel to the sampling surface, where the z axis is perpendicular to the sampling plane, and where the x axis points in the general direction of the co-acting plane, the angles of the normal to the first reflecting plane with respect to the x, y, and z axes are 54° 34.5′, 46° 52′, and 116° 20′.

The orientations of the reflecting planes are completely specified if the directions cosines of the normals to these planes are known. These are determined in the following way. The light beam, after being reflected from the sampling surface, approaches the reflecting mirror in the yz plane; and the direction cosines of the incoming beam, λ_1, μ_1, ν_1, are determined by the angle of incidence on the sampling surface. After reflection from this oblique surface, the light beam travels in the xy plane to the co-acting plane with direction cosines λ_2, μ_2, ν_2. These direction cosines are determined by the number of passes (i.e., number of reflections from the sampling surface) since the co-acting plane has an angular displacement of π/N from the first plane. Here N is the number of reflections. The angle between the incoming and reflected beam at the reflecting plane is 2θ, where θ is the angle of incidence on the first oblique plane. It is well known that

$$\cos 2\theta = \lambda_1\lambda_2 + \mu_1\mu_2 + \nu_1\nu_2 ; \tag{8}$$

therefore θ can be determined.

There are now the following three equations involving the direction cosines λ, μ, ν of the normal to the reflecting plane from which λ, μ, ν can be determined; viz.,

$$\lambda\lambda_1 + \mu\mu_1 + \nu\nu_1 = \cos\theta, \tag{9}$$

$$\lambda\lambda_2 + \mu\mu_2 + \nu\nu_2 = \cos\theta, \tag{10}$$

and

$$\lambda^2 + \mu^2 + \nu^2 = 1. \tag{11}$$

Fig. 18. Photograph of rosette showing path of laser beam inside and outside of the IRE.

These have been solved for the case in which the angle of incidence on the sampling surface is 45° and $N = 4$. It is found that

$$\lambda = \cos\alpha = 0.5796 \qquad \alpha = 54°\,34.5'$$
$$\mu = \cos\beta = 0.6836 \qquad \beta = 46°\,52'$$
$$\nu = \cos\gamma = 0.4436 \qquad \gamma = 116°\,20'.$$

Obviously, these angles determine the orientation of every second oblique plane if the references axes are rotated by $2\pi/N$ about a vertical axis through the sampling point. These angles were used in the construction of the rosette shown in Fig. 18.

These angles also determine orientation of the co-acting plane if new reference axes are chosen where the positive direction of the x axis is in the opposite direction, and then the coordinate system is rotated about the z axis by π/N.

Hirschfeld (49b) has proposed a rosette-type structure wherein the angle of incidence can be continuously adjusted. In his structure the coacting mirrors are curved and are cut into the surface of a hemisphere so that they meet a common point at the top of the hemisphere and form a sawtooth-like structure along the periphery. The orientation of the coacting mirrors must be such that at any angle of incidence equations (9), (10), and (11) are satisfied. The variable-angle rosette is, of course, rather more difficult to construct and incorporate in a spectrometer than the fixed-angle rosette.

In addition to the study of submicrogram quantities, the potential sensitivity attainable with the rosette should make it useful for studying solids where adequate contact to a single-reflection internal reflection element or to the broad area of a multiple reflection plate cannot readily be achieved.

d. Other Geometries

(1) **Modified Hemicylinder.** Fahrenfort and Visser (F3,F4) have described a modified hemicylinder which can be constructed for a few reflections (e.g., from 3 to 5) and where the angle of incidence can be varied continuously over a limited range. This structure is part of a regular hemicylinder and is shown in Fig. 19. Its design considerations are discussed in more detail in their paper. A structure of this sort can be molded from soft materials such as AgCl, KRS-5. For other materials it is necessary to resort to optical

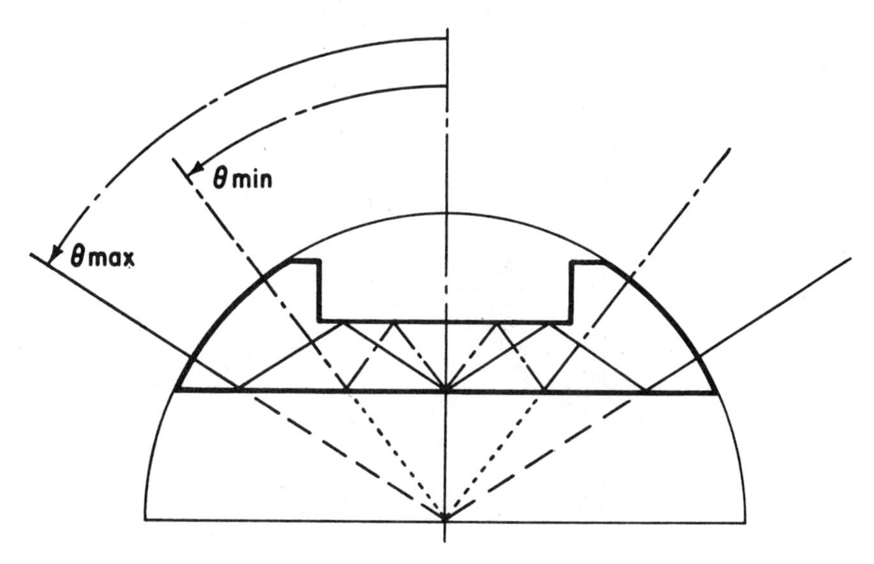

Fig. 19. Modified hemicylinder for five reflections where the angle of incidence can be varied over a limited range from θ_{max} to θ_{min} (F4).

contacting as has already been employed for variable-angle multiple reflection elements.

(2) V-Shaped IRE. Uncollimated light beams are generally employed in spectrometers. Any material of index greater than unity placed in the path of the light beam decreases the optical path length and thus tends to defocus the light at the slit image. In order to maintain focus the actual path length in the material must equal $L = nd$, where d is the distance interrupted by the optical material. (More correctly $L = n_1 d \cos r / \cos i$, where i and r are, respectively, the half-angular spread in the incident and refracted beams at the entrance face. For both i and r near zero, $\cos i \sim \cos r \sim 1$.) No defocusing or displacement of the light beam occurs for a V-shaped structure (H28) similar to that shown in Fig. 20 provided that the condition $L = n_1 d$ is satisfied for materials with refractive index, n_1, greater than or equal to 2 if the internal angle of incidence, θ, is chosen as

$$\theta = \frac{1}{2} \cos^{-1} \frac{N(n_1 - 2)}{n_1 N - 4n_1 + 4} \tag{12}$$

and if the angle between the two arms is 2θ. θ involves both the index of refraction, n_1, and the number of reflections, N. The number of internal reflections is given by

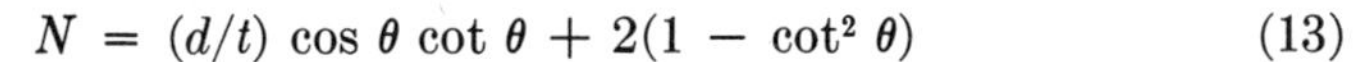

$$N = (d/t) \cos \theta \cot \theta + 2(1 - \cot^2 \theta) \tag{13}$$

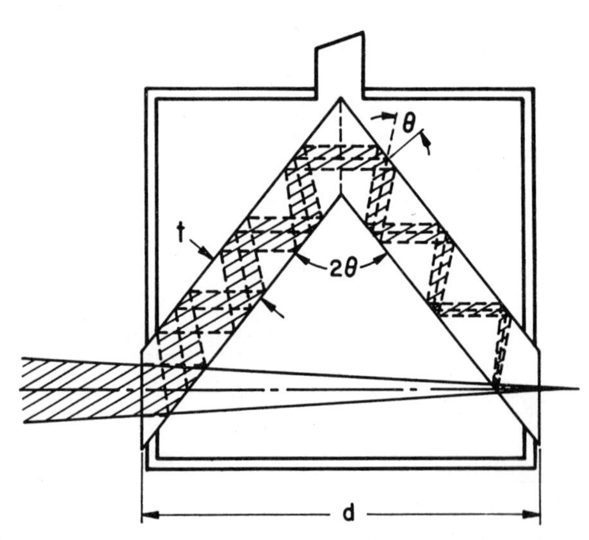

Fig. 20. V-shaped internal reflection element which, when placed in sampling space of monochromator, causes no defocusing or displacement of light beam at entrance slits (H21,H28).

and can be adjusted by adjusting the thickness, t, of the IRE or the distance, d, between the ends of the arms. N must be a multiple of 4 and must be greater than 4 except for $n_1 = 2$. The critical angles and the angles of incidence required for a specified number of reflections are given in Table II for a number of suitable materials as well as the useful wavelength range.

TABLE II
Typical Infrared Transparent Materials ($n_1 \geq 2$) and Parameters for V-Shaped IRE for a Given Value of N

	n_1	θ_c	N	θ	λ range (μ)
Ge	4	14°30′	20	27°15′	2–12
Si	3.5	16°45′	20	30°	1–6
KRS-5	2.5	24°40′	12	39°	0.6–40
AgCl	2	30°	any number	45°	0.5–25

For materials with an index of refraction less than or equal to 2, the appropriate angle of incidence is greater than 45° and is given by

$$\theta = \sin^{-1}\sqrt{\frac{1}{n_1}} \tag{14}$$

and the angle between the two arms is still equal to 2θ. The number of reflections is given by

$$N = \frac{n_1 d \cos\theta}{t}. \tag{15}$$

Appropriate parameters for materials which might be used to construct such IRE's when $n_1 \leq 2$ are given in Table III.

TABLE III
Typical Infrared Transparent Materials ($n_1 \leq 2$) and Parameters for V-shaped IRE (Any number of reflections which is a multiple of 4 can be used.)

	n_1	θ_c	θ	λ-range (μ)
Al_2O_3	1.7	36°30′	50°25′	0.2–5
MgO	1.7	36°30′	50°25′	0.3–9
NaCl	1.5	47°	54°35′	0.25–15

Since there is no defocusing of the light beam by a V-shaped IRE and since the exit beam is coaxial with the entrance beam, this IRE can be placed directly in the sampling space of a monochromator without any additional optical components and without disturbing the optics in the spectrometer. This type of IRE must, of course, be operated at a fixed angle of incidence.

The V-shaped IRE may be made in one piece as shown, or may equivalently be made from two parallelepiped, single-pass plates which may or may not be optically contacted where they meet.

(3) **Cylindrical Rods and Fibers.** Cylindrical rods and fibers can and have been employed as internal reflection elements and refractometers (K12, K13, H5). Here again light introduced at angles exceeding θ_c is propagated down the length via total internal reflection. The rods or fibers can be bent and provided the bend is not too sharp the light will be contained within the fiber. The principal disadvantage of the rod or fiber is that a specific angle of incidence cannot be maintained.

When cylindrical rods are used as IRE's for internal reflection spectroscopy, the light beam should preferably be directed at some angle other than grazing incidence on the cylindrical surface to enhance the number of reflections and thus the strength of absorption. For cylindrical rods, however, a unique angle of incidence cannot be maintained. This can be appreciated by considering a cylinder as shown in Fig. 21 with plane-parallel ends, where for simplicity no refraction is assumed at the entrance and exit faces. If collimated light fills the entrance face and is directed at an angle of incidence of 45° in the median plane, i.e., the plane of incidence along the center of the rod, the angle of incidence will be 60° on the surface of the cylinder where the tangent plane makes an angle of 45° with respect to the horizontal—a substantial change. In fact, the whole spectrum of angles of incidence between

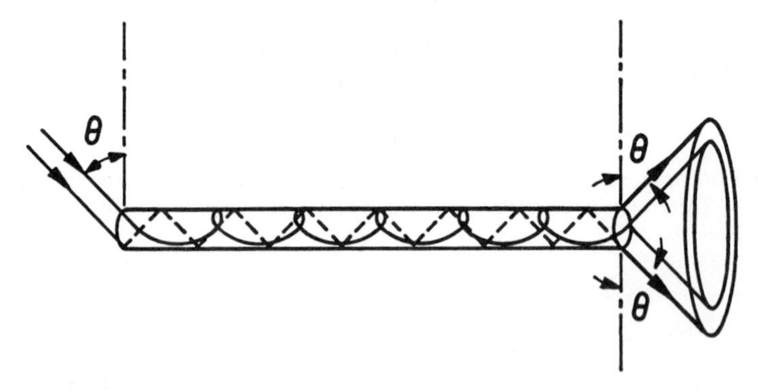

Fig. 21. Cylindrical rod optics (H28). A collimated light beam filling the entire aperture will have angles of incidence between θ and grazing incidence within the rod. The exit beam will be in the form of an annular cone.

45° and grazing is found for such curved surfaces. The light not striking the median plane follows a screwlike path down the rod and all the exit light forms a cone with a hole in the center, as shown in Fig. 21. This light pattern will obviously give rise to complications in conventional monochromators if the cylindrical rod is placed in the sampling space. If only the light representing the desired angle of incidence is collected, there is a considerable loss of power. If more complicated optics are used and all of the light is collected, it will represent a wide spectrum of angles of incidence with inherent distortion and broadening, as was discussed in the previous chapter. Some improvements can be made by appropriately shaping the ends of the rod and by using very high index materials, although it is unlikely that a single mode with a unique angle of incidence can be excited in rods which are large compared to the wavelength of the light being used. The large angular spread within the rods prohibit their operation in a double-pass mode since a good deal of the light will escape from the other end.

The conclusion is that although the use of cylindrical rods for internal reflection spectroscopy may have advantages because of their simplicity in preparation, they should be used with caution. Because of the complicated optical paths, calculations of angles of incidence and hence of effective thickness cannot easily be made. Bends in the rod further complicate calculations; hence calibrations are necessary.

D. Transmission Plates for the Reference Beam

Few crystal materials have a constant transmission over a wide range of wavelengths. Thus it is necessary to place a compensating internal reflection element in the reference beam in order to obtain a flat base line. This reference IRE, however, also tends to cancel signals arising from adsorbed molecules. This cancellation is undesirable, however, when internal reflection spectroscopy is being used to study the surfaces of the IRE. It is possible to construct plates where the light beam passes through them and makes little or no contact with the surface. These "transmission plates" are useful for compensation purposes in the reference beam. Since little contact is made with the surface in these plates, the preparation of the broad surfaces (surface polish) is not critical. This type of plate is also useful in testing the crystal material for bulk absorptions. One possible disadvantage in the use of this type of plate in the reference beam is that it does not compensate for surface scattering in the sample IRE. Partial compensation can be obtained by introducing a suitable scatterer in the reference beam. This lack of compensation for surface scattering is not a real disadvantage because complete compensation for surface scattering generally cannot easily be achieved since it is practically impossible to match exactly two IRE's for surface scattering. It is thus generally necessary to insure that the quality of the surface polish is sufficiently good so that surface scattering is not objectionable.

Some of the single and double-pass fixed angle plates can be employed as transmission plates in the following way.

1. Single-Pass Transmission Plates

A conventional 45° single-pass plate in the form of a trapezoid or parallelogram can be employed as a transmission plate by directing the beam normal to the broad surface towards the inside of the bevel as shown in Figs. 22a and 22b. It is evident that the beam will be deflected so that it passes through the entire length of the plate without contacting the broad surface of the IRE. Even when the beam contacts the broad surface, little or no interaction will

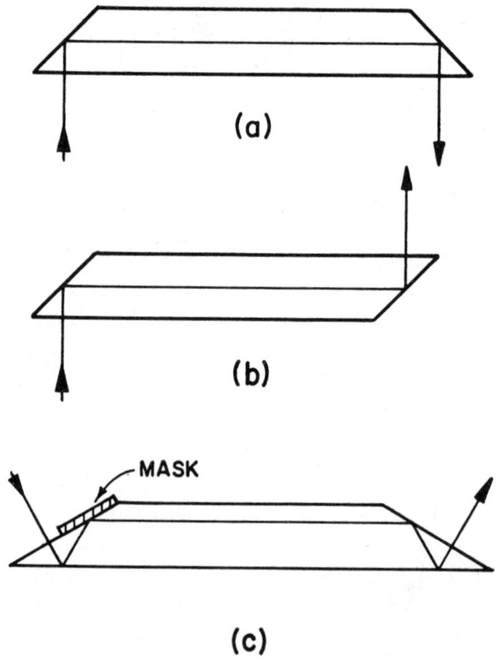

Fig. 22. Single-pass *transmission* plates. (a) 45° trapezoid. (b) 45° rhombus. (c) 30° trapezoid. Mask is used to prevent excitation of TIR modes. After reflection from beveled surface the light beam travels down length of plate parallel to the broad surfaces.

occur with the surface because it strikes the surface near grazing incidence when the effective thickness is small and the reflectivity is high. The distinction between thick and thin plates made for IRE's also apply to transmission plates.

A 30° plate can be employed as a transmission plate as shown in Fig. 22c. Light striking the half of the total aperture nearer the tip of the bevel at normal incidence will be internally reflected from the other portion of the aperture and directed down the plate parallel to the broad areas and will leave the plate via a similar path. The aperture proper should be masked to eliminate any light propagated by multiple reflection.

2. Double-Pass Transmission Plates

One geometry for a double-pass transmission plate is that shown in Fig. 23a where the plate has a 90° roof top at one end and a 60° roof top at the other end. Any light striking the half of the aperture nearer the tip at normal incidence will be internally reflected from the opposing bevel and deflected down the length of the plate parallel to the broad face. It returns via a similar path after striking the retro-prism at the other end and leaves via the exit aperture. In order to eliminate interference from any energy propagated

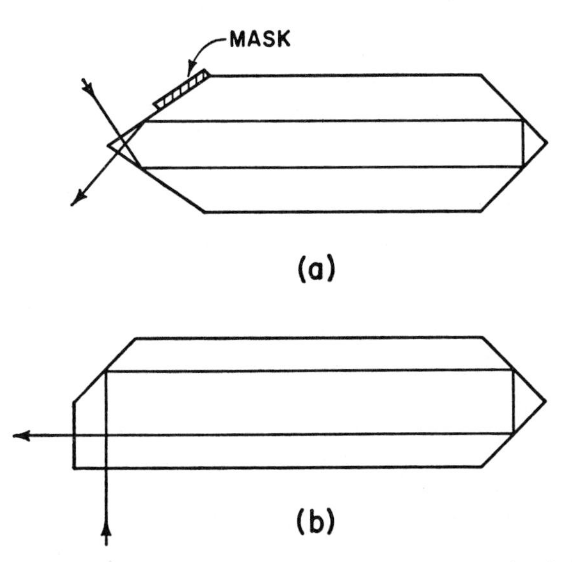

Fig. 23. Double-pass transmission plates. (a) 30° entrance and exit bevels and 90° roof top end-reflecting surface—entrance and exit beams are 120° apart. (b) 45° bevel and 90° roof top—beams are 90° apart.

down the length and back via total internal reflection, the other half of the entrance aperture can be masked as shown or, alternately, the broad area may be purposely left in roughened condition so that the unwanted energy is quickly dissipated.

Another double-pass transmission plate is that shown in Fig. 23b. In this version the 60° roof top has been replaced by a truncated 45° bevel. This version has the advantage over the former in that the entire aperture can be used (i.e., no masking required) although the total useful aperture is the same, and that the entrance and exit beams are 90° apart. Furthermore, the latter plate can be used as a single-pass internal reflection element.

E. Requirements, Preparation, and Test of IRE's

Internal reflection elements place rather severe requirements on transparency of the optical material from which they are made, on the quality of surface preparation, and on the precision on the geometrical tolerances. As will become evident, the stringent requirements are due to the long path lengths within the material and the large number of reflections often employed. The nature of the optical material and the geometry of the IRE are the principal factors to be taken into consideration in the preparation of the internal reflection elements. A number of simple tests are outlined to check the quality of an IRE or to trace down the reason for poor performance.

1. Material Requirements

When choosing an optical material for internal reflection elements consideration is given to its transparency, hardness, brittleness, conductivity, and chemical inertness.

Transparency is a required property of the bulk material and is determined by its inherent absorptions such as lattice bands, absorption edges, free carrier absorption, and purity. The material types available include glass-like materials, pressed materials, polycrystalline, and highly pure, single crystals. For many applications, single-crystal materials are not required, however grain boundaries in polycrystalline materials can lead to considerable power losses because of the long path lengths often required in IRE's. The development of transistor technology was accompanied by the incredible control in the preparation of single crystals of elemental semiconductors. Rather than quoting impurity content in percentages, it can be now controlled (and measured) in parts of 10^{12} per cc; i.e., there may be only one impure atom for every 10^{10} atoms! Many semiconductors materials are readily available in single crystalline form. Single crystals and preferably oriented single crystals are required for surface studies. A number of materials are discussed in more detail in Section F of this chapter.

The properties of hardness and brittleness play an important part in the ease of preparation of the IRE and particularly surface preparation and in the resistance to surface damage through use and breakage through misuse. Soft materials such as AgCl and KRS-5 can be rolled into simple plates or molded into more complicated structures. For most materials the IRE's must be prepared by cutting, lapping, and mechanical polishing, preferably from one piece of single-crystal material.

Conductivity of the material and its chemical inertness are taken into consideration in determining the species that can be studied. Electrode reactions, for example, require a conducting electrode although surface conduction may be adequate. If the IRE is rapidly corroded by the chemical under study, the experiment must be terminated and the IRE repolished or replaced. All these material requirements will become more evident in the later sections of this chapter.

2. Surface Requirements and Preparation

The requirements on the surfaces of the IRE are that they be optically polished so that the reflection is specular rather than diffuse and that the opposing surfaces be flat and parallel. The surface polish should be determined finally by the performance of the IRE. If there is no scattering loss at the shorter wavelengths, the surface is considered to be good. It is not always possible to judge this from a visual inspection. Sometimes the surface looks excellent and yet the performance of the IRE is found to be poor, while at other times the opposite is true.

Soft materials present considerable difficulty in polishing and therefore are often molded. Hard materials must be lapped and polished and this must be done in a sufficient number of steps to insure that the damaged material is removed. A rough rule of thumb is that the depth of damage is about equal to the grit size employed. Exact measurements of the depth of damage resulting from abrasive particles of different sizes have been made for Ge and Si (B36,B37). The final quality of the surface polish must be such that the reflection is perfectly specular and not diffuse so that even after many reflections there is no power loss due to scattering. Many optical firms have the capability of polishing surfaces that can be satisfactorily employed even for hundred of reflections. Polishing techniques have been developed for both hard and soft materials but are rather closely guarded. Polishing is an art so that even if the techniques were published it is unlikely that they would be duplicated without considerable effort. It should be emphasized that the quality of a surface cannot be determined from a single reflection or transmission measurement. If the surface reflection is found to be 99.5%, after 100 reflections the power in the beam is reduced to close to 50%.

The more complicated structures are conveniently made in a number of separate pieces and joined together by optical contacting. When this procedure is employed the surface flatness for the contacting area must be 1/10 wavelength of sodium light or better so that when the cleaned surfaces are pressed together, the attractive van der Waal's forces will hold the components together. To preserve the contact it is helpful to seal the edges where optical contact has been made (with shellac, for example) to retard diffusion of gases between the contacting surfaces.

For surface studies, especially studies of the surface of the IRE itself, mechanically polished surfaces should not be employed. While optical measurements may indicate specular reflection after hundreds of reflections, surface damage is always present on a mechanically prepared surface, although it may extend to only submicron depths. The surface damage results from cold flow of the crystal material near the surface which is inherent in mechanical preparation. On one silicon plate, for example, the reflection was found to be specular for the mechanically polished surface after some 200 reflections. The plate was placed in a vacuum chamber and after pumping and baking considerable power loss was observed at the shorter wavelengths. The reason for the deterioration of this plate was attributed to the possible reorientation of the material near the surface resulting in a deterioration of the optical quality of the surface. For this reason and more significantly because the nature of the bonding to the surface is dependent on the crystalline orientation, the internal reflection element should be cut from a single-crystal material and so oriented that the broad faces represent well-defined crystalline planes. These surfaces must then be polished in such a manner that there is no damage to the surface. Damage-free surfaces can be obtained in a number of ways.

a. Cleavage

Certain materials (e.g., mica and gallium arsenide) can be cleaved to expose a well-defined, optically perfect, crystalline plane. Crystals such as Ge and Si can be cleaved also, although not easily, nor over large surface areas.

b. Removal of Damaged Portion from Mechanically Polished Specimens

For a mechanically polished surface, the damaged portion can be removed in a number of ways.

(1) **Annealing.** It may be possible to heat up a reflection plate to a point that there is a regrowth of the damaged portion and still maintain the optical quality of the surface. This is more likely to be the case for well-defined crystalline planes.

(2) **Evaporation.** Surprisingly, it has been shown (B10) that in certain cases it is possible to heat up an internal reflection plate to remove the damaged portion by evaporation and the optical quality of the surface remains acceptable.

(3) **Ion Bombardment.** Ion bombardment can be employed to remove surface material. Bombardment may result in some surface damage which can be annealed if not too extensive.

(4) **Chemical Etching.** Chemical etching will not in general yield surfaces of optical quality. Preferential etching occurs at defects, dislocations, impurity sites, etc., with the result that a chemically etched surface is usually pitted and wavy. Certain etching procedures, however, which have been developed for the preparation of semiconductor wafers for epitaxial films in transistor technology yield surfaces of reasonable optical quality and might be used in the preparation of internal reflection elements. Here fine mechanical polishing followed by suitable light etch to remove the damaged portion is employed. In a slightly more complicated procedure a combination of mechanical motion and etching has yielded surfaces of satisfactory optical quality. An example of this is the "spin etch" wherein a silicon sample is spun in a suitable etch. A further elaboration of this approach is electropolishing (S33, B26, D16). Here, in addition to the mechanical motion and chemical etching, an electric current through the specimen accelerates the etching of the high spots from the surfaces and thereby yields high quality surfaces. Still another technique that should yield damage free surfaces of good optical quality is oxidation to a depth equal to the depth of damage followed by an etching treatment which will preferentially etch the oxide. This can be employed for semiconductors (e.g., Ge and Si) wherein hydrofluoric acid attacks the oxides vigorously but not the semiconductors.

c. *Surfaces as Grown—Dendrites and Ribbons*

A technique has been developed at Westinghouse (D13,D14) to grow semiconductors in thin film form with excellent surface quality. Two seeds are dipped in a melt. By carefully controlling the temperature gradients and growth rate, wide ribbons of material of controlled thickness are grown between the two seeds as they are withdrawn from the melt. Silicon and germanium ribbons have been prepared in this way. Strips 1 cm $\times$ 30 cm with highly uniform resistivity and thickness over the entire lengths can be made.

3. Geometrical Requirements

a. Length to Thickness Ratio

The index of refraction of the IRE need not be considered in determining the length to thickness ratio when the light beam enters and leaves the IRE at normal incidence and when no attempt is made to obtain a specific optical path length within the IRE. The length to thickness ratio, l/t, of the internal reflection plate is one factor that controls the number of reflections and, assuming that θ is predetermined, it is the only factor which controls N. The ratio l/t should be chosen so that the central ray enters and leaves via the center of the entrance and exit apertures, respectively. This may appear to be trivial yet it has been overlooked in some cases with resulting complications. If l/t is incorrect, a single incoming beam may either yield two spatially separated beams at the exit aperture or may partially or even completely miss the exit aperture. Spatially separated beams may result for either a collimated beam of finite width or for a diverging beam initially

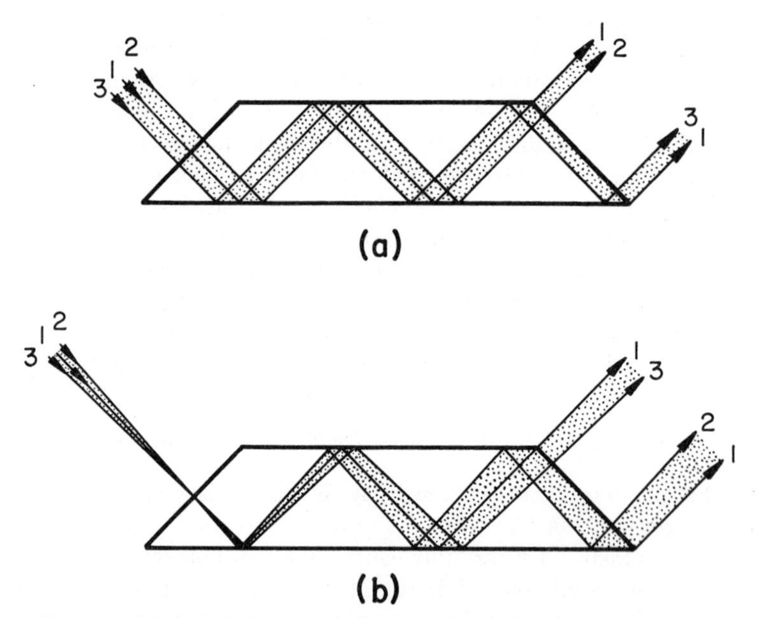

Fig. 24. Decomposition of single input beam into two beams at the output for internal reflection plate of incorrect length. (a) Collimated input beam. (b) Focused input beam.

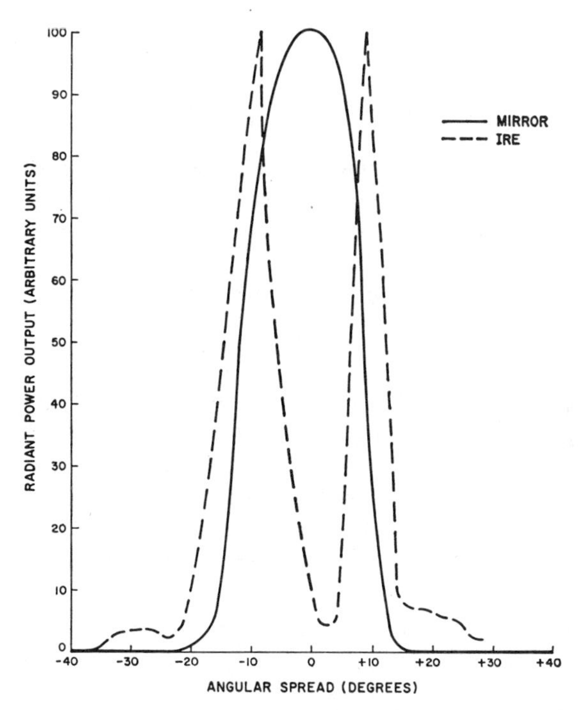

Fig. 25. Measurements of angular beam spread for reflection from a mirror (solid curve) and for an IRE of incorrect length which shows two beams at output (dashed curve).

focused to a point, as shown in Figs. 24a and 24b, respectively, for a single-pass plate. This has been demonstrated in our laboratory. A sample measurement showing a dual-beam output for single-beam input is shown in Fig. 25. Compensation for incorrect length can be made by altering the angle of incidence. However, even for thin plates where the light rays are thoroughly mixed up, an attempt should be made to choose the correct length since most of the energy is carried by the central rays, a result of the central portions of the focusing mirrors being generally more efficient than the outer portions. The beam may partially miss the exit aperture for a single-pass plate for incorrect l/t when $\theta > 45°$ because a portion of the light beam will approach the aperture from the wrong direction and strike the aperture at an angle of incidence of $\pi - 2\theta$, instead of normal incidence, and then be totally reflected by the aperture and be lost instead of being transmitted through it, as shown in Fig. 5c. In double-pass plates, loss of energy can occur at all angles of incidence if l/t is incorrect, since the beam will then tend to strike the entrance, rather than the exit, aperture and be directed back to the source.

The correct geometrical dimensions are determined from the equation for the number of reflections for single-pass plates, i.e.,

$$N = (l/t) \cot \theta. \tag{16}$$

If the length of the plate is defined as the distance between the centers of the entrance and exit apertures, then N must be an *odd* integer for a plate in the shape of a trapezoid and an *even* integer for a plate in the shape of a parallelogram.

For double-pass plates the number of reflections is given by

$$N = 2(l/t) \cot \theta. \tag{17}$$

For these plates l is the distance between the end reflecting surface and the shoulder at the other end where the aperture meets the broad reflecting surface. The exit beam will strike the center of the exit aperture when N is an integer. If the length is incorrect the condition for optimum transmission can be satisfied by adjusting the angle of incidence in this case as well. A series of maxima in transmission via the exit aperture is obtained if θ is changed over a wide range of angles.

It is important to adjust these geometrical dimensions fairly precisely. For slight deviations the central rays will tend to strike the exit aperture nearer the peak or shoulder. These edges of the aperture are often somewhat rounded and this results in a fanning out of the exit beam, especially for high index materials where strong refraction occurs.

b. *Precision in Dimensions, Angles, and Flatness*

Except for the considerations discussed in the previous section, the length to thickness ratio is not all that critical since the required condition on N can be satisfied by adjusting the angle of incidence if the instrumentation permits this. For plates where the light beam does not fill the entire entrance aperture, however, there is an upper limit on the length that should be selected because of lateral extension of the light source image. This upper limit is determined in the following way. For simplicity it is assumed that an incoming beam with angular spread of Δ is focused at the center of an entrance aperture, as shown in Fig. 26. The angular spread of the beam inside of the plate will be approximately Δ/n_1. The length of the path of the beam within the plate is $l \csc \theta$. There will be no lateral extension of the source image if the beam spread within the plate does not exceed the width of the aperture; i.e., provided that

$$l \csc \theta \sin (\Delta/n_1) \leq A$$

or

$$\frac{l}{A} \leqslant \frac{\sin \theta}{\sin (\Delta/n_1)} \simeq \frac{n_1 \sin \theta}{\Delta}. \tag{18}$$

For a greater length than this, or a smaller aperture, there is a mixing of the light rays, as shown at the exit aperture in Fig. 26, and it is no longer possible to focus them to an image size equal to that of the source. If the IRE is long enough the entire exit aperture will become uniformly illuminated and this aperture then acts as the new source image. This source image has the same angular beam spread as the entrance beam but is of greater width. The larger n_1 is, the greater is the permissible length. Obviously the maximum length can be increased by a factor of 2 by locating the focus at the center of the plate rather than at the entrance aperture. As pointed out earlier, for thin plates the slit or source image fills the entire entrance aperture and therefore, a lateral extension of the source image cannot occur.

The tolerance on all angles of the surfaces from which reflection occurs and through which light is transmitted is strict. This is especially true for high index materials. For example, if the angle of the exit aperture of a Ge plate is off by δ degrees, the exit beam will be deflected away from the normal to that surface by $n_1\delta$. The same arguments apply to rounding of beveled edges—any light striking the rounded portion internally is deflected away from the normal and thus increases the angular beam spread. If the broad reflecting surfaces are not strictly parallel but deviate from parallelism by the angle δ, then, after N reflections, the angle of incidence within the plate is changes by $N\delta$ for a single-pass plate; the exit beam will be deflected $n_1N\delta$ degrees (more correctly $\sin^{-1} n_1 \sin N\delta$) away from the normal to the exit

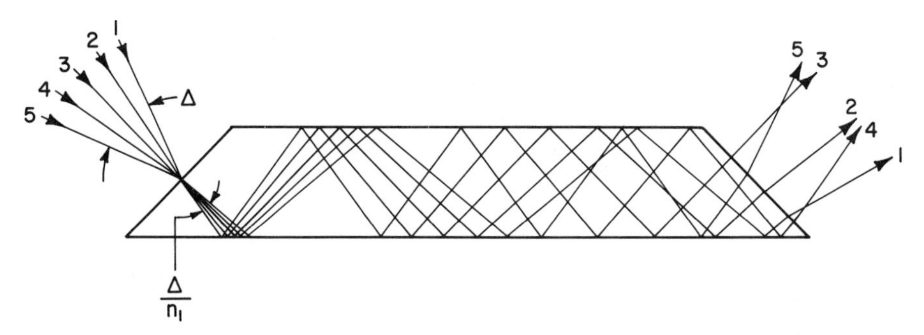

Fig. 26. Lateral extension of source and mixing of rays for plate of intermediate thickness or too great a length. Due to mixing of rays it is no longer possible to focus the beam down to original small dimensions. For an incoming beam with spread Δ degrees the angular spread within the IRE is approximately Δ/n_1.

aperture. For example, if the two surfaces deviate from parallelism 0.1°, after 100 reflections the exit beam for a Ge plate will be deflected 44° away from the normal to the exit aperture! The requirement on the parallelism of the broad faces along the length is not as stringent for double-pass plates—any change in angle of incidence as the beam propagates down the length is compensated for on its return path. It is because of a correction of this sort that a wavy surface for either a single or double-pass plate is not very serious providing average flatness is maintained.

The end-reflecting surface of a double-pass plate must be precisely perpendicular to the broad reflecting faces. If its angle is off perpendicular by $\delta/2$ degrees, in general there will be two exit beams at angles $\theta \pm n_1 \delta$ and none at θ. The reason, as was pointed out in discussion of Fig. 10b, is that an incoming beam propagating down the length at an internal angle θ will in general approach the end surface from both broad faces. The deviation δ will therefore be added to the angle of incidence in one case and be subtracted in the other with the result that there will be two return beams with angles of incidence $\theta \pm \delta$. If the exit aperture is prepared for normal incidence for a beam having an internal angle of incidence of θ on the broad face, the beams strike the exit aperture at angles $\pm\delta$ off the normal and hence will be deflected externally to $\pm n_1\delta$ degrees. A measured, dual beam output due to cocked end surface is shown in Fig. 27. The sharp spikes which are generally observed in the output beam of the IRE may be due to a Schlieren effect because of slight refractive index inhomogeneities in the bulk material. They are not due to interference since their location is not wavelength dependent. Rounding of the end surface also results in multiple beams and increases the beam divergence for the same reason.

c. *Typical Dimensions of IRE's*

The dimensions of the internal reflection elements are determined from the following considerations. Optical material of very high quality is required for the IRE and some of these materials are expensive requiring therefore, the dimensions of the IRE to be small. On the other hand, very small IRE's are difficult to handle and must be positioned very critically in the optical device. Furthermore, some materials are brittle and very thin plates are thus fragile.

For hemicylinders and hemispheres the radius is usually selected in the range from 5 mm to 10 mm. To maintain constant optical path length once the radius of a given hemicylinder is chosen, radii of hemicylinders of other refractive indices should be calculated so that when they are interchanged no

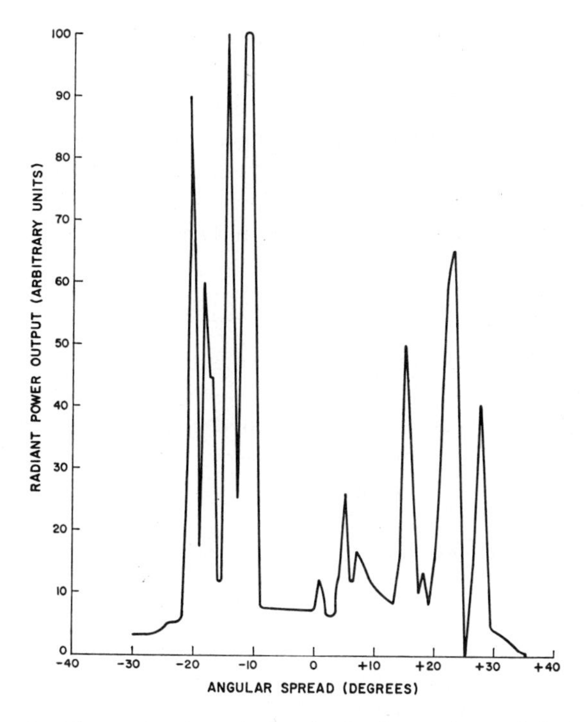

Fig. 27. Two output beams due to cocked end-reflecting surface. Spiked output may be due to refractive index inhomogeneities.

other adjustments are necessary. Hemicylinders are interchangeable providing the distance

$$\frac{r}{n_1 - 1} + r = n_1 r/(n_1 - 1)$$

is the same for both hemicylinders when the light beam is focused at a distance $r/(n_1 - 1)$ in front of the hemicylinder for collimation within the cylinder. For example, Ge ($n_1 = 4$) of $r = 7.5$ mm and KRS-5 ($n_1 = 2.4$) of $r = 5.8$ mm are interchangeable insofar as optical path and focusing within the optical arrangement are concerned.

For multiple reflection plates the angle of incidence and thickness of the plate determine the aperture. The aperture must be at least equal to the maximum width of the spectrometer slits to be employed. Typical range in thickness of plates is from 0.25 mm (250 μ) to 2 mm. Once the angle of incidence and thickness have been selected for the IRE, the number of reflections is determined by the length of the plate. The most common length is about 5 cm; however, lengths up to 10 cm have been employed. It is impractical to make the plates much longer. For a plate 1 mm thick and 10 cm long operated in a double-pass mode at $\theta = 30°$, the light beam undergoes some 350 reflections and traverses 40 cm of the optical material. For the same plate operated at $\theta = 17°$, $N \approx 660$ and the length of path in the IRE is close to 70 cm!

4. Test of IRE's

The quality of an internal reflection element is judged by its transmission level and the dependence of transmission level on wavelength. The maximum transmission expected is determined primarily by considering the reflection losses at the entrance and exit faces. Considering only these losses

$$T_1 \simeq (1 - R)^2 \tag{19}$$

where, at normal incidence for the entrance or exit beam,

$$R = \frac{(n_1 - 1)^2}{(n_1 + 1)^2}. \tag{20}$$

Many internal reflection elements have exhibited transmission levels close to the maximum value predicted by equation (19) even when hundreds of reflections were employed. Optical materials often exhibit some internal losses thus when the surfaces are well prepared the transmission level is controlled more nearly by the length of path in the bulk rather than by the number of reflections. The advantages gained from IRE's of high quality are high transmission levels, which simplify optical alignment, and lack of light scattering, which insures a flat reference base line over a wide wavelength range.

If an IRE does not perform well, it should be possible to determine the reason for the poor performance. There are three reasons for bad performance: viz., poor material, inadequate surface polish, or poor tolerance on length and angles. It is, in principle, possible to test for each of these independently, although in practice it is not quite as simple as it may appear to be.

The quality of the IRE material can be checked by passing the light through long lengths of the material by employing only a few or no reflections and measuring the wavelength dependence of the transmission. For 45° or 30° single-pass plates this can be done by employing it as a transmission plate, as was shown in Fig. 22. The material may also be checked for 45° and 30° double-pass plates, as was shown in Fig. 23. For the 45° plate a small 45°

bevel can be provided along one edge of the reflecting surface so that it can be employed as a transmission plate, as was shown in Fig. 23b. If the bevel is small enough, it will not substantially affect the performance of the double-pass plate as an IRE. For the 30° plate, rather than providing a 90° roof top as was shown in Fig. 23a, it is possible to rely on the natural reflectivity of the end-reflecting surface for the return beam.

Inadequate surface polish can be readily detected from the transmitted power level as a function of wavelength. Scattering, which goes roughly as λ^{-4}, is less severe at longer wavelengths. Examples of transmission characteristics of IRE's with good and poor surfaces are shown in Fig. 28. Curves *a*, *b*, and *c* represent the transmission for good polish, hazy surface, and scratched surface, respectively. The transmission of KRS-5 actually increases with wavelength because the refractive index decreases with increasing wavelength and hence the reflectivity losses decrease at the entrance and exit faces. The falloff at the shorter wavelengths is typical for soft materials like KRS-5 where the best surface polish obtained to date is still wanting. For harder materials like Ge and Si, better surface polish can be achieved and this falloff at the shorter wavelengths can be eliminated.

The tolerances on the angles and flatness can be easily checked by mounting the IRE on a goniometer and reflecting a highly collimated laser beam from the surfaces in question and noting angular displacements. Reasons for poor operation due to these geometrical considerations can also be deduced by a check of the performance of the IRE. For this purpose, a detector mounted on a goniometer is very convenient. Multiple output beams which may be

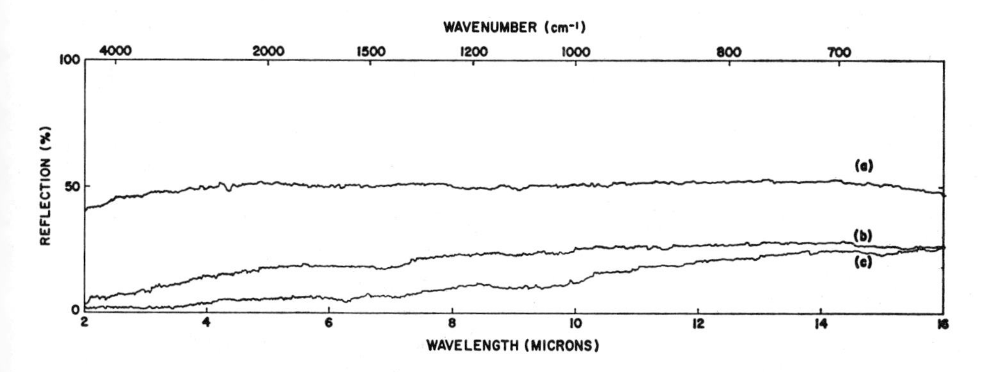

Fig. 28. Comparison of the transmission versus wavelength for a number of KRS-5 single-pass plates with various qualities of surface polish; $N = 26$, $\theta = 45°$. (a) Good polish; (b) hazy surface, needs resurfacing; (c) scratched, poor surface polish, needs repolishing. (Courtesy of G. D. Propster, Wilks Scientific Corp., South Norwalk, Conn.)

due to incorrect length, rounded bevels, or cocked end-reflecting surface for double-pass plate can easily be detected. Increased angular spread in the beam may occur for the same reasons.

Lack of sensitivity of the IRE can generally be traced down to a simple cause. First, the angle of incidence for a portion of the light beam may be higher than desired. For fixed-angle multiple internal reflection elements constructed for angles below 45°, light striking the portion of the bevel which is not part of the aperture, as defined earlier, will travel down the length of the plate at angles of incidence larger than that desired or even at grazing incidence. This energy is mixed in with that propagated at the desired angle of incidence and any information about surface absorption thus becomes diluted. Secondly, an oxide film on the IRE or sample material in general acts as a spacer and separates the material to be investigated from the active surface and thereby reduces the sensitivity. The question of sensitivity is especially important when quantitative measurements are made. For this reason, it is imperative to understand in detail the interaction mechanisms which involve the performance of the IRE.

Figure 6 of Chapter Three demonstrates how an incoming beam is decomposed into many reflected and transmitted components by the natural reflectivity of the entrance and exit surfaces. The exit and reflected beams of an IRE are made up of similar components. The higher order components are usually neglected as has been the case in this chapter thus far. For high index IRE's the neglect of these components can cause considerable error in quantitative measurements of absorption as will now be shown. For small absorption the reflected components and the total reflected component may be written as

$$I_{R1}/I_0 = R \tag{21}$$

$$I_{R2}/I_0 = (1 - R)^2 R \, e^{-2N\alpha d_e} \tag{22}$$

$$I_{R3}/I_0 = (1 - R)^2 R^3 \, e^{-4N\alpha d_e}, \text{ etc.,} \tag{23}$$

$$I_R/I_0 = \sum_{n=1}^{\infty} I_{Rn}/I_0 = R + \frac{R(1 - R)^2 \, e^{-2N\alpha d_e}}{1 - R^2 \, e^{-2N\alpha d_e}}. \tag{24}$$

The transmitted components and total transmitted component may be written as

$$I_{T1}/I_0 = (1 - R)^2 \, e^{-N\alpha d_e} \tag{25}$$

$$I_{T2}/I_0 = (1 - R)^2 R^2 \, e^{-3N\alpha d_e} \tag{26}$$

$$I_{T3}/I_0 = (1 - R)^2 R^4 \, e^{-5N\alpha d_e}, \text{ etc.} \tag{27}$$

$$I_T/I_0 = \sum_{n=1}^{\infty} I_{Tn}/I_0 = \frac{(1 - R)^2 e^{-N\alpha d_e}}{1 - R^2 \, e^{-2N\alpha d_e}}. \tag{28}$$

It is evident that the multiple reflected components, i.e., components which have traversed the length of the IRE more than once, yield a higher contrast spectra than the first component. For Ge, for example, the intensity of the first transmitted component is 41% of the incident beam and that of the second (i.e., the component that travels down the length of the plate, is reflected from the exit aperture, returns to the entrance aperture, is reflected from it, and is propagated back down the length for the third time to leave via the exit aperture) is 5.3%. However, the second component is absorbed three times as strongly as the first component. Therefore, it is the equivalent of 16% of the total energy in contributing to the net spectral contrast. The spectral contrast due to the first plus the second components thus corresponds to an effective power level of 57% (i.e., 41% + 16%) which is $57/46.3 = 112\%$ of the spectral contrast in the first component alone. The second component if neglected can thus contribute to an error in the measurement of the strength of absorption of greater than 12% for weak absorbers. For KRS-5, this error amounts to 0.5%. Effects of this sort must not be neglected for quantitative measurements and especially in the measurement of optical constants.

F. Optical Materials for Internal Reflection Elements

1. Solids

Internal reflection spectroscopy places much more stringent demands on both the quality and preparation of the optical materials for IRE's than has heretofore been required for optical windows for example. The reasons for this are the long path lengths and the large number of reflections employed.

There is a wide range of optical materials from which IRE's can be fabricated. Many of these materials are discussed by Wolfe, Ballard, and McCarthy (W11,M11) in the chapter on optics in the American Institute of Physics Handbook, and also in their reports from the University of Michigan on this subject as well as in a series of articles by McCarthy (M7,M8,M9, M10). Additional optical information, especially on semiconductors, may be found in the book by Moss (M18). The indices of refraction and transmission limits of the materials considered by Wolfe, Ballard, and McCarthy are shown in Figs. 29 and 30. The first consideration in selecting an IRE material is the wavelength region of interest, viz., UV, visible, IR or far IR. It should be emphasized that the transmission level for IRE's must now be quoted for path lengths of a few centimeters or even tens of centimeters in bulk of material (we have employed Si plates where the path length in the material was as much as 40 cm) compared to 1 or 2 mm often required for optical window materials. Thus weak lattice bands with absorption coefficients of 0.01 cm^{-1} cannot be tolerated. For example, it is shown in Fig. 31 that the

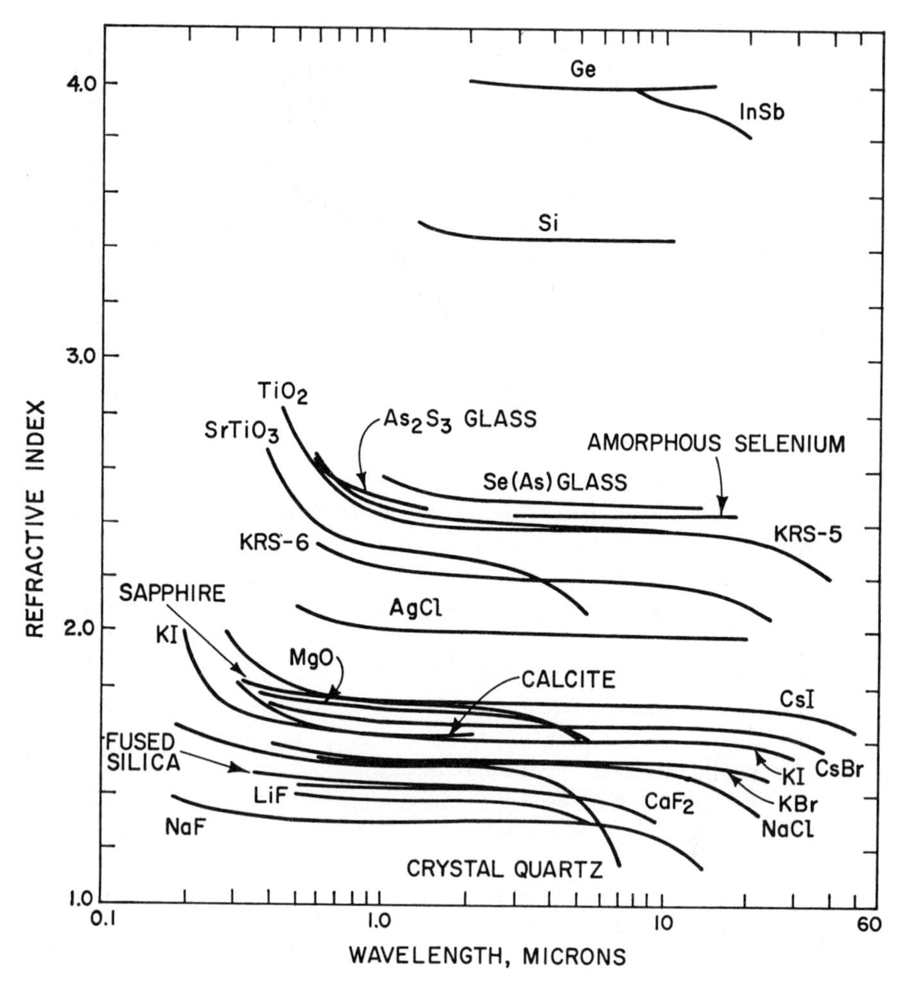

Fig. 29. Refractive index versus wavelength for selected optical materials. (From reference W11 by permission.)

long wavelength cutoff for Si and Ge is 6 and 12 μ, respectively, for their use as IRE's for a path length in the material of 15 mm compared to the cutoff of 15 and 23 μ indicated in Fig. 30 for their use as window material. For this same reason pressed materials (e.g., Irtran series), while they are excellent for optical windows, are generally not suitable for IRE's especially where multiple reflections are employed and long path lengths in the material are required because of excessive scattering by the bulk. Many of these Irtran materials are available in single crystalline form, which is more preferable for IRE's.

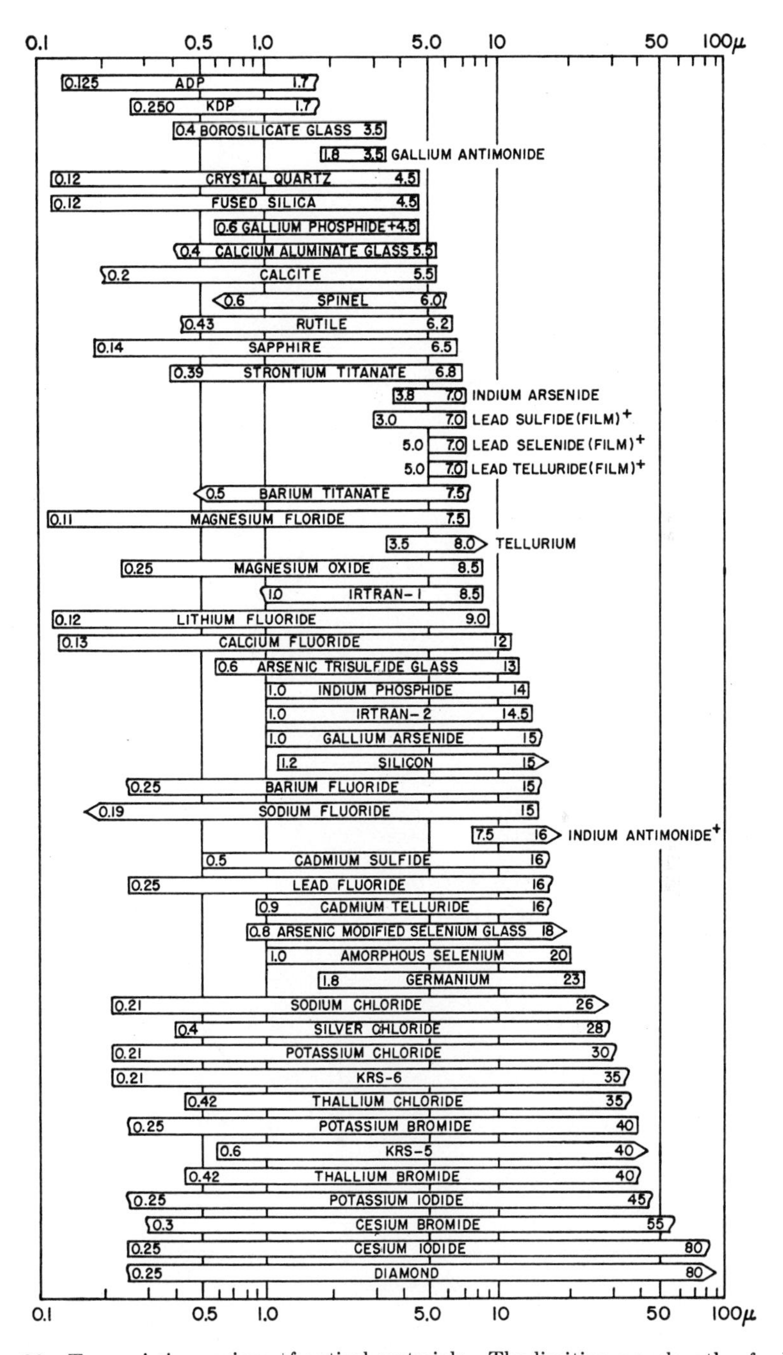

Fig. 30. Transmission regions of optical materials. The limiting wavelengths, for both long and short cutoff, have been chosen as those wavelengths at which a sample 2 mm thick has 10% transmission. Materials marked with a cross (+) have a maximum transmission less than 10%. (From reference M11 by permission.)

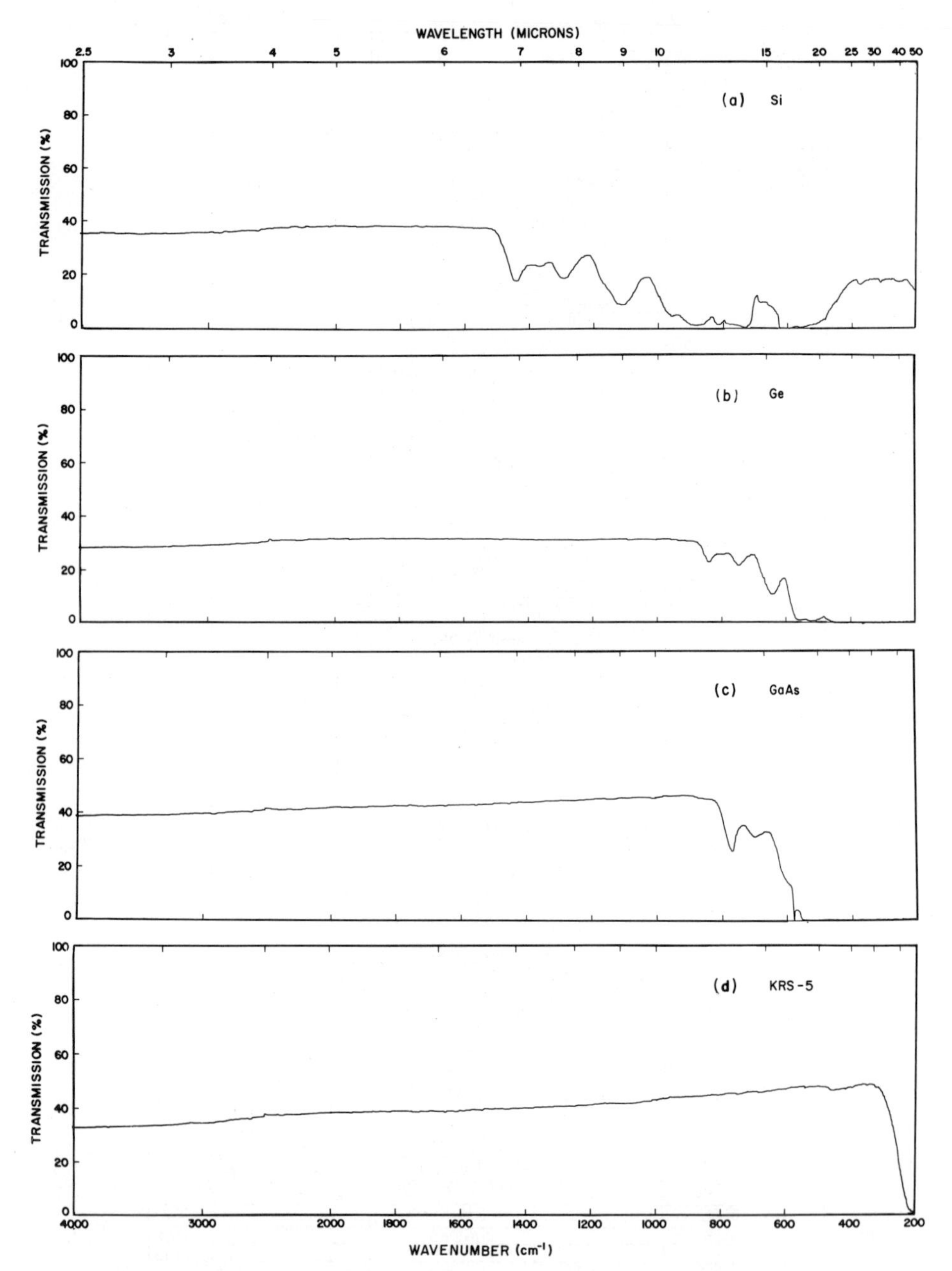

Fig. 31. Transmission versus wavelength for a number of materials, each 15 mm thick. (a) Si, (b) Ge, (c) GaAs, (d) KRS-5. The transmission levels may not be correct due to defocusing in the instrument when the samples are interchanged. (Measurements made by R. W. Hannah, Perkin-Elmer Corp., Norwalk, Conn.)

Another consideration, so far as semiconductors are concerned, is the absorption of energy by free carriers. This absorption follows a λ^2 dependence and may become very large at longer wavelengths. Intrinsic semiconductors should be selected where possible because the free carrier density is low in these materials. When the holes have a larger absorption cross section than the electrons, slightly n-type material is preferable. Where intrinsic materials are not available, compensated materials, i.e., materials in which the free carriers are frozen out, should be prepared. The GaAs used to obtain the curve in Fig. 31c was compensated material. Although polycrystalline materials in many cases have proved to be quite satisfactory for optical components, excellent single crystals of many materials are available and should be selected where possible because of freedom from grain boundaries, inclusions, etc. A material like KRS-5 sometimes has a hazy internal condition which contributes to losses especially at the shorter wavelengths. This may explain in part the increase in transmission with increasing wavelength indicated by the KRS-5 curve shown in Fig. 31d. Another part of this increase in transmission ($\sim$8%) is attributed to a decrease in reflection losses because of the decrease in refractive index with increasing wavelength.

When there is a choice in the refractive index, it should be so selected that measurements on bulk materials made at the desired angle of incidence will not yield distorted spectra, as was discussed in Chapter Three. It should be recalled, however, that for thin films the lowest possible index should be employed because of the absence of distortion and because of the enhanced absorption. Low index will also yield higher transmission because of a reduction in the reflection losses at the entrance and exit faces.

Other considerations include hardness and chemical inertness. Hard materials can be polished more easily than soft materials although they tend to be brittle and fracture more easily. The system to be studied determines to some extent the choice of the IRE material since the surfaces must not be attacked chemically. Although the Irtran materials have the disadvantage of excessive bulk scattering, they are attractive for certain applications because of their chemical inertness.

Table IV provides information on a few materials which have been or may be used to prepare IRE's. This table is not intended to be complete but is only meant to provide some guide lines in selecting materials for IRE's. Most of the information is self-explanatory. The reflectivity R is calculated from equation (20). The transmission is given for the first transmitted component T_1 as well as for the second T_2. T_1 is calculated from equation (19) and T_2 is determined from equation (26) with $\alpha = 0$; i.e.,

$$T_2 = R^2(1 - R)^2. \qquad (29)$$

TABLE IV

Properties of Typical Optical Materials for Internal Reflection Spectroscopy

Material	λ range (μ)	n_1 (mean value)	θ_{ca} (°)	R (%)	T_1 (%)	T_2 (%)	Comments
Quartz	0.3–2.3	1.43	44.5	3.1	93.5	0.01	Hard and inert. Good for low-index materials in visible and UV.
Al_2O_3	0.22–4.5	1.7	36.5	6.7	87.0	0.4	Very hard and inert. Good for UV, visible, and near IR.
MgO	0.35–7.0	1.7	36.5	6.7	87.0	0.4	Hard and inert. Good for visible and near IR.
AgCl	0.4–20	2.0	30.0	11.1	80.0	0.9	Very soft, can be molded but difficult to main surface finish.
AgBr	0.45–30	2.2	27.0	14.0	74.0	1.45	Soft (slightly harder than AgCl), otherwise attractive material for IRS.
KRS-5	0.6–40	2.4	24.6	16.8	69.0	1.95	Toxic, relatively soft, has convenient index and useful over wide λ range.
ZnTe (S24)	0.57–52(?)	2.7	21.75	21.4	62.0	2.8	Limited information is available. ZnTe should be interesting if it transmits over entire range indicated.
GaAs	1.0–17	3.3	17.6	28.6	51.0	4.2	Use compensated materials (semiinsulating). Good beyond 15 μ. Properties similar to Ge. Very expensive.
Si	1.1–6	3.5	15.6	30.8	47.7	4.5	Hard, easy to prepare and maintain surfaces. High resistivity material (>1000 Ω-cm) available. Excellent for near IR.
Ge	2–12	4.0	14.5	36.0	41.0	5.3	Good and relatively inexpensive. Not as hard as Si. Preferable to use near intrinsic slightly n-type material. Free carrier absorption and weak lattice bands bothersome beyond 11.5 μ.
Te	5–25	$n_{\parallel} = 4.8$ $n_{\perp} = 6.3$	9.0 12.0	43.0 53.0	32.5 22.0	6.0 6.15	Has not been used for IRE's. The very high index may make it useful for certain applications.

Many high index glass-like materials that are under current development for the infrared should be of interest for preparation of IRE's.

2. Liquids

The ease of making good contact between solid and liquid for internal reflection measurements suggests the use of liquids for IRE materials for analysis of solid samples. It is only necessary to find a liquid that is transparent over the wavelength region of interest and one that has a sufficiently high refractive index.

Liquid IRE's have not yet been employed; however, there are numerous liquids of relatively high refractive indices that might be used for this purpose. A number of examples are listed in Table V which is provided to show that liquids of relatively high refractive indices are indeed available and that they are transparent in some spectral regions of interest. Of the materials listed, several are transparent only in the visible region. The transparency in the visible is potentially advantageous since, because of the smaller penetration depth, adequate contact between sample and IRE is more difficult to obtain in this spectral region than in the infrared.

TABLE V

Several High Index Liquids that Might be Employed for Liquid IRE's

(Most of the transmission ranges are courtesy of R.W. Hannah, Perkin-Elmer Corporation.)

Liquid	n_D	λ range (μ)
Chlorinated biphenyl (Hla)	1.62	~0.4–0.75
Carbon disulfide	1.627	0.35–13 (except for bands at 3.5, 4.5, 7, and 11.8)
Monobromonaphthalene	1.657	~0.4–0.75
Methylene iodide	1.738	~0.4–0.75, 10–12
Sulfur	1.929	2–10

The liquids can be placed in hollow prisms with a slot in the hypotenuse, where the solid sample material is to contact the liquid. If multiple reflections are required, the liquid can be placed between two polished surfaces of the solid sample. In the use of liquid IRE's care must be exercised because of changes in refractive index due to thermal gradients.

CHAPTER FIVE

OPTICAL CAVITIES FOR ENHANCED ABSORPTION

A. Introduction

Optical spectra of minute quantities and thin films can be recorded easier via internal reflection spectroscopy than via conventional transmission spectroscopy because of the ease of sample handling and also because of the greater sensitivity. As discussed in Chapter Two, Section E (on effective thickness of thin films), there can indeed be an increased absorption for a single reflection over that observed in a single transmission. For thin films where the area of material is not limited, the absorption can be increased by increasing the number of reflections according to $N = (l/t) \cot \theta$. According to this equation, the number of reflections can be increased by increasing length l and decreasing thickness t of the internal reflection plate. However, it is not practical to make the reflection plate longer than, say, 10 cm. The thickness of the plate controls the aperture and should not be less than, say, 100 μ; furthermore, thin plates are fragile. The angle of incidence also controls the aperture and therefore a reduction in the angle of incidence is practical only insofar as the reduced aperture can be tolerated. A small angle of incidence requires the use of high index internal reflection elements, in which case the index matching to the absorbing medium becomes poor (see Chapter Two) and the coupling is then reduced. These are the practical factors which limit the degree of absorption that can be obtained for thin films via internal reflection spectroscopy using simple internal reflection elements. It should be noted that in all the conventional IRE's the light beam is introduced through a beveled edge and it skips along the surface with a skip distance between reflections equal to at least the beam width. The light beam thus interacts with a given portion of the surface or sample only once. To enhance the absorption for thin films it is therefore desirable to have the beam of light interact with a given point of the film more than once. This type of enhancement is very important for minute quantities, where it is the amount of material that is the limiting factor. (In principle the absorption can be enhanced until the lower energy levels of the absorbing species become depleted more rapidly than they can be replenished by natural relaxation process from the upper levels. This population inversion causes a saturation in absorption with increasing power levels such as is commonly observed in nuclear magnetic and paramagnetic resonance experiments. There is thus an optimum power level which results in spectra of highest contrast. In conventional optical spectroscopy such saturation is not observed because of the fast relaxation times and low power levels generally employed.)

Enhancement of absorption by multiple interaction of the light beam with the sample at one point can be obtained with the rosette type of structure discussed in Chapter Four. The optical cavity, which will be discussed in this chapter, can also be used to achieve enhancement of absorption over that obtainable using conventional internal reflection elements. The optical cavity consists of a very thin film IRE into which a wide beam of light is introduced at angles above the critical angle. The electric field amplitude within and outside the film is shown in Fig. 1 for the optical cavity. Because the film is thin the skip distance is small and therefore a large number of reflections are obtained over an area equal to the width of the incoming beam. The electromagnetic waves can be introduced into the optical cavity (thin film) through one of the large surfaces via frustrated total reflection, for example. Strong coupling of these waves into the film occurs when certain resonance conditions are fulfilled. At resonance the multiply reflected components of the light beam within the film superimpose to strongly amplify the standing wave pattern for total internal reflection shown in Fig. 1, and strong coupling of the evanescent field can be obtained to a sample which

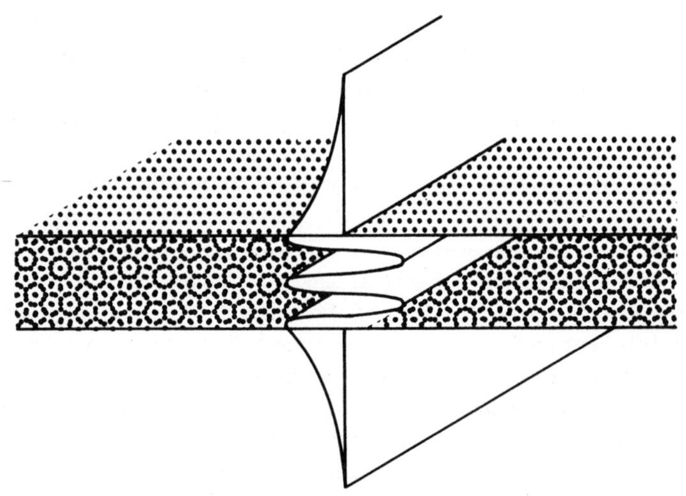

Fig. 1. The optical cavity. The standing wave pattern of the intense electric field amplitude in the thin film, and the evanescent waves outside the film which exist when resonance conditions are satisfied, are illustrated.

may be the thin film optical cavity itself or an absorbing medium outside the film. This is analogous to microwave cavities, where strong interaction can be obtained with weakly absorbing media properly located inside the cavity if the Q of the cavity is high when very intense fields are established.

Optical cavities have just recently been proposed for optical spectroscopy. The first structures constructed for this purpose will be described and some results will be given.

The optical cavity utilizes the principles of the Fabry-Perot interference filter, the FTR filter, and the generalized Fabry-Perot filter. These filters will be discussed in the following section so that the operation of the optical cavity can better be appreciated.

B. Interference Filters

1. Fabry-Perot Interference Filter

Interference phenomena in thin films are well known in optics. It is, for example, the cause of color in thin oil films, and also the cause of no color in very thin so-called "black soap films." It is a nuisance in transmission spectroscopy since it leads to band distortions and lack of precision in the measurement of intensity levels. On the other hand, advantage is taken of interference phenomena to construct narrow-band optical filters. In one of its simplest forms an interference filter consists of a thin film with parallel surfaces of equal reflectivities. When light strikes this film it is decomposed into many reflected components because of multiple reflections from the top and bottom surfaces as shown in Fig. 2. It is straightforward to prove that when the reflected amplitudes are the same for the two surfaces, i.e., $r_1 = r_2$, the sum of the amplitudes of multiply reflected components, i.e., components $2 + 3 + \ldots \infty$, is exactly equal to r_1, i.e., equal to the amplitude of the first reflected component. When the multiply reflected components arrive at the top surface 180° out of phase with r_1 there is phase matching and perfect cancellation of the reflection at the top surface and then 100% transmission is obtained. Thus, provided two conditions are satisfied, viz., that there is amplitude matching, i.e., $r_1 = r_2$, and phase matching, i.e., the optical thickness is correct, all the power is transmitted through the film.

For a dielectric film with a refractive index higher than that of its surroundings, it is well known that the external reflection (first reflected component) undergoes a phase change of π whereas there is no phase change for the internal reflections or for transmission through a surface. The condition for the net reflectivity to be zero thus is that the optical thickness be either zero or an integral number of half-waves. When this is the case, all of the multiply

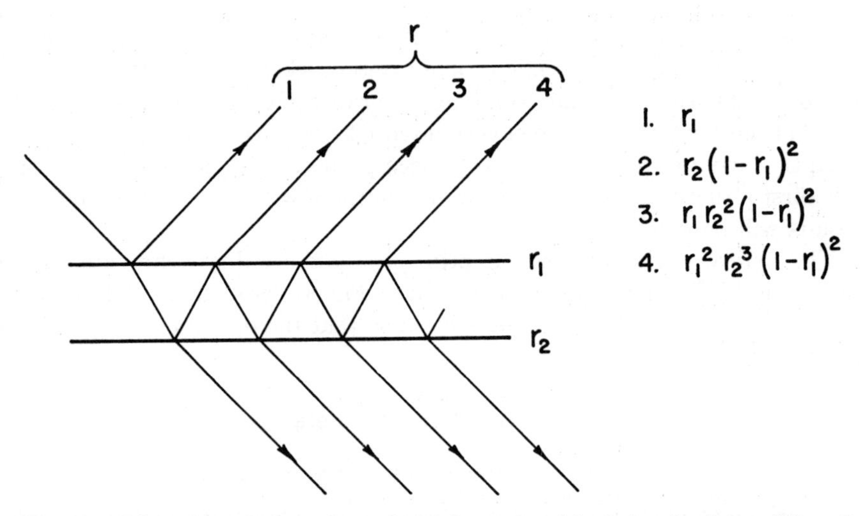

Fig. 2. Reflected components from the surfaces of a thin dielectric plate. When the amplitudes $r_1 = r_2$, the sum of the components $2 + 3 + \ldots \infty$ is exactly equal to r_1, and complete cancellation of the reflected amplitude r can be obtained.

reflected components arrive in phase but exactly out of phase with r_1. The dependence of the net reflected power from a thin film on reflectivity, R_1, and phase difference γ is expressed by the following equations (B27):

$$R = \frac{F \sin^2 (\gamma/2)}{1 + F \sin^2 (\gamma/2)} \tag{1}$$

where

$$F = \frac{4R_1}{(1 - R_1)^2}, \qquad R_1 = r_1^2 = r_2^2$$

and

$$\gamma = \frac{4\pi nt \cos \theta}{\lambda}. \tag{2}$$

Here n is the refractive index of the film, t its thickness, θ the internal angle of incidence, and λ the vacuum wavelength. The total reflected power R is zero when $\gamma = 0$. This occurs for $t \rightarrow 0$, which is the case of the "black soap films." In general the reflected power is zero when $\gamma = 2\pi m$, where the order is an integer, i.e., $m = 1, 2, 3$, etc. For normal incidence ($\cos \theta = 1$) zero reflected power, or 100% transmission, occurs when the "optical thickness" equals an integral number of half-waves, i.e.

$$nt = m(\lambda/2). \tag{3}$$

It should be noted that in spite of the actual increase in path length within the film as the angle of incidence increases, the phase difference γ *decreases*; i.e., the transmission maximum moves to shorter wavelengths as θ increases.

The total reflected power, as determined from equation (1), is plotted versus phase change in Fig. 3 for a number of values of R_1. The phase change plotted along the abscissa can, of course, be expressed in terms of t, λ, or θ, via equation (2). The reflected power is zero when the phase change is equal to 2π or any multiple thereof. The reflectivity rises to a maximum value of $4R_1/(1 + R_1)^2$ at the midpoints. When $R_1 = 0.5$, for example, $R_{max} = 89\%$. The transmission remains 100% for $\gamma = 2\pi m$ regardless how high R_1 may be. However, the transmission half-width, $\Delta\gamma$, becomes small as R_1 increases. Advantage is taken of this decrease in half-width for high R_1 in constructing narrow-band filters.

The curves shown in Fig. 3 represent an ideal case where there is no absorption loss. In many cases, e.g., where half-silvered mirrors are used for the reflecting surfaces, there is an absorption loss when the light passes through the metal film and a transmission level of 100% *cannot* be achieved by such a

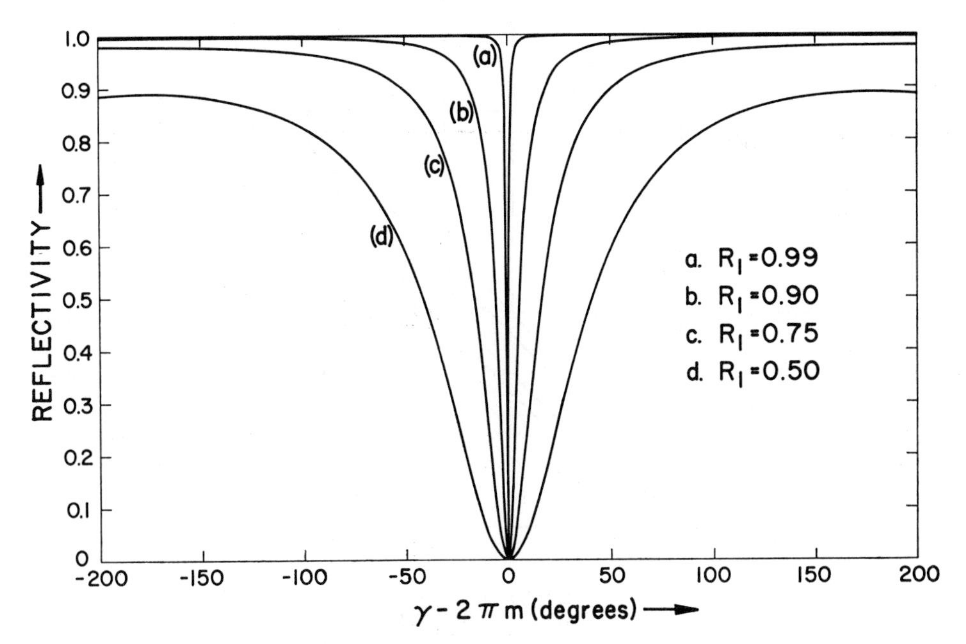

Fig. 3. Net reflected power of a Fabry-Perot structure for several values of R_1 versus phase difference. For larger R_1 the requirements on setting of angle of incidence, collimation, and monochromaticity become very high.

Fabry-Perot structure. Leurgans and Turner (L4) made an ingenious proposal to overcome this limitation with their frustrated total reflection (FTR) filter—an almost ideal Fabry-Perot filter.

2. FTR Filter

The FTR filter (L4,T5,T6,B20,B21,P18) takes advantage of the lossless coupling that can be made to the evanescent wave for total internal reflection. As has already been demonstrated in Chapter Two, the reflectivity can be continuously adjusted between 0 and 100% by adjusting the distance separating the two prisms. The FTR filter utilizes this type of coupling at two surfaces and is constructed as shown in Fig. 4. The central plate is of high refractive index and is the interference film or the phase layer. The other two layers are the FTR spacers and have lower refractive indices than that of

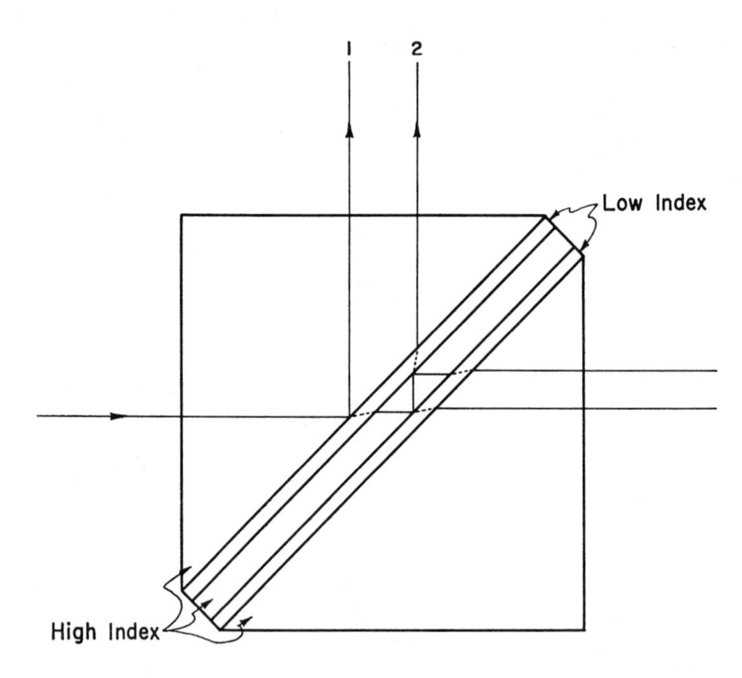

Fig. 4. The frustrated total reflection filter. The reflection of the surfaces of the high-index phase layer is determined by frustrated total reflection and the phase layer is equivalent to the thin film shown in Fig. 2.

either the phase layer or the prisms. For light striking the hypotenuse of the prism at angles exceeding the critical angle, the thickness of the FTR film controls the reflectivity of the prism-surface or the amount of power transmitted into the phase layer, in exactly the same way as already described for the lossless coupling in Chapter Two. The amount of power transmitted from the phase layer into the second prism is determined by the thickness of the second FTR layer in the same way. The phase layer can thus be analyzed exactly as the film shown in Fig. 2 except that the reflectivities are adjusted by frustrated total reflection rather than metallic or dielectric reflection. The behavior of the FTR filter is also described by equation (1). When the two prisms have the same index and the two FTR layers have the same thickness, $r_1 = r_2$ for Fig. 2, then $R = 0$ or $T = 100\%$ when

$$\frac{4\pi nt \cos\theta}{\lambda} - \delta_1 - \delta_2 = 2\pi m. \tag{4}$$

Here δ_1 and δ_2 represent the phase changes for total internal reflection at the internal surfaces *1* and *2* of the phase layer, respectively, and are equal in the present case. These phase changes are different for $\|$- and $\perp$-polarization and are given respectively by:

$$\tan\frac{\delta_\|}{2} = \frac{(\sin^2\theta - n_{21}^2)^{1/2}}{n_{21}\cos\theta}$$

and

$$\tan\frac{\delta_\perp}{2} = \frac{(\sin^2\theta - n_{21}^2)^{1/2}}{\cos\theta}. \tag{5}$$

The phase shifts for the Si–SiO_2 interface, where $n_{21} = 0.415$, are plotted in Fig. 5. The characteristics of the FTR filter are given by curves similar to those shown in Fig. 3, where r_1 is determined by the thickness of the FTR layer. (The exact dependence of r_1 on the thickness of the frustrating layer is rather complicated and is given by Court and Willison (C10), for example.)

The FTR filter is an almost ideal Fabry-Perot filter because there is no loss at the reflecting surface. It is not completely ideal, however, because of the "walk-off" (I4,B16) problem which is inherent in filters operated at oblique incidence with light beams of finite width. (The FTR filter must, of course, be operated at angles exceeding the critical angle.) Walk-off within the phase layer is clearly depicted in Fig. 2, where it is evident that for an incoming beam of finite width at non-normal incidence, many of the multiply reflected components become displaced to a region not illuminated by the incoming beam. This displacement makes complete destructive interference

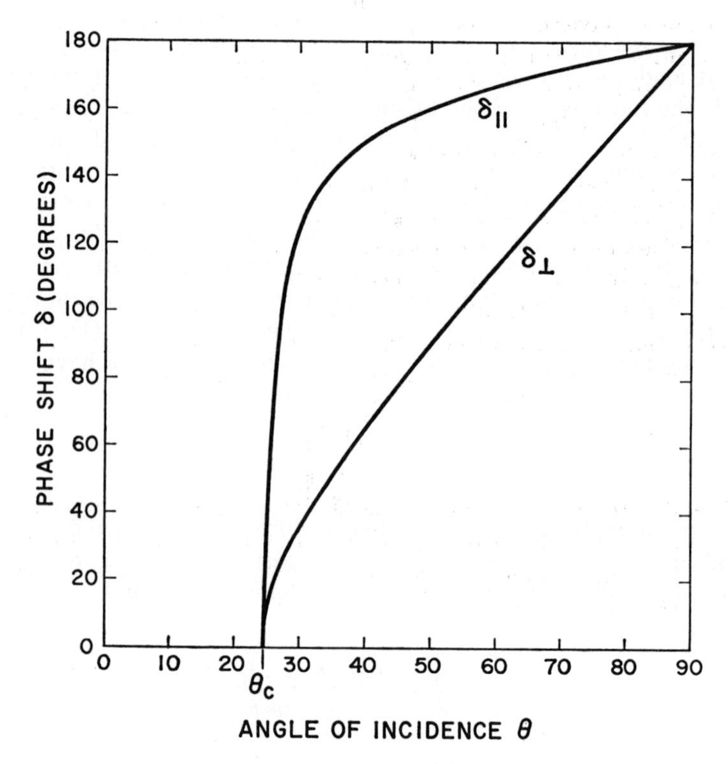

Fig. 5. Phase shift for total reflection of light polarized ⊥ and ∥ to plane of incidence versus angle of incidence for a Si–SiO_2 interface ($n_{21} = 0.415$).

impossible for a beam of finite width since many of the multiply reflected components can then not interact with the first reflected component. An increase of the beam width tends to reduce the deterioration in performance due to walk-off. The displacement of the beam in passing through the FTR layer (M19) discussed in Chapter Two also contributes to a degradation of the performance of the FTR filter. Both of these displacements play a more significant role in high Q filters where a high degree of destructive interference is required.

3. Generalized Fabry-Perot Filter

The filters described in the two previous sections both represent the case where the two opposing surfaces have identical reflectivities and is the case generally treated in textbooks. Complete destructive interference is possible at the resonant frequency because the sum of amplitudes of the multiply reflected components equals exactly the amplitude of the first reflected component. If r_1 is not equal to r_2 this requirement cannot be satisfied because the sum of the amplitudes of the multiply reflected components will either be less than or exceed the first reflected component; i.e., there is no amplitude matching. There is still a minimum in the reflectivity when the phases are matched; however, complete destructive interference is impossible.

At resonance the multiply reflected components arrive exactly out of phase with the first reflected component. The net reflected power can be calculated by summing up all of the multiply reflected components and is found to be:

$$R = \frac{(r_1 - r_2)^2}{(1 - r_1 r_2)^2}. \tag{6}$$

Here r_1 and r_2 represent the reflected amplitudes for the top and bottom surfaces, respectively, as shown in Fig. 2. It should be noted that $R = 0$ when the two surfaces are identical (i.e., when $r_1 = r_2$) and equation (6) then applies to the conventional Fabry-Perot filter as already discussed. The total reflected power, $R = r^2$, is plotted in Fig. 6 versus $R_2 = r_2^2$ for a few specific values of $R_1 = r_1^2$ using equation (6).

It should be noted that when $R_2 = 0$, $R = R_1$. As R_2 increases, R decreases and becomes zero when $R_2 = R_1$ regardless of the values of R_1, as predicted by equation (1). When R_2 increases above R_1, R increases and becomes 100% when $R_2 = 100\%$. It should also be noted that for high R_1, R changes sharply when R_2 deviates slightly from R_1. Thus a high-Q Fabry-Perot filter, in addition to being very selective to wavelength and angle of incidence, requires very critical matching of the reflectivities for the surfaces. A simple method of relaxing these critical requirements on λ, θ, and matching of reflectivities will be discussed in the next subsection.

4. Multiple Reflection Fabry-Perot Filter

As discussed in the preceding subsections and clearly shown in Figs. 3 and 6, high-Q filters place stringent requirements on monochromaticity, setting of angle of incidence, collimation, and matching of reflectivities. Some of these requirements are advantageous for filters but may be severe limitations for some applications of the optical cavity. These stringent requirements can be relaxed by achromatization through the use of a suitable stack of thin films for both the conventional Fabry-Perot filter (T5) and the FTR filters (K14,K15).

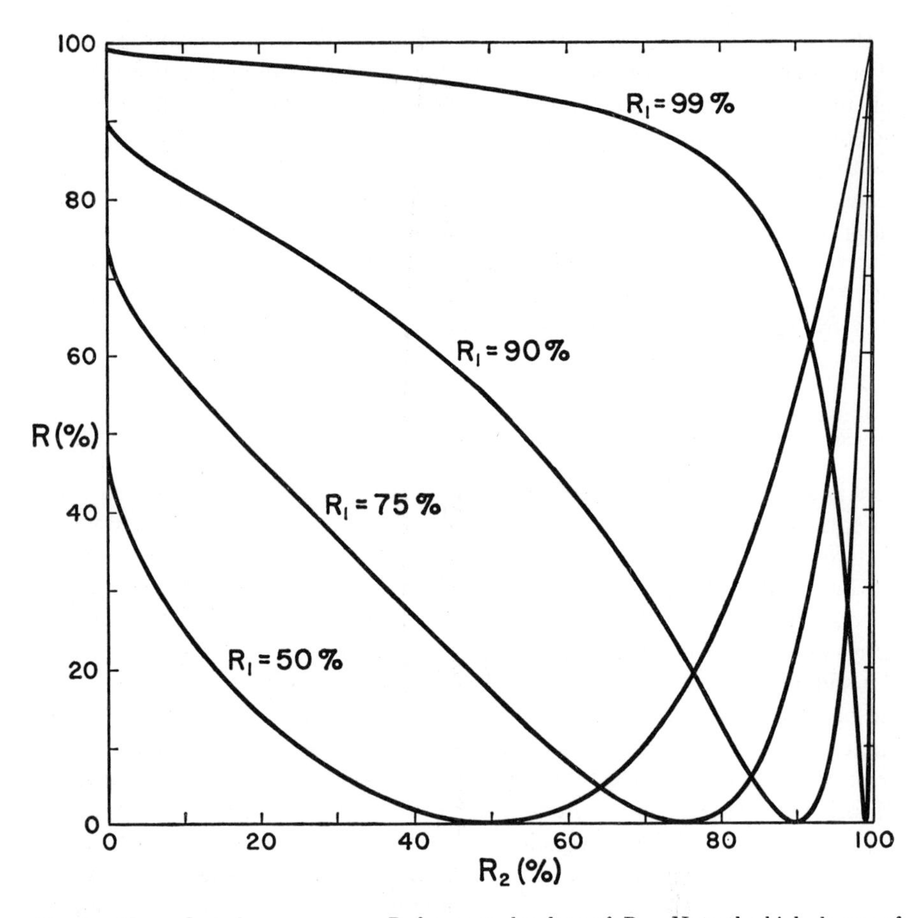

Fig. 6. Net reflected power versus R_2 for several values of R_1. Note the high degree of matching required for high-Q (large R_1) structures.

Another simple method of relaxing these requirements is to reflect the light from the filter a number of times. This can be accomplished very simply for the optical cavity by constructing the cavity on internal reflection plates where the light beam can be coupled into the optical cavity repeatedly. The relaxation of the above-mentioned stringent requirements by multiple reflection or multiple coupling is clearly shown by Figs. 7 and 8, where the response for ten reflections is compared to that for a single reflection. For a single reflection and $R_1 = 99\%$, the reflectivity drops to 50% at a wavelength only 0.05 μ off the "resonant wavelength" or an angle of incidence 3° off the required angle of incidence. For ten reflections, on the other hand, the 50% reflectivity point occurs for $\Delta\lambda = 0.2\ \mu$ and $\Delta\theta = 6°$, as is evident from Fig. 7. The requirement on the matching is also considerably relaxed after ten reflections as shown by Fig. 8.

C. Optical Cavities for Enhanced Absorption

The optical cavity is a thin film structure into which light is introduced at angles above the critical angle. The resulting standing electric wave pattern normal to the film is that shown in Fig. 1. There is a sinusoidal electric field pattern within the film and an evanescent field on either side. Very intense electric field amplitudes are developed at resonance in this structure, and strong coupling of the evanescent field to weakly absorbing media can then be obtained. According to Fig. 6, when there is amplitude matching, i.e., $R_1 = R_2$, complete absorption is induced in the absorbing medium regardless how low the absorption coefficient is. Another way of explaining the strong absorption is that the optical cavity is a means of obtaining a very large number of internal reflections in a thin film, thereby obtaining many

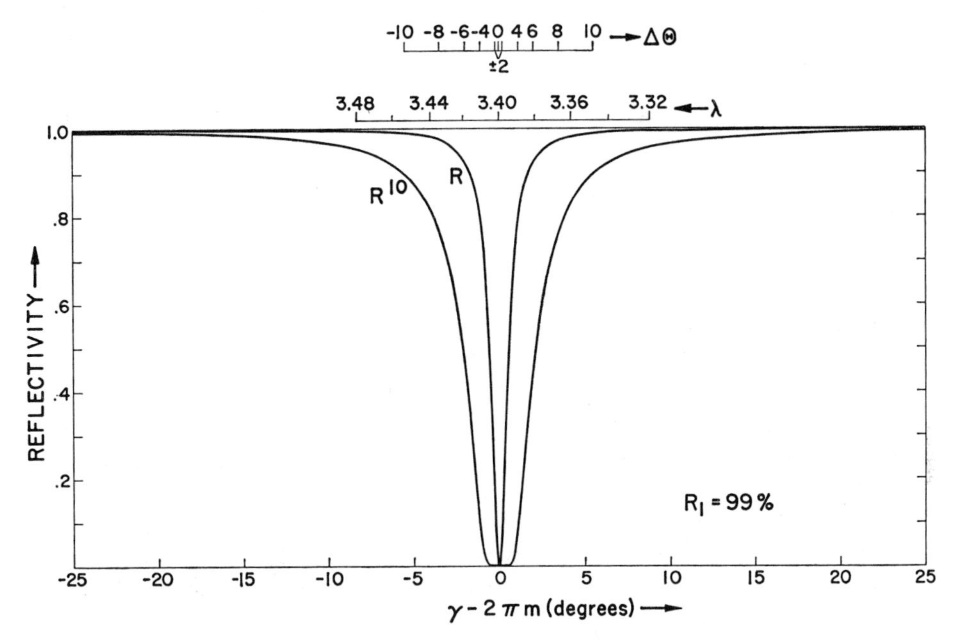

Fig. 7. Reflectivity versus phase difference for single and multiple (10) reflections. Note relaxation in stringent requirements on θ and λ when multiple reflections are employed.

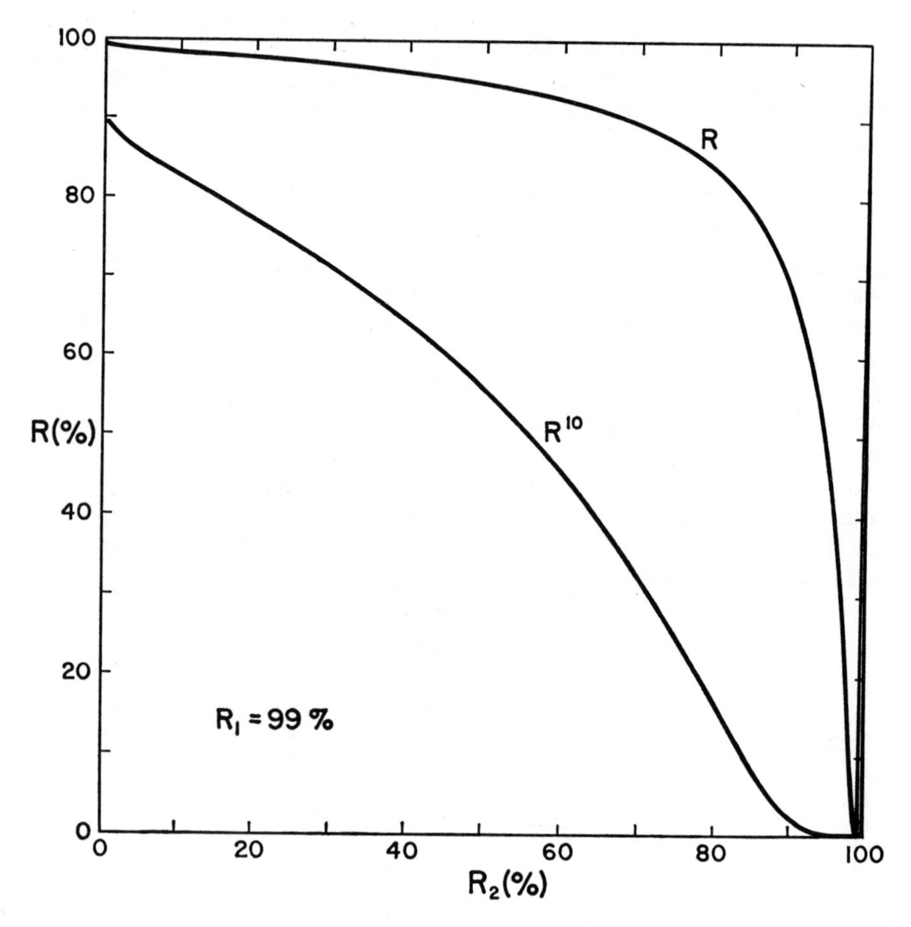

Fig. 8. Reflectivity versus R_2 for single and multiple (10) high reflection ($R_1 = 99\%$) Fabry-Perot structures. The relaxation of the requirement $R_1 = R_2$ for $R = 0$ in the multiple reflection structure should be noted.

encounters with the absorbing material. When there is amplitude matching the light is trapped within the film, i.e., $R = 0$, and it must be totally absorbed by the sample.

As already pointed out, the conventional IRE does not represent such a resonant structure since the light is introduced in it through a beveled edge and the thickness of the plate and beam widths are such that the light beam must walk down the plate with a skip distance equal to or exceeding the beam width in order to maintain a constant angle of incidence. Thus there can be no interference. Therefore conventional methods cannot be used to introduce the beam of light into the optical cavity. In the next two subsections two methods are discussed for adjusting the reflectivity of the top surface and thus coupling a wide beam of light into a very thin film so that the angle of incidence exceeds the critical angle at least at the sampling surface of the film. In one method the reflectivity of the top surface of the film is controlled by frustrated total reflection (H35) (FTR optical cavity). Here there are enough adjustable parameters so that the necessary conditions for total absorption can be realized. In another method the reflectivity of the top surface of the film is determined by the natural reflectivity of the film and another suitable medium of higher index (B18) (light condenser). In this latter case complete absorption cannot generally be obtained. Because it is simpler, the later structure will be discussed first.

Although the thin film (phase layer) is really the optical cavity, the method of coupling light into it is an essential part of the structure and therefore the entire structure will henceforth be called the optical cavity.

1. Light Condenser

One way of coupling energy into a thin film is to place it in contact with a higher index prism and to conduct the light into the prism at angles below the critical angle for the prism–film interface, but at an angle such that the refracted beam inside the film will strike the outer surface above the critical angle, as shown in Fig. 9. The film then has reflectivities of R_1 and R_2 on the top and bottom surfaces, respectively. R_2 is total because θ exceeds θ_c, and R_1 is determined by the natural reflectivity of the prism–film interface and is dependent on polarization and angle of incidence. Berz (B18) has analyzed this case and shown that for $\perp$-polarization and for a one-quarter wavelength, low-index film on a high-index prism, amplified electric fields can be obtained in the evanescent field in medium *3* and within the film. (For the quarter-wave film there is a node ($E = 0$) at the *1–2* interface.) A potential enhancement in the absorption of an order of magnitude can be obtained even though in this structure amplitude matching ($R_1 = R_2$) is not generally obtained. Berz called this structure a "light condenser."

In the light condenser the light enters the prism as shown in Fig. 9 and strikes the interface *1–2*, is refracted into the film *2* and totally reflected at the interface *2–3*. When the angle of incidence is changed, the optical path length and the resonant wavelength both change in accordance with equation (4). The range of angles of incidence for this structure is small. For the *1–2* interface, θ is limited from $\sin^{-1} n_{31}$ to $\sin^{-1} n_{21}$, since total reflection must

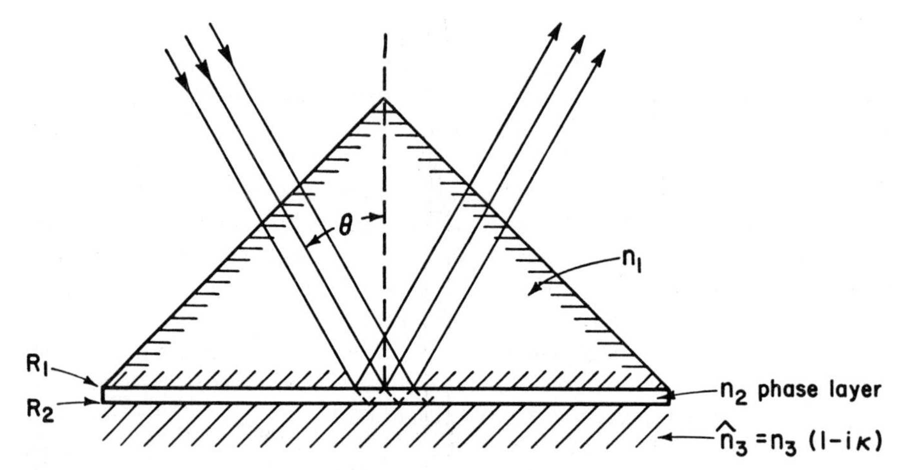

Fig. 9. The light condenser consisting of a low-index, one-quarter-wave film on a high-index prism. At resonance enhanced absorption is observed in medium *2* or medium *3*.

occur at interface *2–3* so that the light is not transmitted into medium *3*. However, total reflection must not occur at the interface *1–2* since the light must enter the film. The range of angles within the phase layer, θ_2, from similar considerations, is $\sin^{-1} n_{32}$ to $\pi/2$. Berz (B18) has shown that amplifications of the E-field at interface *2–3* for $\perp$-polarization over that obtained for an uncoated prism is given by

$$A = \left(\frac{n_1^2 - n_3^2}{n_2^2 - n_3^2}\right)^{1/2}. \tag{7}$$

For a typical case, e.g., SiO_2 ($n_2 = 1.45$) film on a Si ($n_1 = 3.5$) prism and $n_3 = 1$, the amplification of the E-field is 3.2. The E-field is substantially constant over the range of angles that can be employed, viz., $\theta = 16.5°$ to $24.5°$, just because this range is small. Since absorption goes as E^2, the absorption can thus be enhanced by about an order of magnitude over that obtained for a single total internal reflection from an uncoated prism. For $\|$-polarization R_1 is low and only weak amplification is obtained.

Turner and Berning (T7) have discussed a somewhat similar structure. They observed strong absorptions in thin Inconel films separated by a high-index film from a low-index prism. Calculations by du Pré (D23) show that a strong E-field at the outer surface of the high-index film cannot be obtained; hence, absorptions in weakly absorbing materials should not be greater than that obtainable via a single reflection near the critical angle.

Turbadar (T4) has shown that enhanced absorption in metal films may also be obtained by a resonance within the metal film itself. By placing a film of well-defined thickness on a glass plate and selecting the angle of incidence, high absorptions were obtained in certain films.

Effects of this sort have complicated the interpretation of experimental results for Hansen et al. (H11,H11a) where they employ glass plates coated with tin oxide as the electrode in electrode studies via internal reflection spectroscopy. When the wavelength changes, the absorption by the solution or species adsorbed on the surface is enhanced at wavelengths where there is resonance in the tin oxide film, i.e., when the effective film thickness is $\lambda/4$, $3\lambda/4$, etc. This enhanced absorption severely distorts the spectrum and corrections must be made. For this reason, when spectra over a wide range of wavelengths are required, coated IRE's should be avoided if possible.

Experimental results showing that the light condenser enhances the absorption when the condenser is operated at resonance are given in Fig. 10. The structure consisted of a 1.1 μ, SiO_2 film thermally grown on a Si plate. The O—H absorption in the oxide or on the oxide surface was measured as a function of angle of incidence for both polarizations. For about 45 reflections the spectrum for parallel polarization at $\lambda = 2.74\ \mu$ showed an absorption of about 20% and was substantially independent of angle of incidence. For perpendicular polarization, on the other hand, the absorption $(100 - R_1)$ was about 10% at 17° but increased abruptly to an excess of 50% near $\theta = 21°$ and then decreased as the angle of incidence was increased further, as shown in Fig. 10. Thus an absorption which would show a contrast of only 0.2% for a single reflection is amplified by a factor of about 250 by a combination of about 50 multiple reflections and an enhanced absorption by about a factor of 5.

The light condenser has the advantage that it is a simple structure with which a modest but useful enhancement of the absorption can be obtained. The absorbing medium may be the quarter-wave phase layer itself, a very thin layer of any refractive index on the quarter-wave layer (e.g., adsorbed molecules), or a thick layer of low refractive index in contact with the quarter-wave layer. The limitation on the refractive index in the latter case arises because total reflection is required at the outer surface of the quarter-wave layer. If the layer is SiO_2, for example, the index of the absorbing medium must be less than 1.4, which restricts the materials that can be investigated via the light condenser and also further restricts the angles of incidence that can be employed. For a thin absorbing film on the quarter-wave layer there is no limitation on the refractive index. For the higher index films, however,

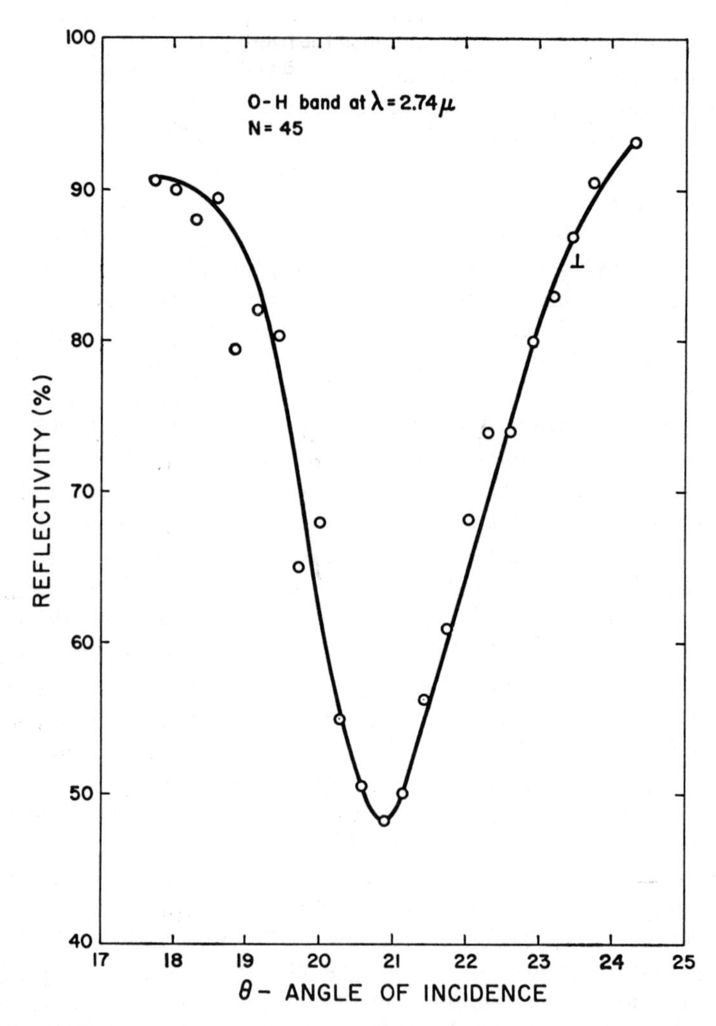

Fig. 10. Reflectivity versus angle of incidence for a light condenser consisting of a Si plate covered with a 1.1 μ SiO_2 film for ⊥-polarization. Note that the absorption for ⊥-polarization at resonance ($\theta = 21°$) is enhanced by a factor of about 5 compared to the absorption off resonance.

the film itself forms part of the resonant structure and the film thickness must be known to determine the resonant wavelength of the cavity.

This structure suffers from the limitation that it has only one adjustable parameter, viz., thickness of the phase layer, since the reflectivity of one surface is determined by the materials selected, e.g., Si–SiO_2. In the FTR cavity (H35,H38a), to be discussed in the next subsection, the reflectivity, R_1, can be adjusted independently of the materials employed and hence total absorption can be induced in any material.

2. FTR Optical Cavity

Another method of coupling light into the phase layer is frustrated total reflection. This method is employed in the FTR optical cavity, shown in Fig. 11, where the thickness of the low-index FTR spacer determines the reflectivity R_1. This structure can be considered as an FTR filter with one prism and one FTR spacer removed to expose one surface of the high-index phase layer. (It is convenient to use a hemicylinder, rather than a prism, so that the angle of incidence can be readily changed. When the light is brought to a focus in front of the curved surface as shown in Fig. 11, the beam becomes collimated within the hemicylinder, as discussed in Chapter Four.)

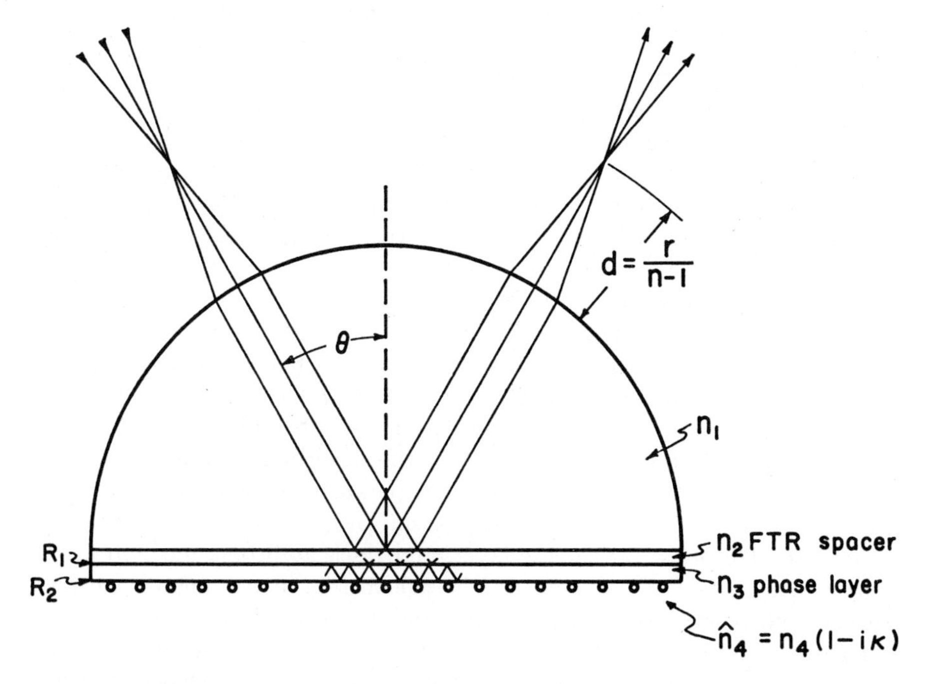

Fig. 11. FTR optical cavity and method of getting the radiation into it. At resonance the very intense electric fields found in the phase layer and in the evanescent wave result in enhanced absorptions.

Media *1* and *3* are most conveniently, although not necessarily, made from the same high-index material, while medium *2* is a suitable low-index material. The absorbing sample material to be detected may be medium *3* itself or another medium, *4*, which may either be of semiinfinite extent or may be in thin-film form. The highest E-fields, hence maximum sensitivity, are obtained by working as near the critical angle as possible which is given by $\sin^{-1} n_{43}$ or $\sin^{-1} n_{21}$, whichever is larger.

To minimize walk-off in the phase layer, media *1* and *3* should be made from the highest index material available for two reasons. First, since the optical path length is proportional to refractive index (see equation (4)), the thickness required for the phase layer is small. Second, the critical angle is small and therefore a small angle of incidence within the phase layer can be employed. When a small angle of incidence is employed, the thickness of the FTR spacer must be increased. This increase, however, results in a greater displacement of the light beam within the spacer. Therefore some compromise on choice of angle of incidence must be made.

Maximum absorption is achieved when two conditions are satisfied, viz., when there is amplitude matching, i.e., $R_1 = R_2$, and when there is phase matching, i.e., the thickness of the phase layer is adjusted so that there is resonance at the wavelength and angle of interest (see equation (4)). R_2 is determined by absorption by medium *4* on the outer surface of layer *3* or by absorption within layer *3* itself. Largest amplification of the absorption for a given cavity, however, is obtained when $R_2 < R_1$. Because the phase changes $\delta_\perp$ and $\delta_\parallel$ are different for total internal reflection, the resonant thickness is different for perpendicular and parallel polarization. These thicknesses become equal as θ approaches the critical angle. It should be recalled that for a given absorber R_2 depends on polarization and therefore the optimum values of R_1 will be different for different polarizations.

The thicknesses of the FTR spacer and phase layer required for complete absorption at any wavelength can be determined precisely with the aid of a computer when the optical constants of the absorbing medium *4* or *3* are known. As an example, these optimum parameters have been computed (T8) for $\theta = 45°$ for a Si ($n_1 = 3.5$) prism, SiO_2 ($n_2 = 1.45$) FTR spacer, evaporated Ge ($n_3 = 3.8$) phase layer, and thick absorbing medium *4* with optical constants $\hat{n} = n - in\kappa$. The thicknesses in microns of the FTR spacers and phase layers required for total absorption in medium *4* at $\lambda = 3.4\ \mu$ are given in Table I. It should be noted that, because $\delta_\parallel > \delta_\perp$, the thickness of the phase layer is greater for parallel than it is for perpendicular polarization. The FTR layer, on the other hand, is thinner for $\parallel$-polarization. Slight changes in the thickness of the phase layer for different absorbers should be noted. This occurs because δ changes as $n\kappa$ changes.

TABLE I

Thickness (in microns) of Phase Layers and FTR Spacers Required to Give Total Absorption at $\lambda = 3.4\ \mu$ for Various Thick Layer Absorbers

	$\|$-Cavity	$\perp$-Cavity
1. Absorber $\hat{n} = 1.4 - i(0.04)$		
Phase layer (Ge)	0.513	0.230
FTR spacer (SiO_2)	0.374	0.680
2. Absorber $\hat{n} = 1.4 - i(0.08)$		
Phase layer (Ge)	0.506	0.230
FTR spacer (SiO_2)	0.272	0.578
3. Absorber $\hat{n} = 1.4 - i(0.16)$		
Phase layer (Ge)	0.500	0.231
FTR spacer (SiO_2)	0.208	0.476

The response of the optical cavity versus normalized frequency (T8), ν/ν_0, is shown in Figs. 12a and 12b for $\|$- and $\perp$-polarization. Total absorption is obtained for the resonant frequency $\nu = \nu_0$. (The shift in the minima of the curves is caused by small numerical errors.) Also shown in these figures is the response expected for an uncoated Ge prism at $\theta = 45°$. The strong enhancement in absorption due to coating the prism is clearly evident.

The thicknesses of the FTR spacer and phase layer can also be calculated in a straightforward manner without the aid of a computer. These calculations are quite valid if the absorption does not exceed 10% per reflection. First R_2 can be estimated or determined from a measurement employing an uncoated IRE. For example, for 5% absorption $R_2 = 95\%$ and complete extinction is achieved by making R_1 also equal to 95%. R_1 can be adjusted to the desired value by adjusting the thickness of the FTR layer as described for the double prism shown in Fig. 12a of Chapter Two. The thickness of this spacer will depend on the angle of incidence and the polarization and refractive indices involved and can be calculated from equations given by Billings (B21) or Court and Willisen (C10), for example. The thickness, t, of the phase layer is determined from equation (4), where λ is the resonant wavelength and is adjusted to the peak absorption of an absorption band. In the first order ($m = 0$) the thickness is given by:

$$t = \frac{(\delta_1 + \delta_2)\lambda}{4\pi n_3 \cos\theta}. \tag{8}$$

In general it is necessary to know the refractive indices of all of the materials to determine t because they enter into the equations for δ_1 and δ_2. It is

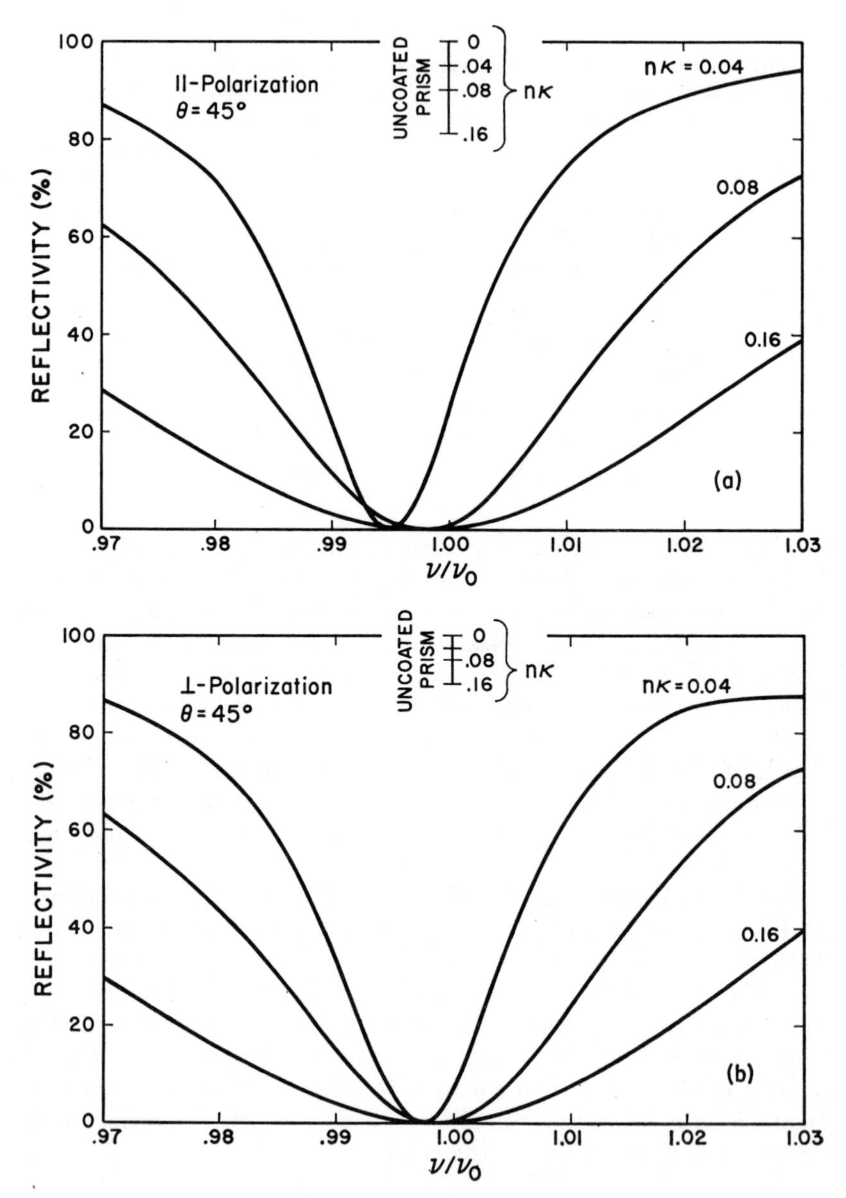

Fig. 12. Calculated reflectivity for ||- and ⊥-polarization versus normalized frequency for optical cavities consisting of a Si prism, SiO_2 FTR spacer, and Ge phase layer. It is designed to resonate at $\lambda = 3.4\ \mu$ for $\theta = 45°$ and to detect a thick layer of $n_4 = 1.4$ and various values of $n_4\kappa_4$. Total absorption is induced at the resonant frequency. The much smaller response for an uncoated prism should be noted.

possible to make the cavity resonate at the same wavelength for both polarizations by choosing a suitable birefringent material for the phase layer as has been done for the FTR filter (B21) or by working at $\theta \sim \theta_c$ when $\delta_\perp \sim \delta_\parallel$.

Because high fields and low walk-off are obtained for small angles, it is preferable to operate the optical cavity near the critical angle. The FTR cavity can, however, be operated for angles ranging from $\theta = \sin^{-1} n_{21}$ to grazing incidence with, of course, a change in resonant wavelength given by equation (4). If medium *1* is made in the form of a hemicylinder of radius r, as shown in Fig. 11, first-order collimation can be obtained within the hemicylinder by focusing the beam at a distance of $d = r/(n_1 - 1)$ in front of the entrance surface. The angle of incidence can then readily be changed as required for "tuning." For a cavity consisting of a Si phase layer imbedded in SiO_2, the tuning range, i.e., change of resonant λ with θ given by equation (4), is shown in Fig. 13 for the first three orders. The tuning range is not small; it is a factor of 20, 6, and 4 for the first, second, and third orders, respectively. Changing θ also changes R_1 and hence the peak absorption for the cavity is shifted to a different degree of absorption.

Although the FTR optical cavity is a more complicated structure than the light condenser, it has a number of advantages. Because the phase layer is of high index, it can be operated at a wider range of angles, viz., from $\theta = \sin^{-1} n_{21}$ to $\pi/2$ and thus it can be tuned over a wider range of wavelengths and materials with a greater range in refractive indices can be studied. Since there are two adjustable parameters, high Q can be obtained for any angle of incidence and total absorption can be induced in any sample. It can also be constructed for either polarization.

The main features of the FTR optical cavity have been qualitatively verified in some preliminary experiments on single-reflection optical cavities constructed of the type shown in Fig. 11 for both $\perp$- and $\parallel$-polarization. Thickness in microns of the FTR and phase layers computed for both polarizations (D23,T8) are given in Table II for cavities consisting of Si ($n_1 = 3.5$) hemicylinders, SiO_2 ($n_2 = 1.45$) FTR spacers, and evaporated Si ($n_3 = 3.1$) phase layers which were designed to give complete absorption at $\lambda = 3.4\ \mu$ for thick layer absorbers with complex index $\hat{n} = 1.4 - i(0.04)$ at $\theta = 29°$.

TABLE II

Thickness (in microns) of Phase Layers and FTR Spacers Required for Total Absorption at 3.4 μ of a Thick Layer Absorber, $\hat{n} = 1.4 - i(0.04)$

	$\parallel$-Cavity	$\perp$-Cavity
Phase layer (Si)	0.422	0.146
FTR spacer (SiO_2)	0.885	0.885

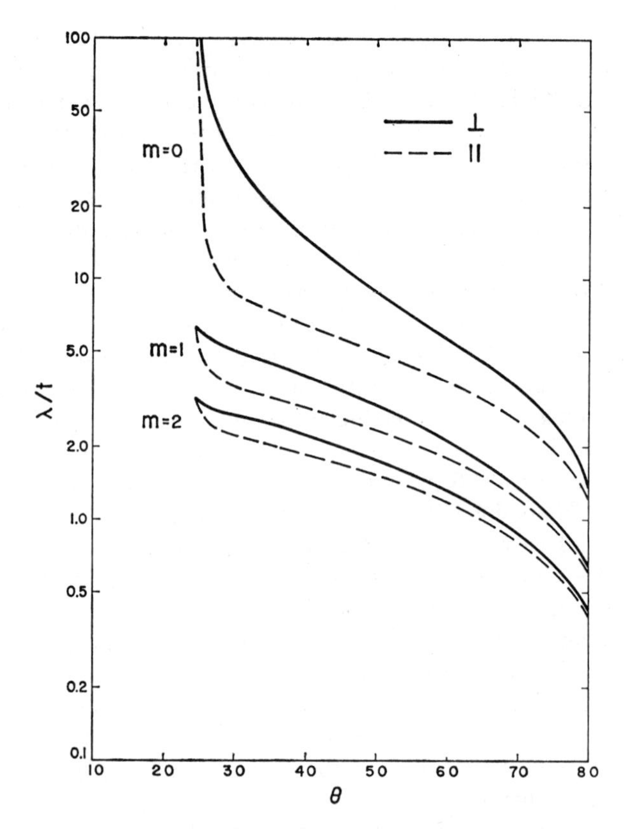

Fig. 13. The dependence of the resonant wavelength-to-thickness ratio of a Si film in contact with SiO_2 versus angle of incidence in the Si film for ⊥- and ||-polarization in first ($m = 0$), second ($m = 1$), and third ($m = 2$) orders.

A number of results demonstrating enhanced absorption and taken with the ||-cavity of Table II will now be discussed. Because of the difficulty experienced in controlling the thickness of thin-film absorbers, e.g., oil films, for testing purposes, thick films were employed where the absorption coefficient was changed.

Figure 14 compares the sharp C—H band at 3.3 μ of chloroform recorded using an uncoated Si hemicylinder (curve *a*) to that obtained with the optical cavity (curve *b*) using ||-polarized light in both cases. The 4% absorption for the uncoated prism is enhanced by more than an order of magnitude with the cavity.

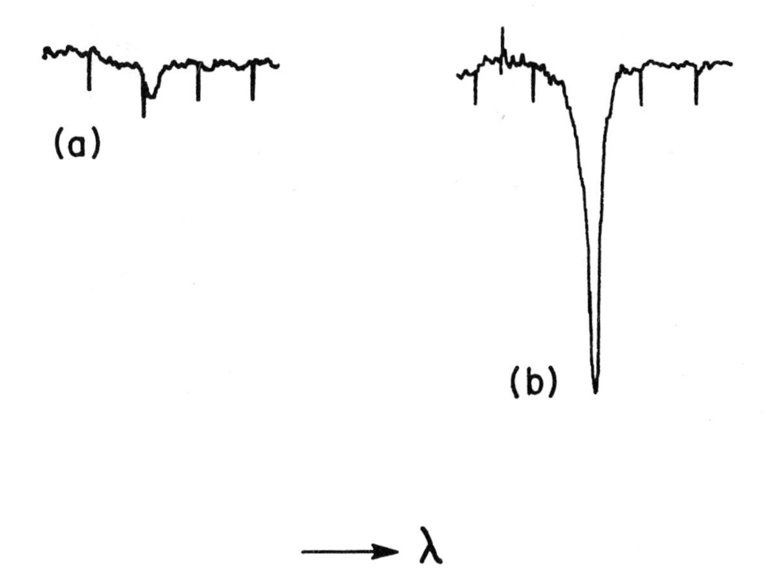

Fig. 14. Comparison of the absorption by the C—H band of chloroform ($\lambda = 3.3\ \mu$) for ||-polarization at $\theta = 29.5°$ using (a) an uncoated Si prism and (b) the ||-cavity specified in Table II. The absorption of 4% in curve (a) is enhanced by over an order of magnitude in curve (b).

Figure 15 compares the absorption of a 50% solution of Nujol in CCl_4 for ||-polarization for (*a*) an uncoated Si hemicylinder at $\theta = 29°$ to that obtained via (*b*) the optical ||-cavity. The absorption at $\lambda = 3.4\ \mu$ is enhanced by a factor somewhat greater than 2. The maximum absorption of about 90% for the cavity occurs at $\lambda = 3.5\ \mu$, which should be compared to an absorption of about 23% for the uncoated hemicylinder at the same wavelength. The cavity has caused some distortion of the absorption band. By changing the angle of incidence it was possible to shift the resonance of the cavity to other regions of the absorption band.

The angular dependence of the absorption for a 3.39 μ laser beam for the Nujol solution in contact with the ||-cavity is shown in Fig. 16. The sharp increase in the absorption to 87% at $\theta = 29°$ should be noted. The absorption versus θ for an uncoated prism qualitatively follows the dashed curve in Fig. 16.

The measured dependence of the reflectivity, R, versus R_2 for the ||-cavity is shown by the dashed curve of Fig. 17 for $\lambda = 3.4\ \mu$. (Similar results were

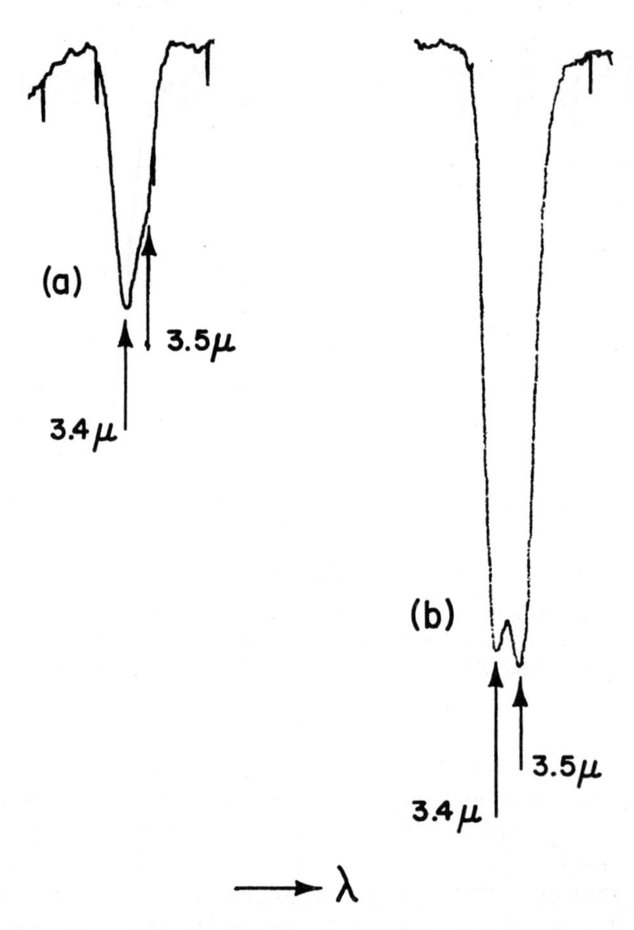

Fig. 15. Comparison of the absorption by the C—H band of a 50% solution of Nujol in CCl_4 for ||-polarization at $\theta = 29°$ using (a) an uncoated Si prism and (b) the ||-cavity specified in Table II. The absorption of curve (b) at $\lambda = 3.5\ \mu$ is 90% compared to about 23% for curve (a).

obtained for the ⊥-cavity.) The concentration of Nujol in CCl_4 was changed to alter the reflectivity R_2 in this study. The change in absorption for an uncoated, Si prism at $\theta = 29°$ as a function of concentration is shown by the solid line. The dashed curve qualitatively follows those shown in Fig. 6, indicating that the absorption passes through a maximum as the reflectivity changes. For this cavity the maximum absorption is calculated (D23) to

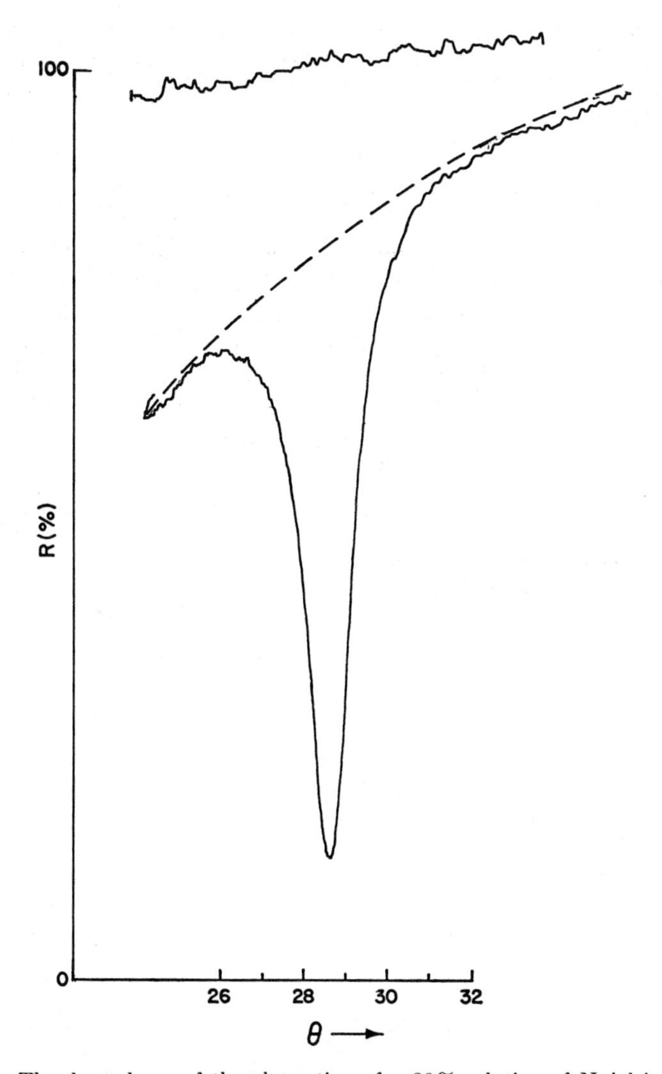

Fig. 16. The dependence of the absorption of a 30% solution of Nujol in CCl_4 at a wavelength of 3.39 μ on angle of incidence for the ||-cavity of Table II. The absorption at the peak which occurs at 29° is 87%. The dashed curve qualitatively shows the dependence of the absorption on θ for an uncoated Si prism. The top curve represents the 100% level versus θ for the cavity in the absence of the solution.

occur for $R_2 \sim 84\%$. The maximum amplification of the absorption over that for an uncoated prism that could occur would then be a factor of 6 for total absorption by the cavity. The measured values (dashed curve) show a maximum in the absorption at the correct value of R_2 and an amplification of the absorption of about a factor of 5. This is considered to be rather good agreement with theory in view of some of the factors, discussed in the next section, which lead to a deterioration of the performance of the optical cavity. (Walk-off, lack of collimation, stray light, incomplete polarization, and depolarization of the light beam can all contribute to incomplete absorption at resonance.) It should be noted that a higher amplification of the absorption is obtained for values of R_2 higher than that required for resonance (lower concentration of Nujol). Figure 17 shows an amplification of a factor

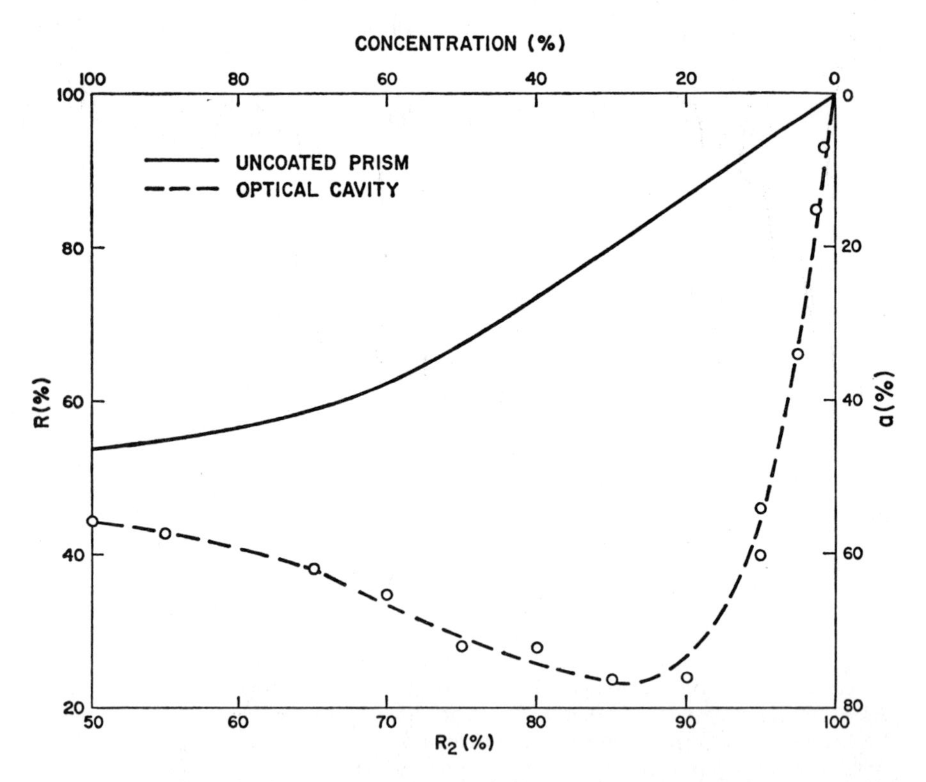

Fig. 17. Reflectivity for an uncoated prism (solid curve) and an optical cavity (dashed curve) versus concentration of Nujol in CCl_4 at $\lambda = 3.4\ \mu$. The enhanced absorption by the cavity should be noted. The dashed curve resembles those of Fig. 6, showing a minimum in the reflectivity when $R_1 = R_2$.

of 10 with the cavity at the 5% absorption point for the uncoated prism whereas theory predicts (D23) a factor of 15.

Another cavity which was tested consisted of a Ge hemicylinder ($n_1 = 4$), followed by a BaF_2 FTR film ($n_2 = 1.47$) of thickness $t = 0.435\ \mu$, and then an evaporated Ge film ($n_3 = 3.8$) of thickness $t = 0.35\ \mu$ designed for resonance at 2.9 μ for the $\|$-component at $\theta = 30°$ and complete extinction for a film of water $\lambda/2$ thick where (C3) $\hat{n} = 1.367 - i(0.0637)$. It was not found possible to place water films of controlled thickness on the Ge film in order to properly test its performance. Tests were therefore made with bulk water where a maximum absorption of 95% was found at $\theta = 26°$ compared to 55% for the uncoated Ge prism using $\|$-polarization.

These results thus show that the FTR optical cavity behaves, within certain limitations, as predicted. Some of the limitations will be discussed in the next subsection.

3. Limitations

For certain applications some limitations of the optical cavity may, for example, be that it is substantially a fixed-frequency device and requires highly collimated and monochromatic light beams, precise angular setting, and critical matching of reflectivities of the opposing surfaces of the phase layer. These limitations can be relaxed by employing multiple reflections, as discussed earlier. It was also pointed out, in connection with Fig. 17, that the reflectivity of the opposing surfaces need not be perfectly matched for absorption enhancement. In fact, when $R_2 > R_1$ the amplification is greater than it is when $R_2 = R_1$. For a weak absorber, therefore, the cavity should be designed for the amplification required rather than for perfect matching.

A fundamental limitation of the optical cavity is walk-off in the phase layer, especially for cavities of high Q. Walk-off becomes more severe for higher orders (thicker phase layers) and larger angles of incidence, and therefore the cavity should be operated in the lowest order ($m = 0$) and at the smallest angle possible to reduce this effect. It is obvious that increasing the beam width should reduce the walk-off and therefore enhance the absorption. This was found to be the case. For the $\|$-cavity specified in Table II, a beam of width less than 1.5 mm resulted in reduced spectral contrast, presumably due to walk-off.

Although a small angle of incidence is required to reduce walk-off in the phase layer, with small angles thicker FTR spacers are required for high-Q cavities, and the displacement in the FTR layer then increases. There are thus conflicting requirements and some compromise on the angle of incidence must be made.

Since the reflection in the phase layer is not perfect, there is some reflection loss in high-Q cavities at resonance even in the "absence" of absorbers. For the $\|$-cavity specified in Table II this loss was between 5 and 10%. Corrections were made for this loss in preparing Fig. 17.

A high-Q cavity will strongly distort broad absorption bands since it will amplify the absorption band only within the resonance width of the cavity. The cavity designed for the O—H band of water, described in the previous subsection, was of relatively low Q, and showed no noticeable distortion of the O—H band. The Q of the $\|$-cavity of Table II was calculated (D23) to be

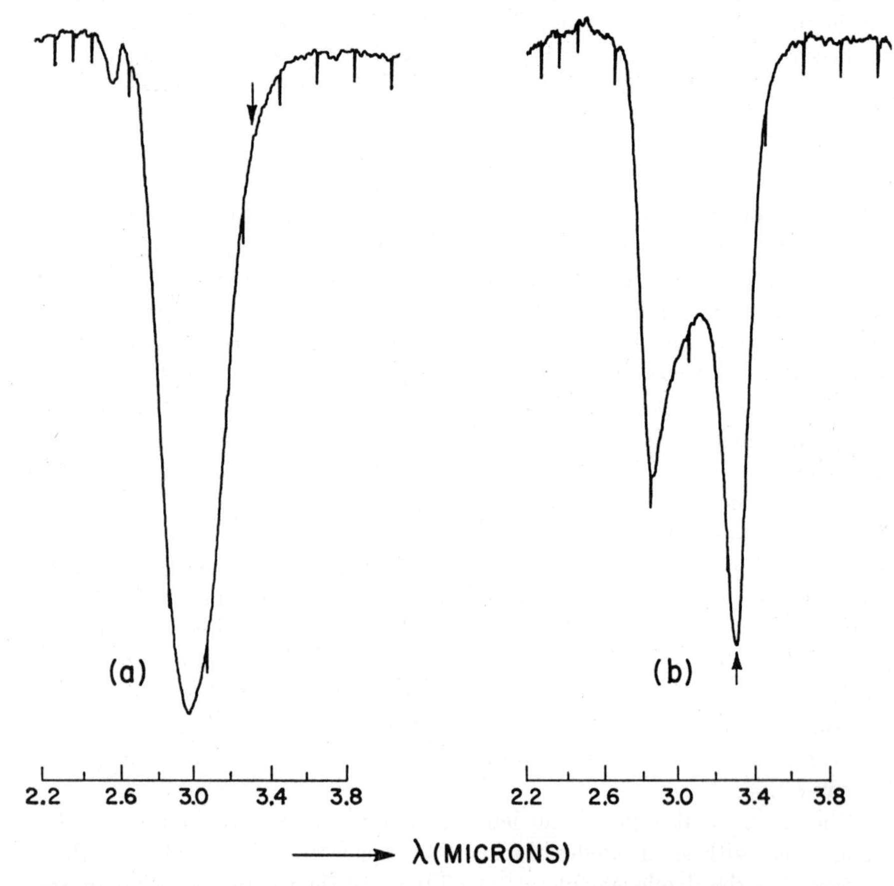

Fig. 18. The O—H absorption band of water at $\theta = 29°$ for $\|$-polarization using (a) an uncoated Si prism and (b) the optical $\|$-cavity of Table II. The strong amplification for curve (b) at 3.3 μ leads to the distortion of the broad O—H band.

about 35, i.e., $\Delta\lambda/\lambda \sim 35$, hence at $\lambda = 3.4\ \mu$ the resonance half-width $\Delta\lambda \sim 0.1\ \mu$. This small half-width should not noticeably affect the band shape of the C—H band of chloroform whose half-width is considerably less than 0.1 μ, and hence the band shown in Fig. 14b should be undistorted. The half-width of the Nujol band however, is about 0.2 μ and some distortion of this band by the optical cavity is clearly evident in Fig. 15. Strong distortion of the broad O—H band of water using this cavity is shown in Fig. 18. The half-width of the enhanced peak at 3.3 μ in Fig. 18 is about 0.1 μ and is determined by the Q of the cavity. Here a narrow portion of the band (at 3.3 μ and depicted by the arrow) is amplified by a factor of about 7, leading to the distortion shown. The amplified peak could be moved to other wavelengths by changing the angle of incidence. Although one should be aware of these possible distortions, they are not a serious limitation since high-Q cavities will generally be designed and employed as detectors for predetermined materials and not to study band profiles.

In spite of these limitations the optical cavity may have a number of important areas of applications such as the ones listed below.

4. Potential Applications

There is a wide range of potential applications of the optical cavity. Some of these areas require the enhancement of the absorption that can be achieved while another one, in particular, also takes advantage of the unique direction of the E-field that can be achieved. The more important areas of potential application of the optical cavity should be in the detection of minute quantities, enhancement of photoemission, and optical pumping of thin films.

(1) **Detection of Minute Quantities.** For adsorbed molecules the necessity of preparing large surface areas is alleviated since, with the aid of the optical cavity, strong interaction can be achieved in small areas. For example, the equivalent of 10^3 reflections can be obtained in a double-pass plate 5 cm long and 1 mm thick at $\theta = 45°$ with an enhancement of a factor of 10. Multiple reflections in this case serve to increase the sampling area and to relax the limitations on λ and θ of the single-reflection optical cavity.

For detection of submicrogram quantities, strong amplifications are desirable. The optical cavity should be designed taking into consideration the manner in which the sample can be placed on the detecting surface, i.e., whether it is localized at one point or spread out thinly over the surface. In most cases, however, it is advisable to employ multiple reflection. An ideal IRE for minute quantities is a combination of the rosette and the optical cavity. Since there is a rotation of the plane of polarization in the rosette, the optical cavity must be achromatized so that both polarizations resonate at the same wavelength. For example, a rosette with 10 reflections and a cavity with an enhancement of a factor of 10 is equivalent to 100 reflections at one point.

The results of this chapter indicate that the optical cavity should be helpful in the detection of minute quantities because of the enhanced absorptions.

(2) **Photoemission.** An important potential application of the optical cavity is in the enhancement of photoemission. If the optical cavity consists of a suitable photoemissive material or if a thin-film photoemissive material is placed on the optical cavity, this structure may be employed as an efficient photodetector. If R_1 and R_2 are adequately matched, total absorption of incoming collimated radiation may be obtained at any predetermined wavelength. Such a fixed-wavelength detector should be useful in a number of cases such as in conjunction with a laser source where the light beam is generally highly collimated and monochromatic and especially where weak signals are to be detected. (Interference film structures have previously been considered for enhancing photoemission (D15).) Even a modest enhancement of the absorption, a factor of 5 or less, can be of considerable interest in the application of the optical cavity to photodetectors.

If the outer film is a photoemissive material and the cavity is designed for $\|$-polarization and $\theta \sim \theta_c$, the optical cavity can possibly be employed as a source of monoenergetic electrons. For $\|$-polarization at angles just above the critical angle, the only E-field present at the reflecting surface is one normal to the surface; hence electrons will be ejected primarily normal to the surface. Since the photoemissive material may be very thin there will be little or no straggling of the electrons emerging from the film, and electrons with energy determined by the quantum process should be obtainable.

(3) **Optical Pumping of Thin Films.** The optical cavity may potentially be employed for efficient pumping of large quantities of energy in thin films where either the absorptions are low or the relaxation times are very short and therefore little or no effect is obtained via conventional illumination.

Optical pumping in thin-film materials with low absorption coefficients is of interest, for example, in obtaining laser action in thin films and also in the enhancement in the photoconductivity in extrinsic photoconductors.

Photoconductivity associated with transitions involving the fast surface states in semiconductors has not been observed because of the short relaxation times involved. The optical cavity may be a means of achieving this because of the possibility of enhancing the number of transitions.

The results on the optical cavity described in this chapter indicate that it is now possible to enhance absorption at optical frequencies by constructing resonant structures and thus creating very intense electromagnetic fields just as has been done at microwave and radiofrequencies for years. The list of potential applications show that there are many areas where even a modest enhancement of absorption at optical frequencies can be used with advantage.

This concludes the discussion of internal reflection elements. The next chapter, devoted to instrumentation, will indicate the type of optical layouts required to utilize the IRE's described in the present and previous chapters.

CHAPTER SIX

INSTRUMENTATION FOR INTERNAL REFLECTION SPECTROSCOPY

A. Introduction

In general adequate instrumentation for internal reflection spectroscopy was not commercially available before 1965 which hampered its early development. A number of workers developed their own instrumentation; but many others who did not want to embark upon an instrumentation program shelved their ideas—at least temporarily. The requirements of internal reflection spectrometers include the ability to vary easily the angle of incidence over a wide range (e.g., 15°–75°), readily accessible IRE's, and adequate space for auxiliary equipment such as polarizers, vacuum or heating chambers, etc.

Instrumentation for internal reflection spectroscopy can be developed in one of four ways, all based on the use of existing commercial spectrometers. These are as follows:

1. The use of special IRE's which do not substantially displace or defocus the light beam at the entrance slit and therefore can be placed in the existing sampling space of a conventional spectrometer without employing additional optical components.

2. The development of special attachments utilizing transfer optics which can also be inserted in the sampling space with no disturbance of the optical alignment.

3. The development of completely new layouts for the source optics of the spectrometer which will include the necessary components for internal reflection measurements.

4. The extraction of the monochromatic beam from the monochromator.

Each of these approaches will be discussed. In addition, a spectroscopic technique in which the absorption can be modulated will be described, as well as some instrumentation for special problems. Polarizers will also be discussed briefly because of their importance in quantitative measurements via internal reflection spectroscopy.

In most of the spectrometers in use, double-beam operation is employed. Double-beam operation is more sensitive than single-beam because, with the resulting flat base line, higher amplifications can be employed and then source fluctuations and atmospheric absorption bands are cancelled to a high degree. For a high degree of balancing, it is necessary that the same portion of the infrared source contributes to both beams to ensure identical spectral compositions. For internal reflection, surface roughness of the IRE contributes to unbalance. Equal lengths of optical material should be traversed by both the reference and sample beams to compensate for any absorptions by the optical material—e.g., due to lattice vibrations and free carriers. The power of double-beam operation is clearly demonstrated in Fig. 1. Here curves *a* and *b* represent the power in the sample and reference beams, respectively. The sample beam passed through a silicon plate where it suffered 165 internal reflections. Information about the silicon surface cannot readily be obtained from curve *a* because of the large variations in power level and the presence of atmospheric bands. When *b* is subtracted from *a*, a flat base line is obtained and the atmospheric bands are cancelled, as shown by curve *c*. The gain of the amplifier system can now be increased and information concerning the silicon surface is clearly evident in curve *d* which shows the presence of O—H and C—H groups on the surface.

Internal reflection instrumentation is currently available from a number of commercial firms, viz., Barnes Engineering, Stamford, Connecticut; Beckman Instruments, Inc., Fullerton, California; Perkin-Elmer Corp., Norwalk, Connecticut; Research and Industrial Instruments Co., London, England (previously marketed by Limit Corporation, Darien, Connecticut. RIIC has been acquired by Beckman Instruments); and Wilks Scientific Corp., South Norwalk, Connecticut. Some of their instrumentation will be discussed in the following sections.

B. Special IRE's

The simplest way of preparing a spectrometer to record an internal reflection spectrum is to insert a suitable internal reflection element in the sampling space of the spectrometer and then to place the sample material in contact with the reflecting surface of the IRE. This can be done by the use of a dove or achromatic prism, for example, if the beam is sufficiently well collimated and if the refractive index of the IRE is not too high so that defocusing of the light beam at the spectrometer slits does not become objectionable. A more satisfactory approach is to design an IRE which when placed in the sampling space (with no additional optical components) does not defocus or displace the light beam at the spectrometer slits. This cannot be accomplished with a simple achromat such as that shown in Fig. 3c of Chapter

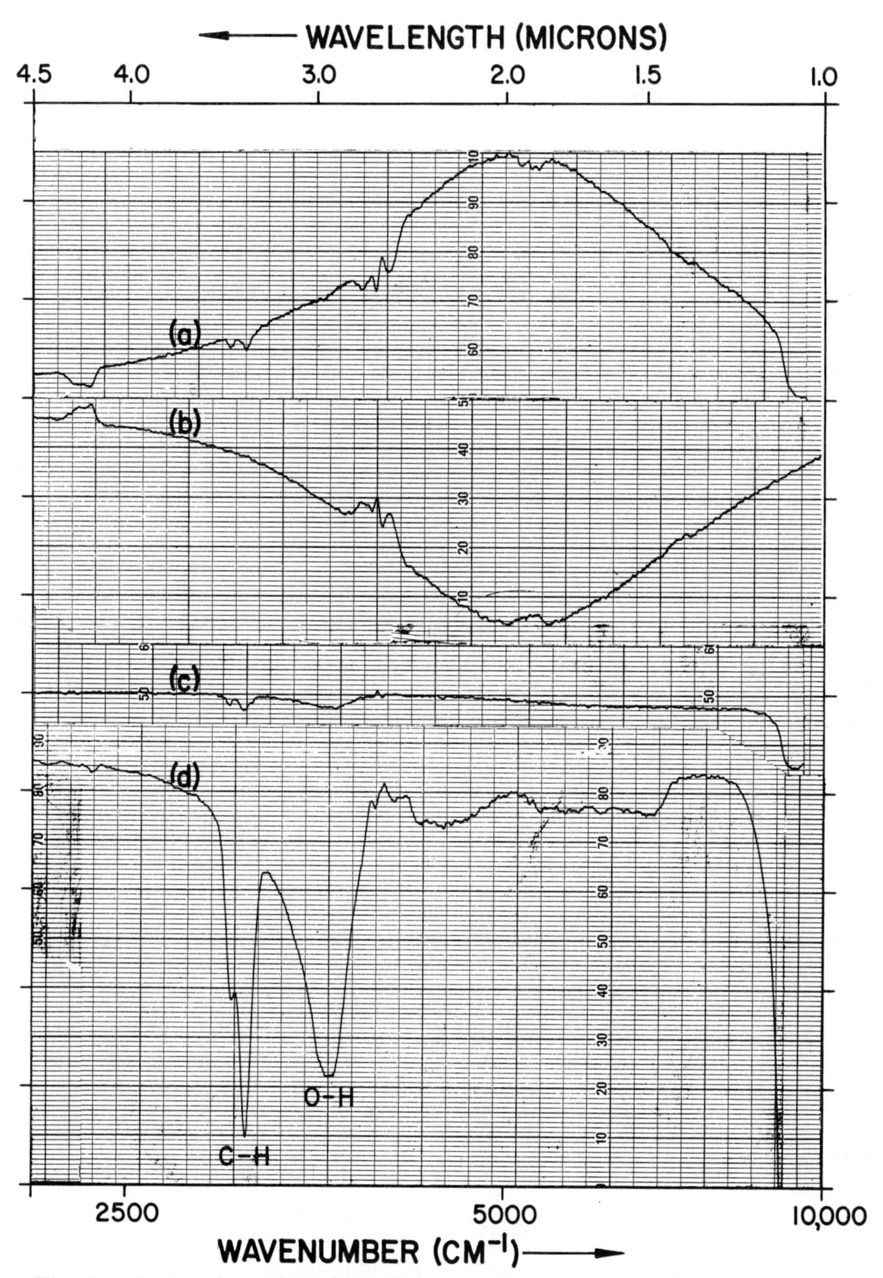

Fig. 1. Series of spectra which illustrate advantages of double-beam operation. (a) Radiation in sample beam. (b) Radiation in reference beam. (c) Subtraction of (a) from (b) giving flat base line. (d) Same as (c) except increased gain of 25, clearly showing surface spectrum of a silicon plate, $N = 165$, $\theta = 45°$.

Four but has been accomplished with the V-shaped IRE, for example, shown is Fig. 20 of Chapter Four (or, equivalently, with two parallelepiped single-pass plates). This type of approach does not take full advantage of internal reflection spectroscopy because the possibility of varying the angle of incidence, a powerful tool if used properly, is excluded.

C. Attachments Utilizing Transfer Optics

Most of the workers using internal reflection techniques have employed attachments which were designed to be placed in the limited sampling space of conventional spectrometers with no modification of the spectrometer. This approach was the one most widely used in the beginning and does work satisfactorily for many applications. For many problems requiring ovens, vacuum systems, or large volume polarizers, however, this approach is inadequate because of the already rather limited sampling space in most spectrometers. A number of attachments for the sampling space of commercial spectrometers that have been developed will be described. Any one of these attachments may also be placed in the reference beam to compensate for absorptions or surface scatter in the IRE or to measure difference spectra. The attachments can be classed in two groups, viz., variable-angle, single internal reflection attachments and fixed-angle, multiple internal reflection attachments.

1. Variable-Angle, Single Internal Reflection Attachments

Many of the internal reflection attachments for the sampling space of commercial spectrometers were initially designed to be used with prisms or hemicylinders employing a single reflection. Some of these units were later modified so that IRE's with a few reflections (e.g., three) could also be used. If the light beam is brought to a focus near the reflecting surface of the IRE in any single-reflection unit, then the prism or hemicylinder can be replaced by a fixed- or variable-angle, double-pass plate, described in Chapter Four, and any number of reflections can then be employed. Many of these attachments can be employed for conventional external reflection by replacing the IRE with a mirror.

a. Internal Reflection Accessory for Hemicylinder

A variable-angle accessory designed by Fahrenfort and Visser (F4) and used to measure optical constants is shown in Fig. 2. The hemicylinder is

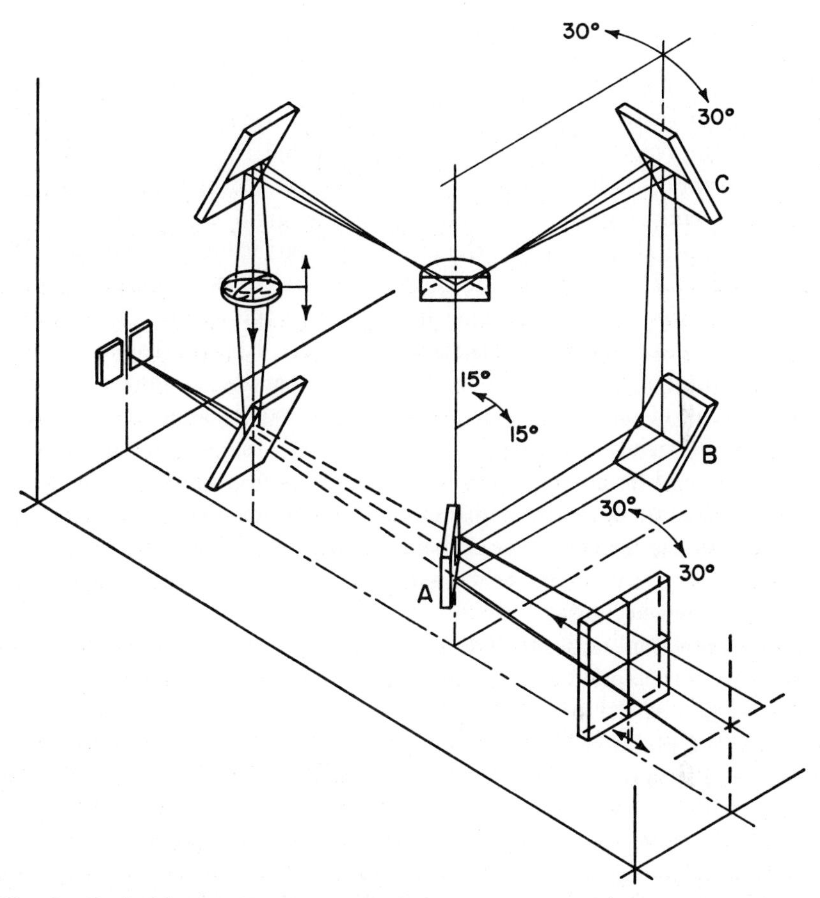

Fig. 2. Optical layout of internal reflection accessory for hemicylinder developed by Fahrenfort and Visser (F4). Mirrors *B* and *C* are mounted on a common arm which can be rotated via an angle-dividing mechanism about the common axis of the IRE and mirror *A*.

mounted directly above and on the same axis as mirror *A* which intercepts the sample beam. Mirror *B* deflects the beam upwards and mirror *C* directs the beam to the vertical reflecting surface of the IRE. Mirrors *B* and *C* are mounted together on a vertical arm which can be rotated about the common axis of the IRE and mirror *A*. The IRE and *A* are connected to *B* and *C* by an angle-dividing mechanism which allows θ to be set to any value between 30° and 60°. After the light beam leaves the reflecting surface of the IRE it is deflected to and refocused at the spectrometer slits as shown.

b. Twin Parallel-Mirror Attachment

The first commercial internal reflection attachment, which was developed at Connecticut Instruments (now marketed by Barnes Engineering), is a twin parallel-mirror system (D10). It is similar to that shown in Fig. 3a where the two mirrors on the right compose one set of parallel mirrors and the mirror and hemicylinder on the left form the equivalent of a second set of parallel mirrors. Interestingly, the idea for this attachment was based (W9) on the V-shaped IRE (H28) or, its equivalent, two parallelepiped, single-pass multiple reflection plates. Parallel mirrors have the unique property that the incoming and reflected beams remain parallel, although displaced, as the mirrors are rotated, provided the mirrors remain parallel, as shown in Fig. 3a. The second set of parallel mirrors, which is rotated through the same angle as the first set, brings the light beam back to the same axis as the incoming beam. It should be noted that rotation of the twin parallel mirrors in this way does not alter the path length of the light beam. In a system such as that shown in Fig. 3a the angle of incidence can be varied over a wide range and there is no displacement or defocusing of the light beam at the entrance slit of the monochromator.

In the commercial unit (ATR-1) shown in Fig. 3c, the rotation of the two sets of mirrors is coupled and a range of angles of incidence from 30° to 65° is achieved. One of the mirrors is made slightly convex in order to correct for the increase in path length which is caused by the introduction of the unit in the sampling compartment. Prisms, corrugated plates, or four reflection rhombus (S19) are employed in the commercial unit as IRE's with an unfocused beam at the reflecting sampling surface. Because the optical path length in a prism changes with rotation, there is some defocusing of the light beam at the spectrometer slits. It should be recalled (see Chapter Four) that the internal angular variation in a prism is substantially less than the external variation (because of the refraction of the beam as it enters the prism) and hence prisms cannot be readily employed over a wide range of angles of incidence. A unit of similar design (TR-3) is made by Research and Industrial Instruments Co.

With a change in the focusing optics this unit could obviously be modified to accept hemicylinders, as shown in Fig. 3a, or double-pass, multiple reflection plates. Figure 3b shows that fixed or variable-angle, single-pass multiple reflection plates may be employed in this basic system if one set of parallel mirrors is removed and replaced by the single-pass plate.

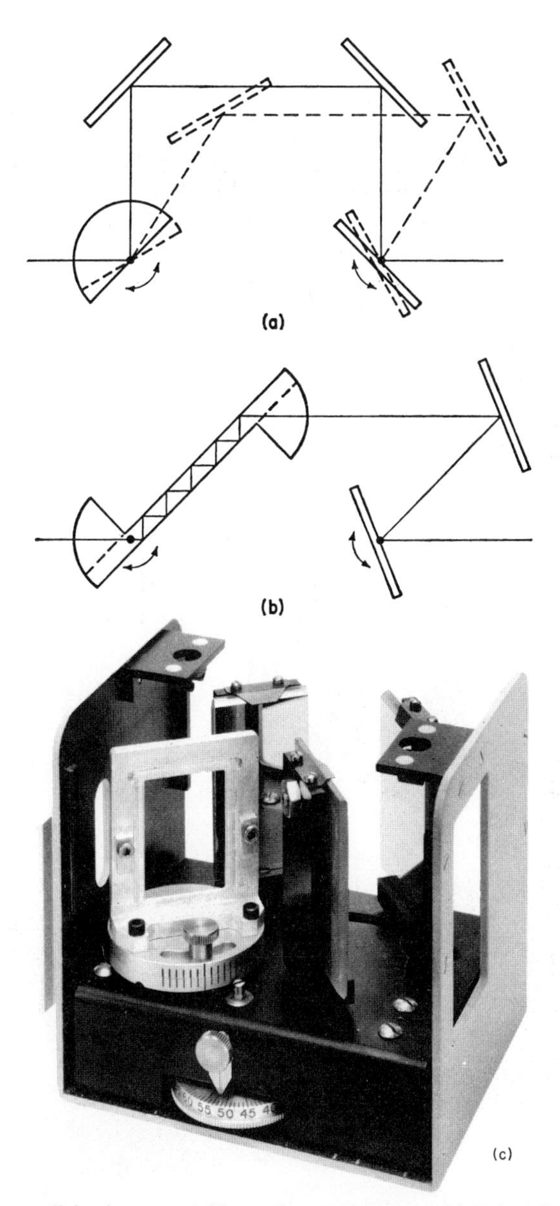

Fig. 3. Twin parallel-mirror, variable-angle attachment. (a) Principle of operation for single reflection IRE. (b) Proposed use with multiple reflection plates. (c) Photograph of CIC (Barnes Engineering) twin parallel-mirror unit employing prism (prism removed).

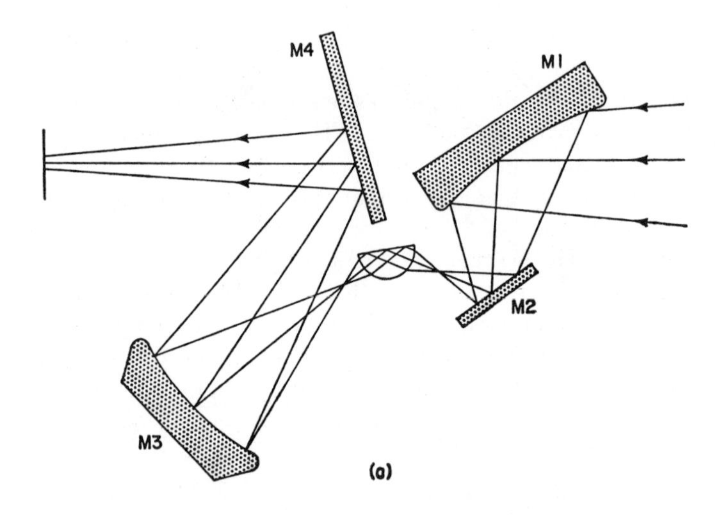

Fig. 4. Tracking toroid, variable-angle internal reflection attachment with hemicylinder. (a) Optical layout. (b) Photograph of Perkin-Elmer unit. (c) Photograph of Research and Industrial Instruments Co. unit.

(c)

c. Tracking Toroid Attachment

The optical layout and photograph of a variable-angle, single-reflection attachment for internal reflection spectroscopy marketed by Perkin-Elmer is shown in Figs. 4a and 4b, respectively. Similar attachments were developed by CIC (acquired by Barnes Engineering) and RIIC (acquired by Beckman). A photograph of the latter unit (TR-5) is shown in Fig. 4c. One advantage of this unit is that the number of reflecting surfaces is kept to a minimum. The internal reflection element used in this attachment may be a prism or hemicylinder. The angle of incidence can be changed over a fairly wide range (e.g., from 25° to 65°) with no serious defocusing. Light from the source optics is deflected by toroid $M1$ in Fig. 4a and strikes mirror $M2$ and is focused at a specified distance from the hemicylinder to achieve collimated light within the hemicylinder. The emerging rays are collected by a tracking toroid M3 and after reflection from tracking mirror *M*4 are brought to a focus at the same place as the focus for the original beam in absence of the attachment. The angle of incidence of the light at the IRE–sample interface is varied by rotating the hemicylinder. The necessary rotation and translation of *M*3 and *M*4, respectively, are achieved by suitable coupling of the optical components. Designs similar to this have been employed, by some of the previously mentioned firms, with microhemicylinders for microsampling. Obviously, the fixed- or variable-angle, double-pass multiple internal reflection element can be inserted in place of the hemicylinder of a device such as shown in Fig. 4a. This design has also been modified for single-pass plates employing a few (e.g., three) reflections. In this case, the range of angles of incidence was severely curtailed.

d. Single Retro-Prism Attachment

Figures 5a and 5b show the optical layout and Fig. 5c shows the photograph of an attachment marketed by Beckman. They employ a 90° prism (retro-prism) and the sample makes contact with one of the reflecting surfaces, as shown in Fig. 5a. The retro-prism has an advantage analogous to that of the parallel mirrors since the reflected ray remains precisely antiparallel to the incoming ray as the prism is rotated, as shown in Fig. 6. This simplifies optical tracking as the angle of incidence is changed. Collimated light is employed in the Beckman attachment and the prism can be rotated over a range of angles from 15° to 80°. The range in the angles of incidence on the reflecting surface will, of course, be much less because of the refraction of the light as it enters the prism. This refraction also results in a change in optical path length and a displacement of the return beam. The displacement is eliminated by a translation of the prism.

e. Double-Prism Variable-Angle Attachments

Hansen (H10) has described a versatile variable-angle, "double-prism" attachment for internal reflection spectroscopy which also takes advantage of the retro-action of a 90° prism; i.e., the reflected beam is anti-parallel to the incoming beam, and thus simplifies the optical tracking required for a variable-angle internal reflection element. He suggests placing this optical assembly directly in the sampling space of a spectrometer where, if the beam is sufficiently well collimated, defocusing of the source image at the entrance slit of the spectrometer due to the increased path length is not serious. As pointed

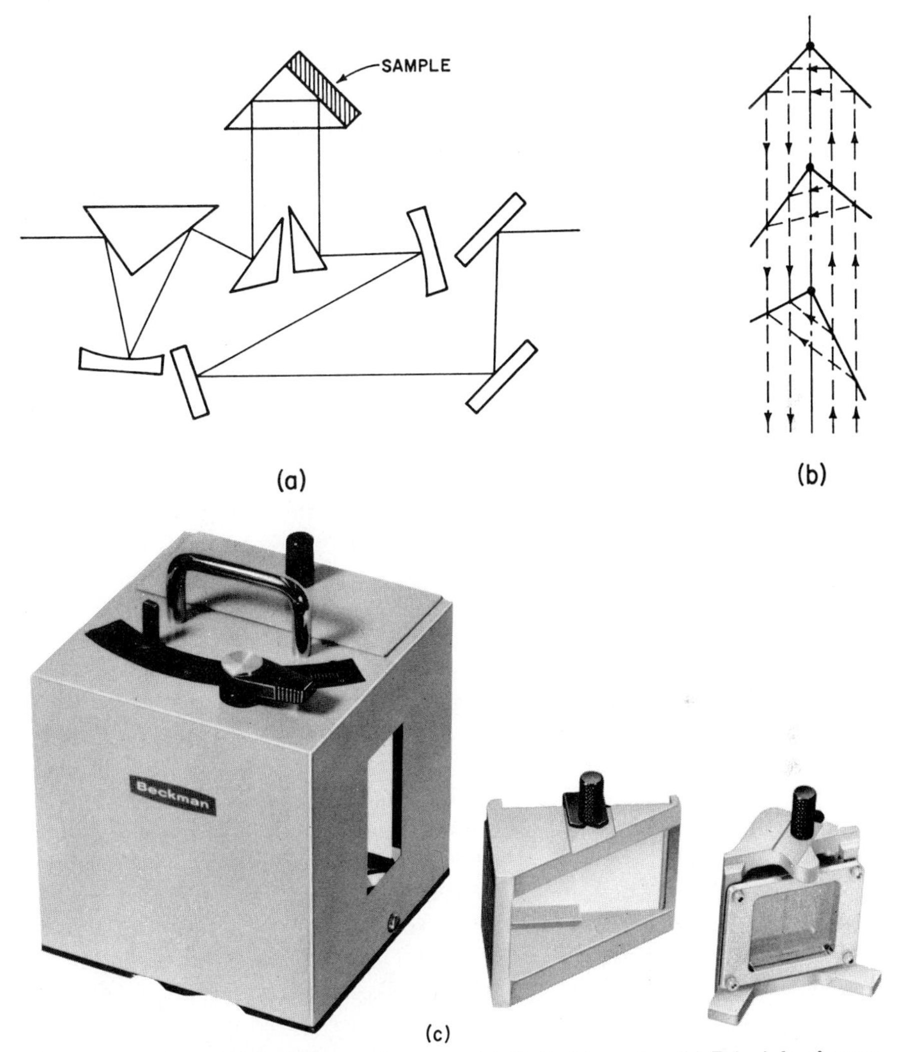

Fig. 5. Beckman VAR-ATR attachment. (a) Optical layout. (b) Principle of operation of retro-mirrors (prism). (c) Photograph of attachment (left), mirrors for external reflection (center), and prism for internal reflection (right).

out by Hansen, the entire assembly can be moved parallel or normal to the light beam without displacing, or further defocusing, the light beam at the spectrometer slit. This device is designed for a single reflection since the light beam is not focused at the reflecting surface of the IRE. The angle of incidence is changed by rotating prism $X\,O\,X'$ of Fig. 6a. It will be noted that this rotation also displaces the light beam at the monochromator slits. This displacement is eliminated by translating XOX' horizontally relative to prism $A\,C\,A'$, as shown in Fig. 6b. In this assembly the light is of course refracted at surface AA' for nonnormal incidence. It is interesting to note that the twin parallel mirror system shown in Fig. 3 can also be analyzed as a rotation of two 90° prisms and a translation of one of the prisms.

There are variations of this double prism assembly which have advantages in certain applications. To change the angle of incidence, it can be shown that by rotating prism $A\,C\,A'$ of Fig. 6 about the vertex C, instead of rotating the silvered prism $X\,O\,X'$ about O, there is *no* change in the distance d; hence there is no displacement of the light beam at the entrance slits of the spectrometer (H31). Furthermore, for wide ranges of angles of incidence (e.g., 15°–75°), there is only a very small change in optical path length; thus, any defocusing of the source image at the entrance slit is negligible. No motion of prism $X\,O\,X'$ relative to prism $A\,C\,A'$ is required; therefore measurements at other angles of incidence can be made with the rotation of a single component. By employing the necessary transfer optics and focusing the beam near the surface of the arm AC, this assembly can be used for variable-angle, either single or multiple, internal reflection elements, as shown in Fig. 7a, with no refraction at the entrance and exit surfaces. The prism $A\,C\,A'$ is replaced by a variable-angle internal reflection element, along the surface AC, and a plane mirror, along the surface CA', which is normal to AC. When the angle of incidence is changed by rotating $A\,C\,A'$ about the vertex C, the light beam will intercept the arm AC at a different location and would thus miss the entrance aperture of a multiple reflection element, fixed on the arm AC. This displacement can be compensated for in one of two ways. The reflection element can either be mechanically constrained to move in a vertical path in the figure, in line with the light beam as the assembly $A\,C\,A'$ is rotated; or, if the reflection element is rigidly fixed on the arm AC, the entire assembly can be moved vertically until the light again strikes the entrance aperture. Any defocusing of the light beam near the entrance aperture of the reflection element in either of these two cases can be corrected by moving the entire assembly to the left or right in the figure. Thus, in the case that the element is fixed on the arm AC, the only adjustments required after the desired angle of incidence is selected are two translations, each not more than $\frac{1}{4}''$, for the design shown in Fig. 7a. These translations could, of course, be coupled to the rotation. As pointed out earlier, these motions neither displace nor defocus the light beam at the entrance slit of the spectrometer. A photograph of this attachment is shown in Fig. 7b.

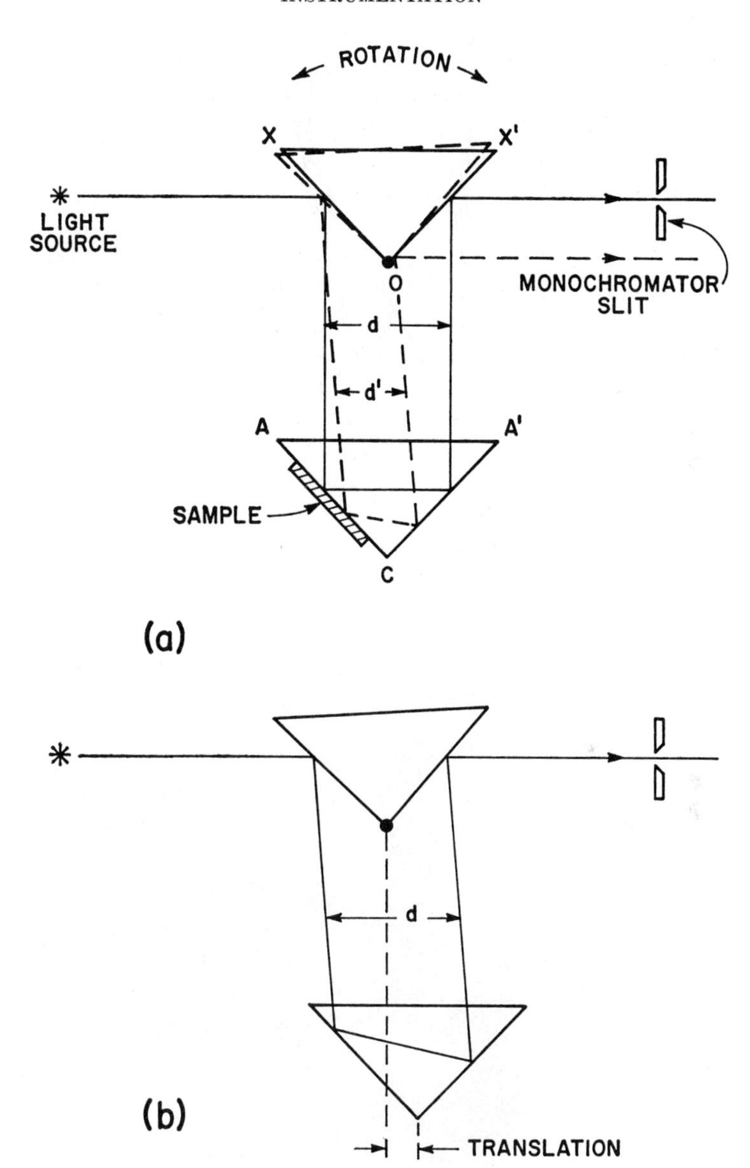

Fig. 6. Double-prism variable-angle attachment developed by Hansen (H10). (a) Rotation of prism $X\ O\ X'$ about O changes angle of incidence but also displaces beam at entrance slit. (b) Translation of $X\ O\ X'$ relative to $A\ C\ A'$ eliminates displacement.

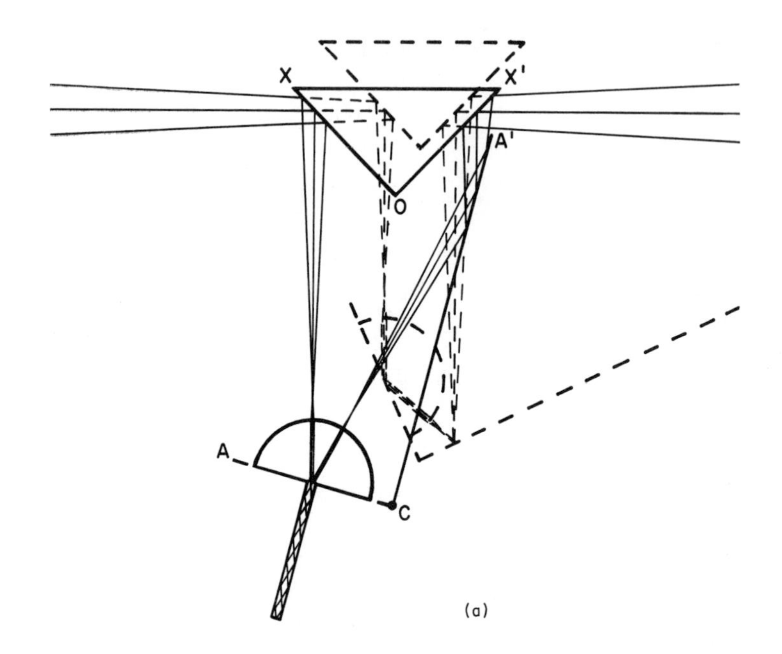

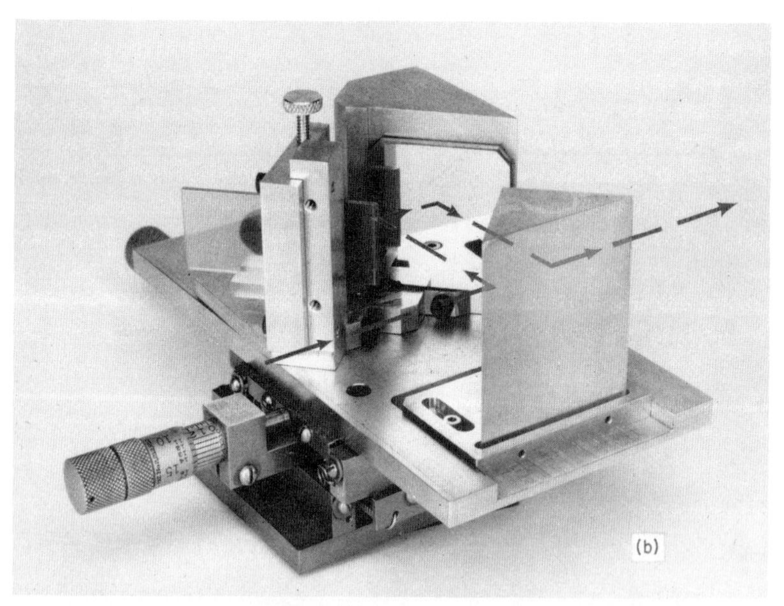

Fig. 7. Modified double-prism assembly employing single or multiple internal reflection element (H31). (a) Rotation of $A\ C\ A'$ about C does not displace beam at entrance slit. Translation of entire assembly is required to relocate focus of beam relative to IRE. (b) Photograph of double-prism assembly.

2. Fixed-Angle, Multiple Internal Reflection Attachments

In a number of cases especially where multiple reflections are employed, fixed-angle attachments for the sampling space of a spectrometer have been developed. In most instances the mirrors were preset and fixed except for possible rotation of one or two mirrors to optimize the energy transmitted through the IRE. Obviously, many different optical layouts might be employed. The practical realization of a few which have previously been discussed elsewhere will be described here.

a. Trapezoid Plates in Double-Beam Layout

Flournoy and coworkers (F10) of E. I. du Pont de Nemours & Co., Wilmington, Delaware have developed and employed the layout shown in Fig. 8. The light path is initially folded using mirrors and retro-mirrors and brought to a focus at one end of a fixed-angle (45°) multiple (19 reflections) reflection Ge plate in the form of a trapezoid. The exit beam is refocused and directed to the entrance slit of the monochromator. For their work utilizing polarized light they placed a Brewster angle Ge reflection polarizer just before the

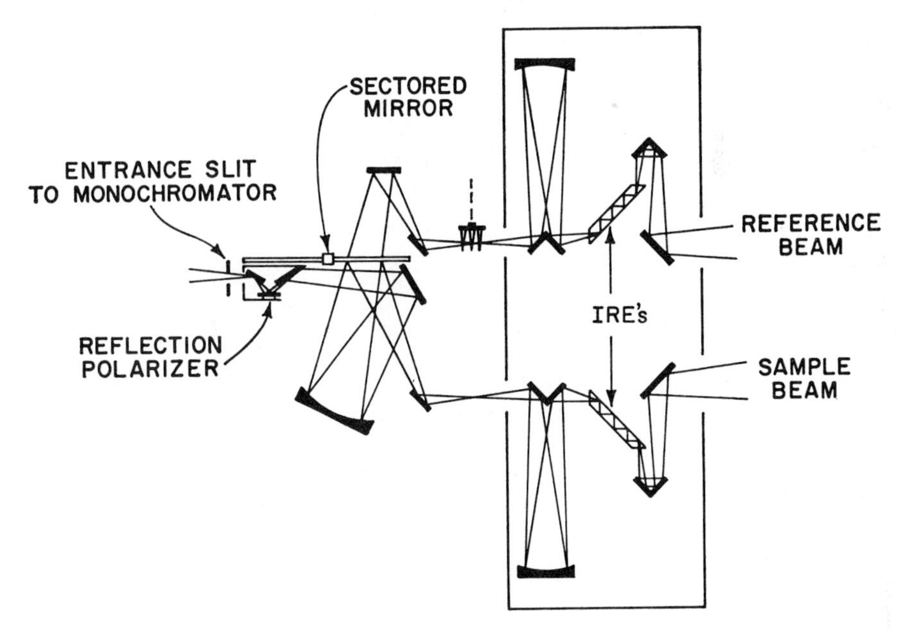

Fig. 8. Fixed-angle internal reflection attachment employing 19 reflection Ge trapezoid plates, $\theta = 45°$ for a double-beam instrument (F10).

entrance slit of the monochromator as shown. A sample was usually placed on both sides of the IRE.

b. Parallelepiped Plates in Double-Beam Layout

Sharpe (S17) of Bell Telephone Laboratories, Murray Hill, New Jersey has converted his double-beam spectrometer for internal reflection work in the manner shown in Fig. 9. Initially he employed 8-reflection Ge plates in the form of parallelograms at $\theta = 45°$. He later modified the system to accept internal reflection plates with 30 reflections.

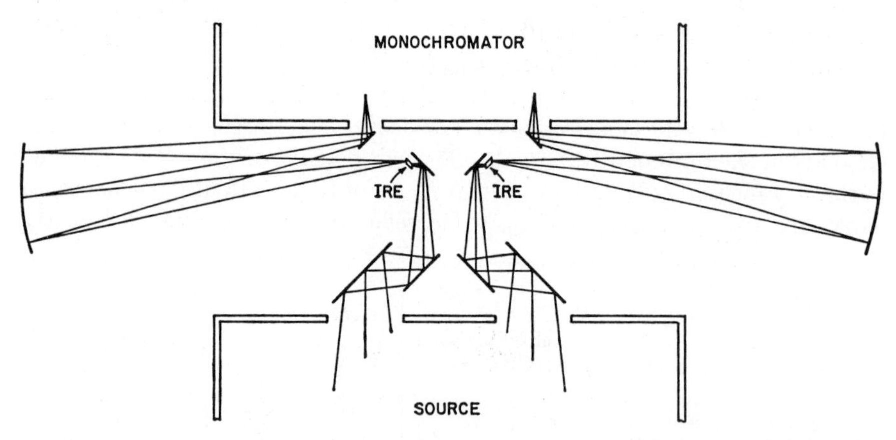

Fig. 9. Fixed-angle internal reflection attachment employing 8-reflection Ge parallelogram plates, $\theta = 45°$ for a double-beam instrument. (Courtesy of L. H. Sharpe, Bell Telephone Laboratories, Murray Hill, New Jersey.)

c. Commercial Attachments for Trapezoid Plates

Barnes Engineering, Perkin-Elmer, and Wilks Scientific supply fixed-angle multiple internal reflection attachments which may be placed in the sampling space of commercial spectrometers. The optical layout and photographs of a unit (ATR-4) marketed by Barnes Engineering is shown in Figs. 10a and 10b, respectively. The optical layout and photograph of another attachment (Model 9), marketed by Wilks Scientific, is shown in Figs. 11a and 11b, respectively. The photograph (Fig. 11b) shows how it is mounted in the sampling space of a commercial spectrometer with a fiber sample pressed against the IRE. The Perkin-Elmer attachment is similar to the one marketed by Wilks Scientific.

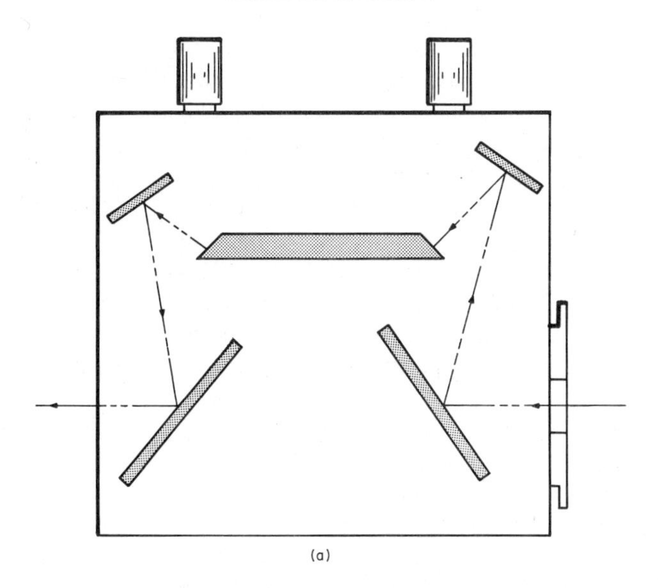

(a)

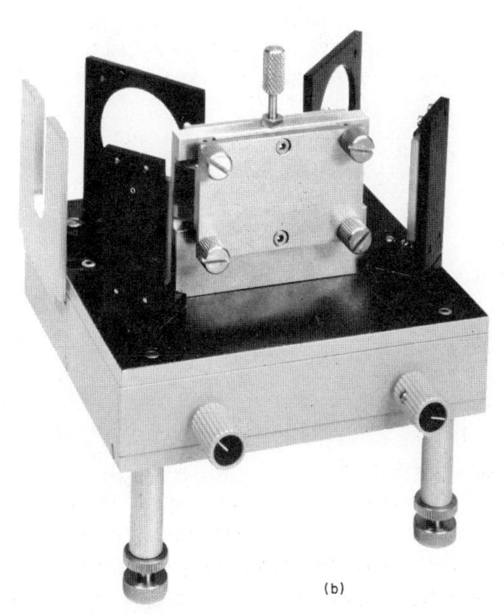

(b)

Fig. 10. Fixed-angle multiple reflection attachment (ATR-4) marketed by Barnes Engineering. The knobs control the movement of the two small mirrors. (a) Optical layout. (b) Photograph.

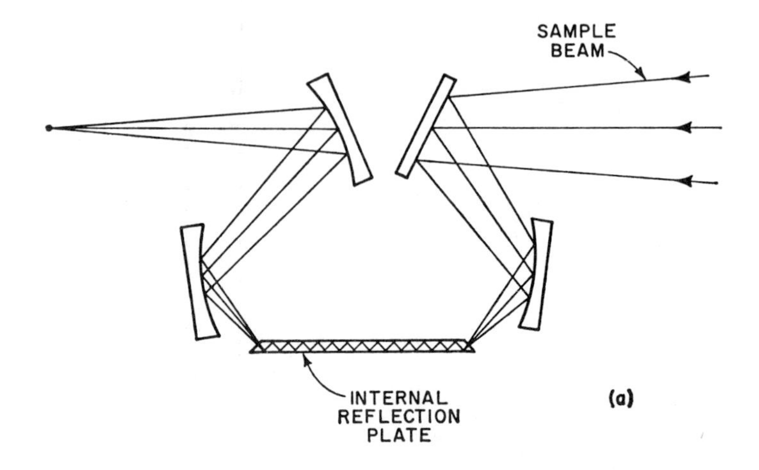

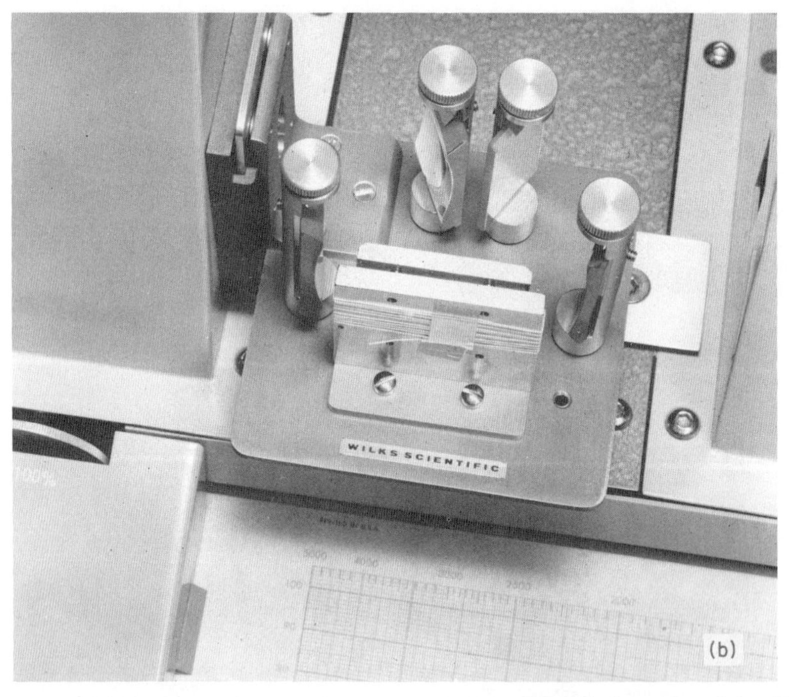

Fig. 11. Fixed-angle multiple reflection attachment (Model 8) marketed by Wilks Scientific Corp. (a) Optical layout. (b) Photograph showing unit mounted in spectrometer with fiber sample prepared for analysis.

D. Rearrangement of Source Optics

The methods discussed above for converting existing spectrometers into internal reflection units result in instrumentation that is satisfactory for certain applications. However, these internal reflection spectrometers are not completely satisfactory because they suffer from severe space limitations. By relocating the source optics it is possible to develop much more versatile equipment. Good designs of rearranged systems have the following advantages: (*1*) unlimited sample space; (*2*) readily accessible internal reflection element surface; (*3*) possibility of varying angle of incidence over wide ranges (e.g., 15–75°); (*4*) space for other components such as polarizers, ovens, vacuum systems, etc.; and (*5*) can still be used for conventional transmission or reflection measurements. A number of systems that have been used will be described.

1. Rotating Sectored Mirror Systems Employing Double-Pass Plates

Figure 12a shows one layout that meets some of these requirements and also converts a monochromator into a double-beam instrument. The transfer optics of the spectrometer utilizes two rotating, coupled, sectored mirrors (M_1 and M_2) which are operated 180° out of phase with each other (H33). The first rotating sectored mirror (M_1) acts as a beam splitter and the optical layout permits the beam to be alternately directed and focused onto the entrance windows of the sample and reference internal reflection plates. The exit beams from these two double-pass multiple reflection plates are subsequently recombined by the second rotating sectored mirror (M_2). The recombined beam is then focused onto the entrance slit of the monochromator. The power in each of the two beams (sample and reference) is initially equalized, via optical attenuators, so that a zero signal is obtained when no absorption occurs at the sample reflection plate. High sensitivity can be achieved utilizing phase-sensitive detection techniques or narrow band amplifiers. A "vertical" double-pass plate can be inserted directly in place of the "horizontal" plate without the need for additional optical components. This would permit the plate to be dipped into the liquid or powder being investigated. Single-pass plates of fixed lengths can be employed if located as shown in Fig. 12a.

A simplified version utilizing a single rotating sectored mirror (H33) as both beam splitter and recombiner is shown in Fig. 12b. This sectored mirror is silvered on both sides, and the relative beam displacement caused by the mirror thickness is compensated for by displacing the reference plate

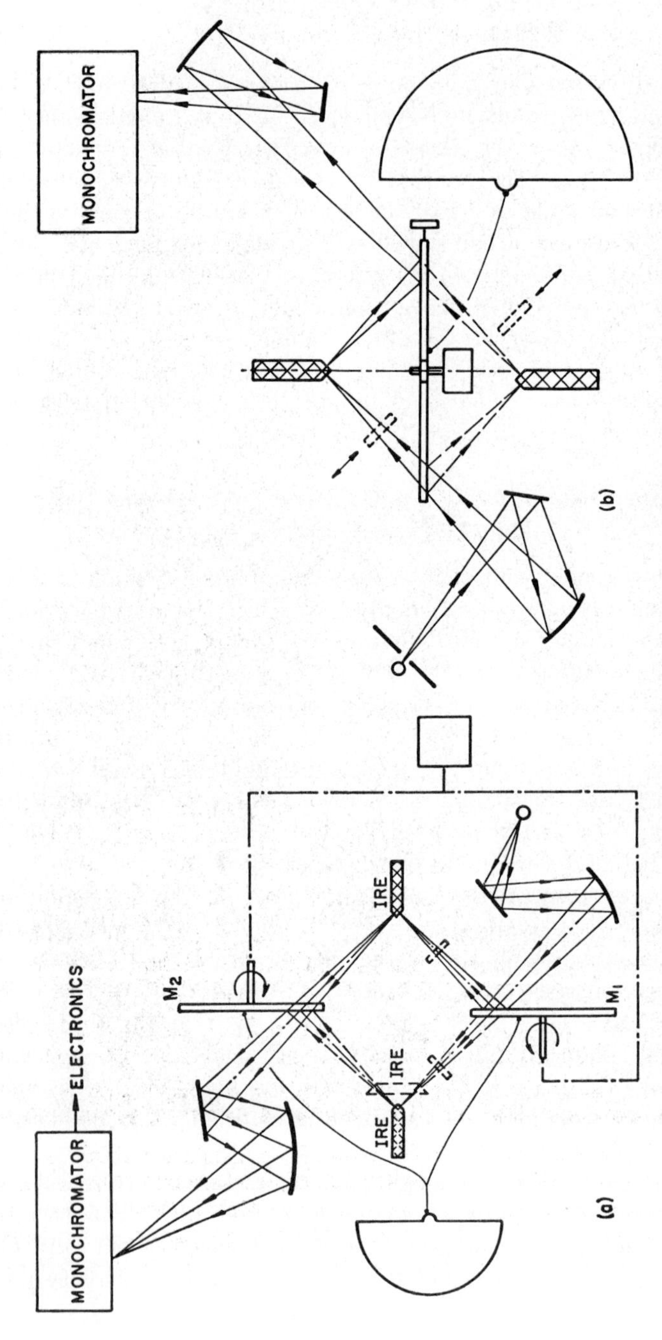

Fig. 12. Schematic diagram of balanced double-beam system employing double-pass plates and rotating sectored mirrors for 180° chopping. Single-pass plates may also be employed as shown. (a) Two synchronized, rotating, sectored mirrors. (b) One rotating, sectored, two-sided mirror (H33).

with respect to the sample plate as shown. In either of these rotating sectored mirror systems the angle of incidence can be changed by moving the IRE's further apart or nearer together and rotating other optical components to redirect the light beam to the IRE's and the monochromator slit.

2. Variable-Angle Internal Reflection Spectrometer with Variable Chopping Phase

One disadvantage of the system described above and other monochromators employing sectored mirrors is that they are limited to 180° out-of-phase chopping. It has been shown that certain advantages can be gained by employing 90° out-of-phase chopping (G11). This is achieved by mounting the two chopping paddles on a common shaft but staggered 45° with respect to each other as shown in Fig. 13. In the electronic system the amplitude variations are converted to variations in phase. The final output represents the ratio of the power in the sample beam to that in the reference beam. This is accomplished without slit drives and optical nulls for a power level range in excess of ten to one and thus the overall instrumentation is considerably simplified, an obvious advantage. It does, however, put more severe requirements on phase stability of the chopping system and on the optical alignment. The optical layout of a double-beam internal reflection spectrometer employing such a phase null photometric system is shown in Fig. 13. The phase null photometric system was built by Instruments and Communications, Inc., Wilton, Connecticut. The variation in angle of incidence over a range of 15° to 65° is achieved by employing the "double-prism" arrangement shown in Figs. 7a and 7b. This double-prism attachment is mounted on a two-stage micromanipulator which provides the motions necessary for optical alignment of the IRE. The beam recombiner employed here is a germanium mirror. This beam recombiner has advantages over many other systems because it is passive, it samples the entire source for both the reference and sample beams and it transmits and reflects about equal quantities of energy (precisely, for $n = 4$ and $\alpha = 0$, it transmits about 47% and reflects about 53% as may be determined from equations 28 and 24 of Chapter Four). This system is not limited to 90° out-of-phase chopping. The advantages of other chopping phases have been discussed by Golay (G11).

3. Variable-Angle Spectrometer for Single- or Double-Pass IRE's

A commercial variable-angle, internal reflection spectrometer (Model 18) developed by Wilks Scientific is shown in Fig. 14. The optical system is

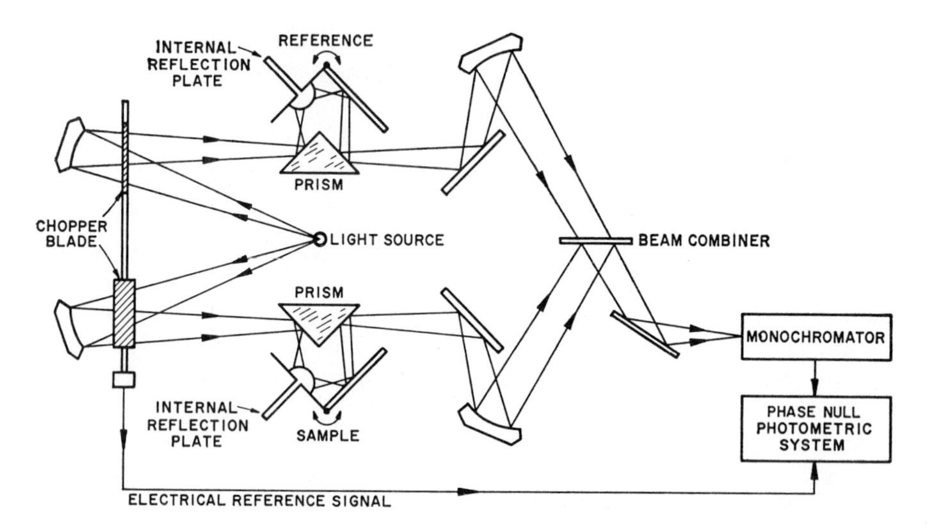

Fig. 13. Optical layout of internal reflection spectrometer employing double-prism variable-angle attachments shown in Fig. 7 and 90° out-of-phase chopping.

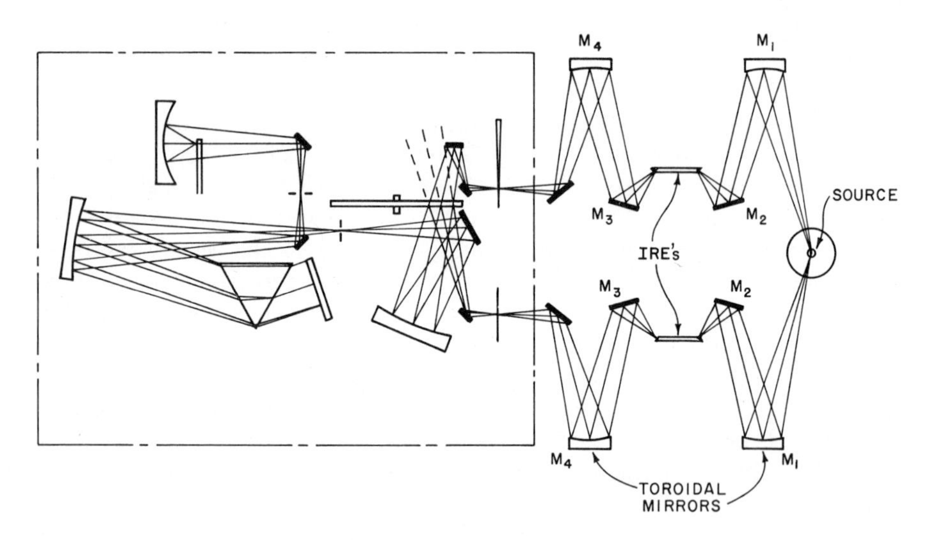

Fig. 14. Wilks Scientific Model 18 variable-angle internal reflection spectrometer for single-pass or double-pass plates.

designed to permit variation of both the angle of incidence and the IRE length. The source and mirrors M_1 and M_2 are mounted on a movable platform. M_2 and M_3 can be rotated independently. The position of the IRE is coupled to the rotation of M_3. This combination of motions permits the use of single- or double-pass plates of any length and angles of incidence ranging from 25° to 75°.

4. Single-Beam, Variable-Angle Instrument for Hemicylinder or Double-Pass IRE

For the determination of optical constants the setting and the reproducibility of the angles is important. An instrument has been designed and built (G8) where the setting of the angles is reproducible to within about 0.5′ of arc and a calibration with an accuracy of about 5′ of arc was achieved. The angle of incidence can be varied from 11° to 75°. In this system, by providing the necessary pivots and coupling gears, the change in angle of incidence was accomplished by rotating the hemicylinder and a coupled rotation at twice the rate of the entire source optics. Details of this system can be found in a paper by Gilby, Burr, and Crawford (G8).

E. Extraction of Monochromatic Beam

The most versatile instrument, so far as working space and range in angles of incidence that can be employed are concerned, is obtained by extracting the monochromator beam, directing it to the IRE and then to the detector, which may be located inside or outside of the monochromator housing. Various arrangements might be employed for double-beam operation. One double-beam system that has been used (H28) both with single-pass and double-pass IRE's is shown in Fig. 15. The double-pass plates make alignment very simple, since the entrance and exit beams have a common focal point especially when the detector for the sample beam is mounted on a goniometer with the pivot point directly below the focal point of the IRE. Collecting the reflected component from the entrance window of the IRE as the reference beam insures that both detectors see the same portion of the infrared source. However, effects of dispersion in the refractive index of the IRE contribute to a sloping base line. For balancing, the detector signals can be equalized by using external beam attenuators or they can be equalized electrically. The use of the reflected beam to generate the reference signal, as shown in Fig. 15, requires that that beam strike the IRE at non-normal incidence. Furthermore, some radiation which has sampled the surface and

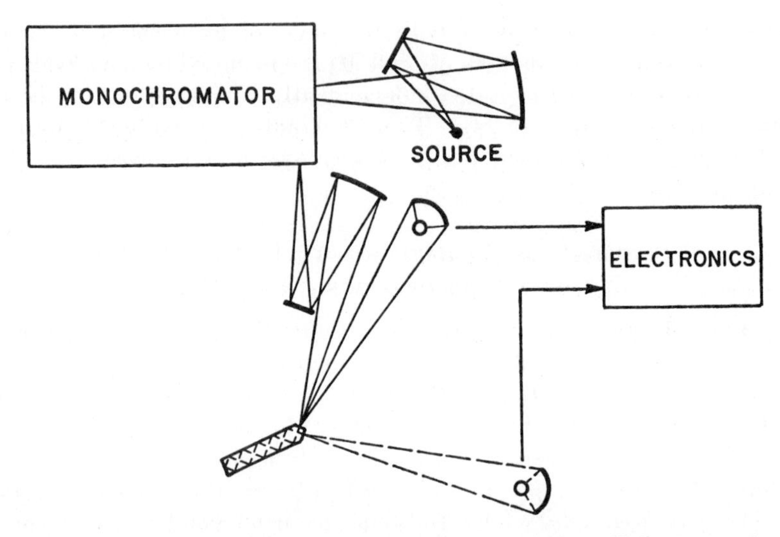

Fig. 15. Optical layout of internal reflection spectrometer utilizing external monochromatic beam (H28). The monochromatic beam is extracted from the instrument and directed to the IRE and then to the detector. The reflected component from the IRE entrance aperture is employed as a reference beam.

leaves via the entrance aperture may be collected by the reference thermocouple and cancels some of the sample absorption observed. These objections can be eliminated by placing a beam splitter (Si or Ge plate) in front of the entrance aperture of the IRE.

The type of layout described above where the goniometer assembly can be moved separately on a large table (machinist's magnetic table for example) is very useful for setting up an experiment quickly since there are no limitations on space, angle of incidence, or type of IRE. Because of the versatility it is also useful in testing IRE's. The optical layout employed in the studies of Becker and Gobeli (B10) was similar to this.

F. Modulated Absorption

The ability to modulate the absorption making it possible to use special narrow band and phase sensitive electronic amplifiers is one of the principal reasons responsible for the high sensitivity achieved in many experiments. These include nuclear and paramagnetic resonance experiments where either the magnetic field or the oscillator frequency can be modulated through the absorption band. In semiconductor surface physics the ability to electrically modulate the surface conductivity is responsible for the high degree of sensitivity achieved (M5). It is also the ability to electrically modulate the population in semiconductor surface states that made possible the direct observation of optical transitions involving semiconductor surface states (H23). In the latter case the sensitivity easily achieved was a surface reflectivity change of one part in one million. More recently a sensitivity of the same order of magnitude has enabled workers to measure external reflectivity changes attributed to interband transitions which promise to shed considerable light on band theory (S13,S16).

In general it is not possible to obtain with electric or magnetic fields a sufficient shift in the location of an absorption band to achieve any modulation in absorption. It should be recalled that Stark and Zeeman effects show only slight shifts in very intense fields. Modulation of absorption via Stark or Zeeman effect may, however, now be possible with the use of highly monochromatic laser sources. However, the inability to continuously tune lasers over wide ranges of frequencies is unattractive for spectroscopy. For this reason the light is chopped in the optical instrumentation so that ac techniques can be employed. Chopping the entire radiant energy has the disadvantage that all of the radiation is modulated and not only that portion which is absorbed. Therefore very small absorptions, e.g., less than 1%, cannot easily be studied. It was previously proposed (H26) that a modulated absorption could be achieved by moving the sample material in and out of the region of the evanescent field for total internal reflection. This has already been achieved with the aid of magnetostrictive (A7) and piezoelectric (A18) materials for the purpose of modulating light. Modulation of the absorption can also be realized by constructing a condenser system as shown in Fig. 16a where the sample material is the thin dielectric film. Application of a dc biasing field and an ac field between the semiconducting IRE and the external field plate causes the thin film to become charged and to oscillate in the intervening space if spacers are provided and the film is not too tightly clamped. A spectrum of a Mylar film obtained in this way with a *single-beam* spectrometer is shown in Fig. 17. The band at 5.8 μ represents about 25% absorption. It should be noted that no signal is observed except in the absorbing regions of the sample material. A flat base line is maintained in spite of the strong wavelength dependence of the radiation intensity. The ratio $\Delta R/R$ could easily be obtained by monitoring the dc as well as the ac level at the detector using modern electronic techniques. The relative band intensities will not necessarily closely resemble those obtained in transmission because even if the absorption were constant the modulation would be wavelength dependent—a characteristic of internal reflection spectra. This example demonstrates that optical spectra can be recorded by modulating

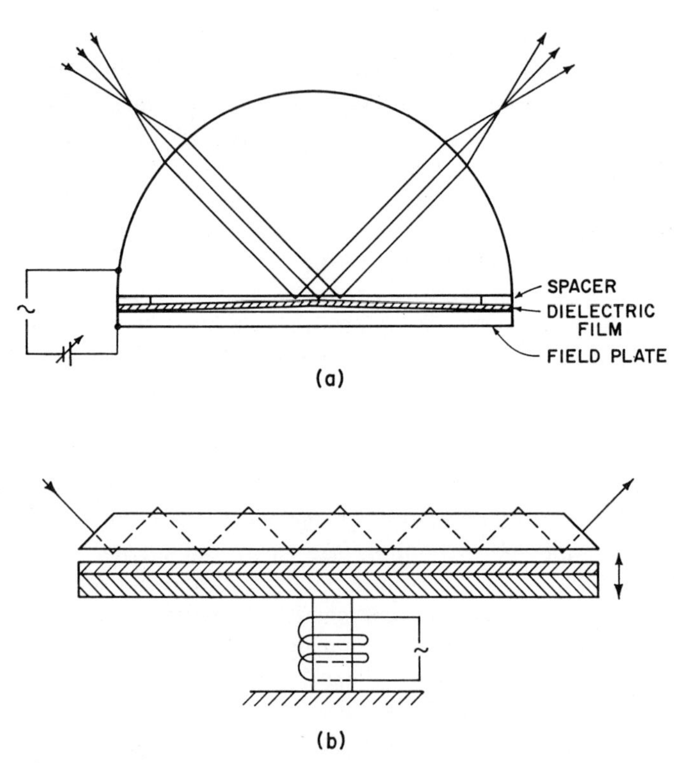

Fig. 16. Condenser arrangement for modulated absorption. (a) Dc bias and ac field causes dielectric film to move in and out of region of evanescent field and thus modulate the absorption. (b) Piezoelectric, magnetostrictive, or ultrasonic device is employed to move absorber and thus modulate the absorption.

the absorption. Other more sophisticated approaches might involve mounting the sample material on a piezoelectric, magnetostrictive, or ultrasonic head which would in turn be brought close to the reflecting surface of the IRE, as is shown in Fig. 16b. This type of modulation permits operation at very high frequencies if fast detectors are employed with the resulting increase in signal-to-noise ratio.

G. Special Instrumentation and Techniques

For certain applications of internal reflection spectroscopy special instrumentation and techniques are required. Some of these are discussed in this section and others in Chapter Seven in the subsection entitled "Miscellaneous Applications." The choice in assigning some of these topics to

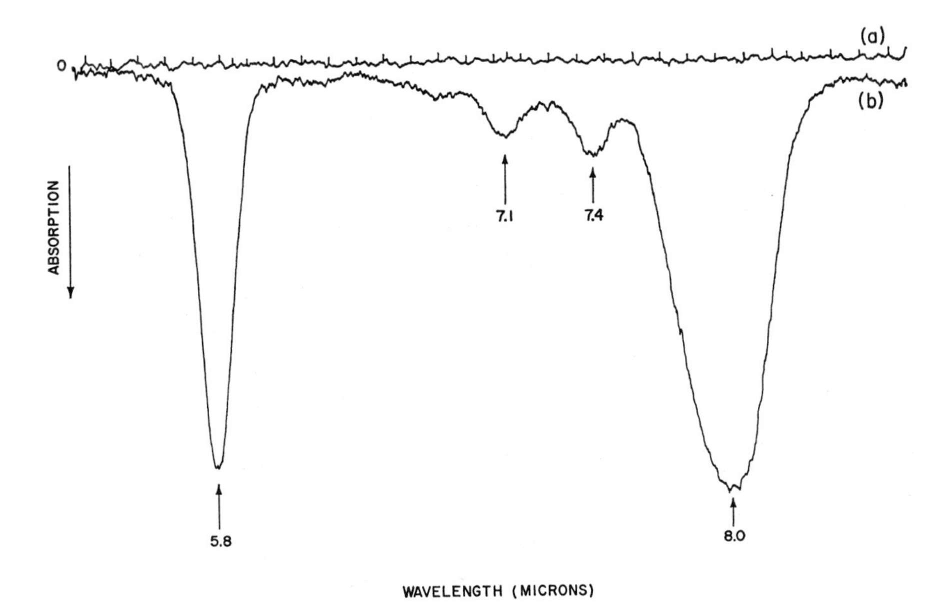

Fig. 17. Spectrum of Mylar obtained via modulated absorption condenser system shown in Fig. 16a using Ge IRE, $N = 1$. (a) Modulating field off. (b) Modulating field on.

this chapter or Chapter Seven was quite arbitrary. Where results are presented, or if the technique is very specialized, the technique is discussed in Chapter Seven.

1. Stack of Internal Reflection Plates

For a fixed angle of incidence and a fixed length of internal reflection plate, the number of reflections can be increased by decreasing the thickness of the plate. This procedure is practical only as long as the aperture of the plate does not become less than the slit width of the monochromator. This limiting aperture is thus one to two millimeters for the infrared. With grating instruments where wide slits are generally required, even larger apertures may be necessary. The number of reflections is therefore restricted. One means of overcoming this restriction, proposed by Wilks (W9), is to employ a stack of thin plates, as shown in Fig. 18. The number of reflections can then be increased by reducing the thickness of the plates and wide apertures can be maintained by stacking the plates. The sample material, films or liquid, is sandwiched between the plates. This method is ideal for liquids which are contained between the plates by capillary action.

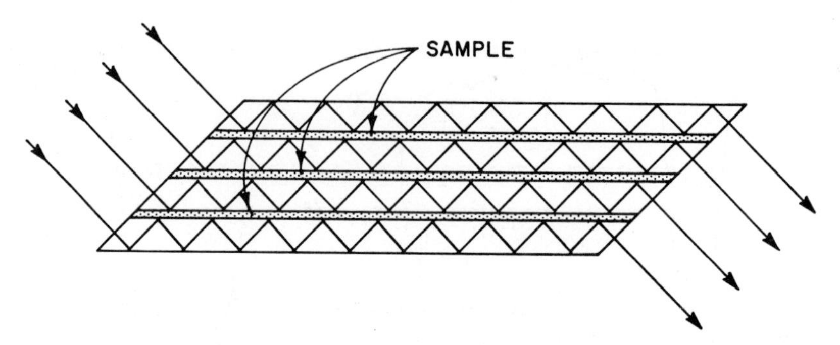

Fig. 18. Stack of internal reflection plates for wide apertures and large number of reflections. Sample (liquid or film) is sandwiched between the plates.

2. Liquid Cells, Variable Area Cells, Flow-Through Cells, and Reaction Vessels

For these applications the double-pass internal reflection plate is ideal because *any* vessel can be employed to contain the liquid and the signal strength for contrast or compensation purposes can be controlled by controlling the depth of immersion of the plate in the liquid in the manner shown in Fig. 8 of Chapter Four.

A liquid cell can be built for any IRE by employing suitable gasket material and adjusting the area of contact for contrast control. A number of these have been described in the literature (F4,H5,M6). Any of these cells can be employed as reaction vessels or flow-through cells by providing the necessary plumbing to conduct the liquid to and from the IRE.

3. Wire Mesh Surface Wetting

When the forces associated with surface tension of a liquid are greater than the attractive forces between the liquid and the surface of the IRE, small quantities of a liquid on the surface of the IRE will form spherical droplets with a small contact area between the liquid and the IRE. Only a small fraction of the material will then be sampled by the evanescent wave and the sensitivity to small quantities will be low. One method of increasing the contact area and hence the sensitivity is to employ closely spaced internal reflection plates when the forces due to capillary action overcome the surface tension forces and the liquid flows into the intervening space. The liquid must be carefully placed at the edge of the plates when capillary plates are employed. Another method which takes advantage of capillary action to increase the contact area and still preserves a large area for sample collection, proposed by Dreyfus (D17), is to place a wire mesh *near* the broad surface of the IRE. Any liquid drop striking this surface will tend to spread over a large area. The mesh should be made from a dielectric or a metal of high conductivity (e.g., Cu) to minimize attenuation losses. For a metal mesh the attenuation loss need not be prohibitive since the effective area of coverage by the metal may be small and furthermore any attenuation loss drops off sharply when there is a space between the wire and the surface of the IRE (Y2). By employing thin wires parallel to the length of the plate there should be no attenuation for $\perp$-polarization due to their presence as will become evident in the discussion of wire grid polarizers (H2, this chapter). Wires parallel to the length should also tend to aid spreading of the liquid along the length of the plate. A suggested means of liquid removal (D17a) is to pass an electrical current through the wires to evaporate the liquid. Wire mesh surface wetting of the IRE is of particular interest in collection and analysis of aerosols where high sensitivity is required.

4. Sample–IRE Contact Control

The contrast of the internal reflection spectrum depends on the nature of the contact between the sample and the IRE. For liquids and pastes good physical or optical contact is readily obtained. For solids, on the other hand, it is necessary to apply some pressure between the sample and the IRE to obtain uniform contact. This is particularly important when attempt is made to obtain spectra of reproducible contrast.

A number of methods have been employed to improve contact or to obtain reproducible contact between the sample and the IRE. It is desirable to distribute the pressure uniformly over the IRE; this is particularly necessary when the IRE is made from a brittle material (e.g., Ge). The distribution of the pressure can be achieved by placing a piece of relatively soft neoprene rubber between a metal pressure plate and the sample. Pressure can then be applied to the pressure plate by a thumb screw.

Internal reflection attachments from Barnes Engineering are supplied with torque wrenches for applying uniform pressures. The torque wrench can be preset to any desired value. The resultant pressure is distributed over an area of about 10 cm^2. The same setting is used for Ge and KRS-5 plates.

A hydraulic pressure cell developed by workers at du Pont (B4) is shown in Fig. 19. The free piston, held within the cell by an O-ring, is operated by varying the oil pressure behind the piston. This pressure is applied after the cell has been assembled by attaching the valve to a small hand pump with an accurate pressure gauge and pumping the oil pressure to any desired value.

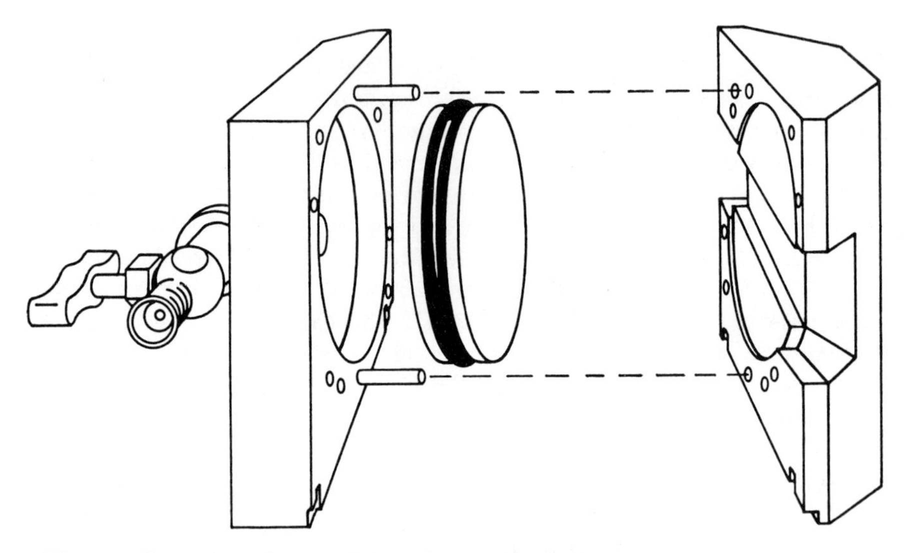

Fig. 19. Hydraulic pressure cell for adjusting pressure between sample and IRE (B4). The internal reflection plate with a sample on both sides is placed in channel on right-hand side and then cell is assembled.

Usually, 100–150 psi is adequate. The assembled cell normally contains the internal reflection element, samples on both sides of the IRE and two thin rubber pads to distribute the pressure between the aluminum body and the IRE.

5. Difference Spectra

Internal reflection spectroscopy offers a convenient way of recording difference spectra. If, for example, the sample material consists of a mixture $A + B$ and the spectrum of A is desired, the spectrum due to B can be cancelled by placing some B-material on the reference IRE. The degree of cancellation at any wavelength can be adjusted by controlling the amount of material, pressure of the material against the IRE and/or angle of incidence on the reference plate. It follows from the discussion in Chapter Two on relative band intensities and profiles that poor contact and band shifts from use of different angles cannot lead to good compensation over a wide range of wavelengths.

Figure 20a shows the spectrum of Millipore filter paper obtained by pressing it against a Ge plate. By pressing another section of paper against the reference internal reflection plate almost exact cancellation of the absorption band is achieved as shown in Fig. 20b.

Difference spectra can be obtained in some cases via transmission techniques

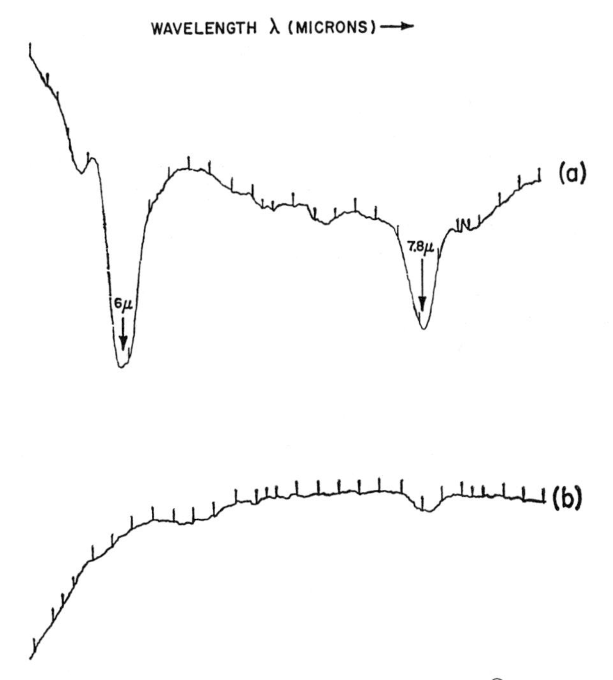

Fig. 20. Difference spectrum. (a) Spectrum of Millipore® filter paper. (b) Restoration of flat base line by pressing similar filter paper against reference plate.

where the length of path in the sample is adjusted to compensate for or cancel the unwanted bands. As pointed out, however, there are more variables which can be used for cancellation via internal reflection techniques. Furthermore, rough and uneven samples, such as filter paper, cannot be studied as easily via transmission techniques. (Transmission measurements can be made directly on very thin "membrane" filter paper and scattering by rough paper can be reduced by soaking it in a suitable liquid such as Nujol.)

Instrument operation can be affected when difference spectra are recorded especially when strong absorbers are involved because of energy limitations and the resultant deterioration of the signal-to-noise ratio.

H. Polarizers

The use of polarized light and the ability to change the state of polarization can considerably enhance the power of internal reflection spectroscopy and is almost essential in quantitative work. There are two principal reasons for this. First, the reflectivity, hence spectral contrast, is dependent on polarization, as discussed in Chapter Two. Since the light in a spectrometer is generally partially polarized, particularly in grating spectrometers, the state of polarization must be known when quantitative measurements are made. The simplest approach is to use completely polarized light. Secondly, also as shown in Chapter Two, since electric fields are found for all three spatial directions at the reflecting surface, by combining measurements made using unpolarized (or partially polarized) light and light polarized perpendicular and parallel to the plane of incidence, the absorption coefficients for all three spatial directions can be determined for a single anisotropic sample without reorienting it. This cannot be done via transmission techniques without reorienting the sample because there can be no absorption parallel to the direction of propagation. These points serve to emphasize the importance of polarizers in internal reflection spectroscopy.

Polarized light and polarizers are treated in detail in the book devoted to this subject by Shurcliff (S21a). This subject will be treated only briefly here with specific mention of the Brewster angle reflection and transmission polarizers as well as the wire grid polarizer.

1. Brewster Angle Polarizers

A high degree of polarization is obtained for reflection or transmission at Brewster's angle, as was discussed in Chapter Two. It is advantageous, however, to employ materials of high refractive index because, as is clearly evident in Fig. 21, for a reflection polarizer the power in the polarized reflected beam is high and for a transmission polarizer the rejection of the unwanted component is high. For transmission polarizers the number of plates can then be reduced and the device simplified. For instance, according to Fig. 21 the degree of polarization for the transmitted energy per surface (not per plate) defined as $(T_\parallel - T_\perp)/(T_\parallel + T_\perp)$ at Brewster's angle for AgCl ($n = 2$) is 22%; for Ge ($n = 4$) it is 64%.

Brewster angle polarizers, because of the large angle of incidence required ($\theta_B = 76°$ for Ge), have the disadvantage that they are long and hence cumbersome. Transmission polarizers have the advantage over reflection polarizers that there is no power loss for the wanted component, but a number of reflections are required to completely reject the unwanted component. Reflection polarizers yield complete polarization at $\theta = \theta_B$ for one reflection, however there is power loss since the reflectivity is considerably less than 100% for the wanted component.

For transmission the internal angle, θ_p, is also a polarizing angle thus there are two polarizing angles per plate. As the light beam passes through the first plate it is laterally displaced, as shown in Fig. 22a, and this displacement results in a precession of the beam as the polarizer is rotated about the axis

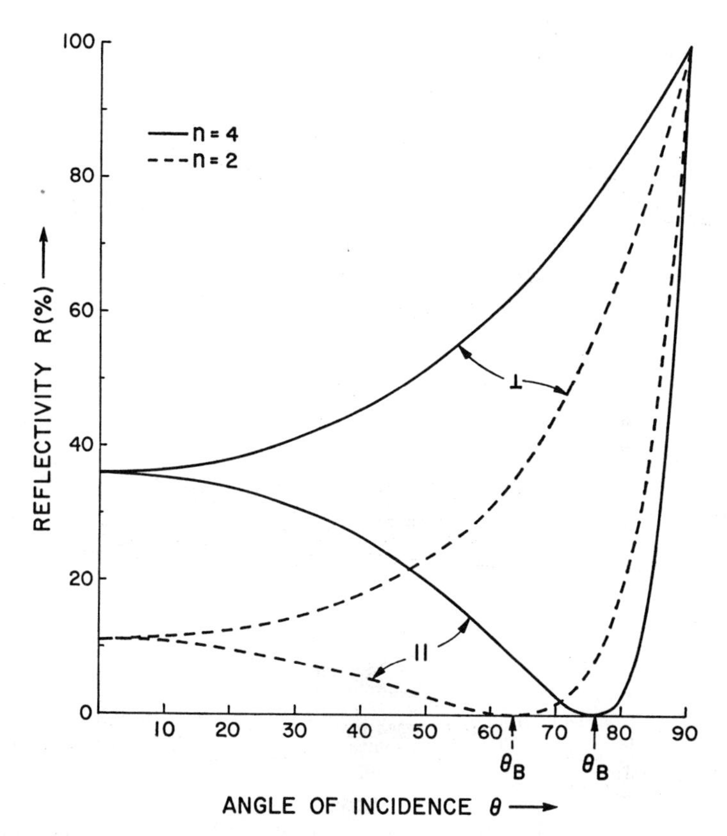

Fig. 21. Comparison of the external reflectivity curves for Ge ($n = 4$)–air (solid lines) and AgCl ($n = 2$)–air (dashed lines) interface (H29). θ_B is Brewster's or polarizing angle, where $R_{\parallel} = 0$. Note that a higher degree of polarization is obtained for the transmitted beam for the medium of higher refractive index.

of the beam to change the state of polarization. For this reason, a second plate is added, as shown in Fig. 22a, to eliminate the displacement and the precession. Such a structure, especially when many plates are employed, results in a cumbersome device with small acceptance angle, θ_A. A device of half the length with a larger acceptance angle can be constructed in the manner shown in Fig. 22b (H29). This "crossed-plate polarizer" is constructed by cutting one of the plates of Fig. 22a in half and lapping angles on the ends of the half-plates so that uniform contact can be made with the other plate. It is of importance to note that for a collimated beam the region of intersection does not interfere with the performance of the polarizer since the beam is refracted away from the center, and none passes through it. One

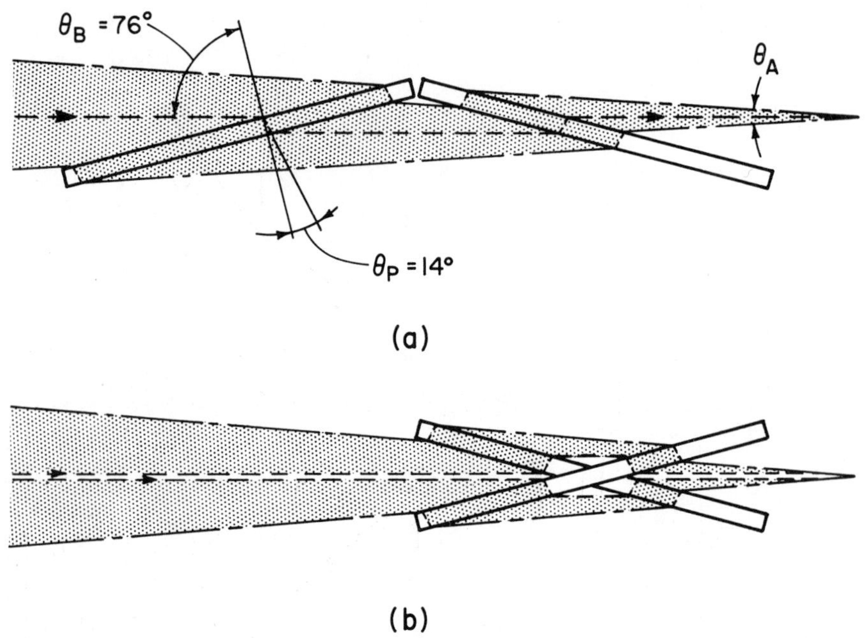

Fig. 22. Brewster's angle transmission polarizers. (a) Conventional symmetrical polarizer. (b) Crossed-plate polarizer (H29)—note that the rays are refracted away from the junction of the plates. The crossed-plate polarizer is one-half the length and has a larger acceptance angle than the conventional symmetrical polarizer.

such polarizer (partially disassembled) employing Ge plates is shown in Fig. 23. The two Ge plates have four polarizing surfaces and, in spite of the reduction caused by scattering, multiple reflections, and lack of collimation, yield a polarization of better than 98%. As is evident from Fig. 21, the transmission level is high for this type of polarizer.

Although complete polarization is obtained at Brewster's angle for the reflected beam, due to lack of collimation not all of the beam strikes the reflecting surface at Brewster's angle and hence polarization is incomplete for a single reflection. For this reason and because it is desirable to have the polarized beam axial with the incoming beam, more than one (minimum of three) reflections are employed. A reflection polarizer using two Ge plates and a mirror was constructed by Flournoy and is shown schematically in Fig. 24. [A similar polarizer was previously discussed employing PbS reflecting layers (G20).] This unit was placed in the monochromator just before the entrance slit, as was shown in Fig. 8. Since it could not be rotated to change the state of polarization, the sample had to be reoriented for this purpose.

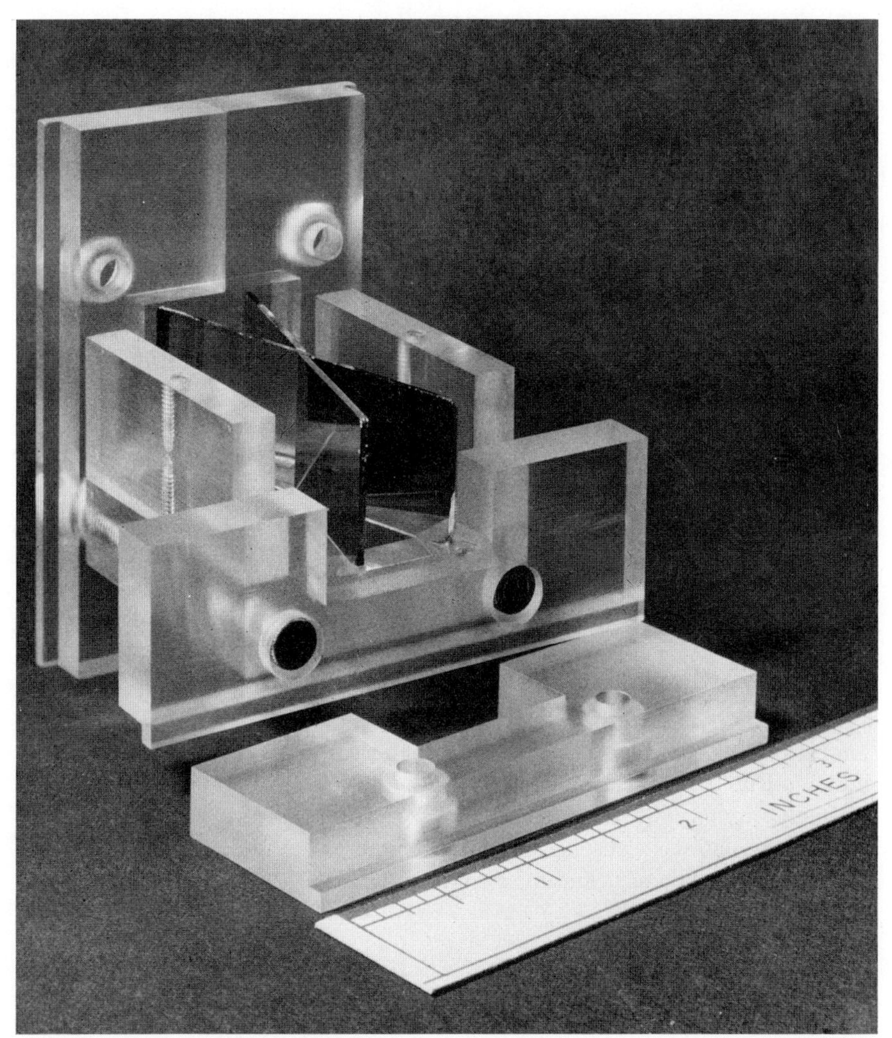

Fig. 23. Photograph of crossed-plate polarizer using Ge plate. State of polarization is changed from || to $\perp$ by turning polarizer end for end and rotating by 90° (H29).

2. Wire Grid Polarizer

Thin film polarizers have the advantages that they take little space in the optical system, do not alter the optical path length upon insertion, and have a large acceptance angle. A thin film wire grid polarizer has recently been developed for the infrared (B23). It consists of a system of closely spaced parallel "wires" (i.e., conductors) which present a high conductivity, therefore high reflectivity for the electric field parallel to the wires and a low con-

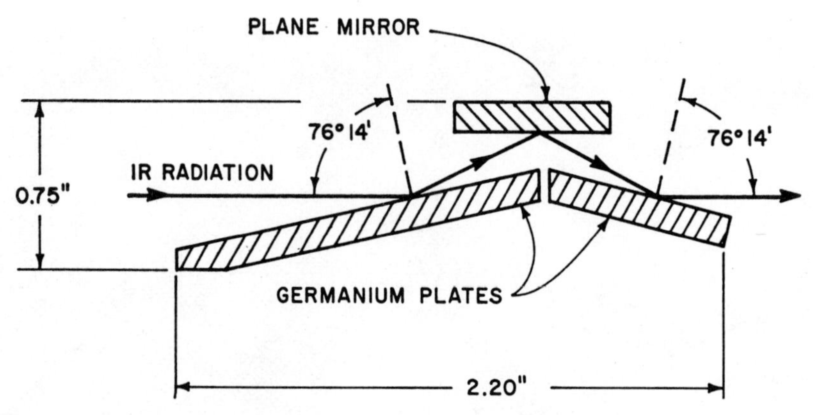

Fig. 24. Germanium reflection polarizer (F10). Although such polarizers produce highly polarized light the power level is lower than that of transmission polarizers (see Fig. 21).

ductivity, therefore high transmission, for the electric field perpendicular to the wires. For the near infrared where the wire spacing must be less than 1 μ, the grid system is prepared by evaporating at oblique incidence a metal (e.g., Au) on a grating replica made of transparent material (e.g., AgCl) as shown in Fig. 25. One such polarizer, marketed by Perkin-Elmer Corp., consists of a Au wire grid on a AgCl (or AgBr) substrate, transmits in excess of 60% in the wavelength range 4–24 μ (4–35 μ for AgBr), and has a polarization ratio ($I_{\parallel}/I_{\perp}$) of about 100 at 4 μ, which rises to more than 500 at 8 μ, as shown in Fig. 26. For the far infrared (20–150 μ), they prepare the wire grid on a polyethylene substrate.

This completes the discussion on instrumentation for internal reflection spectroscopy. The next and final chapter deals with applications of internal reflection spectroscopy.

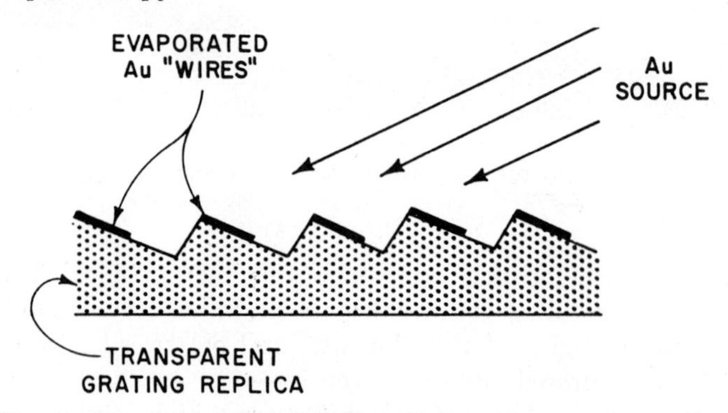

Fig. 25. Evaporation of Au strips on surface of transparent grating replica to prepare wire grid polarizer (G15).

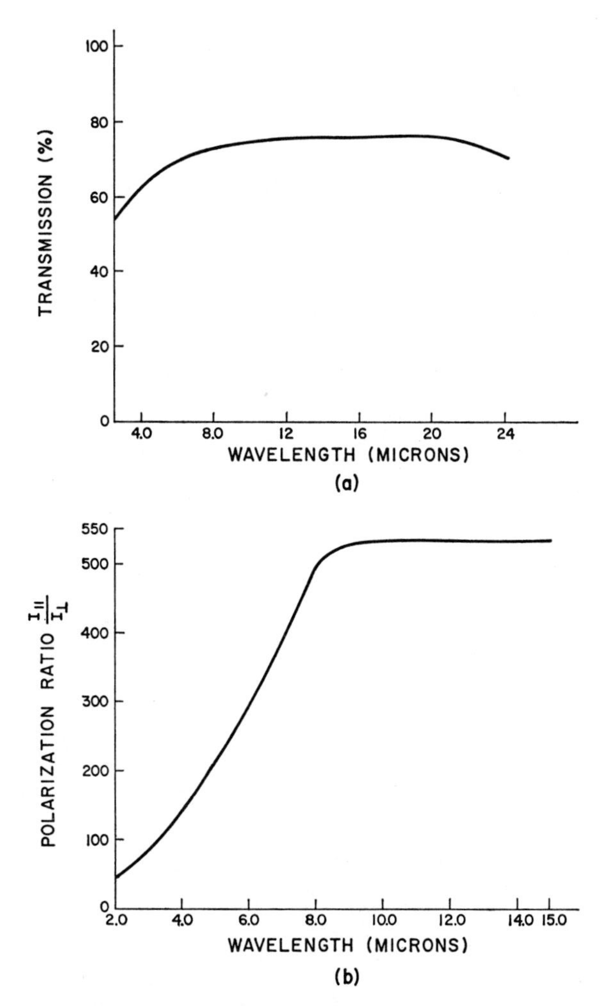

Fig. 26. Performance of Perkin-Elmer wire grid polarizer consisting of Au wire on AgCl substrate. (a) Transmission versus wavelength. (b) Polarization versus wavelength.

CHAPTER SEVEN

APPLICATIONS OF INTERNAL REFLECTION SPECTROSCOPY

A. Introduction

Internal reflection spectroscopy has established itself as a useful analytical tool. It has made possible the application of optical spectroscopy in some areas where it was not previously possible and, in other cases, it has simplified the application of optical spectroscopy techniques. Internal reflection should, however, be considered a supplement to existing techniques and not as a cure-all. Its advantages and disadvantages should be appreciated. It should not be employed in those cases in which conventional techniques work very satisfactorily. Libraries of characteristic transmission spectra are available which facilitate identification via direct comparison with spectra obtained via standard techniques. Libraries of characteristic internal reflection spectra are small at present but are growing. Internal reflection spectra may be compared to transmission spectra with caution, although many similarities exist. Some differences have already been noted. For bulk materials the relative band intensities are different—the ones at the longer wavelengths appear more intense because of the direct proportionality of effective thickness to wavelength and this contrast difference may be even greater if the contact between the sample and IRE is not good, as discussed in Chapter Two. Furthermore, the bands may be displaced towards longer wavelengths. The parameter which adds considerable power to the technique, viz., the angle of incidence, should be adjusted cautiously, since the absorption bands become more displaced to longer wavelengths and more broadened on the long wavelength side as the angle of incidence is decreased towards the critical angle. For thin films, on the other hand, internal reflection spectra resemble transmission spectra rather closely, although the bands may be displaced very slightly toward shorter wavelengths as discussed in Chapters Two and Three. All of these phenomena can be understood from rather simple considerations of the interaction mechanisms discussed in previous chapters. It is therefore recommended that these mechanisms be studied and understood and applied to the interpretation of internal reflection spectra.

Internal reflection spectroscopy offers the following advantages over conventional transmission spectroscopy.

1. No Bothersome Interference Fringes

For propagating waves (transmission measurements), interference fringes arise from the constructive and destructive interference of the multiply reflected components with the first transmitted component or, equivalently, with the first (front surface) reflected component. Fringes resulting from such interaction are shown in Fig. 1 for transmission through Mylar films of several thicknesses. The fringe spacings are related to and can be used to determine the thickness of the film. Fringes of this sort are often present in transmission measurements on thin films and liquid cells and they tend to obviate weak bands and contribute to errors in the location of bands and in intensity measurements. These problems do not arise in internal reflection spectroscopy

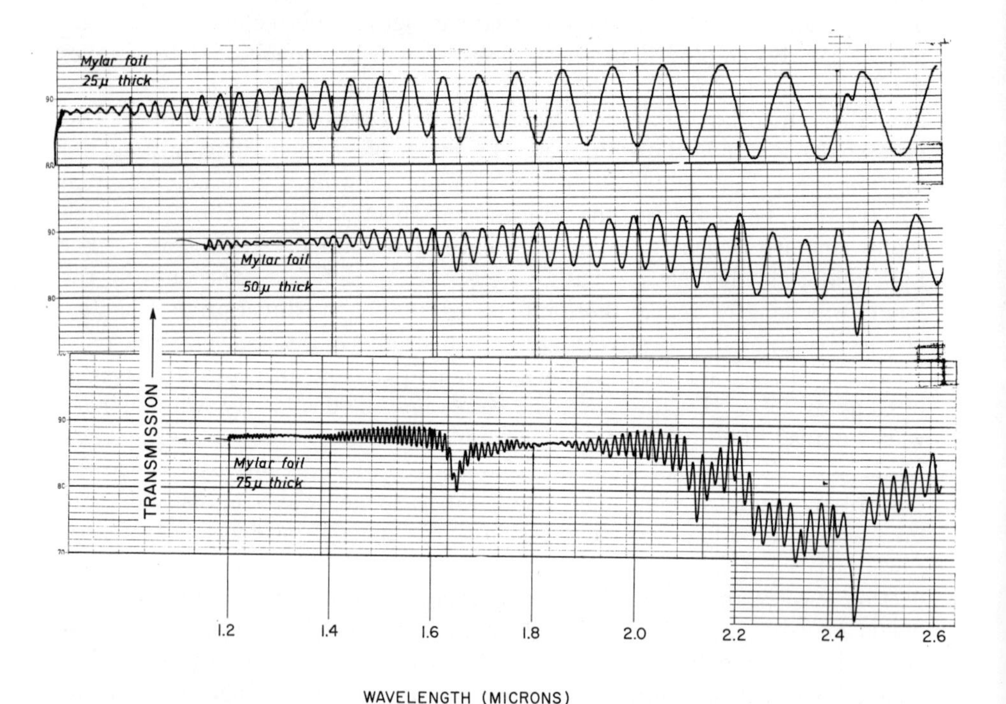

Fig. 1. Fringes resulting from constructive and destructive interference in transmission through Mylar foil of various thicknesses. Note how the fringes tend to obscure the presence of weak bands.

because such interference fringes do not occur even for measurements on thin films. As was discussed in Chapter Two, the fringes are absent because the interaction with the absorbing medium occurs via a nonpropagating wave and there is only a single-reflected component rather than many reflected components to contend with. A comparison of the spectrum of polypropylene film obtained via transmission (Fig. 2a with fringes) and via internal reflection (Fig. 2b without fringes) is shown in Fig. 2. In Fig. 2a it would be difficult to be certain whether the "bands" in the 3.5–6.5 μ region were true absorption bands or interference fringes. The advantage of internal reflection spectra, because of the absence of these fringes, is clearly evident. It should be noted that the location of the bands in Figs. 2a and 2b is about the same for the two spectra; however, the bands at the longer wavelengths in the internal reflection spectrum have a higher contrast, as was discussed in Chapter Two.

2. Ease of Sample Preparation

In conventional spectroscopy sample preparation is an important factor. Except where samples can be used directly (such as liquids in capillary cells), most sampling techniques (such as preparation of mulls, pellets, etc.) are complex and can be considered an art. For internal reflection spectroscopy, on the other hand, the only preparation necessary is that of bringing the material of interest—be it a liquid, an irregular solid, or a powder—to within a penetration depth of the reflecting surface. The material may thus be examined in its natural state, requiring no additional preparation. These statements oversimplify the actual situation somewhat since it is not always easy to obtain adequate contact. As was discussed in Chapter Two, Section D entitled "Coupling to the Evanescent Wave," intimate contact between the sample and the IRE is not required to attenuate the reflection. For quantitative measurements it is preferable to bring the sample and the IRE into good contact. However, the contact need not be optical (i.e., the sample need not wet the surface of the IRE); physical contact is adequate. Quantitative measurements can also be made if there is an intervening layer (e.g., oxide on the sample or on the IRE) between the sample and the IRE; however, it is then necessary to know the thickness and the properties of the layer in order to calculate the coupling to the evanescent wave. The calculations, of course, become more complicated. Adequate contact can be achieved readily for liquids, pastes, and flexible materials (e.g., rubbers, plastics, etc.). For solids, on the other hand, the contact area is determined by surface roughness. A certain degree of surface preparation may therefore be necessary in order to get a sufficiently large area of contact. Sometimes special handling and

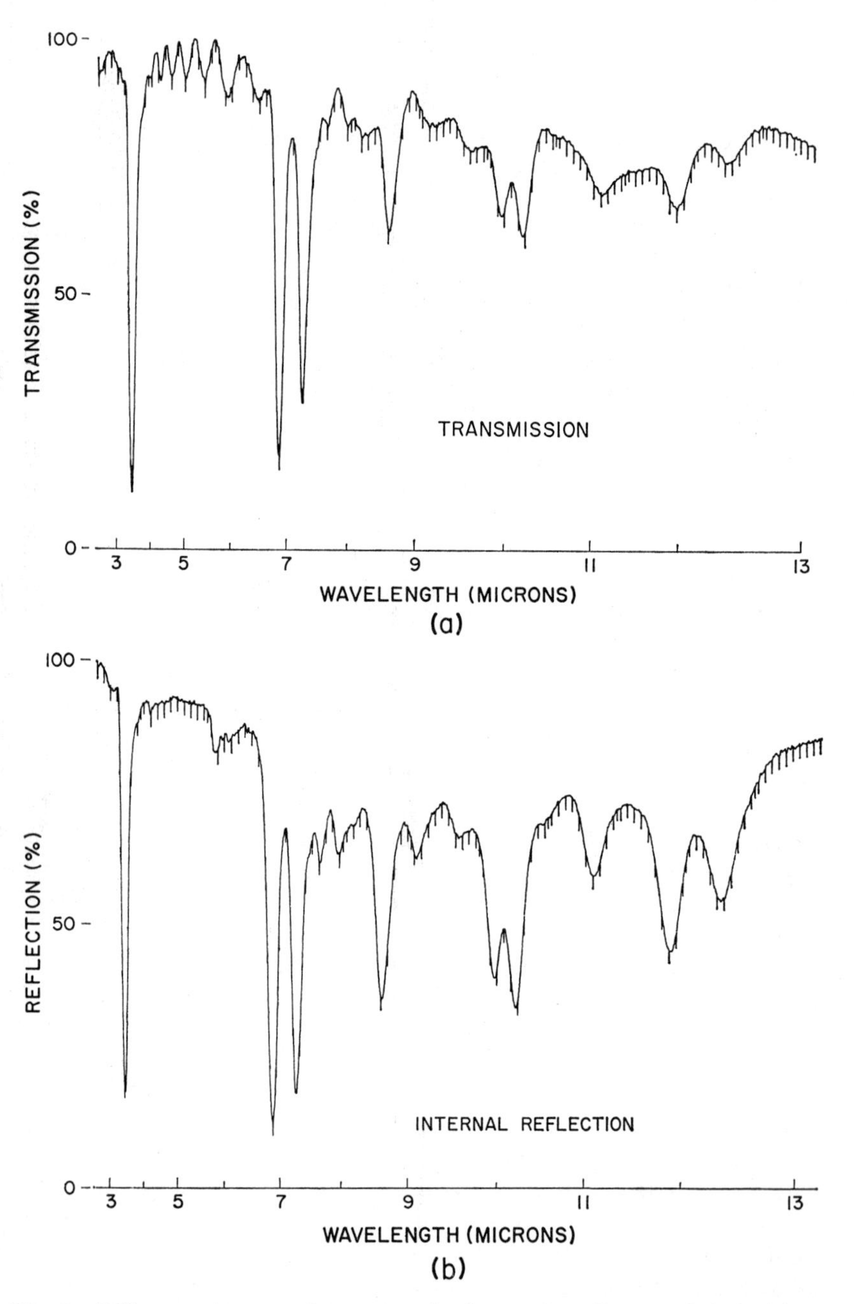

Fig. 2. Differences between the spectra of polypropylene film recorded via (a) transmission and (b) internal reflection using a KRS-5 plate, $N = 37$, at $\theta = 45°$. The interference fringes prominent in the transmission spectrum are noticeably absent in the internal reflection spectrum. The relatively stronger bands at the longer wavelengths in the internal reflection spectrum is another characteristic of the technique.

preparation of the sample is required for internal reflection spectroscopy. Some of these details are covered in this chapter, along with the discussion of the application in which special techniques are required. It is not possible to anticipate or to cover all of the potential applications. Where special techniques are required, the success of the application will depend on the ingenuity of the operator in sample handling. Many sample handling procedures are recommended by the instrument companies. Although ease of sample preparation and handling is a real advantage that IRS has over conventional spectroscopy techniques, there are a number of precautions which the spectroscopist must exercise. For example, sometimes a highly volatile liquid is injected between the sample and the IRE which upon evaporating leaves the two in good contact. This liquid may dissolve a soluble low molecular weight fraction of the sample which would be left on the surface of the IRE after the evaporation of the liquid and be preferentially sampled. The spectrum will then not truly represent the sample. Another example is that of silicone rubber which when pressed against the IRE leaves a deposit which migrates over the surface. The IRE becomes contaminated and must be replaced or carefully cleaned before reusing (H4).

Some excellent examples of ease of sample preparation for internal reflection spectroscopy are provided by the spectra of powdered samples, fibers and fabrics, and sandblasted surfaces, to be discussed later in the text. So far as the examination of powders is concerned, the particle size determines the contact area via the packing fraction—the smaller the particle size, the greater the contrast of the spectrum. For powders, it has been shown that the scattering which usually accompanies conventional transmission or reflection measurements is absent. Another advantage of IRS, applied to strongly absorbing powders, is that large particles can be investigated with ease, which is not the case for transmission spectroscopy for the following reason. For large particles widely dispersed in the mull or pellet, it is impossible to record a spectrum via transmission because there is either total absorption if the light strikes the particle, or no absorption if the light misses the particle. What is observed is thus a general decrease of power level, except for Christiansen transmission peaks in the spectral regions where the index of the powder matches that of the mull.

3. Spectra of Very Thin Films Can Be Obtained with Ease

The material to be analyzed, in many cases, is of necessity in thin-film form. Analyses of this type include investigation of free carriers in a semiconductor space charge region, semiconductor surface states, chemisorbed molecules, oxidation, catalysis, surface reactions, electrode reactions, reactions involving monomolecular films, etc. In these cases it is not that the quantity of material to be analyzed is necessarily small, but that it is spread out very thinly; and in order to record a spectrum of sufficient contrast, the light beam must pass through the surface many times to amplify the very small signal resulting from a single interaction with the surface. The power losses associated with transmission or external reflection are generally much larger than the small signal to be amplified. Therefore, because of the prohibitive loss of power, these techniques cannot be employed. Internal reflection, on the other hand, is essentially lossless; therefore multiple reflections can be employed and weak absorptions adequately amplified. Furthermore, by using polarized light and controlling the angle of incidence, considerable information can be obtained about molecular orientation at the surface. This is one of the potential applications of IRS which has not yet been fully exploited.

4. No Unbalance of Atmospheric Bands Caused by Introduction of Sample

In a well-aligned, double-beam instrument—for either transmission or internal reflection—the path lengths for the sample and reference beams are made precisely equal in order to cancel atmospheric absorptions. The finite dimensions of liquid cells and samples used in transmission spectroscopy may give rise to unequal path lengths in the atmosphere for the sample and reference beams. The atmospheric absorption bands are therefore not always cancelled when the sample is introduced in the instrument. For internal reflection spectroscopy, on the other hand, the introduction of the sample does not *alter* the path length of the light beam in the atmosphere and hence the atmospheric bands remain compensated.

B. Internal Reflection Spectra of Bulk Materials

Internal reflection spectroscopy offers some advantages in obtaining the spectra of a wide variety of bulk materials. In most cases it is the ease of sample preparation which is attractive. For strongly absorbing media, the necessarily small value of the effective thickness (e.g., about 1 μ) can easily be achieved by the proper selection of angle of incidence or the refractive index of the IRE. A single reflection, however, is adequate, but only in a limited number of cases. Multiple internal reflection elements offer the advantage that another parameter, viz., number of reflections, is available for adjusting the effective thickness. The desired number of reflections can be selected by utilizing only a portion of the surface of the IRE. Spectra of bulk materials such as liquids, pastes, pliable or rigid solids, and powders have been recorded with the aid of internal reflection spectroscopy.

1. Liquids

The particular advantage of IRS over conventional transmission for the study of liquids is that the requirements on the liquid container (cell) can be relaxed, especially when small thicknesses are required for transmission measurements. It is only necessary to provide a liquid cell with a suitable gasket material to hold the liquid against the surface of the IRE. Another possibility, requiring no special liquid cell, is to orient a multiple reflection plate so that its broad surface is horizontal and then to place the necessary amount of liquid directly on the surface of the IRE. It is for liquids that either the double-pass plate oriented in a vertical position or the vertical double-pass plate is of particular advantage. No special container is then required since either of these plates can be dipped in a beaker containing the liquid as was shown in Fig. 8 of Chapter Four. The spectral contrast can be controlled by controlling the immersion depth of the plate in the liquid. Other techniques that work well for liquids is to trap the liquid by capillary action either between two or more internal reflection plates (as was shown in Fig. 18 of Chapter Six) or between one plate and a microscope slide or to use "wire mesh surface wetting" (which was also discussed in Chapter Six).

Liquids are one of the easiest class of materials to study quantitatively via IRS because, providing the IRE is not oxidized, a well-defined contact is obtained. As was pointed out in the introduction to this chapter, actual wetting of the surface is not required; physical contact is adequate. Care must be exercised in selecting the optical material from which the IRE is made in order to avoid corrosion of the IRE. Corrosion might be avoided by depositing a very thin non-absorbing film on the surface of the IRE before it is brought into contact with the liquid. In this case, the film thickness must be known and taken into consideration when quantitative measurements are made. Where the liquid contains multiple components, surface potentials can contribute to a segregation of components near the surface. The spectrum recorded in this case will therefore not be a true representation of the mixture.

The transmission spectrum and the internal reflection spectrum of benzene are compared in Figs. 3a and 3b, respectively. The characteristic differences expected between the internal reflection and transmission spectra which was discussed in Chapter Two are clearly evident. The angle of incidence used in the measurements of Fig. 3b was 52°. For an IRE of KRS-5, this angle has

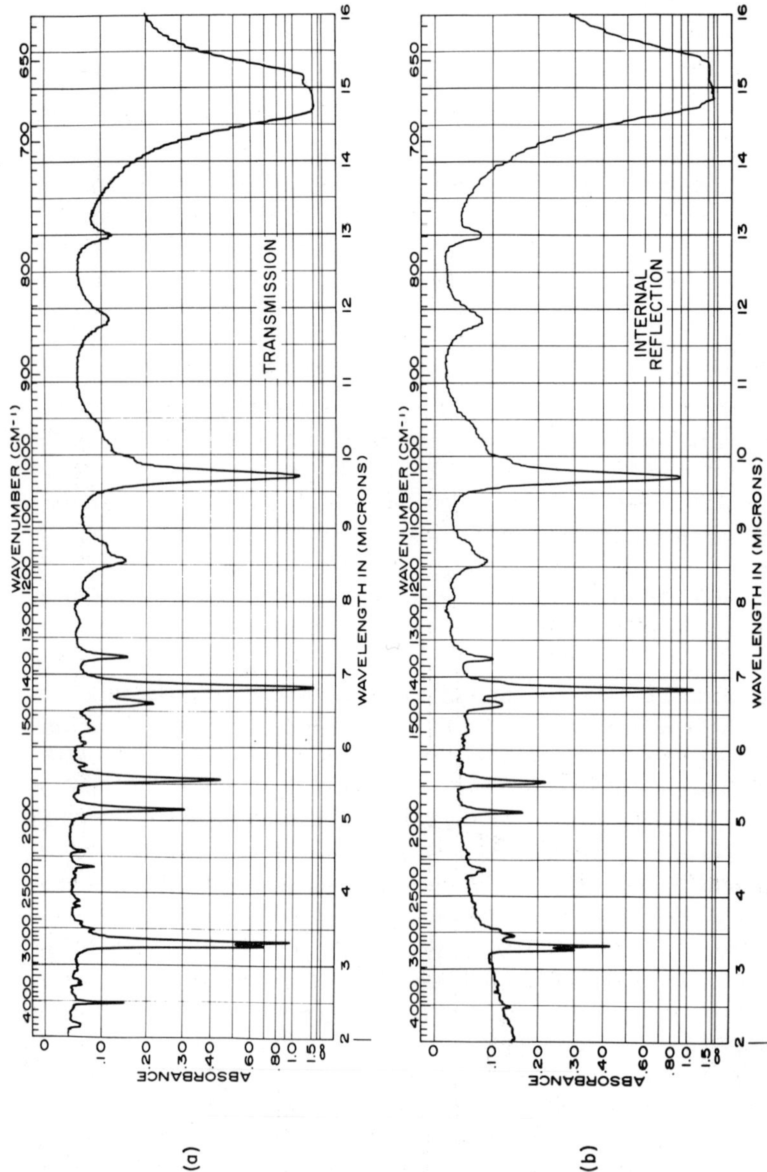

Fig. 3. Comparison of the transmission spectrum (a) through 0.025 mm benzene and the internal reflection spectrum (b) using KRS-5 at $\theta = 52°$ with $N = 20$. Note relatively enhanced contrast at longer wavelengths in latter spectrum. (Absorbance is the logarithm to the base 10 of the ratio of the incident radiant power to the transmitted power.) (Courtesy of S. E. Polchlopek, Barnes Engineering, Stamford, Conn.)

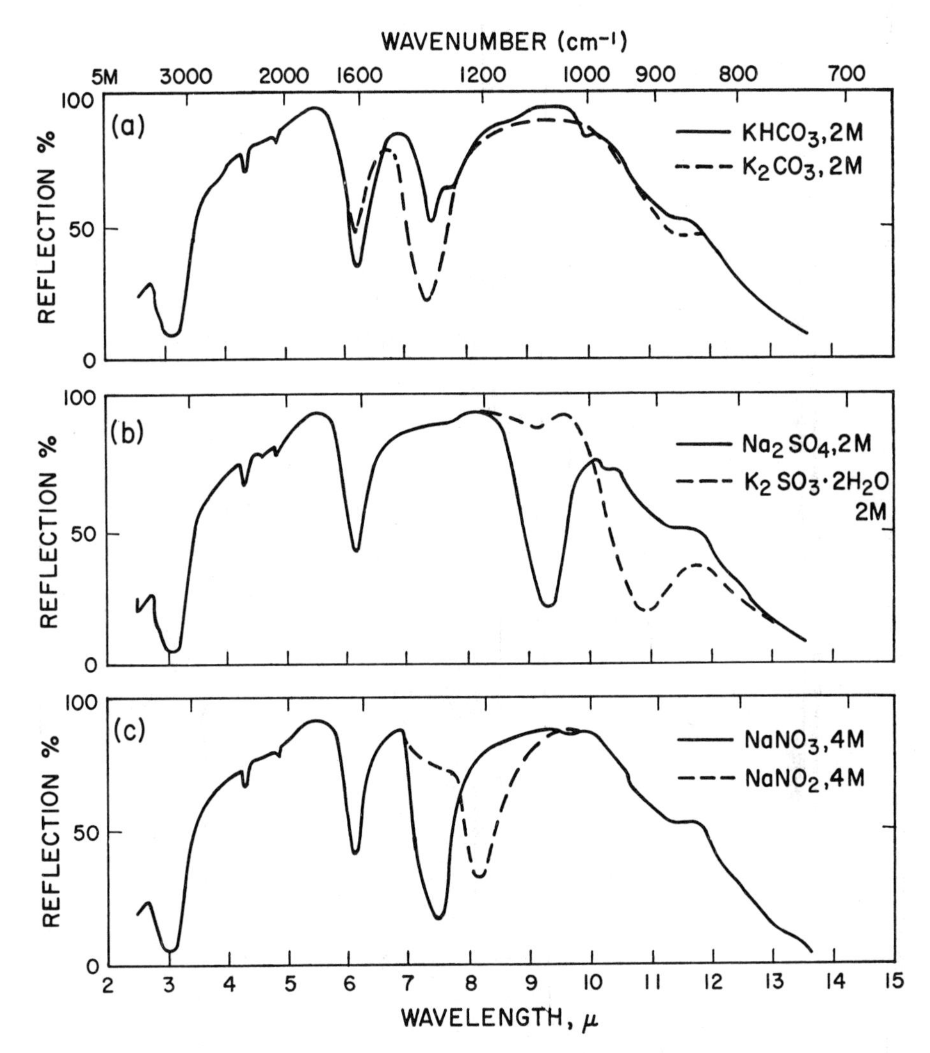

Fig. 4. Internal reflection spectra of several inorganic salts in water using single-reflection Irtran-2 prism, $N = 1$, $\theta = 40°$ (K17).

the advantage over the customary 45° angle in that the distortion, starting about 1000 cm^{-1} for most samples, is reduced or eliminated.

A number of studies of liquids via internal reflection, particularly of aqueous solutions, have been reported in the literature. The work of Katlafsky and Keller (K17) involved solutions of carboxylic acids and salts, sulfonic acids,

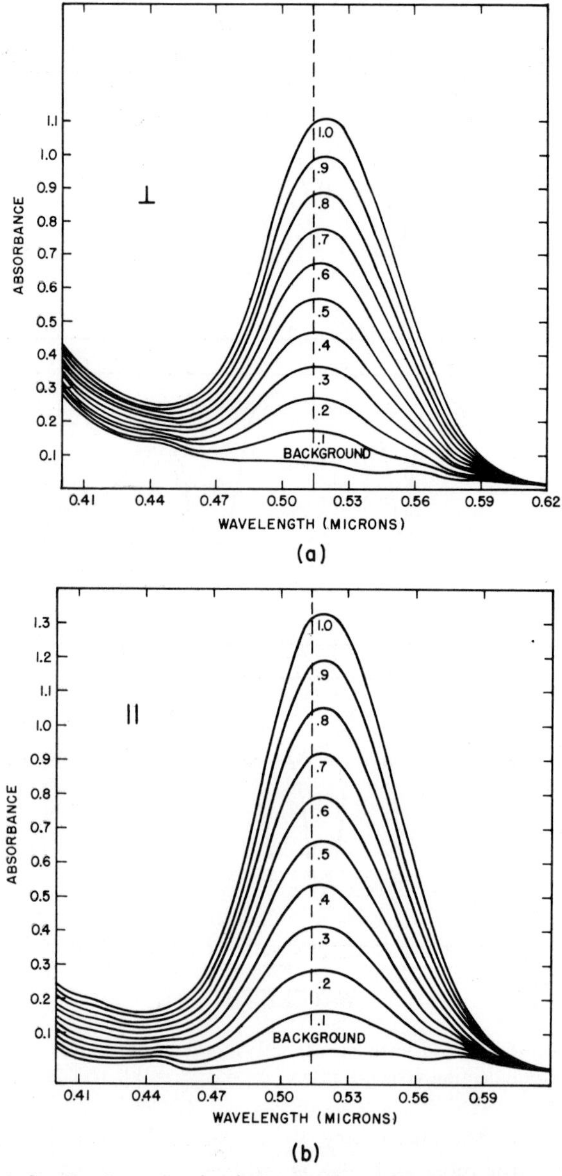

Fig. 5. **Internal reflection spectra in the visible of Eosin-B in H_2O as a function of** increase in concentration in equal steps. A relative concentration of 1 corresponds to a 49 g/liter solution in water. (a) $\perp$-polarization; (b) $\|$-polarization. Eleven reflections were utilized in an IRE of glass (n_D = 1.516) at θ = 72.8° (H7).

amino acids, phenols, amides, carbohydrates, and inorganic components. Figure 4 shows some of the spectra recorded by them. Other papers report a study of amino acids (R10), glycol-L-alanine in aqueous solutions (P1), alcohols in aqueous solutions (M4), eosin solutions (H6,H7,H9,H10), potassium permanganate in water (H5), and the determination of the nitrate ion in aqueous solution (W8). Some of these studies involved wide ranges in concentration such as those of Hansen on eosin solutions (H7) shown in Fig. 5. Many of these studies were not possible previously because water is a strong absorber and sufficiently thin liquid cells could not easily be prepared for transmission measurements.

2. Pastes

Pastes are as amenable as liquids to study via IRS. There is no problem in obtaining adequate contact with the surface of the IRE. In many cases the paste is sufficiently viscous to adhere to the surface of the IRE and no holder is required. Sample spectra of this class of material are that of oleomargarine and butter, shown in Figs. 6a and 6b, respectively (G15). Other typical materials of this class are silicone lubricant and tooth paste.

3. Solids

a. Pliable Materials

Pliable solids such as plastics, rubber, and skin are easily studied via internal reflection spectroscopy. When the carbon content of rubber exceeds 3–5%, spectra of rubbers cannot readily be obtained and techniques such as pyrolysis (discussed in a later section) should be employed. There is no problem in obtaining adequate contact to the reflecting surface of the IRE. As an example, the spectrum of polyurethane foam, which would be practically impossible to measure in its natural state by transmission, is shown in Fig. 7. The ability to record the spectra of such materials with no special preparation has the important implication of nondestructive sampling. This is especially important for recording the spectra of skin, tissue, cells, etc., for medical purposes (S19,H45,Pla).

b. Hard, Brittle Materials

Hard and brittle materials are not so amenable to analysis via internal reflection spectroscopy as are liquids and pastes. However, they can still be handled. For solids it is often difficult to prepare sufficiently thin films for

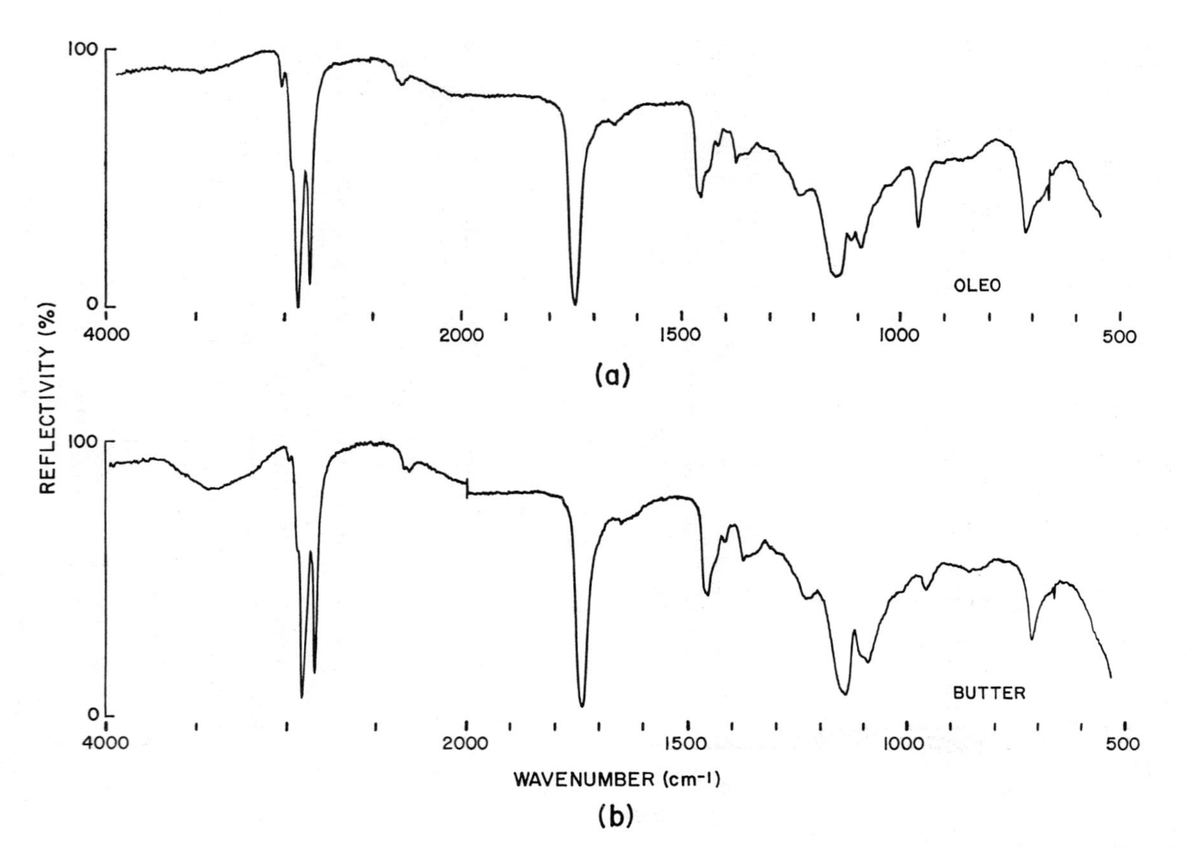

Fig. 6. Comparison of the internal reflection spectra. (a) Oleomargarine and (b) butter recorded using a single reflection KRS-5 IRE at $\theta = 45°$. (Courtesy of R. C. Gore, Perkin-Elmer Corp., Norwalk, Conn.)

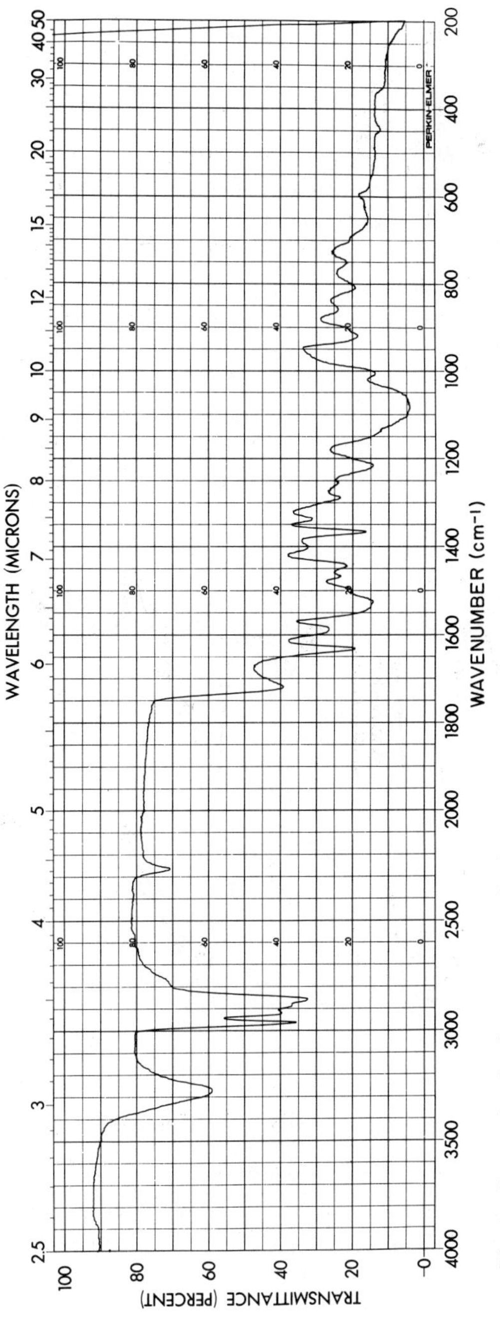

Fig. 7. Internal reflection spectrum of polyurethane foam taken with KRS-5 plate, $\theta = 45°$, $N = 22$. Elaborate sample preparation is required to obtain transmission spectrum of this material. (Courtesy of R. W. Hannah, Perkin-Elmer Corp., Norwalk, Conn.)

conventional transmission measurements and thus some effort in preparing the sample for internal reflection measurement is justified. As an example, the first internal reflection spectrum of a solid, recorded by Fahrenfort (F2), is that of epoxy resin, shown in Fig. 8a, which can be compared to the KBr pellet transmission spectrum shown in Fig. 8b. The surface of the epoxy resin was first polished smooth and then placed in contact with a AgCl hemicylinder. Some CS_2 was injected between the two materials which, upon evaporating, left the epoxy resin in good contact with the AgCl so that the internal reflection spectra could be recorded via a single reflection. Harris and Svodboda (H39) discuss the use of IRS as a means of determining the aromatic constituents of alkyd resins without prior chemical treatment.

The problem in handling solids is that of obtaining sufficient area of contact with the surface of the IRE. Again, it is emphasized that actual optical contact is not required—physical contact is adequate. Smooth flat surfaces are required for quantitative measurements although they are not necessary

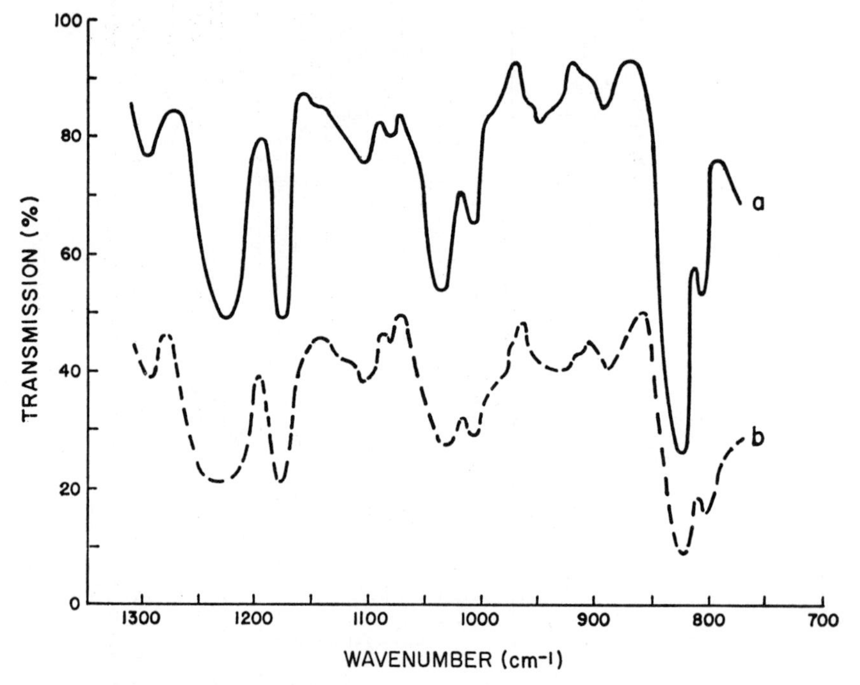

Fig. 8. Comparison of the spectra of epoxy resin obtained via (a) internal reflection using a single-reflection AgCl hemicylinder and (b) KBr pellet transmission (F2).

for qualitative measurements. An example of a spectrum of a material with a rough surface is that of sandblasted fused quartz, shown in Fig. 9, recorded via IRS. Fahrenfort (F5) has pointed out that by the use of a microhemisphere the necessary contact area is reduced and the problem thus alleviated, as was discussed in Chapter Four. The use of a unipoint multiple IRE such as the rosette, which was also discussed in Chapter Four, would also be helpful in this respect.

Another example of a spectrum of a class of material that would be impossible to handle in its natural state using transmission techniques is shown in Fig. 10. The sample material is porous and uneven paper saturated with Rohm and Haas Rhoplex. The fact that the paper has been treated with an acrylic-base resin shows up quite well in the spectrum at, for example, 5.8 μ and 8.7 μ. The sharp slope from 4000 to 2000 cm^{-1} and from 800 to 600 cm^{-1} is indicative of the presence of titanium dioxide.

Many solids, including metals, can be studied by evaporating them on the surface of the IRE. Another way of handling solids is to pulverize the sample material and then to dip a double-pass plate into the powder to record its spectrum. It will become evident in the next section that powders can easily be handled via internal reflection spectroscopy.

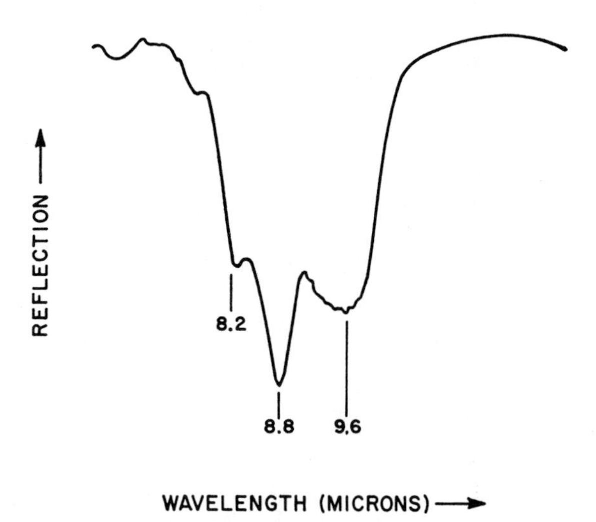

Fig. 9. Internal reflection spectrum of a frosted fused-quartz plate using a Ge internal reflection plate, $\theta = 45°$. The scattering would make a transmission spectrum difficult to obtain.

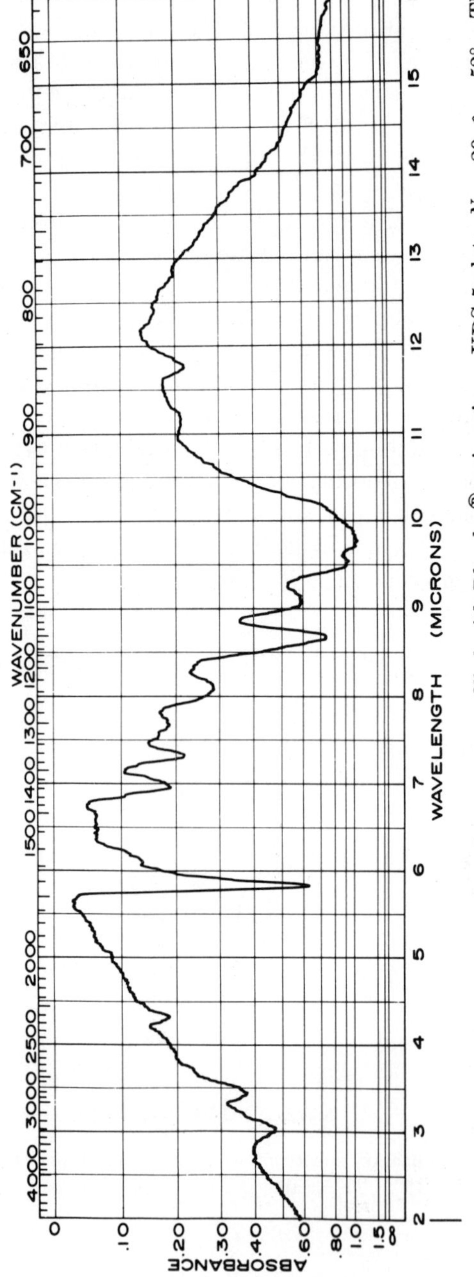

Fig. 10. Internal reflection spectrum of porous paper filled with Rhoplex® resin using a KRS-5 plate, $N = 20$, $\theta = 52°$. The falloff at short λ is due to inadequate surface finish (typical of soft materials) and the falloff at large λ is due to presence of titanium dioxide in paper. (Courtesy of S. E. Polchlopek, Barnes Engineering, Stamford, Conn.)

4. Powders

Many sample materials to be analyzed are available only in powdered form. It is often impossible to record optical reflection or transmission spectra of materials in powdered form in a direct way because of the high degree of scattering which results. Transmission measurements can be made with no further sample preparation if the particle size is very small (e.g., less than 1 μ). Diffuse reflection spectra are sometimes recorded but they are extremely difficult to interpret since the spectra represent a combination of reflection and transmission and are dependent on particle size. Mulls and pellet techniques are commonly employed for transmission measurements; and provided that the refractive indices of the mull and particle can be matched and that the particle size is not too large, good spectra can be recorded by transmission through the pellet or mull. The particles imbedded in suitable materials such as KBr, KI, ThBr, and KRS-5, where the refractive index of the powder in the non-absorbing regions is well matched to that of the mull, do not act as scattering centers in the *non-absorbing* regions. It

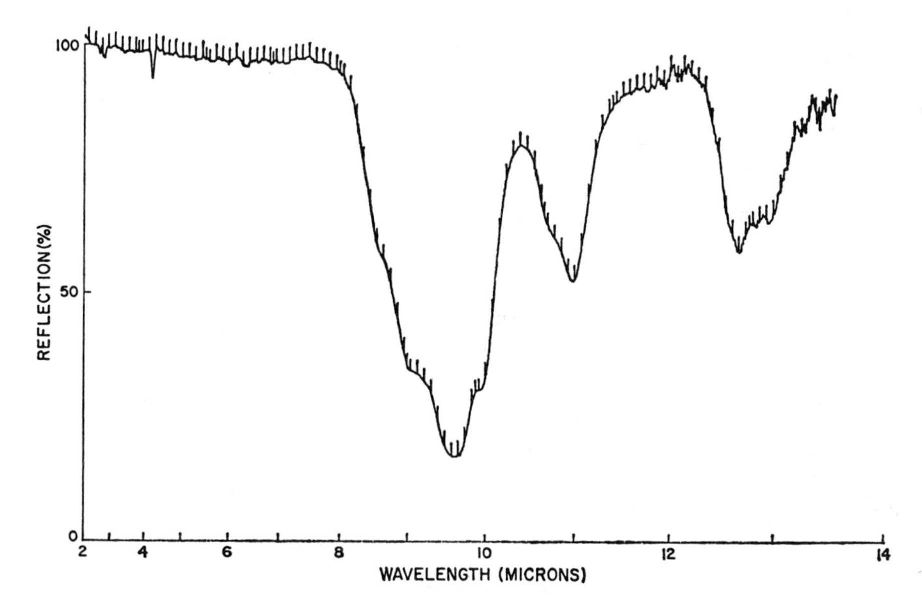

Fig. 11. Internal reflection spectrum of quartz-kaolinite powder, fraction 5–10 μ diam obtained by placing loose powder on a Ge plate, $\theta = 45°$, $N \sim 100$. The lack of scattering observed in the non-absorbing regions is characteristic of internal reflection spectra of powders although the reason for this is not understood.

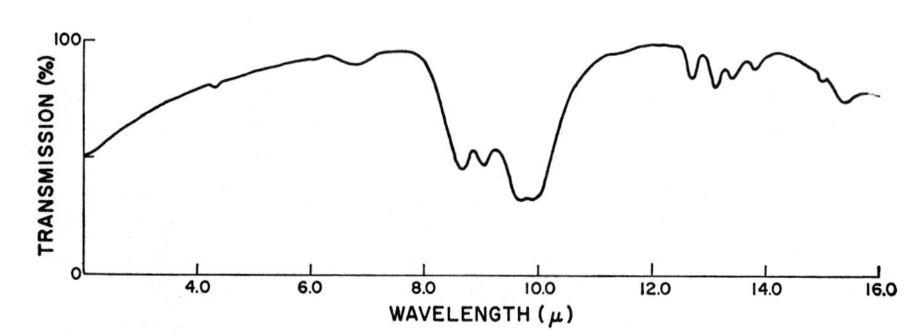

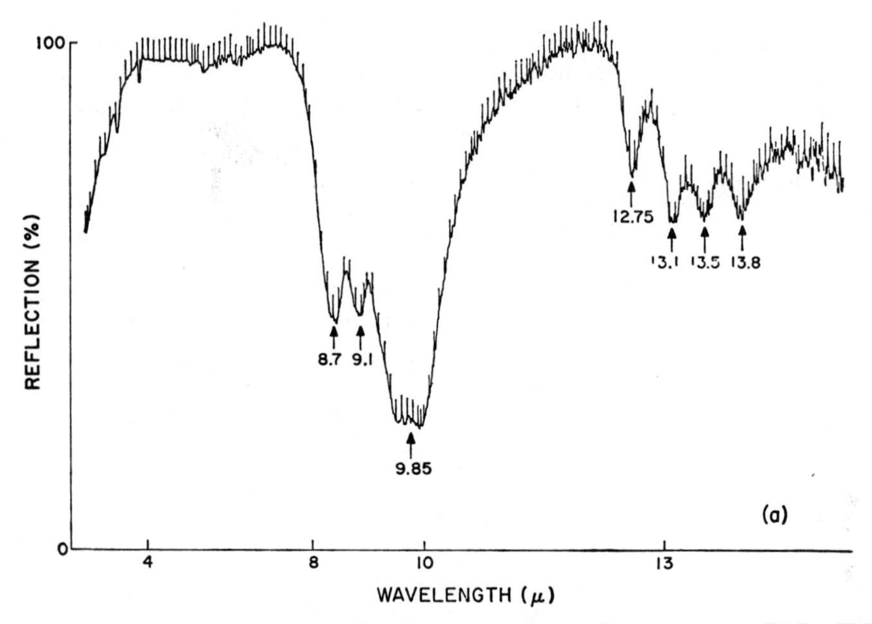

Fig. 12. Comparison of the transmission and internal reflection spectra (KRS-5 IRE, $\theta = 45°$, $N = 20$). (a) Powdered albite. (b) Powdered augite. Transmission spectra (upper curves) were obtained on very fine powders and internal reflection spectra (lower

should be realized that the spectrum recorded in this way, strictly speaking, is not a transmission spectrum. This is because in the absorbing regions the refractive indices are not matched and the particles will thus act as scattering centers. Among the materials studied in this way are powdered minerals (H51,H52,K21,L2,L12,L13).

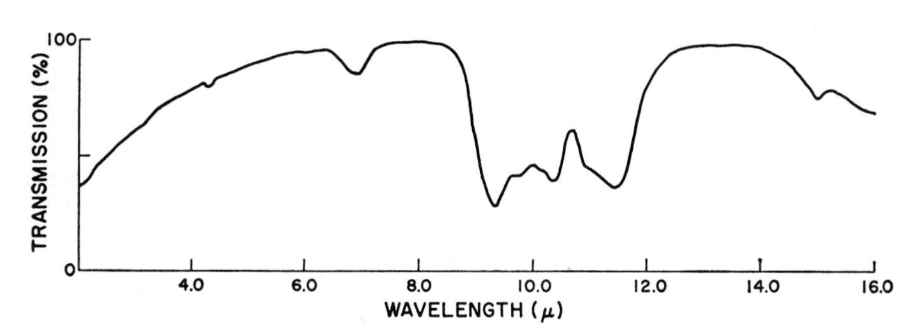

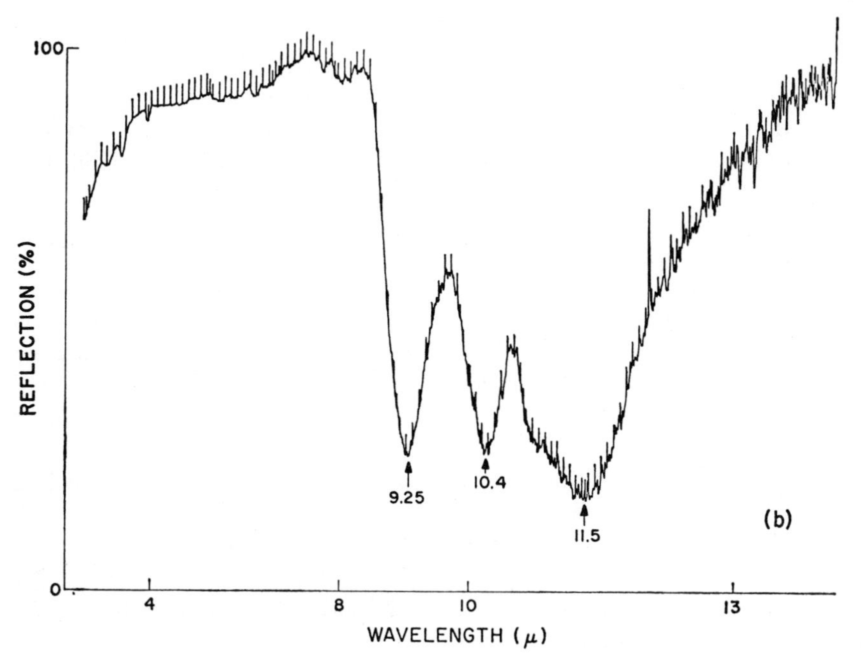

curves) were obtained on unelutriated powders of diameter of 100 μ and less. The scattering which causes the reduction in the transmission spectra at shorter wavelengths is noticeably absent in the internal reflection spectra.

Studies have shown that IRS can be employed to record spectra of powders regardless of particle size and that there is no scattering of light in the *non-absorbing* regions regardless of particle size (H32), provided that an angle of incidence exceeding the critical angle is maintained. A double-pass plate is useful for powders since the free end can be dipped into the powder in order to obtain contact between the sample and the IRE. In some cases the plate may be withdrawn from the powder and enough material sticks to the plate to make an analysis. Another technique that works well for powders is to sprinkle the powder on a suitable adhesive tape and then to press the tape against the surface of the IRE. In this case, excessive or prolonged pressure will cause the adhesive material to flow to the surface of the IRE and to produce an interfering spectrum.

A few examples of such measurements are shown in Figs. 11 and 12. Figure 11 shows the internal reflection spectrum of a quartz-kaolinite mixture for a fraction in which particle sizes range from 5 to 10 μ in diameter. Similar spectra, except of differing contrast, were obtained for a number of fractions in which particle sizes ranged from below 3.5 μ to above 43 μ in diameter (H32). The conclusion from this data was that there is no scattering of light due to the interaction of the evanescent wave with particulate matter regardless of particle size. Other evidence that supports this conclusion is the ability to record the spectra of samples with rough and uneven surfaces without scattering losses such as those of sandblasted glass (Fig. 9), paper (Fig. 10), and fibers (Figs. 16 and 43). Further demonstration of the applicability of internal reflection spectroscopy to the study of powdered materials is provided by the spectra of minerals shown in Fig. 12. Here the transmission spectra of albite (upper curve of 12a) and augite (upper curve of 12b) recorded via transmission (H51,H52) are compared to those recorded via internal reflection (H38). The transmission measurements were made on powders that consisted of particles less than 5 μ in diameter while the internal reflection measurements were made on unelutriated powders of 100 μ diameter and less. The presence of scattering in the transmission curves at the shorter wavelengths and the lack of scattering in the internal reflection curves should be noted. Again, it is emphasized that not only is scattering absent for internal reflection but that it is also possible to record spectra of powders which, because of their large particle size, would not transmit any energy in the absorbing regions and for which therefore it would not be possible to obtain useful transmission spectra.

As might be expected, the spectral contrast depends on particle size. This dependency, attributed to packing fraction, is shown in Fig. 13 for one series of measurements on quartz-kaolinite mixtures (H32).

Although the interaction mechanism of the evanescent field with particulate matter has not yet been theoretically worked out and therefore the exact reasons for the absence of scattering in non-absorbing regions are unknown, it is expected that the answer has to do with the fact that the evanescent field has a nonpropagating nature. There may indeed be a small degree of scat-

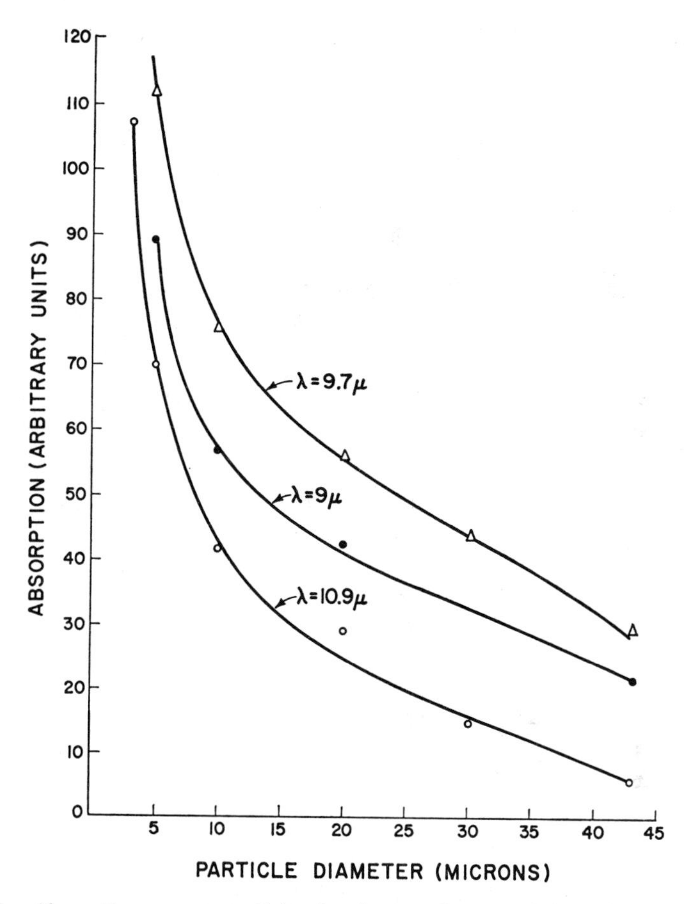

Fig. 13. Absorption versus particle size for powders consisting of quartz-kaolinite mixtures for several bands recorded via IRS. Change in absorption with particle size is attributed to changes in packing fraction (H32).

tering which was not detected; however, for practical purposes, as in the recording of spectra, no measurable scattering losses were observed. These observations of little or no scattering for particulate matter in *non-absorbing* regions are not in disagreement with observations by Frölich (F20) of scattering resulting from the interaction of the evanescent wave for total internal reflection with *absorbing* (soot) particles on the reflecting surface. The experimental results, in any case, are important in themselves, since IRS does provide a convenient means of analyzing many materials which may be found only in powdered form. In some other work, Gottlieb and Schrader (G15a)

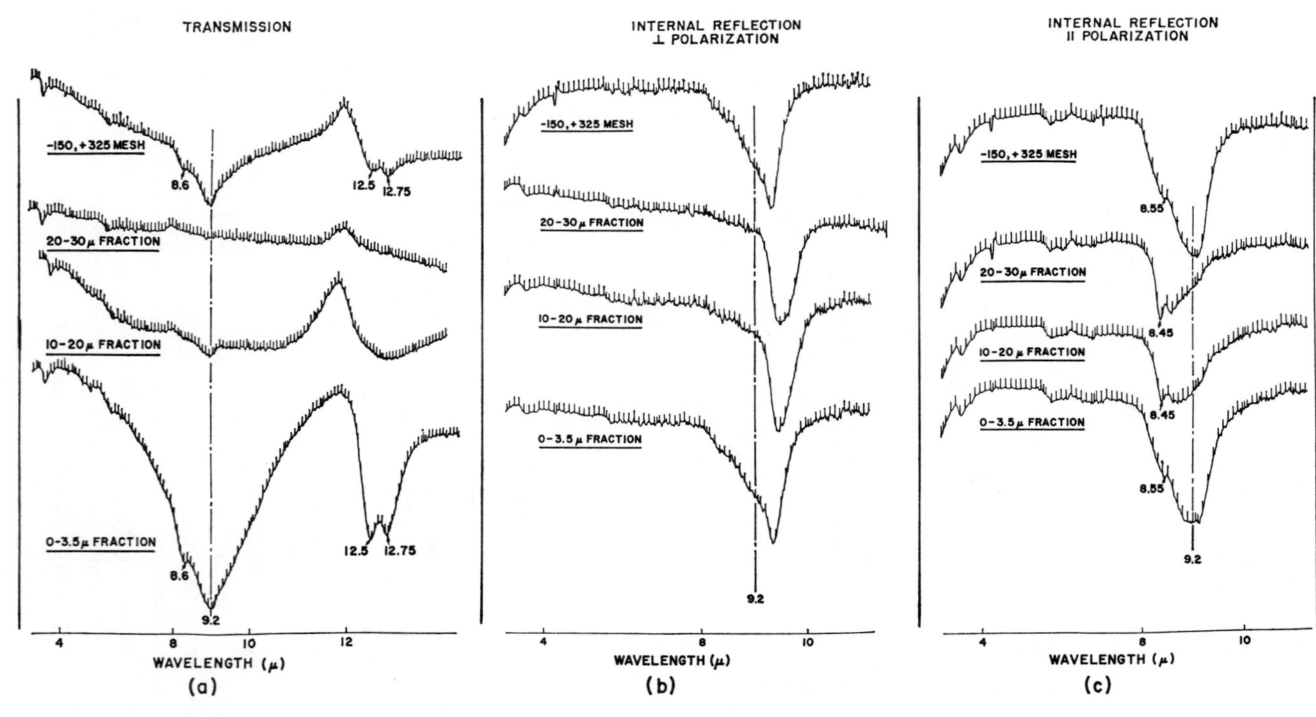

Fig. 14. Comparison of the spectra of several fractions of quartz powders. (a) Transmission spectra of 300 mg KBr pellets containing 0.17% powdered quartz fractions. (b) Internal reflection spectra of loose powders of same fractions using perpendicular polarization. (c) Internal reflection spectra of loose powders of same fractions using parallel polarization. Note that, unlike transmission spectra, internal reflection spectra can be recorded regardless of particle size.

obtained the spectra of powdered materials with no scattering losses by pressing the pure powder (without a matrix) into a pellet and placing it into contact with a single-reflection KRS-5 IRE.

Studies were also made on powders of pure quartz fractions (H38). The results on this material are very difficult to analyze because, first, the material is doubly refracting; second, it has refractive index variations from close to zero to above 7 over an absorption band and therefore the critical angle will move from well below to well above the angle of incidence regardless of the refractive index of the IRE material; and, third, very large variations in extinction coefficient occur and this combined with the low refractive index will make the reflection metallic in certain regions. Results obtained on a number of fractions are shown for transmission through KBr pellets in Fig. 14a and are shown for internal reflection at $\theta = 45°$ using Ge plates for perpendicular and parallel polarization in Figs. 14b and 14c, respectively. The inability to obtain useful transmission spectra for the fractions of larger diameters is clearly evident—only Christiansen transmission peaks appear in these spectra. Internal reflection yields spectra for all fractions; however, it will be noted that the band shapes and their location are dependent on fraction size and polarization. This dependence of band shifts and shapes on polarization and particle size is unexplained and does complicate interpretation of the spectra. It will be recalled that Fresnel's equations for complex refractive index, and especially for anisotropic materials, are very complicated. However, it is emphasized that spectra can be obtained regardless of particle size. It would appear that, for a material such as quartz which has such large variations in refractive index and from which very strong external reflection spectra can be obtained, not much is gained by employing internal reflection if it is in solid form.

Excellent results have been obtained via external reflection at near normal incidence on solid, oriented quartz plates (S28). It is for undamped materials like quartz that Simon (S22,S23) pointed out that the optical constants can be determined from external reflection measurements at two selected angles of incidence.

5. Anisotropic Materials

In the earlier discussion of the absorption mechanisms, the difference in absorption for different polarizations was emphasized. For anisotropic materials this dependence of absorption on polarization can lead to a difference in the spectra between transmission and internal reflection measurements. It was also pointed out that, unlike for propagating waves, *E*-fields are found for all three spatial coordinates at the totally reflecting interface. Furthermore, the E-field direction can be selected by selecting the angle of incidence and the polarization of the incoming waves. This control on the direction of the E-field can be used with advantage in the study of anisotropic materials.

Flournoy and Schaffers (F9) have worked out the theory for the interaction by anisotropic materials with the evanescent field and applied it to oriented polymers (thick films). They showed that quantitative data could be obtained for molecular orientation in some specific cases and that polarized internal reflection measurements offer advantages over conventional transmission measurements for determining the polarization dependence of strongly absorbing bands, for measuring the components of the absorption coefficient in all three spatial directions, and for studying surface orientation independent of bulk properties. Flournoy (F10) then applied their theory in an investigation carried out to determine and to characterize the molecular orientation that takes place in polypropylene during the process of uniaxial drawing and also to compare molecular orientation in the surface layer to that found in the bulk. The surface was found to exhibit radial symmetry about the axis of drawing. From measurements of internal reflection spectra for partially polarized light, as well as for polarized light in which the electric vector was parallel to the axis of drawing or perpendicular to the axis of drawing, it was possible to evaluate the absorption coefficients for the three spatial directions in the film. The dichroic ratios obtained in this way compared favorably to those determined from transmission measurements. Typical internal reflection spectra used in the determination of the dichroic ratios are shown in Fig. 15, where curves a and b are the spectra for the E field parallel and perpendicular to the axis of drawing and curve c is the spectrum for partially polarized light.

Another example of work on anisotropic materials is given by some studies of Barr and Flournoy (B4) on organic fibers. The spectra were obtained using polarized light under essentially the same conditions as for the films. The fibers are initially wrapped around a metal mandrel, one-fiber layer deep. Cellophane adhesive tape is wrapped around the fibers to hold them in place. The fibers are then cut free from the mandrel and applied to the internal reflection plate. Infrared spectra are obtained with the fiber axes arranged first parallel and then perpendicular to the electric vector. An example of the internal reflection spectra of 66 stretched nylon fibers is given in Fig. 16a. From these results, it is possible to calculate the degree of orientation of the fiber surface. The value of the dichroic ratio studies is fully explained by Barr (B5) and Fraser (F16,F17).

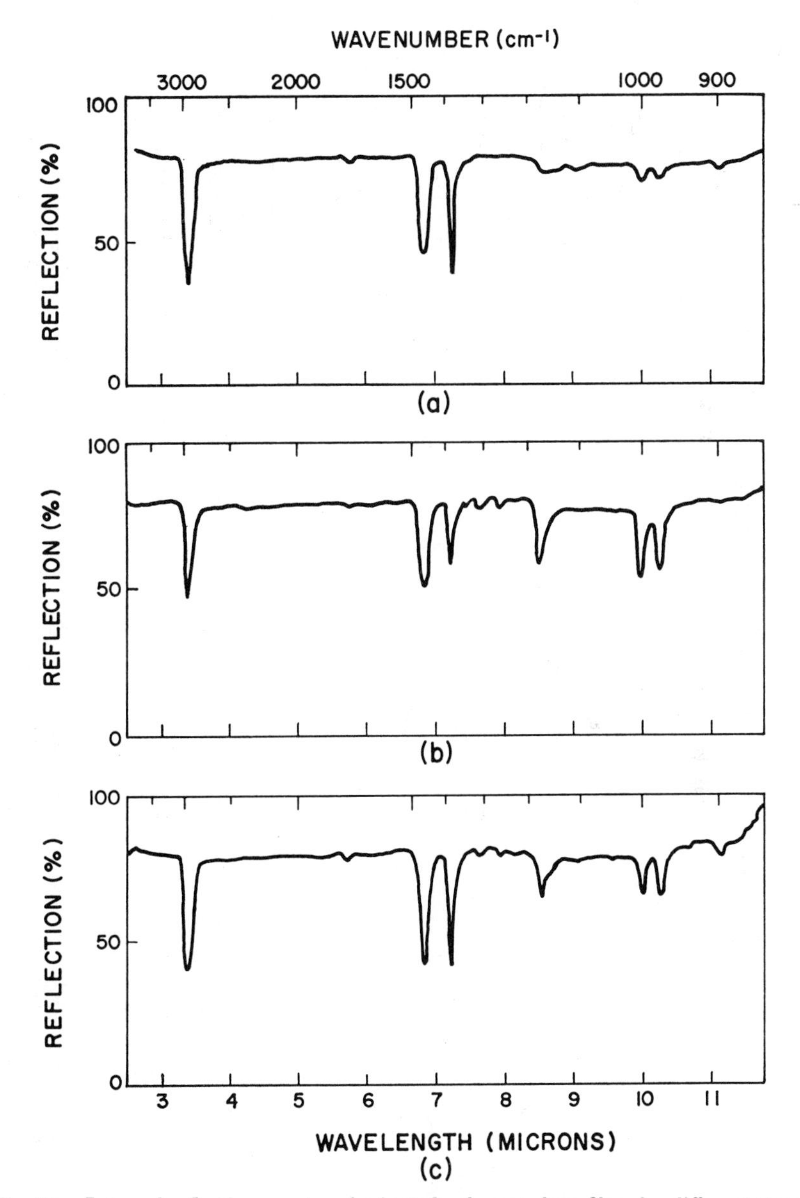

Fig. 15. Internal reflection spectra of oriented polypropylene films for different states of polarization using Ge IRE, $N = 21$, $\theta = 45°$ (F10). (a) E field parallel to axis of drawing. (b) E field perpendicular to axis of drawing. (c) Partially polarized light. These spectra can be combined to calculate dichroic ratios.

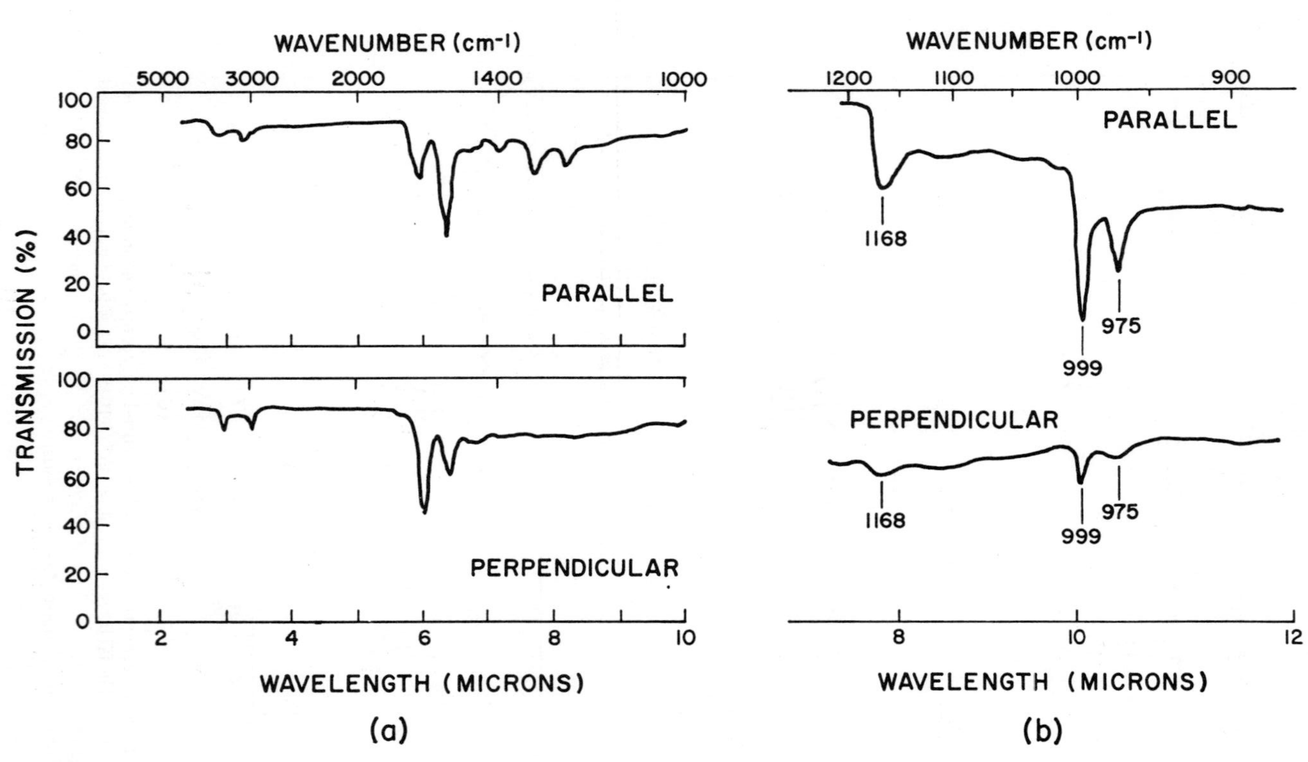

Fig. 16. Polarized internal reflection spectra of organic fibers using Ge IRE, $N = 21$, $\theta = 45°$. (a) Nylon yarn with electric vector parallel and perpendicular to fiber axes. (b) Oriented polypropylene fibers with electric vector parallel and perpendicular to fiber axes.

Figure 16b shows similar spectra of stretched polypropylene fibers over the range 900–1200 cm^{-1}. The difference in the spectra for polypropylene fibers (Fig. 16b) and polypropylene films (Fig. 15) should be noted.

In another application of internal reflection spectroscopy to the study of anisotropic crystals, Yamada and Suzuki (Y1a) have been able to resolve, via IRS, some ambiguities which previously existed in the assignments of normal vibrations for naphthalene.

C. Determination of Optical Constants

One of the most fundamental applications of IRS is in the measurement of optical constants of materials. In this application it has already established itself as a powerful technique. Internal reflection spectroscopy has a number of advantages over conventional techniques when it is necessary to measure both the transmitted and reflected radiation, as well as to contend with interference phenomena. For internal reflection, on the other hand, there is no interference phenomenon. To determine the optical constants it is only necessary to make measurements of $R_\perp$ and $R_\parallel$ at a properly selected angle of incidence or, alternately by using light whose state of polarization is known, to measure the reflected intensity at two angles of incidence. In the latter case, the angles can be optimized for maximum sensitivity. Measurement of optical constants via internal reflection have been discussed by Fahrenfort and Visser (F4,F6), Hansen (H8,H9), Crawford and his students at the University of Minnesota (C7,G8,G9), and also by Kapany and Pontarelli (K13).

Briefly, Fresnel's equations, for a transparent medium 1 and where medium 2 has a complex refractive index $\hat{n}_2 = n_2 - ik_2$, may be written for perpendicular and parallel polarization, respectively, as

$$R_\perp = \left| \frac{n_1 \cos\theta - [(n_2 - ik_2)^2 - n_1^2 \sin^2\theta]^{1/2}}{n_1 \cos\theta + [(n_2 - ik_2)^2 - n_1^2 \sin^2\theta]^{1/2}} \right|^2 \tag{1}$$

$$R_\parallel = \left| \frac{(n_2 - ik_2)^2 \cos\theta - n_1[(n_2 - ik_2)^2 - n_1^2 \sin^2\theta]^{1/2}}{(n_2 - ik_2)^2 \cos\theta + n_1[(n_2 - ik_2)^2 - n_1^2 \sin^2\theta]^{1/2}} \right|^2. \tag{2}$$

These equations give the reflected intensities if the incident wave in medium 1 has unit intensity and if medium 2 is very thick.

Two equations are obtained from separating each of the above equations into real and imaginary parts, making it possible to calculate n_2 and k_2 with the aid of a computer from measurements of $R_\perp$ and $R_\parallel$ at a fixed angle or, preferably, from measurement with fixed polarization at two angles. It turns out that measurements of the reflectivity that are made far above the critical angle resemble $n_2\kappa_2$ fairly closely, while measurements made just below the critical resemble the mirror image of the dispersion in n_2. This has already been discussed in Chapter Three where some measurements exhibiting this change in character of the spectrum with change in θ were also shown. Another example is given in Fig. 17 for the absorption band of silicone lubricant at $\lambda \sim 7.9\ \mu$. Figure 17a shows the internal reflection spectra at various angles of incidence compared to a transmission spectrum, and Figs. 17b and 17c show the internal reflection spectra at various angles of incidence for perpendicular and parallel polarization, respectively. With the aid of a computer, the selection of angles to optimize the measurements can be realized. Internal reflection spectroscopy is the most direct and sensitive way of recording optical constants reported up to the present time. An example of measurements and calculations by Fahrenfort and Visser (F4) of the optical constants for the 1035 cm^{-1} band of liquid benzene is shown in Fig. 18. Figure 18a shows that measurements over the entire absorption band were made at two selected angles of incidence. Figures 18b and 18c show their calculated values of n_2 and κ_2. Crawford et al. at the University of Minnesota (C7,G8,G9) have extended the technique by making measurements at optimum angles of incidence for different regions of the absorption band. Their measurements and results on the 675 cm^{-1} band of liquid benzene are shown in Fig. 19. From the data shown in Fig. 19a (G9), they made their calculations on n_2 and $n_2\kappa_2$, shown in Figs. 19b and 19c, by selecting four different pairs of angles of incidence over the wavelength region of the absorption band. In subsequent work (C7), they related their measurements of the optical constants to "local susceptibilities" calculated from previously published theories. Figure 20 shows some reflectivity measurements and calculated values of optical constants of Hansen (H10) on eosin-Y solutions in the visible region of the spectrum. The reflectivity measurements at 55° (Fig. 20a) and at 45° (Fig. 20c) were combined to calculate the optical constants α_2 (Fig. 20b) and n_2 (Fig. 20d). It should be noted in Fig. 20c that absorbance plots near $\theta = \theta_c$ qualitatively resemble n_2 of Fig. 20d, while reflectivity plots (Figs. 17, 18a, 19a) resemble the mirror image of n_2.

Internal reflection spectroscopy has also been applied to solids for the measurement of optical constants (R7). Here the quality of the contact between the IRE and the sample controls the precision of the measurements. Some indication of the nature and area of the contact can be obtained from a measure of the reflected intensities at two "critical angles"; viz., IRE–sample, θ_{cs}, and IRE–air, θ_{ca}. (θ_{cs} cannot be sharply defined because of the continuous coupling obtained for intermediate spacings between sample and IRE.) A measure of the quality of the contact can also be obtained from

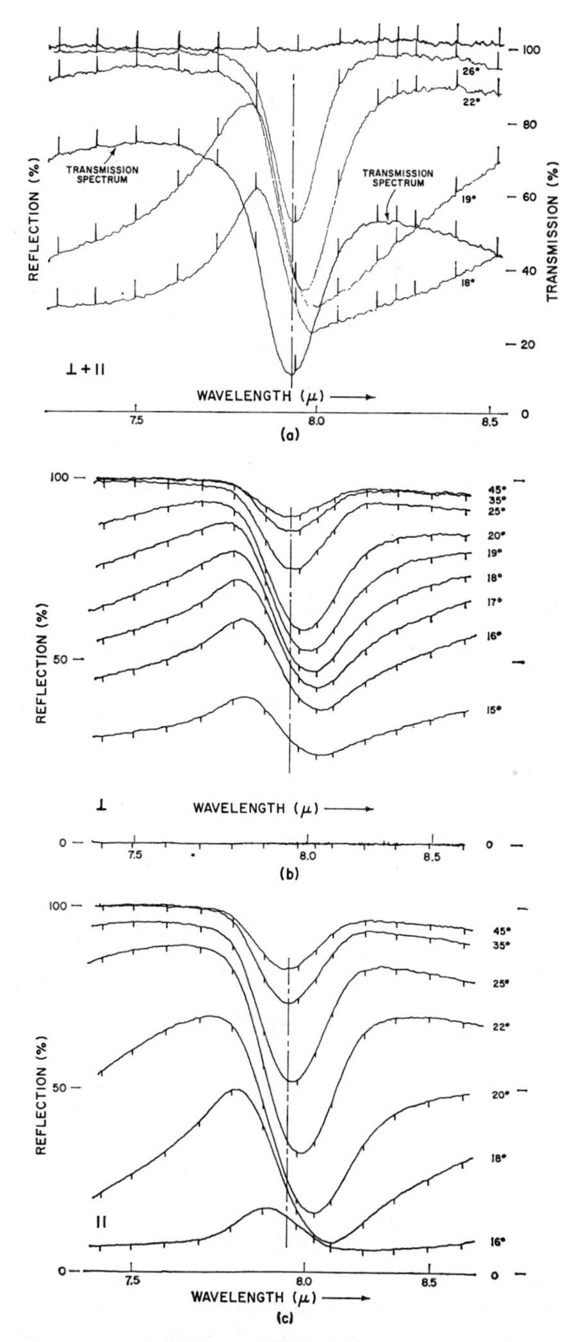

Fig. 17. Spectra of band of silicone lubricant at 7.9 μ. (a) Internal reflection spectra for unpolarized light at various angles of incidence compared to transmission spectrum. (b) Internal reflection spectra at various angles of incidence for $\perp$-polarization. (c) Internal reflection spectra at various angles or incidence for $\|$-polarization.

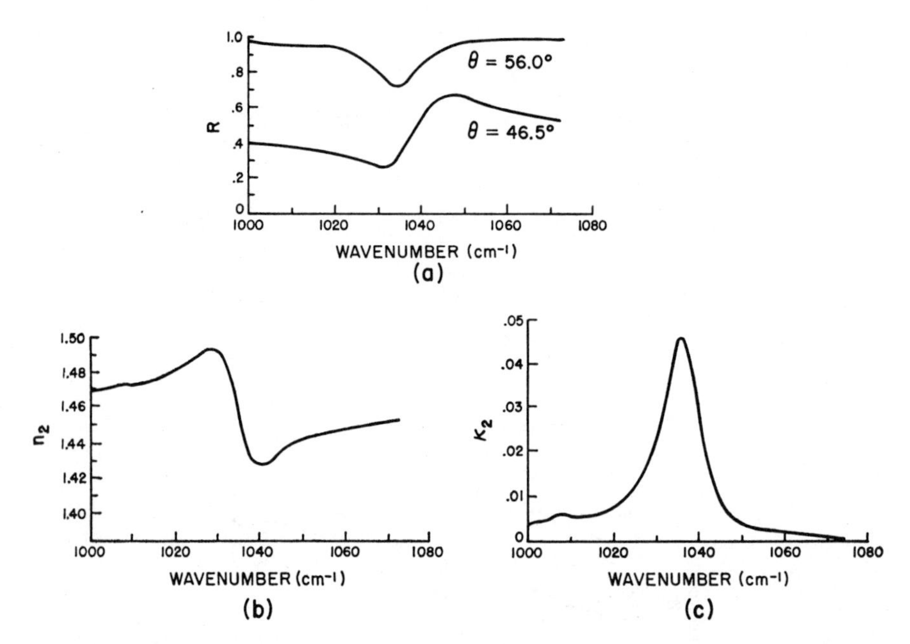

Fig. 18. Internal reflection spectra and optical constants of 1035 cm^{-1} band of liquid benzene. (a) Reflection spectra at two angles of incidence. (b) Calculated values of n_2. (c) Calculated values of κ_2 (F4).

the reflected intensity at the principal angle, θ_p, for parallel polarization in non-absorbing regions. ($R_{\parallel}$ will be zero at θ_p for a good contact.)

Considerable controversy has existed in the past concerning the determination of optical constants of metals. The measurements are difficult because reflectivities are often very high and it is necessary to measure slight deviations from 100%. Furthermore, many metals oxidize easily and there is always a question of whether the measurement represents the metal or the oxide. IRS promises to alleviate both of these difficulties, since the metal can be evaporated on the surface of the IRE and be kept clean indefinitely. In a first approximation, the percentage reflectivity of a dielectric (IRE)–metal interface is given (H16) by

$$R = 100 - 2.1 \times 10^{-4} \, (\nu\epsilon/\sigma)^{1/2}, \tag{3}$$

where ϵ is the dielectric constant of the IRE and σ the conductivity of the metal. This equation shows that the presence of the IRE reduces R, thereby permitting more precise measurements. Hansen (H9) has made internal reflection measurements and calculations of optical constants of metals. He

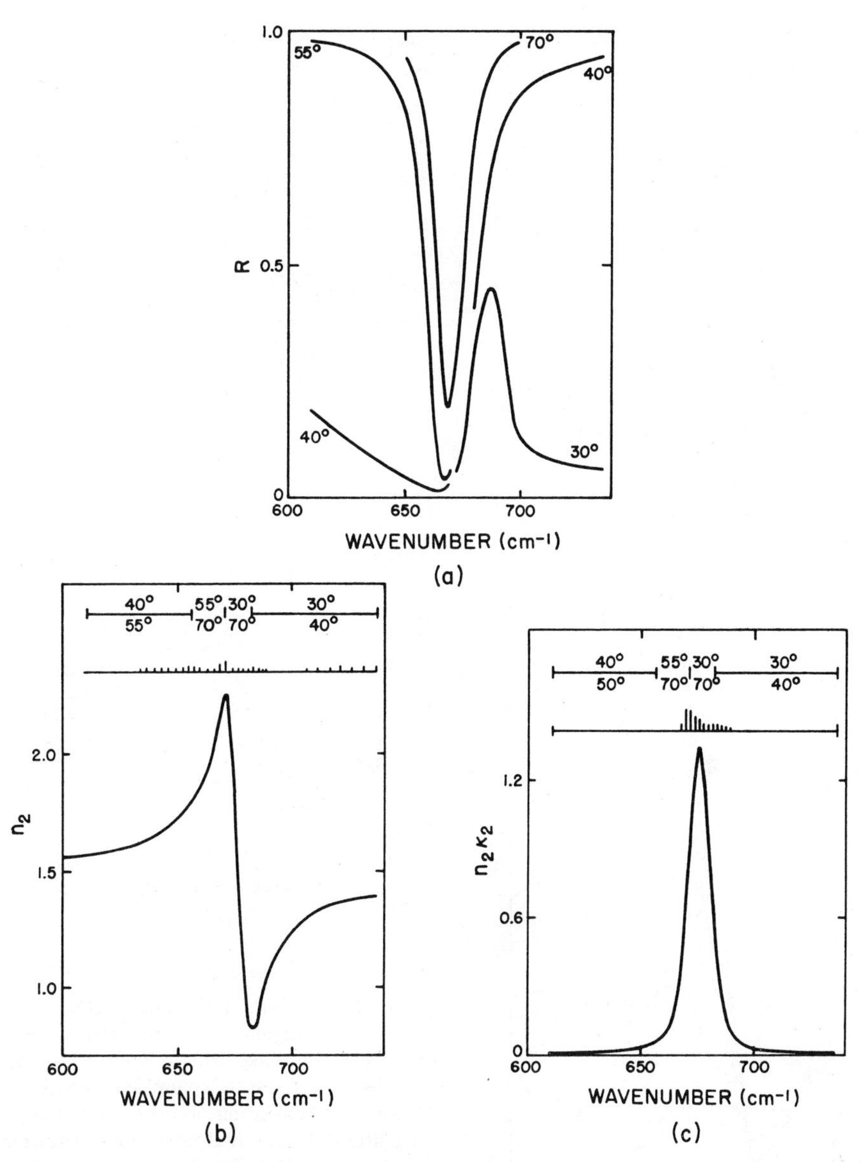

Fig. 19. Internal reflection spectra and optical constants of 675 cm^{-1} band of liquid benzene. (a) Reflection spectra at a pair of angles of incidence. (b) Refractive index calculated from curves in (a)—the numbers above the curve are the pairs of angles of incidence from which data were selected while the vertical lines represent the calculated errors. (c) Extinction coefficient calculated from curves in (a) (G9).

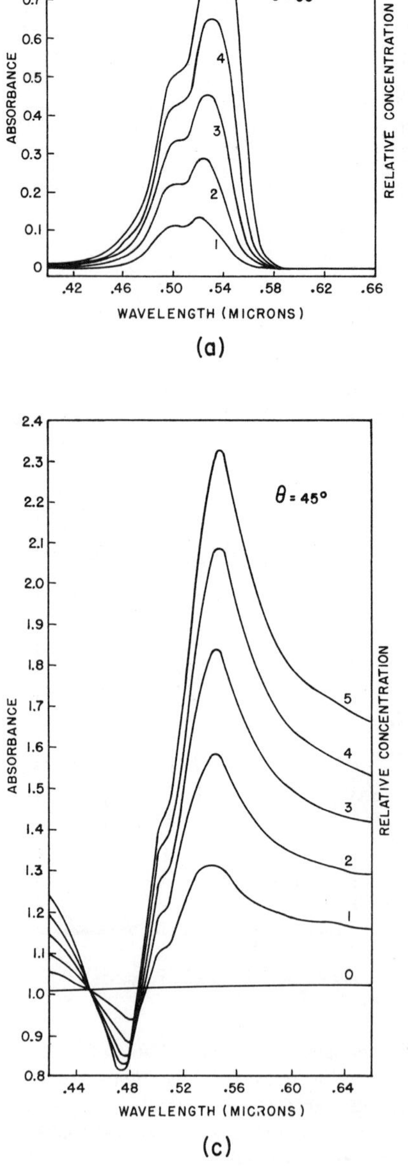

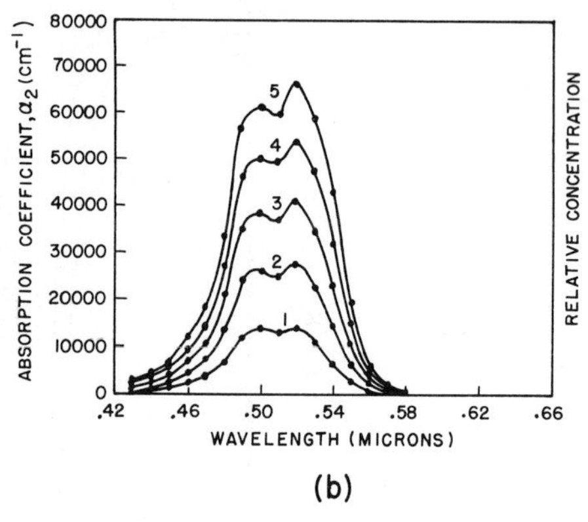

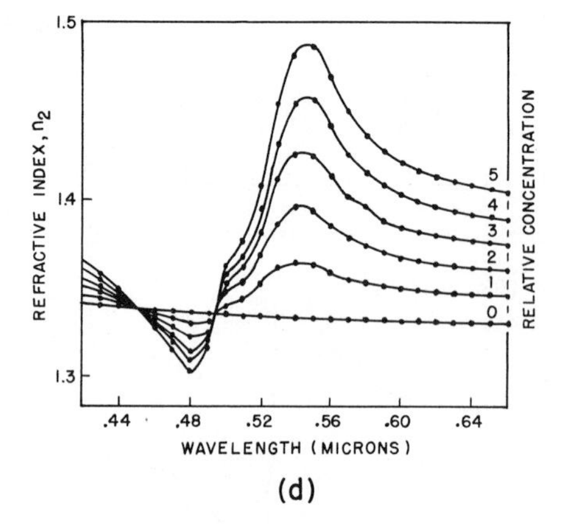

Fig. 20. Internal reflection spectra taken above (55°) and below (45°) the critical angle of eosin-Y solutions, using a glass prism (n_D = 1.787), and calculated optical constants. Relative concentration of 1.0 corresponds to 50 g/liter. (a) Internal reflection spectra for θ = 55°. (b) Calculated absorption coefficients. (c) Internal reflection spectra for θ = 45°. (d) Calculated n_2 (H10). The refractive index of the zero concentration is that of water.

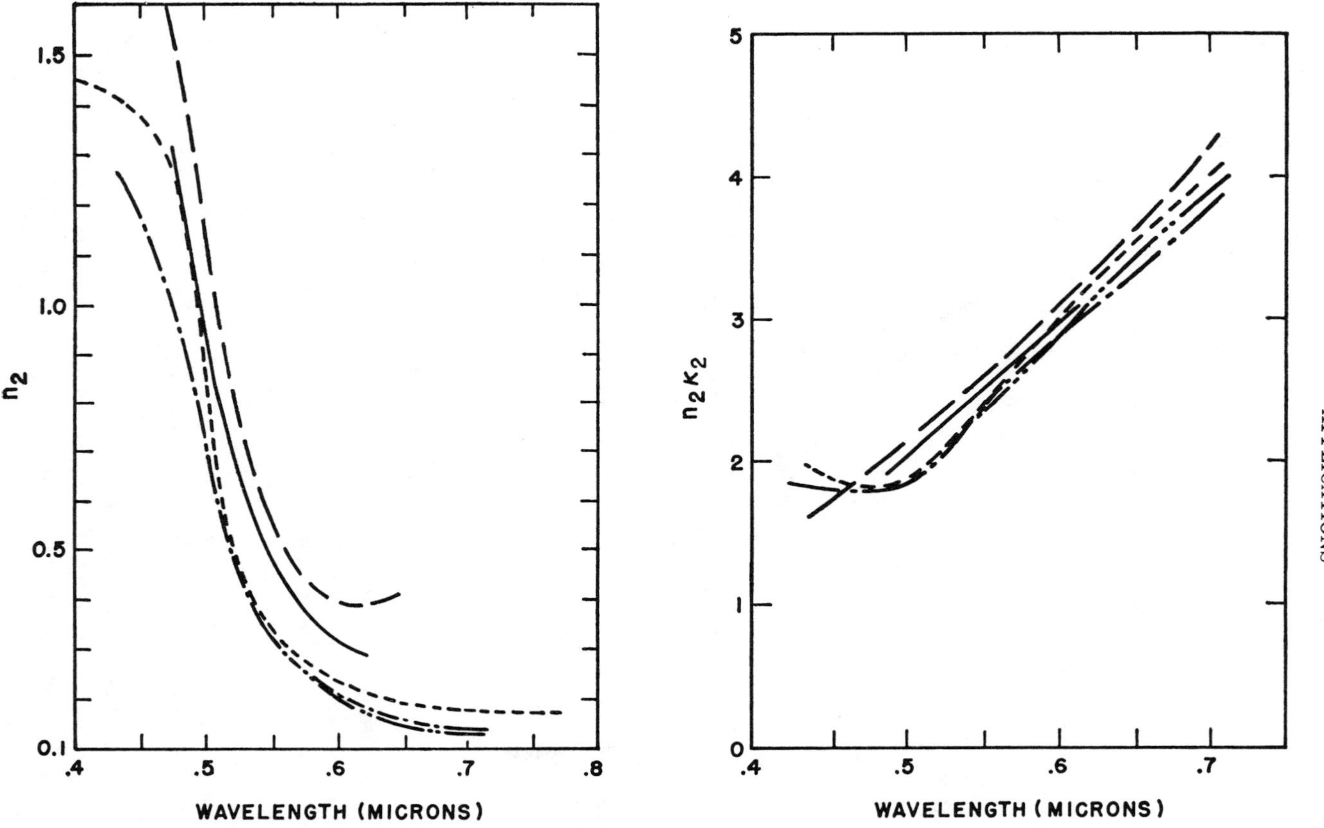

Fig. 21. Optical constants n_2 and $n_2\kappa_2$ of gold. Comparison of external reflection measurements with internal reflection measurements of Hansen. (a) (— —) Hagen and Rubens. (b) (- - -) Schulz. (c) (— · · —) Weiss. (d) (— · —) Fragstein and Kampermann. (e) (——) Internal reflection measurements of Hansen (H9).

was able to obtain data with ease which yielded results in agreement with results obtained from very careful classical measurements of external reflectivity. Hansen's measurements are compared to the earlier measurements in Fig. 21.

The equations for the effective thickness which were discussed in Chapter Two can be used to determine approximate optical constants of thin films. By measuring the reflectivities for parallel and perpendicular polarization at a fixed angle, the effective thickness ratio is obtained from $(1 - R_{\perp})/(1 - R_{\parallel}) = d_{e\perp}/d_{e\parallel}$. If n_1 and n_3 are known, n_2 can be calculated by using the equations for the effective thickness for thin films. [The determination of n_2 is particularly simple when medium 3 is air ($n_3 = 1$) and when $\theta \sim \theta_c$ because, then, $d_{e\perp}/d_{e\parallel} = n_1^2/n_2^4$.] By employing an independent measurement of the film thickness (e.g., by ellipsometry) $d_{e\perp}$ and $d_{e\parallel}$ can be obtained and then from $R_{\perp} = 1 - \alpha d_{e\perp}$ or from $R_{\parallel} = 1 - \alpha d_{e\parallel}$, α can be obtained.

D. Semiconductor Surfaces

The first use of internal reflection techniques for studying surfaces was not dependent on the evanescent field but was concerned with the study of the inside of the surfaces, viz., semiconductor surface space charge regions. Later developments extended the technique to the study of the outside of the surface (H21). Some properties of the semiconductor surface will be discussed and it will become evident that what is referred to as the semiconductor surface has to do with a substantial portion (about 1 μ) of the bulk which cannot be probed via conventional techniques. (Semiconductor surfaces are treated in detail in a recent book by Many, Goldstein, and Grover (M5).)

1. Semiconductor Space Charge Region

The properties of a semiconductor are generally not uniform right out to the surface as shown in Fig. 22a. Here E_c and E_v represent the energy levels of the edges of the conduction and valence bands, respectively. The "forbidden region" or band gap is given by $E_G = E_c - E_v$. The fermi level is represented by E_F. Any charge on the surface is compensated by an equal and opposite charge which may be located in the semiconductor near the surface. The portion of the semiconductor where the compensating charge is found is called the semiconductor space charge region. The depth of this region is typically of the order of 1 μ for semiconductors. The surface barrier height qV_B, is determined by this added charge which is often calculated from conductivity measurements. Conductivity measurements of the space charge region are not always easily made, especially for inversion layers,

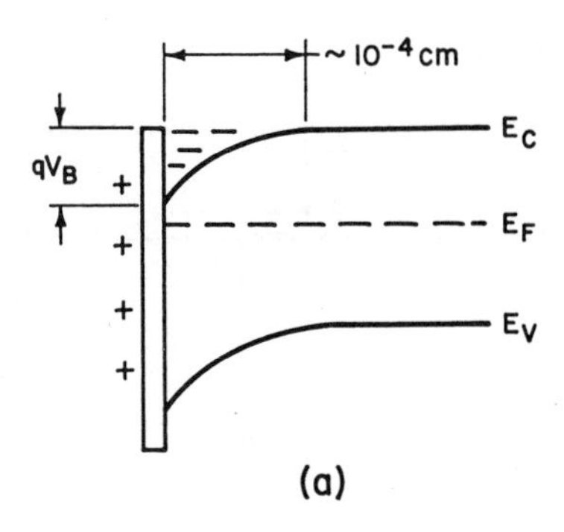

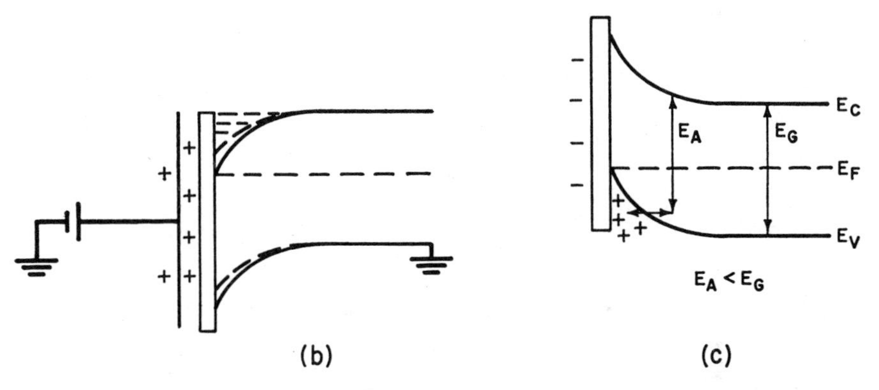

Fig. 22. Schematic representation of (a) a semiconductor surface and (b) control of the surface barrier by means of an external electric field. (c) Schematic representation of field-assisted absorption. See text for explanation of diagrams and symbols.

i.e., where the surface is of opposite conductivity type to that of the bulk, on certain semiconductors (e.g., silicon) when the space charge region becomes highly insulating from the bulk. Furthermore, contacts to the space charge region are not easily made. The excess carrier concentration, hence barrier height, can be measured by the use of internal reflection of infrared radiation. The necessary sensitivity can be achieved by employing multiple internal reflection.

The charge in the surface can be controlled by means of an external field, as shown in Fig. 22b. This is responsible for a large, added sensitivity for these measurements through the use of ac techniques and narrow band amplifiers. The sample arrangement for this field-effect measurement might be that shown in Fig. 23a. By adjusting the dc bias, the carrier type in the

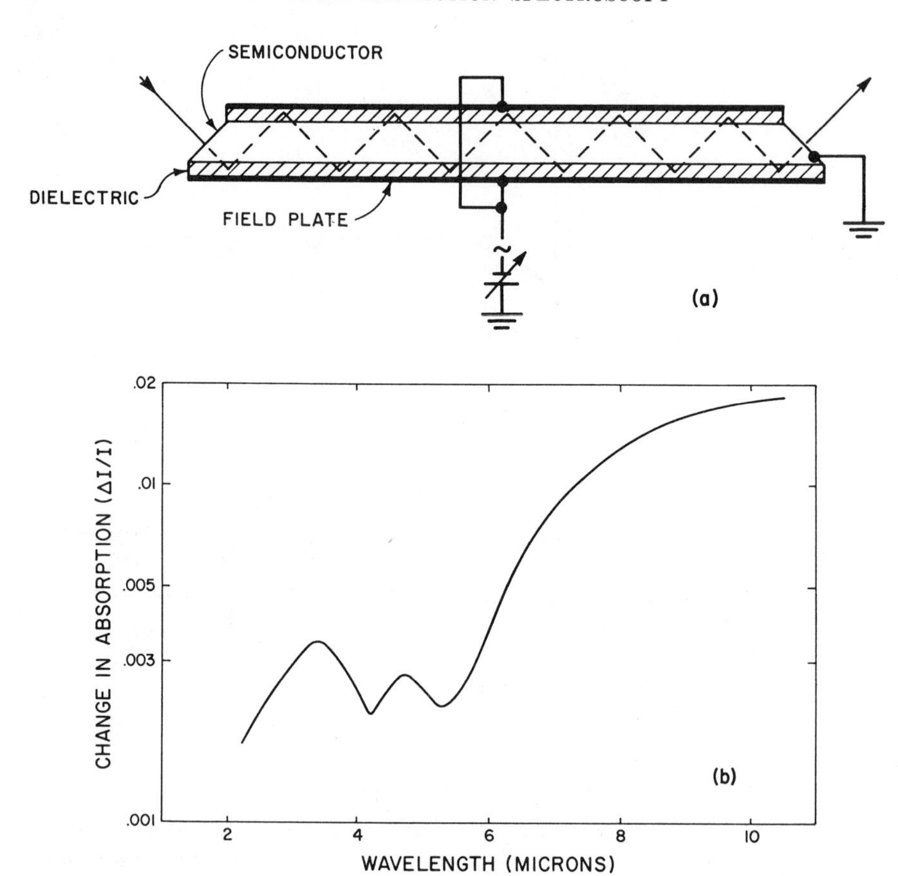

Fig. 23. Optical studies of field-effect modulation of semiconductor surfaces. (a) Condenser system for field-effect modulation of semiconductor barrier height and hence modulation of free carriers in space charge region and population in surface states of semiconductor. (b) Infrared absorption of free holes in the space charge region of intrinsic Ge for a change in hole density of 10^{11} per cm^2, $\theta = 45°$, $N = 100$ (B12a).

surface can be controlled and the absorption of holes and electrons can be studied separately on one and the same sample. This type of study should be important since the infrared absorption by free carriers as studied to date in the bulk, could only be changed by changing the doping of the semiconductor and when this is done other things also change; e.g., mobility is found to depend on the dopant.

The sensitivity that can be attained using internal reflection of infrared radiation is such that for a single reflection a change of the order of 10^9

carriers per cm^2 can be measured in the surface. Thus after, say, 100 reflections, it is possible to measure a change in carrier concentration in the surface of 10^7. Extremely sensitive measurements might thus be made on free carrier absorption in the space charge region. Specifically, the following studies might be made:

1. Compare the absorption of carriers in the bulk to that in the space charge region and thus get some information on the scattering mechanism at the surface and change of effective mass with barrier height using polarized light and the theory outlined in Chapter Two. It should also be of interest to measure the absorption cross section of holes and electrons as a function of barrier height which should shed some light on changes in scattering mechanisms and effective masses as the surface potential changes. An example of a measurement by Beckmann (B12a) showing the change in absorption as a function of wavelength by free holes in the space charge region is shown in Fig. 23b for an intrinsic Ge plate in contact with an electrolyte. The signal is produced by a change in the density of free holes of 10^{11} per cm^2 employing 100 internal reflections and $\theta = 45°$. The well-known hole bands due to interband transitions (K1) are clearly seen in the 2–6 μ region. By changing the dc bias voltage, Beckman was also able to measure the free electron absorption in the space charge region on the same sample.

2. Study of the interband transitions for holes and electrons. The added sensitivity may make it possible to locate the hole absorption bands for silicon in the 20–30 μ region which have not yet been found. (Silicon becomes transparent beyond 25 μ where the lattice absorption bands do not interfere.) This may also turn out to be an easy way to measure the shift of the interband transitions due to electric fields since, with the aid of blocking contacts, high electric fields at the surface can often be easily obtained. In the bulk it is often difficult to develop such high electric fields. Observations of such shifts in the bulk for holes in Ge have been reported (B34).

3. As suggested earlier, the surface barrier heights can be measured and monitored in this way. Some studies of free carrier changes in the space charge region where the relaxation effects are associated with trapping of free carriers in the space charge region by surface states were observed. The barrier heights were changed by bringing liquid metals into contact with the semiconductor and were due to contact potential differences (H15).

2. Field-Assisted Absorption

A shift of the absorption edge toward longer wavelengths can be obtained by means of an electric field and a change in absorption by the lattice can be observed. This may easily be demonstrated with CdS crystals which are normally transparent to sodium light yet become opaque to this light when an electric field is applied to the crystal. This effect may be attributed to a smearing out of the band edge in strong electric fields or a penetration of the electron in the forbidden region. With the aid of Fig. 22c it can be described in the following way. When there is an appreciable curvature of the bands within a distance comparable to an electron wavelength, the electron spends part of its time in the forbidden region as depicted by the horizontal arrow of Fig. 22c. When the electron is in the forbidden region, transitions to the conduction band can take place at smaller energies than that required for flat bands. This effect is most easily demonstrated in semiconductors with very sharp absorption edges (e.g., CdS, GaAs) and is easily measurable for fields exceeding 10^5 V/cm. It has been observed in bulk CdS by Böer (B25) and in Si by Keldyš *et al.* (K20). Williams (W10) has measured it at the surface for CdS and we have demonstrated it for the Si surface. This phenomenon is mentioned here because it is a prominent absorption mechanism at the surface. Also, it might be studied more easily at the surface than in the bulk since the magnitudes of the electric fields required are more easily attained at a surface with the aid of blocking contacts than in the bulk (e.g., fields of the order of 10^7 V/cm at Si surface (H23) have been obtained. Multiple internal reflection lends itself directly to the study of this effect for semiconductors with very sharp absorption edges.

A number of experiments have recently been reported (S14,S15,S16) of external reflectivity changes attributed to effects of this sort. Condenser structures and blocking layers at semiconductor–electrolyte interfaces were employed for these measurements. The value of these measurements is that they provide differential reflectivity measurements which are sensitive to reflection discontinuities giving a much richer spectrum than is obtained in conventional passive reflectivity measurements. This data ought to be useful as experimental verification of band theory calculations.

3. Semiconductor Surface States

It has been assumed in the previous section that the charge in the space charge region can be controlled by means of an externally applied field. This can not always be done, as Shockley and Pearson (S21) found out when they tried to control the conductivity of thin semiconductor samples in this way to make electronic devices. They found that they could control the conductivity through a range of 10% or less of that expected. This discrepancy was explained by the presence of surface states which absorb and immobilize part of the induced charge which cannot then contribute to an excess conductivity. A great deal is now known about surface states. Much of the information has been obtained from these so-called field-effect and surface conductivity measurements. This experiment is rather indirect and there are numerous aspects of the surface states which are still unclear. Different experimental approaches are desirable since it is then more likely possible to make simultaneous measurements on the surface; e.g., electrical and optical and spurious effects can more readily be eliminated.

If absorptions involving the surface states could be detected, it should be possible to obtain directly the optical absorption spectrum of the surface states. The order of magnitude of the signal expected can be determined if some assumptions are made. For example, if the density of states is assumed to be about $10^{10}/cm^2$ and their absorption cross section to be about 10^{-16} cm^2, reflectivity changes of one part in 10^6 or 10^7 must be measured to detect surface state absorption. This obviously can not be measured directly, even after 100 reflections. This can be accomplished, however, if only changes in absorption are amplified and measured just as in magnetic and electric resonance experiments where this is done by sweeping through the resonances periodically. In the present experiment the population in the surface states can be modulated, hence the absorption by the surface states can be changed.

The nature of the signal expected can be determined with the aid of Fig. 24. Transitions can take place from any filled state in the valence band to any empty surface state and from any filled surface state to an empty state in the conduction band. Hence, there will be no sharp absorption bands, only absorption edges. Because of the low density and probably localized character of the surface states, interstate transitions are considered undetectable. To detect the transitions involving the surface states, the charge in the surface is modulated which will alter the population in the states only near the fermi level. Thus only changes in the transitions denoted 1 and 2 in Figs. 24a and 24c will contribute to the signal. When the surface barrier height changes the number of free carriers, hence absorption, may increase or decrease. Consider what happens when electrons are taken out of the surface by the modulating field. For the n-type surface shown in Fig. 24a, when electrons are taken out of the surface, transition 2 becomes more likely since there are more empty states. Hence, there will be an increase of absorption over a wide wavelength range but terminating at the wavelength λ_2 corresponding to minimum energy difference between the empty surface state and a full state in the valence band. Conversely, transitions to the conduction band, denoted by 1, will be decreased because more surface states

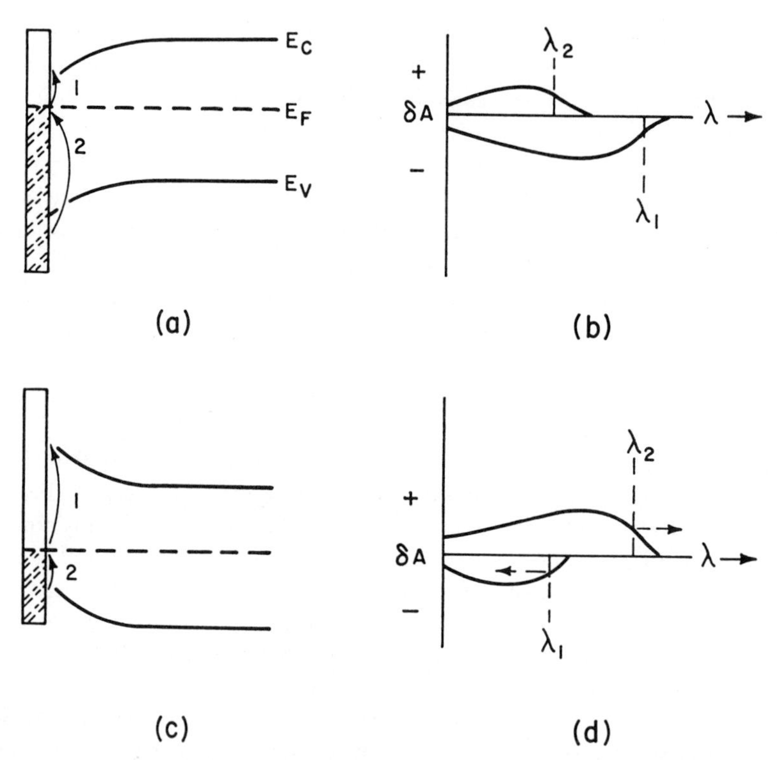

Fig. 24. Transitions involving semiconductor surface states and the nature of absorption expected therefrom. For an n-type surface shown in (a) the transition from the occupied surface states to the empty states in the conduction band, designated by 1, have a longer wavelength cutoff than do transitions from the full states of the valence band to the unoccupied surface states, designated by 2, as shown in (b). The opposite is true for a p-type surface shown in (c) as shown in (d). Note motion of absorption edges as barrier height is changed.

are empty; hence a decrease of absorption will be observed for this transition when modulation is applied.

The absorption edges, which will locate the energy level of the active surface states, will not be very sharp. The lack of sharpness can be attributed to the density of state distributions in the valence and conduction bands, the population distribution in the surface states, continuous distribution of the surface states, any non-uniformity of the surface and the finite depth of modulation.

The surface barrier can be controlled by an external field, ambient gas or composition of electrolyte in contact with the surface. Thus the entire forbidden region can be searched for surface states. When the surface becomes p-type, Fig. 24c, more surface states are empty; hence transition 2 is expected to predominate. The nature of the signals expected is shown in Fig. 24d for the p-type surface. It should be noted that as the surface is driven from n to p-type, the absorption edges for transitions 1 and 2 move to shorter and longer wavelengths, respectively.

For the flat band case the effects on transitions 1 and 2 are about equal and opposite so that little or no signal should be observed.

Since some of the induced carriers will remain in the space charge region, there will always be superimposed on the surface state absorption a broad band signal arising from free carrier absorption due to these free carriers. This component of absorption will generally follow a λ^2 dependence with some deviations due to interband transitions (M17) and its magnitude will be proportional to the number of carriers which remain in the space charge region.

Results showing the change in the free carrier and surface state absorption given in Figs. 25 and 26 were obtained using the technique outlined in Fig. 23.

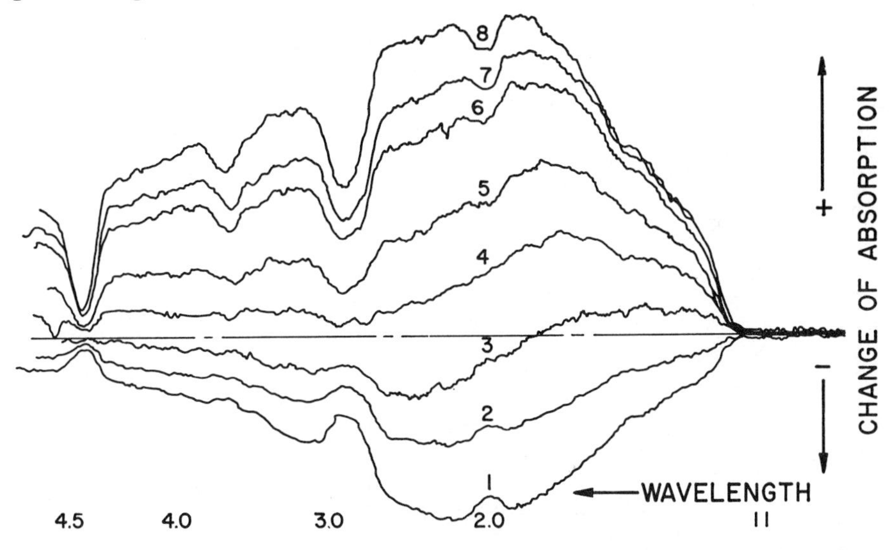

Fig. 25. Change of surface state absorption with wavelength for various values of net charge in a silicon surface for low biases. Each curve from *1* through *8* represents an addition of about 2×10^{11} holes per cm^2 to the surface. The negative signals are observed when the surface is n-type (curves *1* and *2*) and the positive signals when the surface is p-type (curves *4* through *8*). When both positive and negative signals were observed, e.g., curves *3*, the surface was nearly in flat band condition. The largest signals here represent a change in absorption at the surface of about one part in 10^6.

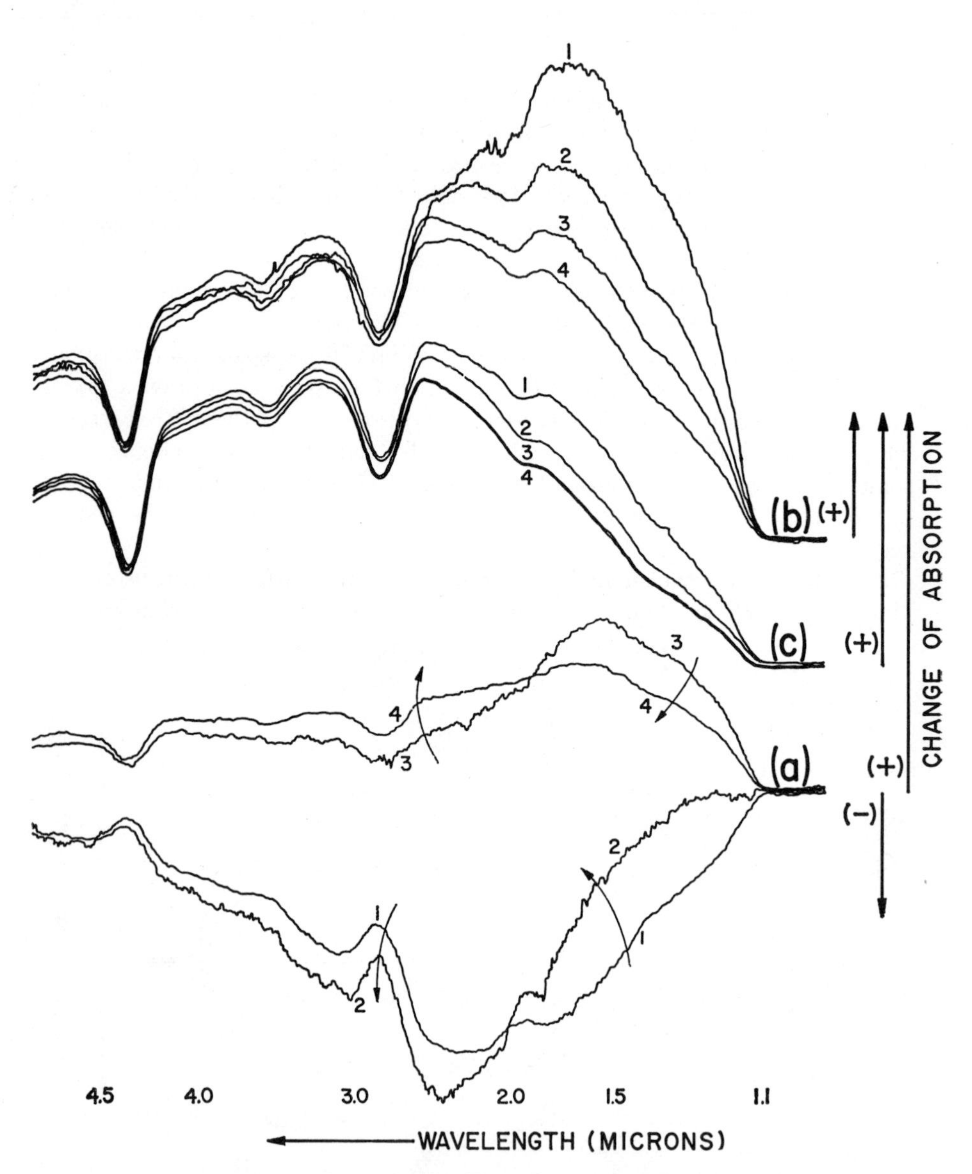

Fig. 26. Surface state and free carrier absorption in a silicon surface. The curves have been normalized at the longer wavelength so that the change in the absorption at the shorter wavelength could be compared more easily. For the low biases (curves *a*, where the dc bias is increased in equal steps from 10 V for curve *1* to 70 V for curve *4*) almost all the transitions involve surface state absorption. For intermediate biases (curves *b*, where the dc bias is increased from 60 V for curve *1* to 160 V for curve *4*) there is surface state absorption only at the shorter wavelengths, the rest being dominantly free carrier absorption. For

Each curve represents the recorder tracing for a different dc bias but the same ac modulating field. The dc bias increases as the numbers designating the curves increase in Figs. 25 and 26. The results are complicated somewhat since the infrared intensity is not constant with wavelength. The apparent absorption bands reflect a decreased infrared intensity arising from absorption by atmospheric water and carbon dioxide. The bias is changed in small steps to drive the surface from n to p-type. In Fig. 25 the amplifier gain was kept constant while in Fig. 26 the gain was adjusted to normalize the curves at the longer wavelengths so that they could be more readily compared at the shorter wavelengths. Since the character of the signal is strongly dependent on bias and wavelength at low biases as shown by the curves of Figs. 25 and 26a, these transitions are attributed to surface state absorption. At the high biases (Fig. 26c) the character of the signal is independent of bias and these signals are attributed to free carrier absorption. The curves of Fig. 26b represent an intermediate case where there is a mixture of surface state and free carrier absorption. Consistent with expectations, the following points should be observed:

1. The signals are of the expected order of magnitude assuming an absorption cross section of 10^{-16} cm^2.

2. A negative signal is observed for n-type surfaces (Fig. 25 curves 1 and 2) and positive for p-type (Fig. 25 curves 4 through 8). (The surface type was checked independently for all biases by measuring the surface photovoltage.)

3. For the flat band case (Curve 3 of Fig. 25), there is a great deal of compensation so that the observed signal is very small and a mixture of signals (both positive and negative) is observed.

4. Part of the signal is always changing character. This part of the signal is attributed to surface state absorption and the change in character can be accounted for in terms of the relative magnitude of transitions 1 and 2 and the motion of their absorption edges.

5. For a large bias the character of the curve has become independent of bias which suggests few or no surface states in this part of the forbidden region. When the signals are normalized for infrared intensity variations, it is found that they follow a λ^2 dependence very closely. This λ^2 dependence is expected for holes in silicon in this wavelength range.

---

high biases (curves c, which represent a dc bias range of 160–230 V) there is little change in surface state activity at all wavelengths and the absorption tends to be independent of bias. Curves *3* and *4* of group c follow a λ^2 dependence very closely when adjusted for the variation of the infrared intensity with wavelength.

It is necessary to measure the free carrier contribution to each curve and subtract it from the total signal to determine the surface state absorption. This can be done for each bias by considering the measurements at long wavelengths where it is expected that free carrier absorption will predominate because of the λ^2 dependence. This has been done for low biases in an approximate way only, since the measurements were not carried out to long enough wavelengths so that the degree of free carrier absorption could be unambiguously determined. When this is done correctly, it is evident that absorption edges in the remaining signals will appear. These results show that there is a continuous distribution of surface states but that their density decreases or even becomes zero near the top of the valence band.

Other applications of similar techniques (C6,S1) to the study of Ge surfaces revealed narrow absorption bands which are attributed to transitions involving surface states.

E. Adsorbed Molecules and Surface Reactions on Semiconductors and Insulators

There are many surface effects which have escaped thorough investigation and therefore understanding. For semiconductor surfaces, for example, one-tenth monolayer coverage (i.e., one impurity in every ten atoms) causes drastic effects on the physical properties of the surface and strongly influences the performance of transistors (M5). Optical spectra of such surfaces can be of value in more than one respect. Not only do they serve to identify the impurities by comparison to known spectra, but exact location of the bands and the appearance of new ones shed some light on the nature of the bonding of the impurities to the surface and chemical reactions with the surface. Recent reports indicate that emission spectra in the visible and infrared regions yield some information on the nature of the surface (L7,L8, L9,L10). More data must, however, be gathered on this approach. It is difficult to obtain useful information from transmission measurements on samples in very thin film form because of the necessity of traversing the film many times to amplify the weak absorption and the associated power losses. Eischens and Pliskin (E4) have successfully employed transmission techniques on finely divided powders to study surface absorptions and reactions. There are two reasons why it is possible to record surface spectra using pulverized samples. First, fine powders have the necessary large surface area, and second, for sufficiently small particles scattering of light is absent (even very fine metal powders behave as nonconductors). Pulverizing is not recommended for semiconductors since not only does the nature of the semiconductor change, but also its properties are unknown when the particle size becomes smaller than a Debye length and, furthermore, crystalline orientation is lost. A number of experiments have demonstrated that internal reflection techniques can be employed with advantage to identify and study adsorbed molecules. These areas of application of IRS will now be discussed.

Many semiconducting materials are ideal materials for studying surface effects. Because of the massive effort in both preparation and study of semiconductors following the invention of the transistor, high quality specimens are available and their bulk properties are generally understood better than those of other materials. Many of these materials are transparent over a large portion of the infrared region, viz., the so-called "fingerprint region" (2–15 μ), and thus can be used for making the IRE's. Furthermore, these materials can be considered as conductors for many purposes and thus electrode reactions, etc., can be studied using these materials.

For surface studies of this type it is preferable to work with single crystal materials of known purity and so oriented that the crystalline planes on the broad surfaces are known since the bonding to the different planes will be different. Furthermore, the surfaces should be free of mechanical damage to preserve the crystalline orientation.

1. Adsorbed Molecules

The first suggestion that the evanescent wave might be used to measure the spectra of adsorbed molecules was made in 1959 at the Second International Conference on Semiconductor Surfaces (H20). Although there is definite evidence that in certain cases internal reflection techniques can be used for this purpose, they have not been widely employed because of experimental difficulties and lack of suitable commercial instrumentation. Internal reflection spectroscopy is beginning to be more widely used for this purpose as equipment becomes more readily available.

Results showing that surface spectra of solid transparent materials can be obtained are given in Figs. 27, 28, and 29. Figure 27 shows the internal reflection spectrum ($N = 165$, $\theta = 45°$) of a mechanically polished silicon surface exposed to the atmosphere. The two bands represent hydroxyl (O—H band) and hydrocarbon (C—H band) components on the surface at 2.9 and 3.4 μ, respectively. For a surface exposed to the atmosphere the O—H is always present and the C—H is generally present except on a freshly cleaned surface. Figure 28a shows some results of Becker and Gobeli (B10) in which they monitored the formation of SiH_4 by bombarding the surface of a silicon plate with atomic hydrogen. Figure 28b shows the decrease in the intensity of the absorption band as surface layers are removed via argon

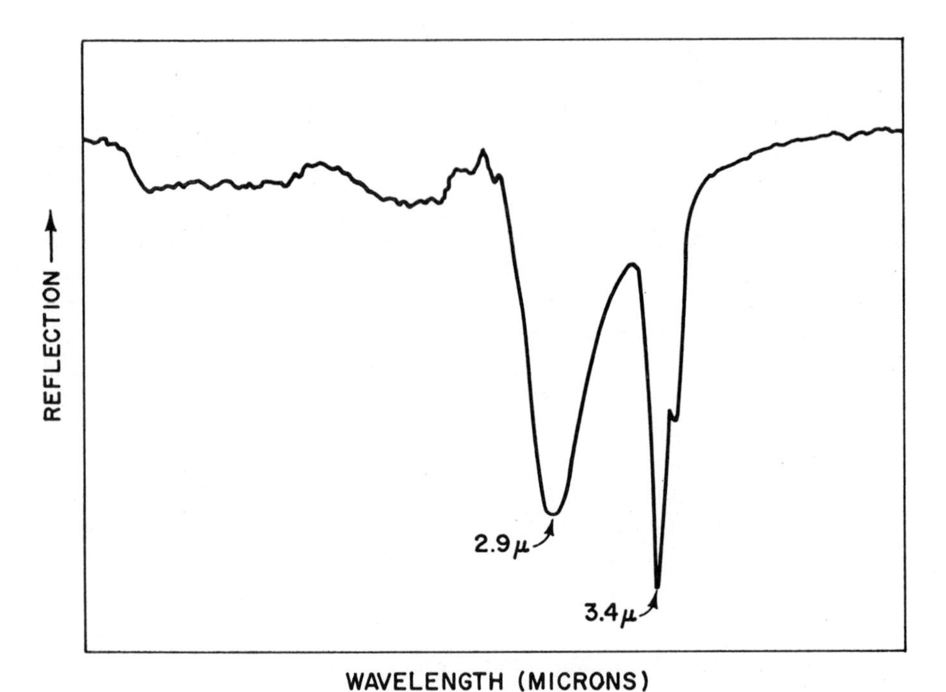

Fig. 27. Surface spectrum of a silicon internal reflection plate, $N = 165$, $\theta = 45°$. Note the presence of O—H and C—H bands at 2.9 and 3.4 μ, respectively.

bombardment. Their results showed that the location of the band depended on the energy of the hydrogen ions. This can be explained by the depth of penetration of the H^+ ions, hence change of bonding to the Si. Measurements such as these are not limited to semiconductor surfaces but can be made on any transparent material. In some other measurements, Beckmann (B12) employed internal reflection spectroscopy to determine the composition of surface films produced on germanium in different etchants. From the spectral behavior he concludes that films prepared in HF/HNO_3 consist of amorphous dioxide. He also finds germanium hydride and germanium hydroxide bands, as well as some water and parts of the etch in these films. Films produced in HF/H_2O_2, on the other hand, contain a high number of hydride bands. An internal reflection spectrum of a Ge plate etched for 20 sec in a mixture consisting of 7 parts HF (40%) and 3 parts HNO_3 (65%) is shown in Fig. 29 for $N = 50$, $\theta = 45°$. A transmission measurement through the plate (two surfaces) yielded a spectrum for the GeO and GeO_2 bands of about one-thirtieth of the contrast of the internal reflection spectrum (B12a).

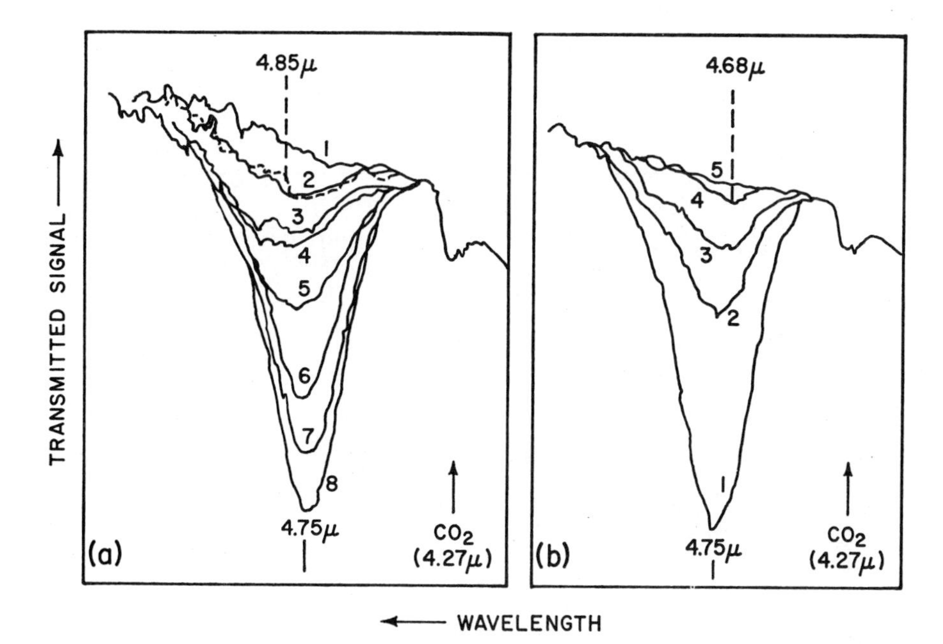

Fig. 28. Internal reflection spectra of silicon surface $N = 200$, $\theta = 45°$ (B10). (a) Curve *1a* an initially clean Si surface after sputtering in argon and annealing. The dashed curve, nearly superposed on *2a*, shows the maximum absorption peak resulting from exposure of silicon to atomic hydrogen. Curves *2a* to *8a* due to bombardment with hydrogen ions of increasing energy and for longer times. Note shift in absorption peak. (b) Series of spectra showing decrease in strength of silicon hydride band as the silicon was bombarded with argon ions for various lengths of sputtering. Curve *1b* thick surface layer, same as curve *8a*. Note band shift for curve *4b* relative to curve *2a*.

It is possible to make such measurements even through the wavelength region of some of the weak lattice bands by employing small, thin plates, hence short path lengths in the optical material, and by placing a clean IRE or a transmission plate in the reference beam to cancel the lattice bands.

2. Photoenhanced Adsorption and Desorption

It is well known that light can catalyze the absorption and desorption process of gases on the surface of a solid. Such effects have been measured indirectly to date (K22). Although IRS has not yet been employed to study effects of this sort it is an obvious application for semiconductors and other transparent materials.

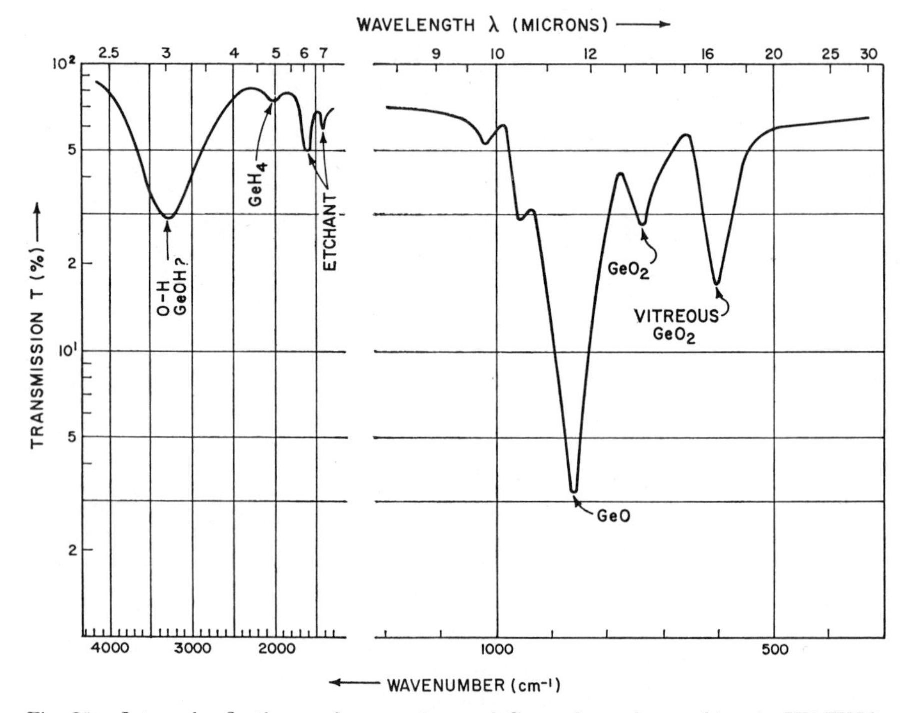

Fig. 29. Internal reflection surface spectrum of Ge surface after etching in HF/HNO_3, $N = 50$, $\theta = 45°$ (B12). The complexes formed on the surface are clearly detectable.

3. Oxidation

Internal reflection spectroscopy offers a means of studying the properties of an oxide especially in its early stages of growth. The solid curve of Fig. 30a shows the single-beam transmission of an Si plate at $\theta = 45°$ after some 50 reflections and the dotted curve shows the deviations when *N*-methylacetamide surrounds the plate. Figure 30b is the transmission after the surface was electrolytically oxidized with *N*-methylacetamide. Electron microscope studies of an oxide produced in this way indicated the oxide to be very dense with no traces of the electrolyte (P18). Yet, the internal reflection measurements show absorption bands in the oxide which correspond to those of *N*-methylacetamide. From this, the presence of the electrolyte in the oxide in some form is suspected. Silicon, unfortunately, is transparent only out to 6 μ for long path lengths. As was pointed out earlier, by using short path length IRE's and suitable reference plates, surface spectra can be recorded through the weak lattice bands.

Some measurements using conventional transmission have been recently reported for silicon (B11). Germanium, which is transparent over a longer wavelength range, is ideal for studying its oxides, GeO and GeO_2, via IRS as has been shown by Beckmann (B12). He was able to record the spectrum at $\theta = 45°$ with only 50 reflections of the Ge–O valence vibration of germanium dioxide of films as thin as 15 Å determined from ellipsometry measurements (B12a).

4. Electrode Surface Reactions

Electrode reactions are of considerable interest because of their importance, for example, to fuel cells. Internal reflection spectroscopy offers a means of studying such reactions for certain systems. Semiconductor plates, especially double-pass plates, provide excellent electrodes for this purpose because they are sufficiently good electrical conductors and also optically transparent. Reactions can be studied *in situ* in the wavelength region where the electrolyte has a window, i.e., where it is optically transparent. This is necessary because the surface film on the electrode may be only a few angstroms thick while the effective thickness of the electrolyte may be more than one micron. A possible means for extending the investigation to wavelength regions where the liquid is absorbing is to withdraw the electrode from solution in order to record the surface spectrum. Withdrawing the electrode is generally undesirable because it upsets the chemical reactions. In any such investigation corrosion of the electrode will eventually terminate the experiment. The reaction can be monitored only as long as sufficient optical surface polish of the electrode (IRE) is maintained.

The possibility of monitoring such electrode surface reaction was demonstrated recently by Mark and Pons (M6) employing a Ge electrode. Figure 31 shows the change in the internal reflection spectrum of 8-hydroxyquinoline (saturated solution in dimethylformamide—0.1M $LiClO_4 \cdot 3H_2O$) before electrolysis (Fig. 31a) and after (Fig. 31b). In other work Mark and Pons are attempting to prepare electrodes by depositing thin coats ($\sim 1\ \mu$ thick) of Pd, Pt, or Au on KRS-5 plates. The use of metal films on the IRE will severely limit the number of reflections because of the enhanced reflectivity loss.

Hansen, Osteryoung, and Kuwana (H11) have extended such measurements to the visible and UV regions using glass electrodes coated with semiconducting SnO_2 to make the electrode conducting. Total internal reflection occurs at the SnO_2–electrolyte interface and the reaction between the SnO_2 and the electrolyte is then monitored. The use of coated IRE's over a wide wavelength range complicates the interpretation of the spectra because of

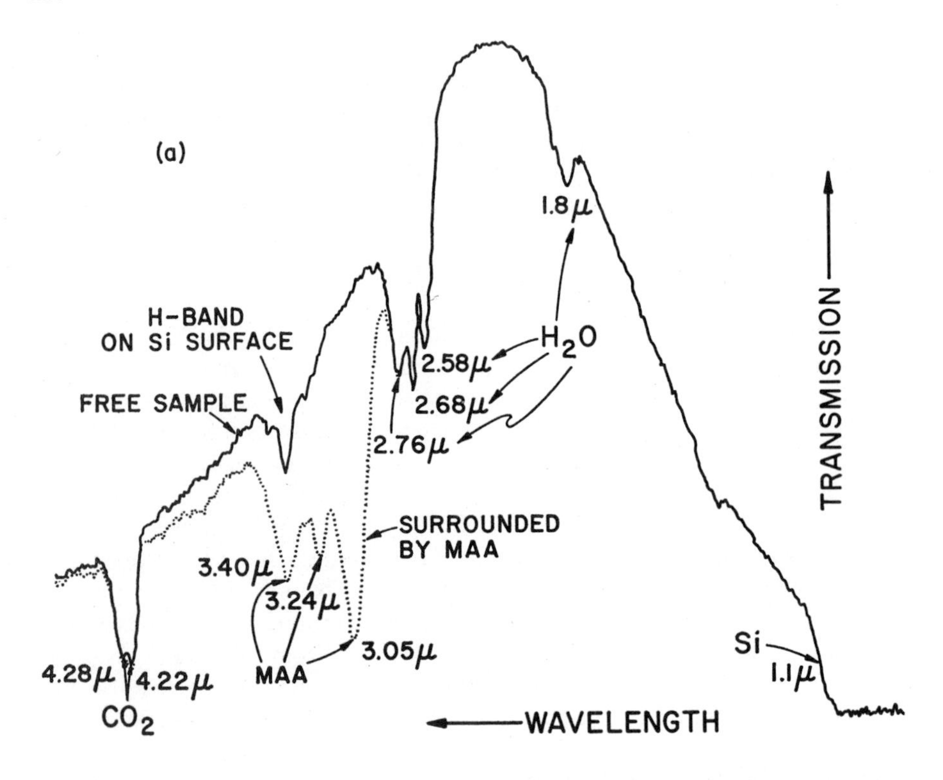

Fig. 30. Transmission of silicon plate before and after oxidation. (a) Transmission of a silicon sample after 50 internal reflections. The dotted curve indicates the deviations that occur when the unoxidized silicon plate is surrounded by the electrolyte, *N*-methylacetamide. The absorption bands are characteristic of the electrolyte. (b) Transmission of a

the resonance phenomenon in the thin film, as discussed in Chapter Five and by Hansen et al. (H11a); therefore uncoated IRE's are preferable. The energies in the visible and UV regions permit the study of the electron transfer process. There are a number of advantages of working in the visible. First, the electrolytes are often non-absorbing in this wavelength region; second, the short wavelengths make the effective thickness correspondingly small and thus it is possible to measure thinner films even when the electrolyte is absorbing.

5. Catalysis

Internal reflection techniques might find general use in the investigation of catalysis for semiconductors and dielectrics.

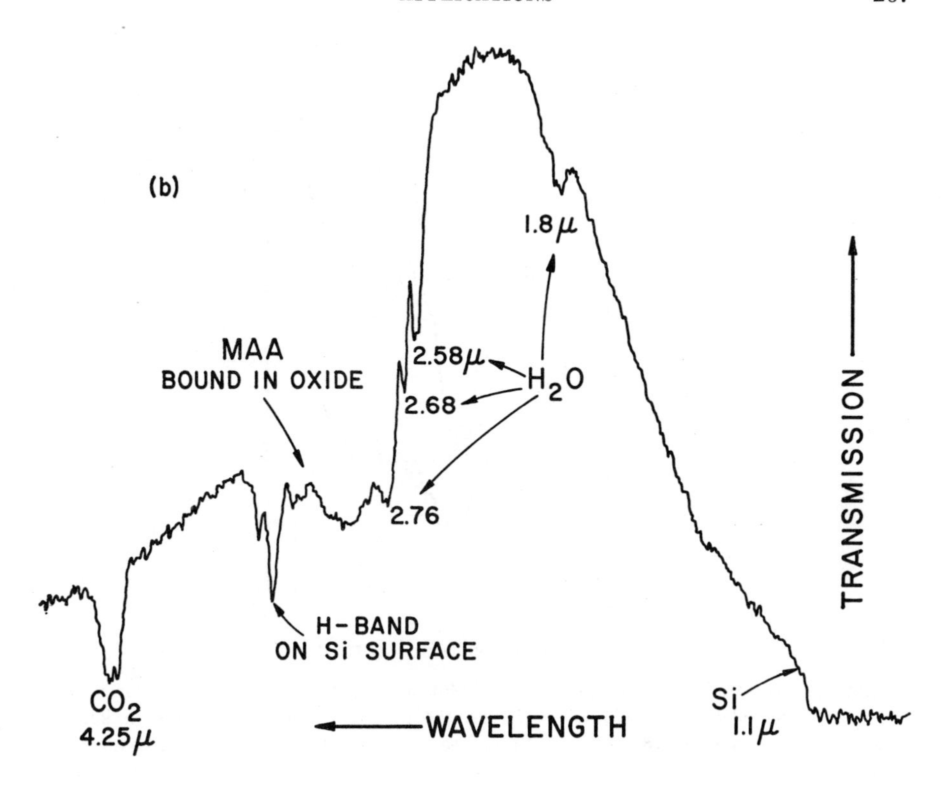

silicon plate after 100 internal reflections after it had been oxidized via *N*-methylacetamide. By comparison with Fig. 30a, the spectrum suggests that some *N*-methylacetamide is bound in the oxide in some (unknown) form.

6. Flotation

Flotation is a process of ore beneficiation, wherein the mineral of interest is concentrated in the froth from an ore pulp. This is achieved by conditioning the pulp with an organic reagent, which selectively coats the mineral with a hydrophobic (or aerophyllic) coating of a monolayer thickness. The reagent is called the collector. When air is introduced into such a collector conditioned pulp, the hydrophobic particles get attached to air bubbles and are collected in the froth. The particle sizes normally subjected to flotation will be around 75 μ. There is considerable interest (P2,R4) in understanding the nature, physical or chemical, of the formation of the

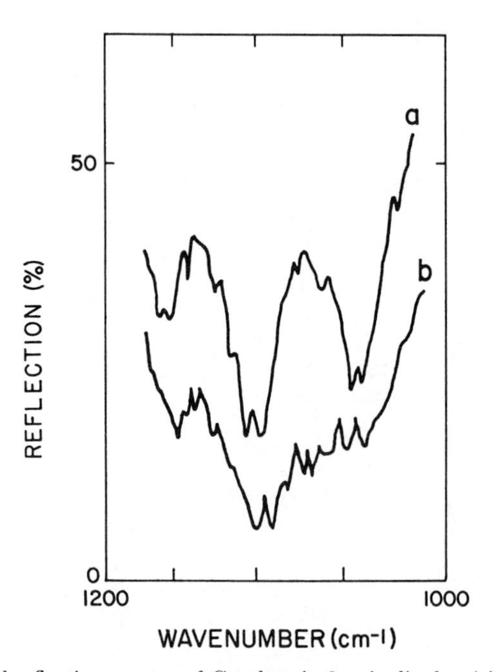

Fig. 31. Internal reflection spectra of Ge plate in 8-quinolinol. (a) Before electrolysis. (b) After brief electrolysis (M6). Although the results are not completely understood, these curves show that IRS can be employed to obtain *in situ* spectra of species at or near electrode surface during actual electrolysis.

collector coating over the mineral particle. If it is chemical, infrared spectroscopy might be used to determine the species and the molecular orientation of the reagent. The minerals of interest include zircon ($ZrSiO_4$), rutile (TiO_2), and sapphire (Al_2O_3) and the collector is sodium dodecylbenzene sulfonate. The problem here again involves measuring a surface layer on an absorbing substrate since many of the reactions occur in a wavelength region where the mineral is opaque. Infrared transmission has been used in a number of cases where the particle sizes were made 0.15 μ or less. Internal reflection spectroscopy might be used in the transparent regions of the mineral where initially it would be of advantage to make the IRE of the mineral itself so that its surface could be sampled more efficiently.

F. Very Thin Films

The possibility of recording the spectrum of a very thin film placed on the surface of the IRE extends spectroscopy techniques to many areas where it was previously not applicable. Even though the sensitivity required here is of about the same order of magnitude as that required for monitoring adsorbed molecules and surface reactions, a differentiation is made between this type of study and the study of very thin films since in the latter case the IRE is not necessarily involved in the reactions but serves only to obtain the conditions necessary to record internal reflection spectra. Mechanically prepared surfaces for the IRE are thus acceptable for these studies.

Sharpe (S17,S18) was the first to extend IRS to studies of monomolecular films transferred to the surface of the IRE principally because of his interest in adhesion. Figure 32a shows the internal reflection spectrum of a film of hydrogen octadecanoate 2.9 molecules thick placed on Ge plate via a modified Langmuir–Blodgett (B24) technique. (He actually recorded spectra of monomolecular films in other measurements.) The capability for recording the spectra of very thin films is clearly demonstrated. The acid carbonyl absorption, strongly present in the bulk at 1705–1715 cm^{-1}, seems to be virtually absent in the spectra of the oriented films from which certain conclusions regarding the orientation on the surface can be made. Of particular interest is the appearance of a new intense band (at 1593 cm^{-1}) in Fig. 32b after a few hours contact whose intensity grows with time. This new band is attributed to a reaction of the carboxyl groups with the surface to form germanium salt by chemisorption. Sharpe has also observed chemical reaction between different monomolecular films stacked on a Ge IRE.

Loeb (L6) is also experimenting with fatty acid films transferred to Ge-plates to study polymer molecules whose spectra are dependent upon molecular configuration. Poly(γ-benzyl-L-glutamate), for example, exhibits the amide I-band frequency associated with the α helical configuration when a monolayer is transferred from the air–water interface.

There are many areas in the medical field which are really surface problems involving thin films. The sense of smell and taste are examples. The conditions to monitor the reactions involved can be set up in the laboratory by placing cephalin, which is the phospholipid that makes up the outside of the olfactory membranes, on the IRE and then exposing it to the aromatic of interest (e.g., benzene, chloroform, acid aldehyde, etc.) (F18).

Interest has also been expressed in the study of the Gouy layer (R8) via IRS. The Gouy layer is the layer in an electrolyte adjacent to an electrode where ion concentrations change rapidly with distance. It extends a distance of only a few angstroms from the surface of the electrode. This distance is small compared to an effective thickness; therefore here, as in a number of the experiments already discussed, the bulk material (electrolyte) must be substantially transparent in spectral regions where effects associated with the

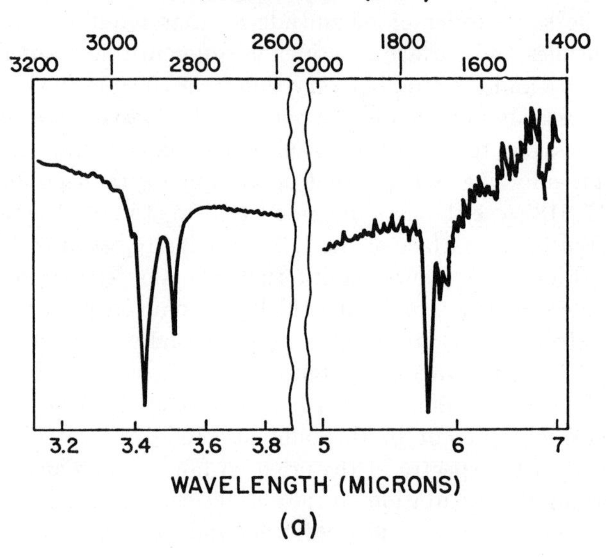

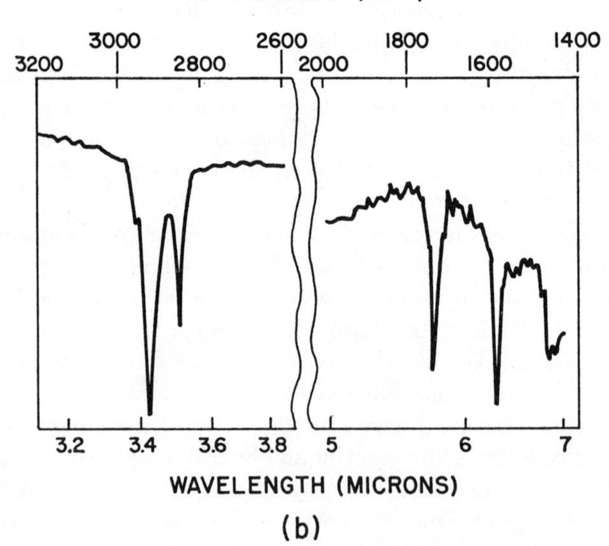

Fig. 32. Internal reflection spectrum of film of hydrogen octadecanoate on Ge plate, $N = 8$, $\theta = 45°$. (a) Initial contact of film, 2.9 molecules thick. (b) 24 hours after contact of film, 3.5 molecules thick. Note appearance of new band (S17).

Gouy layer are to be observed. Furthermore, because of the small effective thickness such measurements might be made with advantage in the UV.

G. Submicrogram Quantities

Often only a very minute quantity of a sample material is available for the experimentalist to work with. In attempting to obtain the optical spectrum of these samples, condensing systems have been employed in which the source image has been reduced to a size of 1×4 mm or smaller. It is found convenient, in some cases, to dissolve the sample material in a suitable transparent solvent and place the solution in a microcell. In other cases, micro KBr disks of 1.5 or 0.5 mm diameter have been used with excellent success. Microgram quantities can be handled fairly readily in this way and for strong absorbers, 0.1–0.01 μg quantities have been analyzed.

Another technique that has been employed to record the spectra of minute quantities (S25) is that of the so-called "double transmisssion." In this case, the solution is placed on a front surfaced mirror; the solvent evaporates leaving the solute on the mirror. On using a condensed light beam that is reflected from the mirror but through the residue, the spectrum can be recorded. The advantage in this technique is that the solvent is absent and, provided that the sample is thick enough, a sensitivity can be obtained twice as great as that via a single transmission. A sensitivity corresponding to "double-transmission" is achieved if the sample thickness is $\lambda/4$ or greater. For smaller thicknesses the sensitivity decreases and for very small thicknesses it approaches zero. It would be advantageous to place a $\lambda/4$ dielectric film on the metal mirror and then to place the sample on the dielectric in order to locate the thin sample at the absorption-sensitive loop of the standing wave. (Recall the experiment of O. Wiener which was described in Chapter Two.) For thicknesses greater than $\lambda/2$, interference phenomena will be present resulting in the usual complications. The results are further complicated somewhat by the fact that the front surface reflection ($\sim$4%) is mixed in with the doubly transmitted component giving a mixed spectrum (reflection plus transmission). In addition, relative band intensities for thin films on a metal mirror will not be the same as that observed in transmission measurements. The reason for this is that the distance of the loop from the surface, viz., $\lambda/4$, will be different at different wavelengths and hence the location of the film relative to the loop will also change. Thus a film positioned for maximum absorption at $\lambda = 3\ \mu$ will show a minimum in absorption at $\lambda = 6\ \mu$.

Internal reflection spectroscopy has a number of advantages over the approaches described in the foregoing for investigating submicrogram quantities. Just as in the "double-transmission" technique, the sample material can be placed free of the solvent on the sampling area. In addition, for films thinner than $\lambda/4$, a maximum in the interaction with the sample material can be achieved for a single reflection because the sample can be placed at the loop of the standing wave for $\theta \sim \theta_c$. A small angle of incidence also has the advantage of a narrow beam width at the reflecting surface for samples of limited extent. With the aid of special IRE's such as the optical cavity or the rosette, enhanced absorptions can be achieved because of the multiple reflections of the light beam from one point. The expected gain in sensitivity is at least one, and possibly two, orders of magnitude. Such enhanced sensitivity has already been demonstrated (see Chapter Five on optical cavity). Even for a single reflection the feasibility of handling submicrogram quantities has been demonstrated. A sensitivity of one-tenth microgram is clearly shown in Fig. 33 for the C—H band of polystyrene at a wavelength of 3.4 μ (H33). Measured amounts of a solution containing polystyrene were placed on the IRE which left a known quantity of solute on the IRE when the solvent evaporated.

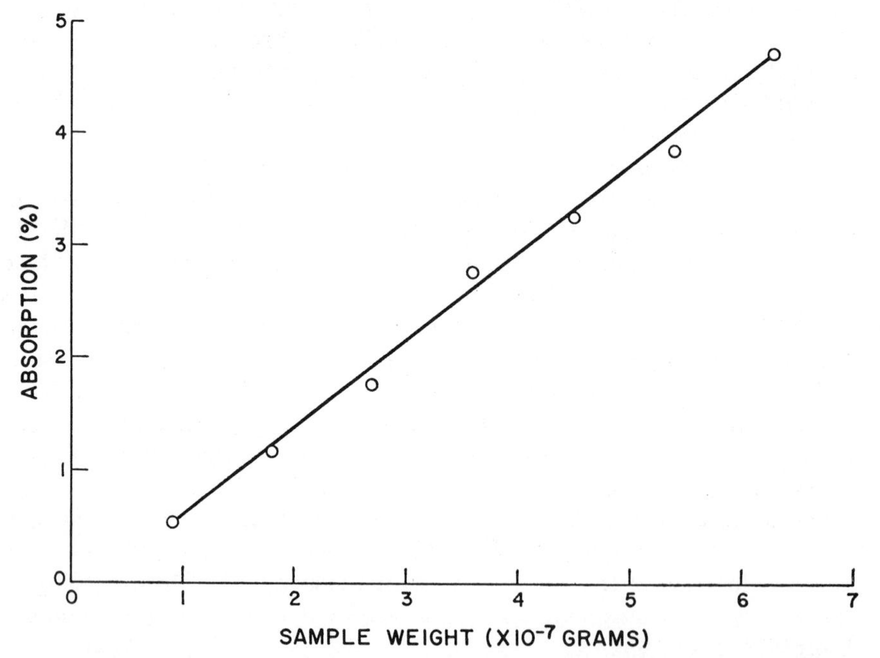

Fig. 33. Absorption by C—H band of polystyrene at 3.4 μ versus sample weight observed via internal reflection. Similar results were obtained for the 9.5 μ band of Saran.

An application of IRS to the study of microgram quantities of organophosphorus pesticides via IRS has been described by Hermann (H43). It should be noted that his internal reflection spectra resemble transmission spectra rather closely and do not show the relatively stronger absorption for the bands at longer wavelengths characteristic of bulk spectra. Presumably, this is so because his samples are in very thin film form and therefore the spectra represent those of thin films rather than bulk. A typical result is shown in Fig. 34 where the transmission spectrum (Fig. 34a) is compared to the internal reflection spectrum (Fig. 34b). The power loss in Fig. 34b at the shorter wavelengths is typical of KRS-5 plates which, because of their softness, are difficult to polish adequately.

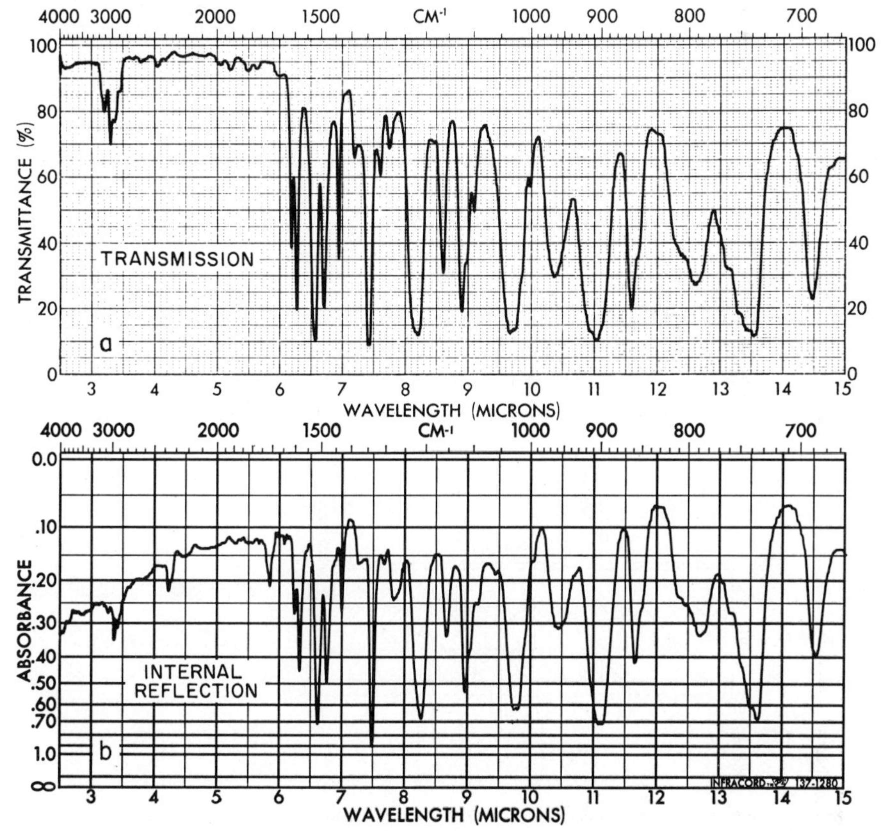

Fig. 34. Comparison of transmission and internal reflection spectrum of pesticide EPN. Curve *a* transmission and curve *b* internal reflection using KRS-5 IRE, $N = 28$, $\theta = 45°$ (H43).

H. Miscellaneous Applications

Many of the applications discussed in this section are special cases of the more general applications already discussed and some of these possible applications have not yet been demonstrated. These special applications, however, are each of sufficient interest that they merit individual consideration.

1. Condensed and Frozen Species

It is a straightforward matter by means of some refrigerator to vary the temperature of the IRE to almost any desired low temperature. Peltier coolers can be used to produce temperature differences between the cold and hot junctions of about 60°C. Other closed-cycle coolers (such as the Cryogem), can be used to produce temperatures down to 20°K and below (D22). For fixed low temperatures, condensed gases may be used in suitable cryostats. One design for temperature control of the IRE via Peltier cooling is shown in Fig. 35. For efficient cooling thermal contact is made between one of the broad faces of the IRE and the Peltier cooler. In order to prevent attenuation of the light beam, optical contact must be avoided but good thermal contact must be maintained; therefore a low index transparent film about 5 μ in thickness is placed between the two. Semiconducting materials such as Si, Ge, and GaAs have high thermal conductivities and high refractive indices and can be used for the IRE. Other high index materials such as KRS-5 or AgBr may also be used; however they have lower thermal conductivities. The spacer may be made from AgCl, CsI, or CsBr. The angle of

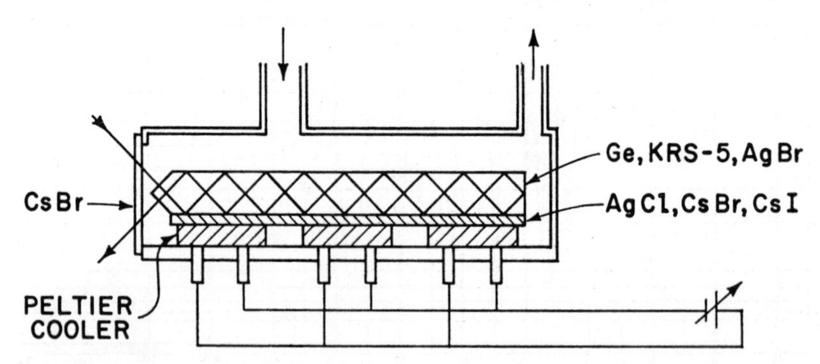

Fig. 35. Peltier cooling of IRE for collecting gas chromatographic fractions. IRE can be cooled or heated by controlling direction and magnitude of current through thermoelectric junctions. Fraction is collected on cold surface of IRE, analyzed, and then allowed to evaporate by heating IRE.

incidence in the IRE must be adjusted so that it exceeds the critical angle of the IRE–spacer interface. For the IRE's which have high thermal conductivities, sufficient cooling capacity is obtained by cooling via the long edges. No spacer is then required and both reflecting faces of the IRE are then exposed. Any material of sufficiently high boiling point can therefore be trapped on the surface of the IRE and analyzed or studied as a function of temperature. For well-designed systems, the quantity of material required may be only in the submicrogram and submicroliter ranges. The possibility of handling such minute quantities has important implications in many areas.

Some of the areas wherein a cooled IRE can be employed with advantage are the following:

a. Analysis of Gas Chromatographic Fractions

One of the first practical applications suggested for IRS was its use in identifying gas chromatographic (GC) fractions. There is little doubt that a well-designed system will do the job. Peltier cooling is quite adequate for many of the higher boiling point fractions. The GC fraction is conducted via the inlet tube of Fig. 35, into the space adjacent to the exposed surface and is quickly trapped on the surface if the temperature of the Ge plate is low enough. After analysis the IRE plate is heated, by reversing the polarity of the power supply, to vaporize the GC fraction so that it can be pumped out of the chamber.

Another approach, developed at Wilks Scientific Corp. (W9), is to cool two internal reflection plates whose broad faces are in contact. The GC fraction is then injected between the two plates and initially condensed but due to capillary action is retained for sufficient time for analysis, even after the plates become warm. A photograph showing the collection of a GC fraction where it is injected between two cooled KRS-5 plates is shown in Fig. 36. The cooled plate assembly is subsequently mounted in a spectrometer for infrared analysis of the fraction. Typical spectra are shown in Fig. 37.

b. Breath Analysis

Experiments indicate (S31a) that analysis of breath promises to be a good approach for early medical diagnosis. Carbon monoxide is readily detected in the breath of a smoker. Acetone is present in the breath of a diabetic. Obviously, the same instrumentation as that developed for analysis of gas chromatographic fractions can be applied to analyze some high boiling point components in the breath. A gas chromatograph may be used just as well to remove some of the interfering components such as H_2O and CO_2.

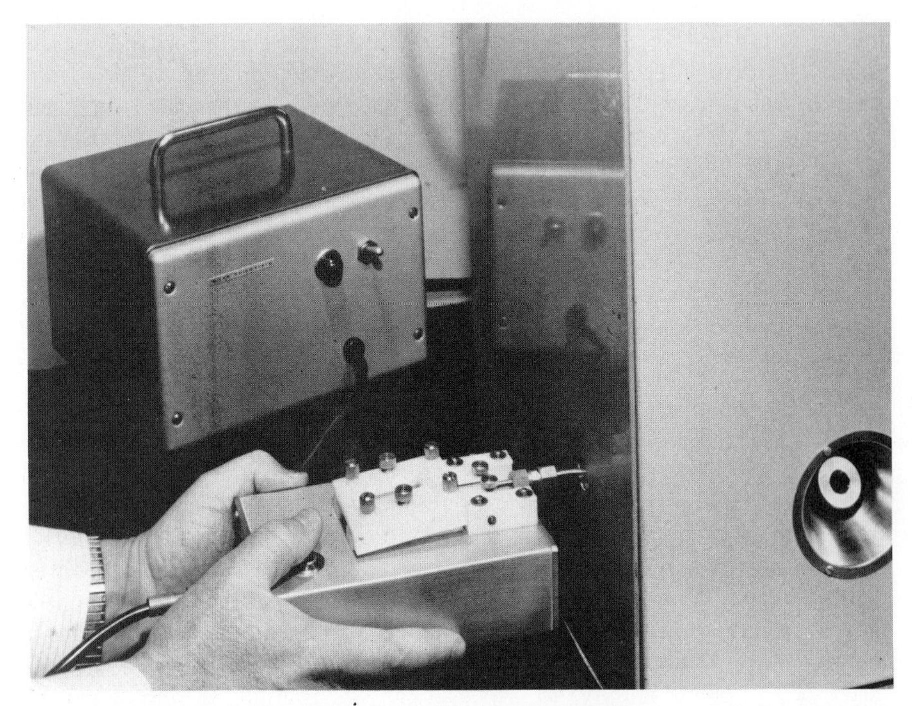

Fig. 36. Injection of GC fraction between two cooled KRS-5 plates for infrared analysis via IRS. The reduced temperature and capillary action both aid in trapping GC fraction for times long enough to record spectrum. (Courtesy of Wilks Scientific Corp., So. Norwalk, Conn.)

c. Dew Point Meter

Another application of a cooled IRE is in the measurement of dew point. This approach has the advantages over the misty mirror systems (H50b) in that it is specific and will indicate regardless of the nature of the condensation (i.e., whether the form is droplets, thin uniform film, or even ice). Furthermore, this approach can be used to study the condensation process which is still not fully understood.

For the detection of a specific component (e.g., H_2O) a monochromator is not required and can be replaced by two simple optical filters—one tuned to the O—H band and the other, to some suitable reference wavelength in a non-absorbing region. A schematic diagram of the optical layout and photograph of a compact dew point meter are shown in Figs. 38a and 38b, respectively. The light from the light source (S) passes through a double filter (F) and then is focused on the entrance aperture of the IRE. It is then

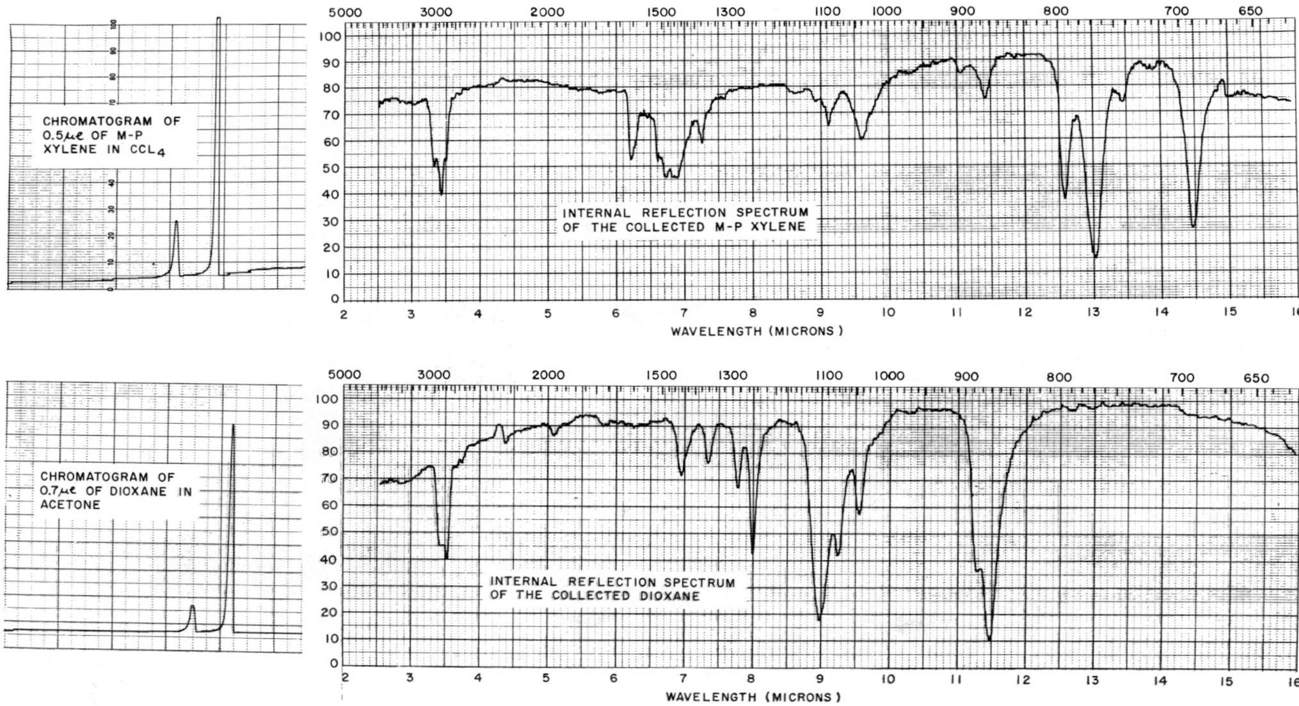

Fig. 37. Chromatograms (left) and internal reflection spectra (right) of GC fractions obtained using capillary collection. (Courtesy of Wilks Scientific Corp.)

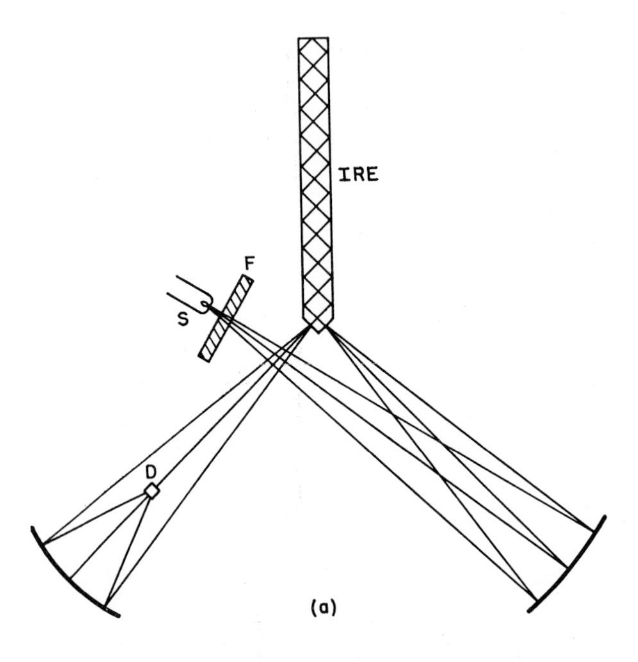

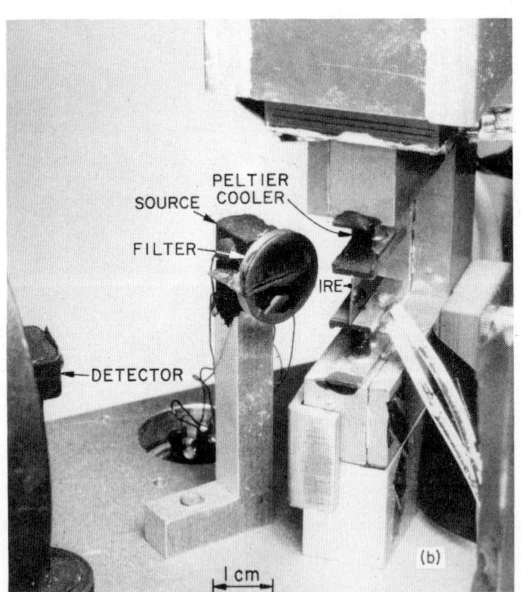

Fig. 38. Internal reflection dew point meter. (a) Optical layout. (b) Photograph. The double-pass silicon plate is mounted between two Peltier coolers. Two filters are placed side by side in front of the light source to select the proper wavelengths for the O—H band and the reference beams.

collected by a mirror and focused onto the detector (*D*). Peltier coolers are utilized to control the temperature of the IRE. Mechanical light chopping is eliminated; instead two small lamps are employed, one behind each filter, and they are turned on and off at the desired rate and relative phase by means of an ac current. Alternatively, a single light source may be employed and the filters mounted on an electrically driven tuning fork or rotated by a small motor. The signal from the detector is amplified and used to control the temperature of the IRE via the Peltier coolers.

Systems of this sort (Fig. 38) are useful for monitoring the presence of water in ultrapure gases. By selecting suitable filters, this unit can also be employed in a similar fashion to detect other components, e.g., alcohol or acetone in the breath.

d. Air Pollution Study

Still another application of IRS with cooled IRE is to the study of air pollution. It should be realized, however, that conventional transmission techniques utilizing long path gas enclosures work very well for studies of air pollution (by gases but not by particulate matter).

e. Study of Frozen "Hot" Species

Compounds can be preserved in their transition states by a rapid cooling to very low temperatures. The material of interest is evaporated and trapped on a suitable window which has been cooled to liquid helium temperatures. Some excellent work on the study of frozen "hot" species has been reported by Weltner and McLeod (W2,W3) using conventional transmission spectroscopy. These experiments could also be peformed via IRS, which is advantageous because a smaller amount of material is required and because interferences fringes are absent.

2. Films on Absorbing Substrates

There are many instances where it is of interest to obtain the spectrum of a film on an absorbing substrate without destroying the sample. This includes films on opaque substrates (e.g., coatings on metals) as well as films on partially absorbing substrates (e.g., protective coatings on fabrics). Spectra of these films serve to show their presence, to identify them, and sometimes to make it possible to study their aging process. Internal reflection spectroscopy can be used for identifying films on absorbing substrates in a number of cases. The problems of measuring the spectra of films on absorbing substrates is divided into two categories according to whether the film is thick or thin compared to the effective thickness for bulk materials.

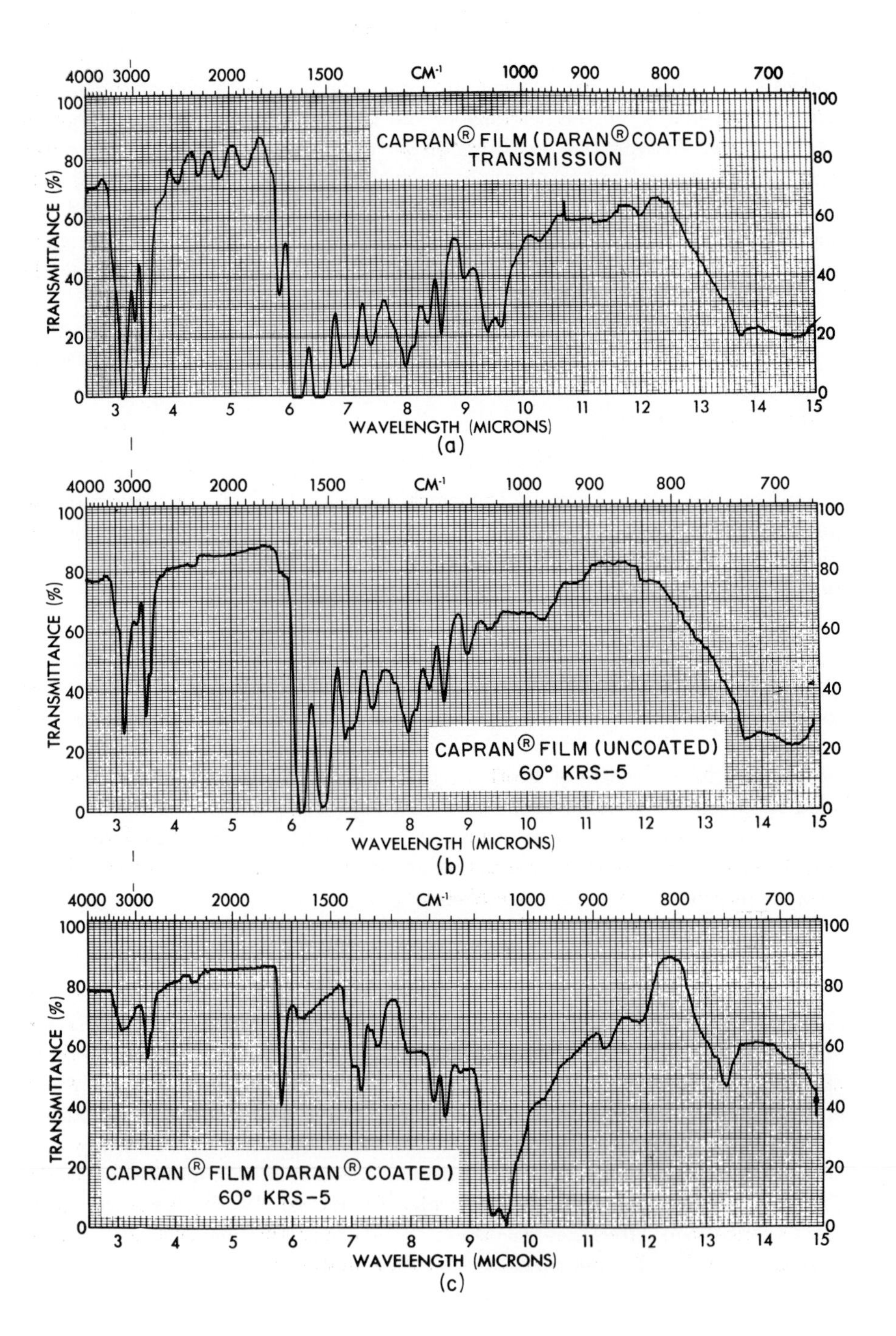

4000
3000
2000
1500
CM⁻¹
1000
900
800
700
100
80
60
40
20
0
TRANSMITTANCE (%)
CAPRAN® FILM (DARAN® COATED)
TRANSMISSION
3
4
5
6
7
8
9
10
11
12
13
14
15
WAVELENGTH (MICRONS)
(a)
CAPRAN® FILM (UNCOATED)
60° KRS-5
(b)
CAPRAN® FILM (DARAN® COATED)
60° KRS-5
(c)

a. Thick Films

When the film is thick the substrate does not produce an interfering spectrum and there is no problem in detecting the film. Examples of this case are thick coats of paint or shellac on wood or metal or coating on wires. It is emphasized that even for thick films, only a thin layer (e.g., 1 μ) near the surface is sampled and the spectrum may not truly represent the bulk. If the surface is sufficiently smooth or if the substrate is sufficiently flexible so that the necessary area of contact can be made to the surface of the internal reflection plate, the spectrum can be readily recorded. If the paint or lacquer is available in liquid form, the easiest way to obtain its spectrum is to paint it on the surface of the IRE.

Reported work in this area includes that of Baxter and Puttnam (B7) on the measurements of the spectra of coatings on paperbacked aluminum foil. Crystalline materials on opaque backings can also be examined with advantage via IRS. Removal of the films for transmission measurements usually destroys the crystallinity.

Figure 39 shows an example of measurements on a coated film wherein the advantages of internal reflection over transmission are clearly evident. The transmission spectrum (Fig. 39a) represents a composite of the spectra of the substrate and the coating, from which it is not possible to determine whether the film is coated or consists of a mixture. The two internal reflection spectra (Figs. 39b and 39c), on the other hand, clearly show that the film is coated. The coating obviously represents a thick film since the spectrum of the substrate is absent in the internal reflection spectrum of the coated substrate (Fig. 39c). Similar results were reported by Reichert (R8a) for Saran films on polyethylene.

Still within this area, it was demonstrated that IRS could be used successfully to measure the tenacity of lotions to skin after repeated washings (W9).

b. Thin Films

It is possible in many cases to record the spectrum of a thin film on an absorbing substrate with the aid of internal reflection spectroscopy. It should be realized, however, that in some cases (e.g., 10 Å film on an absorbing substrate) even if ideal contact can be made to the IRE it is just not possible

Fig. 39. Comparison of spectra of a film consisting of a thick film on an absorbing substrate. (a) Transmission spectrum. (b) Internal reflection spectrum for uncoated film. (c) Internal reflection spectrum of coated film. The transmission measurements give a composite spectrum from which it is not clear whether film is coated or consists of a mixture. The internal reflection measurement shows that the film is coated. (Courtesy of Wilks Scientific Corp.)

to distinguish the surface spectrum from that of the bulk. Whether or not the spectrum of the thin film can be distinguished from that of the bulk is determined from their relative contrast which, in turn, can be calculated approximately by comparing the effective thickness equations for the thin film and bulk material. The film can be considered to be thin if the absorption band due this film has not saturated; i.e., if the degree of absorption still changes with film thickness. This will depend on angle of incidence and wavelength. In the measurements shown in Fig. 7 of Chapter Two, a film up to about 1000 Å can be considered thin. In some measurements of Reichert (R8a) that were made near the critical angle, the absorption did no saturate until the film was of a thickness greater than 5 μ.

For a thin absorbing film on an absorbing substrate, following the designation shown in Fig. 21 of Chapter Two in which the film is medium *2* and the substrate is medium *3*, in the low absorption approximation wherein the effective thickness equations of Chapter Two apply, the reflectivity can be written as (D23)

$$\begin{aligned} R &= 1 - a \\ &= 1 - \alpha_2 d_{2e} - \alpha_3 d_{3e}. \end{aligned} \tag{4}$$

For perpendicular polarization, the total absorption parameter can be written as

$$a_{\perp} = \alpha_2 \frac{4n_{21}d_2 \cos\theta}{1 - n_{31}^2} + \frac{\alpha_3 \lambda_1 n_{31} \cos\theta}{\pi(1 - n_{31}^2)(\sin^2\theta - n_{31}^2)^{1/2}}, \tag{5}$$

where equations (31) and (26) are used for $d_{2e\perp}$ and $d_{3e\perp}$, respectively. The following conclusions, drawn from this equation, serve as approximate rules when considering thin films on absorbing substrates.

1. For angles near the critical angle it is not possible to detect the thin film. The spectrum of the film will be swamped out by absorption by the substrate because the effective thickness of the bulk becomes very large due to the increase in the penetration depth.

2. In order to suppress the spectrum of the substrate it is helpful to use a high index IRE and to make θ large since both of these tend to make the penetration depth small and hence reduce the contribution of the substrate to the spectrum.

The relative contrast of the spectra for the film and the substrate can be determined from equation (5). As an example, for $\alpha_2 = \alpha_3$ and $n_2 = n_3$,

$$a_{\perp} = \frac{\alpha \cos\theta\, n_{21}}{(1 - n_{21}^2)} \left[4d_2 + \frac{\lambda_1}{\pi(\sin^2\theta - n_{21}^2)^{1/2}} \right]. \tag{6}$$

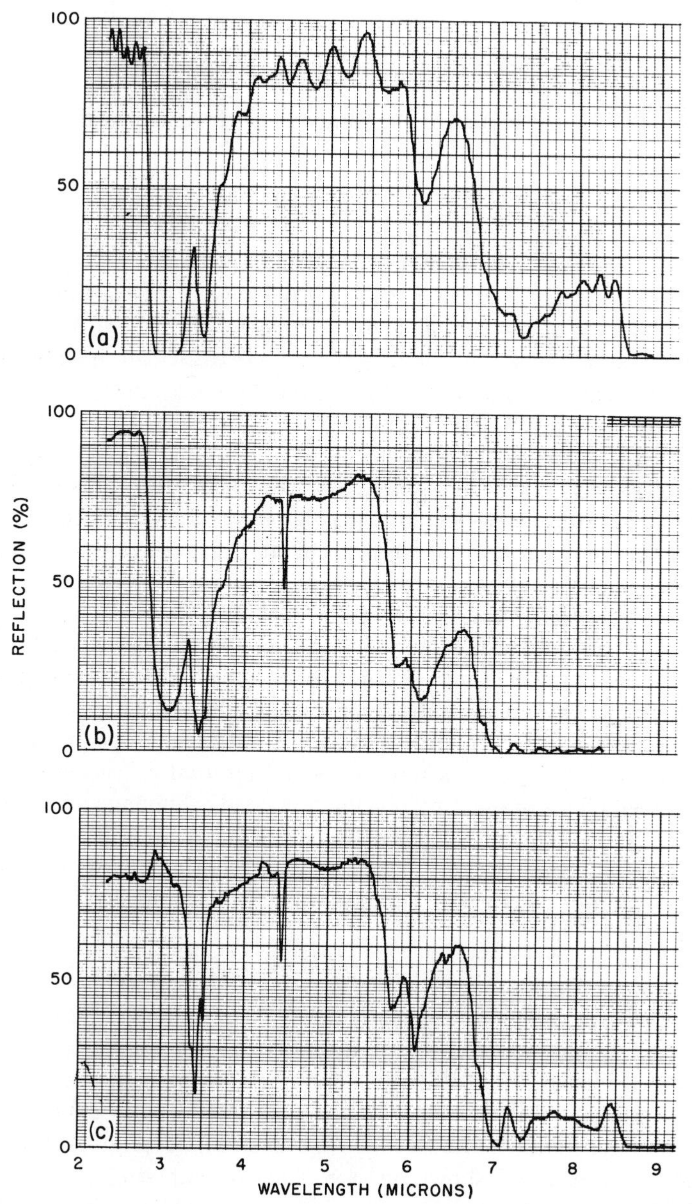

Fig. 40. Comparison of transmission and internal reflection spectra of coated cellophane film. (a) Transmission of coated cellophane film. (b) Internal reflection spectrum of same film, note nitrile band at 4.5 μ. (c) Difference spectrum of coating obtained by placing pure cellophane in contact with reference IRE. Note that the interference fringes present in the transmission spectrum are absent in the internal reflection spectra. (Courtesy of Wilks Scientific Corp.)

The contrast of the spectrum of the film will be the same as that of the bulk when

$$4d_2 = \frac{\lambda_1}{\pi(\sin^2 \theta - n_{21}^2)^{1/2}}. \tag{7}$$

For $n_1 = 4.0$, $n_2 = 1.6$ at $\lambda_1 = 0.75\ \mu$ ($\lambda_{vac} = 3.0\ \mu$); the contrast of the spectra is the same at $\theta = 60°$ when $d_2 = 0.075\ \mu$. Therefore, spectra of films less than 1000 Å thick on an absorbing substrate can be obtained. If measurements can be made in the visible region of the spectrum it should be possible to obtain the spectra of films considerably thinner than 1000 Å.

The difference spectra technique discussed in Chapter Six can also add considerable sensitivity in recording the spectra of thin films on absorbing substrates via internal reflection spectroscopy. If the spectrum of the substrate does not show total absorption at the absorption bands, a material identical to the substrate may be placed against the reference IRE to cancel the absorption band due to the substrate. This is shown clearly in Fig. 40. Curve *a* represents the transmission spectrum of a cellophane film with a thin coating. Curve *b* represents the internal reflection spectrum of the same film. The nitrile band at 4.5 μ, which is very weak and further obscured by the interference fringes in the transmission spectrum, is indicative of the coating. Curve *c* represents the internal reflection spectrum of the coating which is obtained by placing uncoated cellophane on the reference IRE to cancel the unwanted spectrum of the substrate. The power of internal reflection spectroscopy for studying coatings and thin films on absorbing substrates is clearly demonstrated by these spectra.

3. Fibers and Fabrics

Wilks (W9) has shown that fibers and fabrics, among the most difficult materials to handle via transmission spectroscopy, are quite amenable to being studied via IRS. Multiple reflections must be employed because the nature of the material is such that the contact area is small. Typical sample handling for fibers and fabrics is shown in the photograph of Fig. 41 and typical spectra are shown in Fig. 42. Recent studies of fabrics via internal reflection spectroscopy are also reported by McCall et al. (M6b).

4. Paper Electrophoresis—Paper Chromatography

In paper electrophoresis the various components are separated in the substrate material (e.g., filter paper) into which they are absorbed. Each spot

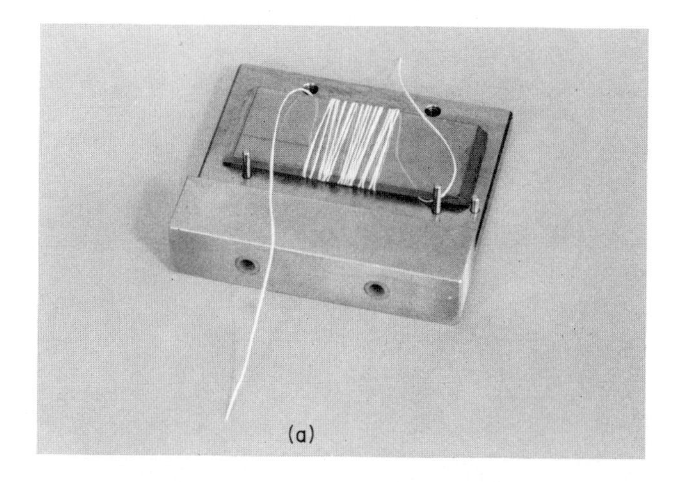

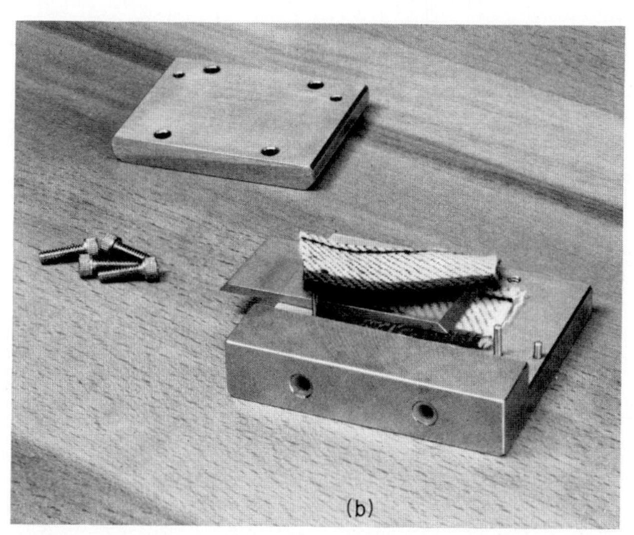

Fig. 41. Preparation of sample (a) fibers and (b) fabrics for analysis via internal reflection spectroscopy. (Courtesy of Wilks Scientific Corp.)

on the substrate represents a different component and can be examined separately by using the techniques for obtaining difference spectra to cancel the spectrum of the substrate. An approach that offers more sensitivity and demonstrated by Wilks Scientific Corp. is to elute the component onto the internal reflection plate via a suitable solvent which is then permitted

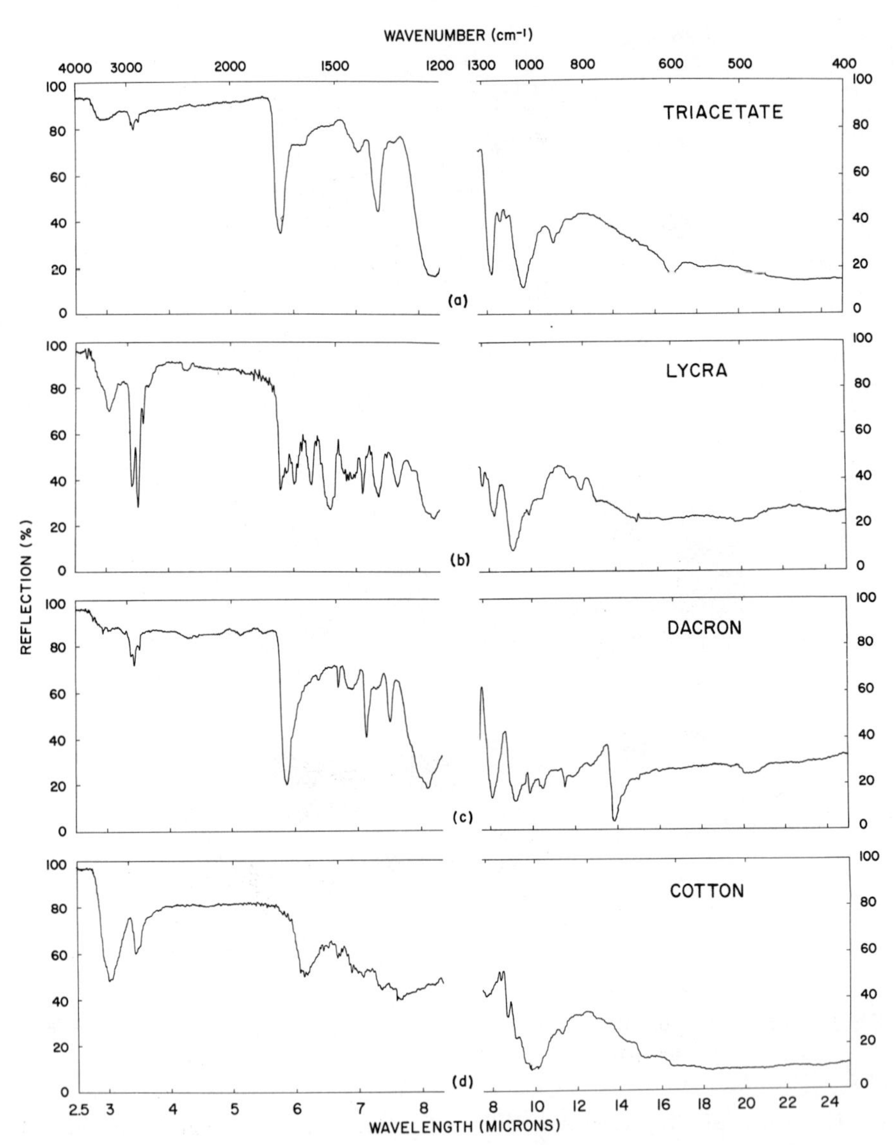

Fig. 42. Internal reflection spectra of various fibers and fabrics obtained using KRS-5 plate, $\theta = 45°$, $N = 26$. (Courtesy of G. D. Propster, Wilks Scientific Corp.)

to evaporate leaving the solute behind for analysis. It is necessary to run a blank to check whether or not extractables from the substrate have also been eluted onto the surface of the IRE.

5. Diffusion Rate Measurements

Diffusion rate measurements have been made to date with the aid of radioactive tracers and preferential etching. Barr (B4) has demonstrated that internal reflection spectroscopy is of particular value in measuring the rate of surface diffusion. Some materials may be covered with a coating or an adhesive and it is desirable that the coating remain permanently at the surface rather than diffuse into the bulk of the substrate. Figure 43 is an example of the case wherein the coating diffuses into the bulk. The absorption band at 1270 cm^{-1} is due to a 0.02% silicone oil treatment of cotton cloth. Over a period of three hours, the absorption band at this frequency decreased, indicating penetration or diffusion of the silicone into the bulk of the fiber. The wetting characteristics of the fabric returned to normal after a few hours, verifying this conclusion. Qualitative studies such as these easily

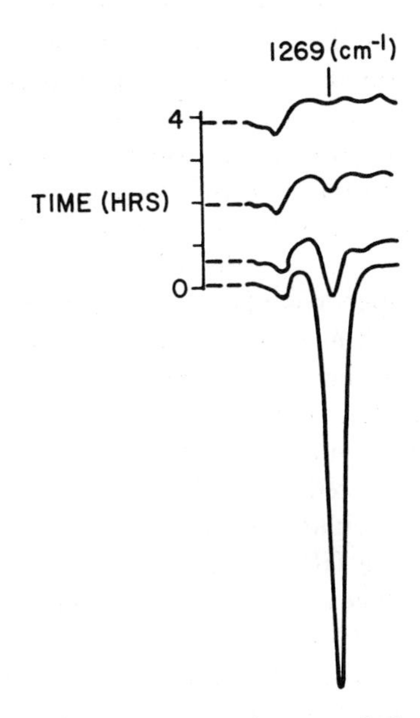

Fig. 43. Internal reflection spectra of cotton cloth taken after various time intervals showing diffusion of surface film of silicone oil into bulk. (Courtesy of J. K. Barr, E. I. du Pont de Nemours and Co., Wilmington, Del.)

determine the effectiveness of coating procedures on fibers and a variety of other surfaces as well.

In some other work Mellow (M16) proposed to measure the diffusion rate of nitroglycerine through nitrocellulose films by placing the film in contact with the IRE and then attempting to detect the presence of the nitroglycerine when it has diffused through the film. Another approach to this problem involving shorter times and perhaps more definitive measurements is to remove the film periodically from the diffusant supply and to place the side of the film where the diffusant enters the film in contact with the IRE after certain intervals of time and thus to observe the growth in thickness of the thin film containing diffusant.

As was discussed in this chapter in Section H-2 entitled "Films on Absorbing Substrates," a diffusion depth from less than 1000 Å to more than one micron can be monitored in the near infrared region via internal reflection spectroscopy.

6. Suspended Particulate Matter

The possibility of studying particulate matter of any size without any sample preparation has already been discussed. Sometimes this matter is suspended in the atmosphere and because of scattering of light cannot be studied using long path infrared techniques. The particulate matter is therefore often collected on filter paper and dissolved in a suitable solution and then studied using conventional transmission techniques. Internal reflection has been employed to measure the spectrum of particulate matter without removing the particles from the filter paper by employing the difference spectra technique which was described in Chapter Six. As has been pointed out, clean filter paper is placed on the reference IRE and any interfering spectrum from the filter paper can be cancelled, leaving only the desired difference spectrum. Other demonstrations of internal reflection for examining suspended particulate matter are reported by Hannah and Dwyer (H3) wherein they collected in membrane filters, powders, trace contaminants in liquids, fumes, etc., and analyzed them via IRS.

The study of suspended particulate matter can be simplified by collecting it directly on the surface of the IRE. This can be done by impacting the suspended particles on the surface and thereby collecting them (M6a,A7a) or by electrostatic precipitation. In the latter case, the IRE must be a conductor (e.g., semiconductor). One design of an electrostatic precipitator that has been employed to collect cigarette smoke and other suspended particles directly on the surface of a Ge plate is shown in Fig. 44. There is slight corona discharge in the vicinity of the tungsten wire and a current flows

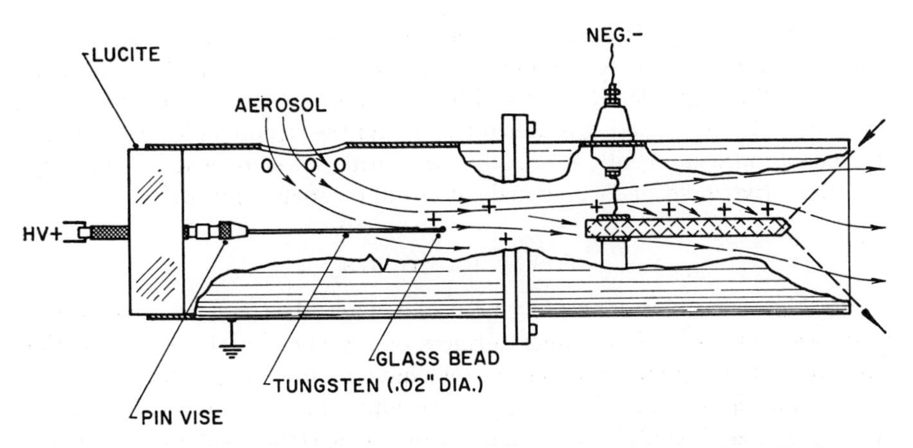

Fig. 44. Schematic diagram of design of electrostatic precipitator for collecting suspended particulate matter on an internal reflection plate for analysis via IRS. The aerosol flows past corona discharge, becomes positively charged, and is deposited on negatively biased conducting IRE.

towards the negatively biased Ge plate. The suspended particles become positively charged and flow towards the plate where they are finally deposited. This electrostatic precipitator may be installed directly in a suitable internal reflection spectrometer for continuous monitoring of suspended particulate matter.

7. Product Control and Reaction Monitoring

The technique of internal reflection spectroscopy can obviously be used for continuous monitoring of solutions for product control and reaction monitoring. The double-pass plates are particularly useful for this application since they can be employed without special vessels. Another means of monitoring reactions is either to use a reaction vessel where the IRE (e.g., the single-pass multiple reflection plate) is an integral part of the vessel wall, or to use special cells where the solution flows through the cell past an IRE.

8. Conductivity of Epitaxial Films

There is a real need for a simple technique for measuring the resistivity of epitaxial films on semiconductors because of their current importance in transistor device technology. An attempt has been made to determine this resistivity via IRS from a measure of the optical constants (R7) for epitaxial films on silicon using a Ge hemicylinder. Unfortunately, the results are not very encouraging. First, the k of these films is very low; second, the refractive indices of the semiconductors are generally very high, making it difficult to find suitable IRE's of still higher index; and third, these materials are hard and brittle making it difficult to obtain the required physical contact for reliable measurements, especially for routine measurements. The very high refractive index of Te may make it useful for such applications.

9. Vacuum Studies

Ultrahigh vacua can be achieved only after adsorbed volatile components have been pumped off the inner surfaces of the vacuum chamber. In the past, mass spectrometers and omegatrons have been employed to study high vacuum physics by monitoring whatever components are pumped out of the system or are still contained as a gas within the system. Internal reflection spectroscopy offers the possibility of measuring what is still left on the surface. Figure 27 shows the adsorbed components on a Si plate. The presence of these components was monitored as a function of baking and pumping down to a pressure of 10^{-8} torr, after which the C—H and O—H complexes could no longer be detected. On opening the system, the O—H component reappeared immediately. These studies might be extended in an attempt to detect components such as methane and carbon monoxide which are formed during ion pumping. A photograph of Si double-pass plate sealed in a vacuum system for this type of study is shown in Fig. 45.

10. Magnetic Studies

The multiple internal reflection plate, and especially the double-pass version, is ideal for magnetic studies since it can be conveniently placed in a narrow gap between magnetic pole faces. The type of studies that might be carried out are magnetic effects on free carriers and surface states. So far as magnetic effects on molecular resonances are concerned, it is known that Zeeman shifts are very small. With the highly monochromatic laser beams available now such measurements may, however, prove fruitful.

11. Pyrolyzates

Pyrolysis is employed in cases in which a sample cannot be conveniently dissolved for transmission measurements or in cases in which the spectrum is too complex for interpretation. Workers at Barnes Engineering have demonstrated that the spectrum of the pyrolyzate can be readily recorded via IRS by depositing it directly on the reflection plate. This also works well for

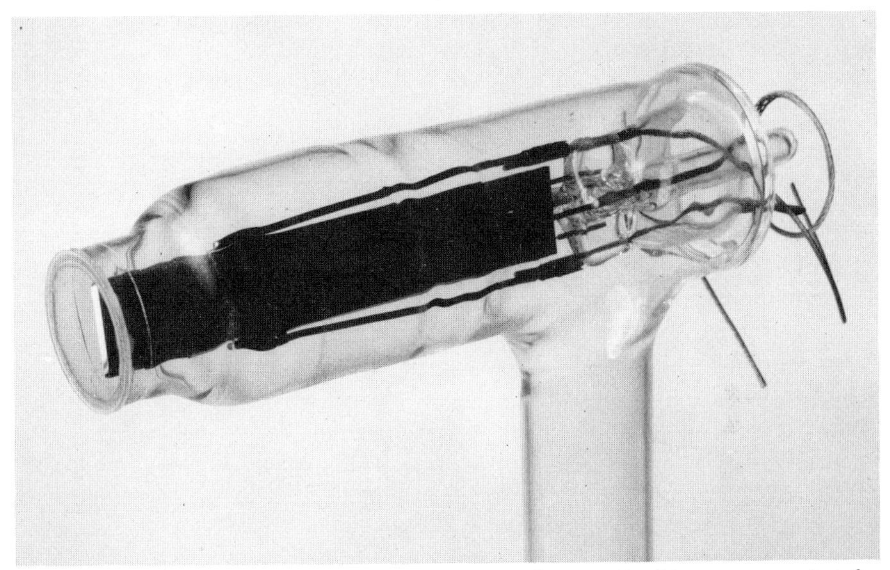

Fig. 45. Photograph showing double-pass silicon plate mounted in vacuum system for study of desorption process in obtaining a high vacuum. The radiation is introduced in and out of the vacuum system through a single sapphire window.

samples which by virtue of their hardness, surface texture, or composition even defy internal reflection techniques. Carbon-filled rubber is a typical example of such a compound. Figures 46a and 46b show the spectra of isoprene rubber and its pyrolyzate, respectively. The isoprene rubber spectrum shows filler bands in the 1000–1125 cm^{-1} region and again at 830 cm^{-1}. The sample was pyrolzyed at 900°C for 10 sec and both sides of the internal reflection plate were exposed. It will be noted that the filler bands have been removed from the spectrum. Spectra of pyrolyzates can readily be recorded using transmission techniques although heavier deposits are required.

12. Biological and Medical Applications

Optical spectroscopy techniques will undoubtedly be widely used in biological and medical studies in the future because of promising initial results. The ease of sample preparation because it is both rapid and convenient makes internal reflection spectroscopy attractive for biological and medical studies. Spectra of muscle, liver, kidney, and stomach recorded via IRS have already been reported (S19,H44,P1a). Hermann (H44) showed that induced chemical changes in the tissues could also be detected

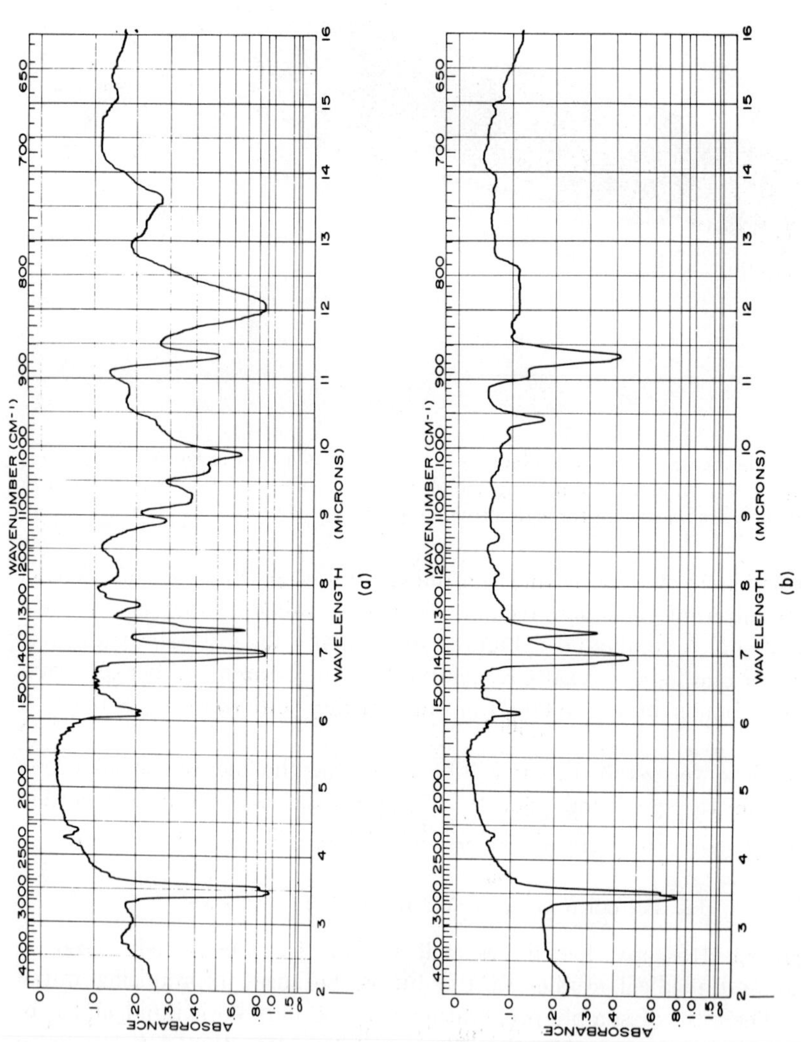

Fig. 46. Internal reflection spectroscopy for study of pyrolyzates. (a) Spectrum of isoprene rubber. (b) Spectrum of pyrolyzate of isoprene rubber. Spectra were obtained using KRS-5 plate, $\theta = 52°$, $N = 20$. (Courtesy of S. E. Polchlopek, Barnes Engineering, Stamford, Conn.)

under certain conditions using these techniques. Obviously, continuous monitoring of perspiration and saliva is straight forward using double-pass multiple internal reflection plates. Continuous monitoring of blood and tissues could also be achieved by making the double-pass plate in the form of a small (1–2 mm on each side) hypodermic needle so that it could be inserted into the blood stream or tissue. This is not unreasonable since fiber optic hypodermic needles are already employed for visual examination of tissue (C1b,H45,K6). Furthermore, by conducting the light to and from the IRE via flexible optical fibers, the IRE could be employed for nondestructive spectroscopic sampling of any part of the body (e.g., stomach) that can now be examined visually via fiber optic techniques.

I. Limitations of Internal Reflection Spectroscopy

The long list of applications discussed for internal reflection spectroscopy is not meant to convey the impression that it can be employed indiscriminately. For the applications mentioned, IRS has, indeed, the advantages noted. However, there are certain areas wherein IRS should not at all be employed and other areas wherein it should be employed only with caution, which often necessitates a thorough understanding of the interaction mechanisms. Although this has been pointed out a number of times before in this book, some of these areas will be enumerated to stress this point. All of these points have been discussed in more detail in earlier sections:

It should be recalled that in recording the spectra of bulk materials via IRS, only a thin film of the material near the surface is sampled. This is particularly so when large angles of incidence are employed. The internal reflection spectrum may thus be strongly influenced by the surface, which may be different from the bulk. Whether or not the surface is different from the bulk can be determined from measurements as a function of angle of incidence and can be of advantage in many problems.

Internal reflection spectroscopy is, insofar as instrumentation is concerned, generally more complicated than conventional transmission, requiring judicious choice in the refractive index of the IRE and/or angle of incidence. Consideration must be given to the possible corrosive attack of the IRE by the sample and periodic replacement of the IRE is generally required because of its deterioration with use. IRE's require a high surface polish and are often expensive.

Because the total effective thickness that can readily be achieved does not exceed a fraction of a millimeter even with hundreds of reflections, IRS should not be employed for weakly absorbing sytems in which long path lengths are required. These include study of materials in the gas phase and titration experiments in which color changes are not intense and a few millimeters of path length are required to record reactions.

Materials which have very large changes in refractive index (e.g., quartz) are generally not suitable for internal reflection measurements because the angle of incidence cannot be maintained above the critical angle.

When good contact between the sample and the IRE is not obtained, and is unknown, relative band intensity data cannot be used reliably.

Caution is suggested in the application of internal reflection in certain areas: Solutions consisting of mixtures, for example, may have a tendency to change their relative concentration near an electrode because of different surface potentials. In such a case the internal reflection spectrum will not be truly representative of the mixture.

Band intensities, profiles, and location recorded via internal reflection depend on the angle of incidence and the index of refraction to some extent and thus should be compared with caution to those recorded via transmission. Although some simple rules have been given, it is advisable to have a good understanding of the interaction mechanisms to aid in the interpretation of the spectra.

The degree of interaction of the light with the sample is dependent on polarization for internal reflection. Therefore, for quantitative measurements it is advisable to work with polarized light since the state of polarization is then always known. In most instruments the light is partially polarized and the degree of polarization is wavelength dependent and often changes when the sample or other optical elements are introduced into the beam, therefore the state of polarization is not always known.

In spite of these limitations, in many cases internal reflection spectroscopy has extended the areas of application of optical spectroscopy and has simplified the application of optical spectroscopy. The ease of sample preparation is an important advantage in many instances. One good example is the ease with which powders can be handled via internal reflection even though the absence of scattering which occurs in the non-absorbing region is still not clearly understood. Another important advantage is the absence of interference fringes. The ability to perform nondestructive sampling via internal reflection has extended the areas of application of optical spectroscopy—films on absorbing substrates, fibers and fabrics, samples on filter paper are good examples. An advantage of internal reflection over transmission that has not yet been fully exploited is the presence of electric fields in all three spatial directions at the reflecting surface, which makes it useful for studying anisotropic materials. Perhaps the most important field of application of internal reflection spectroscopy is to the study of surface reactions such as oxidation, catalysis, adhesion, electrode reactions, and numerous medical problems in which the spectra of monolayer films must be monitored. There will probably be significant applications of internal reflection spectroscopy in this general area in the future.

NOMENCLATURE

The following terms dealing with internal reflection spectroscopy have been approved by the sponsoring committee and accepted by the American Society for Testing and Materials (ASTM) and published in the 1967 ASTM Book of Standards, ASTM Designation E131-66T, Part 31 (copyrighted ASTM publication).

1. Internal Reflection Spectroscopy (IRS). The technique of recording optical spectra by placing a sample material in contact with a transparent medium of greater refractive index and measuring the reflectance (single or multiple) from the interface, generally at angles of incidence greater than the critical angle.

2. Spectrum, Internal Reflection. The spectrum obtained by the technique of Internal Reflection Spectroscopy.
   Note: Depending on the angle of incidence the spectrum recorded may qualitatively resemble that obtained by conventional transmission measurements, may resemble the mirror image of the dispersion in the index of refraction, or may resemble some composite of the two.

3. Frustrated Total Reflection (FTR). Reflection which occurs when a nonabsorbing coupling mechanism acts in the process of total internal reflection to make the reflectance less than unity.
   Note: In this process, the reflectance can vary continuously between zero and unity if:
   (*a*) An optically transparent medium is within a fraction of a wavelength of the reflecting surface and its distance from the reflecting surface is changed.
   (*b*) Both the angle of incidence and the refractive index of one of the media vary in an appropriate manner.
   In these cases, part of the radiant power may be transmitted through the interface into the second medium without loss at the reflecting surface in such a way that transmittance plus reflectance equals unity. It is possible to have this process take place in some spectral regions even when a sample having absorption bands is placed in contact with the reflecting surface.

4. Attenuated Total Reflection (ATR). Reflection which occurs when an absorbing coupling mechanism acts in the process of total internal reflection to make the reflectance less than unity.
   Note: In this process, if an absorbing sample is placed in contact with the reflecting surface, the reflectance for total internal reflection will be attenuated to some value between greater than zero and unity in regions of the spectrum where absorption of the radiant power can take place.

5. Internal Reflection Element (IRE). The transparent optical element used in Internal Reflection Spectroscopy for establishing the conditions necessary to obtain the internal reflection spectra of materials.

   Note: Radiant power is propagated through it by means of internal reflection. The sample material is placed in contact with the reflecting surface or it may be the reflecting surface itself. If only a single reflection takes place from the internal reflection element, the element is said to be a single-reflection element; if more than one reflection takes place, the element is said to be a multiple-reflection element. When the element has a recognized shape it is identified according to each shape, for example, internal reflection prism, internal reflection hemicylinder, internal reflection plate, internal reflection rod, internal reflection fiber, etc.

6. Single-Pass Internal Reflection Element. An internal reflection element in which the radiant power transverses the length of the element only once; that is, the radiant power enters at one end of the optical element and leaves via the other end.

7. Double-Pass Internal Reflection Element. An internal reflection element in which the radiant power transverses the length of the optical element twice, entering and leaving via the same end.

8. Fixed-Angle Internal Reflection Element. An internal reflection element which is designed to be operated at a fixed angle of incidence.

9. Variable-Angle Internal Reflection Element. An internal reflection element which can be operated over a range of angles of incidence.

ABBREVIATIONS

ATR	Attenuated total reflection
FTR	Frustrated total reflection
IRE	Internal reflection element
IRS	Internal reflection spectroscopy
SCR	Space charge region
TIR	Total internal reflection

SYMBOLS

A	Aperture of IRE
a	Absorption parameter, $a = (100 - R)\%$
$a_\perp$, $a_\parallel$	Absorption parameter for $\perp$-, $\parallel$-polarization
α	Absorption coefficient (cm^{-1})
c	Velocity of light
D	Displacement, $D = \epsilon E$
d	Film thickness
d_e	Effective film thickness
$d_{e\perp}$, $d_{e\parallel}$	Effective film thickness for $\perp$-, $\parallel$-polarization
d_p	Penetration depth of electromagnetic field in rarer medium (distance required for amplitude to fall to e^{-1} of its value at the interface)
Δ	Increment
δ	Phase shift of light due to reflection
$\delta_\perp$, $\delta_\parallel$	Phase shift of light for $\perp$-, $\parallel$-polarization
E	Electric field amplitude near reflecting interface for unit incoming amplitude
E_0	Electric field amplitude at reflecting interface for unit incoming amplitude
E_{x0}, E_{y0}, E_{z0}	Electric field amplitudes in x, y, z directions for unit incoming amplitudes
$E_\perp$, $E_\parallel$	Electric field amplitude for $\perp$-, $\parallel$-polarization
E_c	Energy level for bottom of conduction band
E_v	Energy level for top of valence band
E_F	Energy for fermi level
e	Exponential
ϵ	Dielectric constant, $\epsilon = n^2$
γ	Phase difference
I	Light intensity
I_0	Intensity of incoming beam
i	Square root of minus one, $i = \sqrt{-1}$
k	Extinction coefficient
κ	Attenuation index
l	Length of IRE
λ	Wavelength of light in vacuum
λ_1	Wavelength of light in medium *1*
λ_e	Effective wavelength of standing wave pattern normal to reflecting surface
μ	Micron (10^{-6} m)
N	Number of reflections
n	Index of refraction
n_1	Index of refraction of the IRE
n_2	Index of refraction of the second (rarer) medium
n_3	Refractive index of medium *3* (for measurements on thin films)
n_{21}	Refractive index ratio for reflecting interface, $n_{21} = n_2/n_1$
ν	Frequency of light

φ	Angle of refraction
q	Electronic charge
R	Reflection coefficient, $R = r^2$ (%)
$R_\perp$, $R_\parallel$	Reflection coefficient for light polarized $\perp$, $\parallel$ to plane of incidence, i.e., electric vector $\perp$, $\parallel$ to plane of incidence
r	Reflected amplitude for unit incident amplitude
$r_\perp$, $r_\parallel$	Reflected amplitude for $\perp$, $\parallel$-polarization
ρ	Resistivity
σ	Conductivity
T	Transmission (%)
$T_\perp$, $T_\parallel$	Transmission for $\perp$, $\parallel$-polarization
T_1, T_2	Transmission for first, second components
t	Thickness of IRE
θ	Angle of incidence
θ_B	Brewster's angle—polarizing angle for external reflection
θ_c	Critical angle
θ_{ca}	Critical angle for material—air interface
θ_{cs}, θ_{ca}	Critical angle of IRE with respect to sample, air
θ_{c1}, θ_{c2}, θ_{c3}	Critical angles for media *1, 2, 3* with respect to air
θ_p	Principal angle—polarizing angle for internal reflection

BIBLIOGRAPHY

This bibliography includes, in addition to the references cited in the text, all the papers dealing with internal reflection spectroscopy which were published before this book was sent to the printer, as well as many additional papers and some pertinent books dealing with some aspect of total internal reflection. Complete titles are provided to enable the reader to classify and to sort out those articles which may be of particular interest. Only those papers that are published in readily available literature, such as the journals listed by *Chemical Abstracts,* are listed here. In general, papers presented but not published are not included in this list, for the obvious reason that they are not readily available. When material from presented papers was used, a private communication reference is given. Some of the papers listed here were taken from an unpublished list compiled by Tomas Hirschfeld, Assistant Professor of Spectrochemistry, Falcultad De Quimica, Montevideo, Uruguay. The source of every article listed here has been checked.

This bibliography is arranged alphabetically relative to the senior author and the works of the author are further ordered chronologically. An asterisk (*) indicates that the paper deals with internal reflection spectroscopy.

A1. Abeles, F., Formules relatives à une lame transparente baignée par deux milieux transparents, dans le cas de la réflexion totale, *Compt. Rend.*, **224**, 1494 (1947).

*A2. Abeles, F., and C. Bazin, Utilization de la réflexion totale pour l'étude de couches minces faiblement absorbants, *Compt. Rend.*, **254**, 2310 (1962).

A3. Abeles, F., Method for Determining Optical Parameters of Thin Films, in *Progress in Optics*, Vol. II, E. Wolf, Ed., Wiley, New York, 1963, p. 249.

A4. Achs, R., R. G. Harper, and M. Siegel, Unusual Dermatoglyphic Findings Associated with Rubella Embryopathy, *New Engl. J. Med.*, **274**, 148 (1966).

A4a. Achs, R., R. G. Harper, and N. J. Harrick, Unusual Dermatoglyphic Findings Associated with Major Congenital Malformations, *New Engl. J. Med.*, **275**, 1273 (1966).

A5. Acloque, P., and C. Guillemet, Sur l'onde de réflexion totale, *Compt. Rend.*, **250**, 4328 (1960).

*A6. Ahlijah, G. E. B. Y., and E. F. Mooney, The Attenuated Total Reflection Spectra of Polyatomic Inorganic Anions. I. Salts of the Oxyacids of Phosphorus, *Spectrochim. Acta*, **22**, 547 (1966).

A7. Aleksoff, C. C., and N. J. Harrick, Magnetostrictive Light Modulator, *Proc. IEEE*, **53**, 1636 (1965).

A7a. Alexander, L. G., and C. L. Coldren, Droplet Transfer from Suspended Air to Duct Walls, *Ind. Eng. Chem.*, **43**, 1325 (1951).

A8. Archer, R. J., Determination of the Properties of Films on Silicon by the Method of Ellipsometry, *J. Opt. Soc. Am.*, **52**, 970 (1962).

A9. Artmann, K., Berechnung des Seitenversetzung des totalreflektierten Strahles, *Ann. Physik*, **2**, 87 (1948).

A10. Artmann, K., Beugung an einer einbackigen Blende endlicher Dicke und der Zusammenhang mit der Theorie der Seitenversetzung des totalreflektierten Strahles, *Ann. Physik*, **7**, 209 (1950).

A11. Artmann, K., Brechung und Reflexion einer seitlich begrenzten Lichtwelle an der ebenen Trennfläche zweier Medien in der Nähe des Grenzwinkels der Totalreflexion, *Ann. Physik*, **8**, 270 (1951).

A12. Artmann, K., Unter welchen Bedingungen ist der Amplitudenverlauf einer seitlich begrenzten Welle komplex?, *Ann. Physik*, **15**, 1 (1954).

A13. Artmann, K., Zur Reflexion einer Lichtwelle am dünneren Medium weit vom Grenzwinkel der Totalreflexion, *Ann. Physik*, **8**, 285 (1951).

A14. Arzelies, H., La Réflexion Vitreuse, *Ann. Phys.* (*Paris*), **1**, 5 (1946).

A15. Arzelies, H., A Study of the Wave Obtained by Total Reflection in Media with Nonvanishing Magnetic Susceptibility, *Ann. Phys.* (*Paris*), **2**, 517 (1947).

A16. Arzelies, H., Propriétés de l'onde évanescente obtenue par réflexion totale, *Rev. Opt.*, **27**, 205 (1948).

A17. Arzelies, H., Sur l'Intensité Transmise par une Lame Transparente en Regime de Réflexion Pseudototale, *Compt. Rend.*, **226**, 478 (1948).

A18. Astheimer, R. W., G. Falbel, and S. Minkowitz, Infrared Modulation by Means of Frustrated Total Internal Reflection, *Appl. Opt.*, **5**, 87 (1966).

*A19. *ASTM Nomenclature for Internal Reflection Spectroscopy*, *ASTM Book of Standards* E131-66T, Part 31, 1967 (copyrighted ASTM publications).

*B1. Bandy, A., J. P. Devlin, R. Burger, and B. McCoy, Infrared Techniques for Fused Salts, *Rev. Sci. Instr.*, **35**, 1206 (1964).

B2. Barnes, R. B., R. C. Gore, R. W. Stafford, and V. Z. Williams, Qualitative Organic Analysis and Infrared Spectrometry, *Anal. Chem.*, **20**, 402 (1948).

B3. Barr, E. S., Historical Survey of the Early Development of the Infrared Spectral Region, *Am. J. Phys.*, **28**, 42 (1960).

*B4. Barr, J. K., E. I. du Pont de Nemours, Wilmington, Delaware (private communication, 1965).

*B5. Barr, J. K., Molecular Orientation of Fibers by Polarized Internal Reflection Spectroscopy, *Nature* (1967).

B6. Baumeister, P. W., F. A. Jenkins, and M. A. Jeppesen, Characteristics of the Phase-Dispersion Interference Filter, *J. Opt. Soc. Am.*, **49**, 1188 (1959).

B6a. Baumeister, P. W., Optical Tunneling and Its Applications, *Appl. Opt.* (1967).

*B7. Baxter, B. H., and N. A. Puttnam, Multi-reflexion Attenuated Total Reflectance Infra-red Spectroscopy, *Nature*, **207**, 288 (1965).

B8. Bazin, C., Utilisation des déphasages introduits lors de la réflexion totale pour l'étude de couches minces faiblement absorbantes, *Compt. Rend.*, **255**, 2742 (1962).

B9. Beauvais, G., Recherches Expérimentales sur la Réflexion Totale des Ondes Hertziennes, *L'Onde Élec.*, **12**, 161 (1933).

*B10. Becker, G. E., and G. W. Gobeli, Surface Studies by Spectral Analysis of Internally Reflected Infrared Radiation: Hydrogen on Silicon, *J. Chem. Phys.*, **38**, 2942 (1963).

B11. Beckmann, K. H., Investigation of the Chemical Properties of Stain Films on Silicon by Means of Infrared Spectroscopy, *Surface Sci.*, **3**, 314 (1965).

*B12. Beckmann, K. H., On the Chemical Composition of Surface Films Produced on Germanium in Different Etchants, *Surface Sci.*, **5**, 187 (1966).

*B12a. Beckmann, K. H., Philips Zentrallaboratorium GMBH, Hamburg, Germany (private communication, 1966).

*B12b. Beckmann, K. H., Methoden und Ergebnisse optischer Untersuchungen an Halbleitergrenzflächen. *Angew. Chem.* (1967).

*B12c. Beckmann, K. H., Zur Bildung oxidischer Deckschichten auf Germaniumanoden in alkalischen Electrolyten. *Ber. Bunsenges. Physik. Chem.*, **70**, 842 (1966).

B13. Bellamy, L. J., *Infra-red Spectra of Complex Molecules*, 2nd ed., Wiley, New York, 1958.

*B14. Bent, R., and W. R. Ladner, A Preliminary Investigation into the Use of Attenuated Total Reflectance for Obtaining the Infrared Spectra of Coals, *Fuel*, **44**, 243 (1965).

B15. Bergmann, L., and C. Schaefer, Polarisation und Doppelbrechung des Lichtes, in *Lehrbuch der Experimentalphysik*, Vol. III, Chapter V, Part I, de Gruyter, Berlin, 1956, p. 343.

B16. Bergstein, L., and C. Shulman, The Frustrated Total Reflection Filter. I. Spectral Analysis, *Appl. Opt.*, **5**, 9 (1966).

B16a. Bergstein, L., W. Kahn, and C. Shulman, A Total-Reflection Solid-State Optical-Maser Resonator, *Proc. IRE*, **50**, 1833 (1962).

B17. Berning, P. H., and A. F. Turner, Induced Transmission in Absorbing Films Applied to Band Pass Filter Design, *J. Opt. Soc. Am.*, **47**, 230 (1957).

*B18. Berz, F., On a Quarter Wave Light Condenser, *Brit. J. Appl. Phys.*, **16**, 1733 (1965).

B19. Billings, B. H., An Experimental Study of Turner Frustrated Total Reflection Filters in the Infrared, *J. Opt. Soc. Am.*, **39**, 634(A) (1949).

B20. Billings, B. H., and M. A. Pittman, A Frustrated Total Reflection Filter for the Infrared, *J. Opt. Soc. Am.*, **39**, 978 (1949).

B21. Billings, B. H., A Birefringent Frustrated Total Reflection Filter, *J. Opt. Soc. Am.*, **40**, 471 (1950).

B22. Billings, B. H., Les couches minces dans l'infrarouge, *J. Phys. Radium*, **11**, 407 (1950).

B23. Bird, G., and M. Parrish, Jr., The Wire Grid as a Near-Infrared Polarizer, *J. Opt. Soc. Am.*, **50**, 886 (1960).

B24. Blodgett, K., Films Built by Depositing Successive Monomolecular Layers on a Solid Surface, *J. Am. Chem. Soc.*, **57**, 1007 (1935).

B25. Böer, K. W., Inhomogene Feldverteilung in CdS-Einkristallen im Bereich hoher Feldstärken, *Z. Physik*, **155**, 184 (1959).

B26. Booker, G. R., and R. Stickler, Large-Area "Jet" Electrolytic Polishing of Ge and Si, *J. Electrochem. Soc.*, **109**, 1167 (1962).

B27. Born, M., and E. Wolf, *Principles of Optics*, 2nd ed., Macmillan, New York, 1964.

B28. Bose, J. C., On the Influence of the Thickness of Air-space on Total Reflection of Electric Radiation, *Proc. Roy. Soc.* (*London*), **62A**, 300 (1897).

B29. Bourg, M. M., Études de la Propagation des ondes Évanescentes dans une Couche Mince Transparente, *J. Phys. Radium*, **19**, 71S (1958).

B30. Bouasse, H. P. M., *Optique cristalline, double réfraction, polarisation rectiligne et elliptique*, Delagrave, Paris, 1925, p. 482.

B31. Brady, J. J., R. O. Brick, and M. D. Pearson, Penetration of Microwaves into the Rarer Medium in Total Reflection, *J. Opt. Soc. Am.*, **50**, 1080 (1960).

B32. Bremmer, H., Propagation of Electromagnetic Waves. Part IV. Total Reflection by a Continuous Layer: W. K. B. approximation, *Handbuch der Physik*, **16**, 552 (1958).

B33. Briggs, H. B., Semiconductive Light Valve, U.S. Pat. 2,692,952 (Oct. 1954).

B34. Brown, M. A. C. S., and E. G. S. Paige, Electric-Field-Induced Modulation of the Absorption Due to Interband Transitions of Free Holes in Ge, *Phys. Rev. Letters*, **7**, 84 (1961).

*B34a. Brown, G., and C. A. Murray, New Technique for Checking Cure of B-Stage Material, *Plastics Technol.*, **11**, 45 (1965).

B35. Brügel, W., *Introduction to Infrared Spectroscopy*, Wiley, New York, 1962.

B36. Buck, T. M., and F. S. McKim, Depth of Surface Damage due to Abrasion on Germanium, *J. Electrochem. Soc.*, **103**, 593 (1956).

B37. Buck, T. M., Damaged Surface Layers: Semiconductors, *Surface Chemistry of Metals and Semiconductors*, H. C. Gatos, Ed., Wiley, New York, 1960, p. 107.

B38. Buizert, H., Circular Polarization of Millimeter Waves by Total Internal Reflection, *Trans. IEEE*, **MTT-12**, 477 (1964).

C1. Cameo, M., Contribution à l'étude des constantes optiques de liquides absorbants dans l'infrarouge, *Rev. Opt.*, **44**, 507 (1965).

C1a. Cameo, M., Contribution à l'étude des constantes optiques de liquides absorbants dans l'infrarouge, *Rev. Opt.*, **44**, 625 (1965).

C1b. Capellaro, D. F., and N. S. Kapany, A Hypodermic Probe Using Fibre Optics, *Nature*, **191**, 927 (1961).

C2. Carrara, N., Rifrazione di onde evanescenti, *Alta Frequenza*, **19**, 164 (1950).

C3. Centeno, M., V, The Refractive Index of Liquid Water in the Near Infra-red Spectrum, *J. Opt. Soc. Am.*, **31**, 244 (1941).

C4. Chakravarty, B. N., On the Diffraction of Light Incident at Nearly the Critical Angle on the Boundary between Two Media, *Proc. Roy. Soc. (London)*, **99A**, 503 (1921).

C5. Chen, F. S., J. E. Geusic, and S. K. Kurtz, Light Modulation and Beam Deflection with Potassium Tantalate-Niobate Crystals, *J. Appl. Phys.*, **37**, 388 (1966).

*C6. Chiarotti, G., G. Del Signore, A. Frova, and G. Samoggia, Optical Study of Surface Levels in Ge, *Nuovo Cimento*, **26**, 403 (1962).

*C7. Clifford, A. A., and B. Crawford, Jr., XIV. The Relation of Optical Constants to Molecular Parameters, *J. Phys. Chem.*, **70**, 1536 (1966).

C8. Colthup, N. B., and S. E. Wiberly, *Introduction to Infrared and Raman Spectroscopy*, Academic Press, New York, 1964.

*C9. Corsini, A., and R. D. MacFarlane, Some Recent Scientific Developments and Their Effect on Analytical Chemistry, *Chem. Can.*, **17**, 27 (1965).

C10. Court, I. N., and F. K. von Willisen, Frustrated Total Internal Reflection and Application of Its Principle to Laser Cavity Design, *Appl. Opt.*, **3**, 719 (1964).

C11. Culshaw, W., and D. S. Jones, Effect of a Metal Plate on Total Reflection, *Proc. Phys. Soc.*, **B66**, 859 (1953).

C12. Cuthrell, R. E., and C. F. Schroeder, Spectrophotometer Signal Enhancement by Digital Computer, *Rev. Sci. Instr.*, **36**, 1249 (1965).

D1. Daly, R., and S. D. Sims, An Improved Method of Mechanical Q-Switching Using TIR, *Appl. Opt.*, **3**, 1063 (1964).

D2. Dayet, J., and J. Vincent-Geisse, Application à des milieux absorbants des methodes de réflexion totale pour la détermination des indices de réfraction, *Compt. Rend.*, **257**, 394 (1963).

D3. Dayet, J., and J. Vincent-Geisse, Détermination des indices de réfraction par des methodes de réfraction limite. Cas de la transmission à travers des milieux absorbants, *Compt. Rend.*, **257**, 635 (1963).

*D4. Dayet, J., and H. Etchart, Application de la méthode de la réflexion totale atténuée à la détermination des constantes optiques du cyclohexane à l'intérieur de la bande de valance ν(C—H), *Compt. Rend.*, **261**, 5379 (1965).

D5. Daw, H. A., Investigation of Laser Modulation by Modifying the Internal Reflection Barrier, *J. Opt. Soc. Am.*, **53**, 915 (1963).

D6. Daw, H. A., and J. R. Izzat, Internal Reflection Barriers as Reflectors in a Modified Fabry-Perot Interferometer, *J. Opt. Soc. Am.*, **55**, 201 (1965).

D7. de Beauregard, O. C., and C. Goillot, Formule de l'effet inertial de spin du photon dans le cas de la réflexion limite, *Compt. Rend.*, **257**, 67 (1963).

D8. de Beauregard, O. C., and C. Goillot, Autre méthode de calcul de l'effet inertial de spin sur les particules en mouvement, *Compt. Rend.*, **257**, 1899 (1963).

D9. de Jong, A. N., A Novel Prism for Total Reflection, *Opt. Acta*, **10**, 115 (1963).

D9a. de Malleman, R., Réflexion totale sur les couches minces, *Compt. Rend.*, **217**, 533 (1943).

*D9b. Deane, A. M., E. W. T. Richards, and I. G. Stephen, Bond Orientations in Uranyl Nitrate Hexahydrate Using Attenuated Total Reflection, *Spectrochim. Acta*, **22**, 1253 (1966).

*D10. Deley, J. P., R. J. Gigi, and A. J. Liotti, Identification of Coatings on Paper by Attenuated Total Reflectance, *Tappi*, **46**(2), 188A (1963).

D11. DeMaria, A. J., A Multiple Internal-Reflection Folded-Path Optical Maser Geometry, *Proc. IEEE*, **53**, 1757 (1965).

*D12. Denton, S., Attenuated Total Reflection (ATR) Infrared Spectra. Some Applications in Forensic Science, *J. Forensic Sci. Soc.*, **5**, 112 (1965).

D13. Dermatis, S. N., Dynamics of Semiconductor "Web" Growth, *J. Appl. Phys.*, **36**, 3396 (1965).

D14. Dermatis, S. N., J. W. Faust, Jr., and H. F. John, Growth and Morphology of Silicon Ribbons, *J. Electrochem. Soc.*, **112**, 792 (1965).

D15. Deutscher, K., Interference Photocathodes of Increased Sensitivity, with Free Choice of Spectral Maximum, *Z. Physik*, **151**, 536 (1958).

D16. Donovan, T. M., and B. O. Seraphin, Undamaged Ge Surfaces of High Optical Quality, *J. Electrochem. Soc.*, **109**, 877 (1962).

*D17. Dreyfus, M. G., Philips Laboratories, Briarcliff Manor, New York (private communication, 1966).

D18. Dreyhaupt, W., Oberflächenprüfung von Flächen mit hohem Gütegrad, *Werkstattstechnik.*, **33**, 321 (1939).

D19. Drougard, M. E., Optical Inhomogenities in Gallium Arsenide, *J. Appl. Phys.*, **37**, 1858 (1966).

D20. Drude, P., Totale Reflexion an sehr dünnen Lamellen, in *Handbuch der Physik*, Vol. 6, A. Winkelman, Ed., 1906, p. 1275.

D21. Dunajsky, L., Energy Flow through a Thin Dielectric Layer during Frustrated Total Reflection, *Czech. J. Phys.*, **11**, 871 (1961).

D22. du Pré, F. K., and A. Daniels, Miniature Refrigerator Opens New Possibilities for Cryo-Electronics, *Signal Mag.*, **20**, 10 (1965).

*D23. du Pré, F. K., Philips Laboratories, Briarcliff Manor, New York (private communication, 1966).

E1. Edser, E., and E. Senior, The Diffraction of Light from a Dense to a Rarer Medium When the Angle of Incidence Exceeds its Critical Value, *Phil. Mag.*, **4**, 346 (1902).
E2. Eichenwald, A., On the Movement of Energy in the Case of Total Internal Light Reflection. *Zh. Russ. Fig.-Khim. Obsch.*, **41**, 131 (1909).
E3. Eichenwald, A., Über die Bewegung der Energie bei Totalreflexion, *Ann. Physik*, **35**, 1037 (1911).
E4. Eischens, R. P., and W. A. Pliskin, The Infrared Spectra of Adsorbed Molecules, *Advan. Catalysis*, **10**, 1 (1958).
E5. Engelsrath, A., and E. V. Loewenstein, Uncertainties in the Optical Constants Determined from Isoreflectance Curves, *Appl. Opt.*, **5**, 565 (1966).
E6. Exner, F., *Beitrage zur Kenntniss der atmosphärischen Elektricität. I. Messungen des Potentialgefälles in Oberägypten*, Bd. 108, Abt. II. A, Akad. der Wissenschaften, Vienna, Feb. 1899.
*F1. Fahrenfort, J., Attenuated Total Reflection—A New Principle for Production of Useful Infrared Reflection Spectra of Organic Compounds, *Molecular Spectroscopy* (Proc. IV Intern. Meeting, Bologna, 1959), Vol. 2, A. Mangini, Ed., Pergamon, London, 1962, p. 701.
*F2. Fahrenfort, J., Attenuated Total Reflection. A New Principle for the Production of Useful Infrared Spectra Of Organic Compounds, *Spectrochim. Acta*, **17**, 698 (1961).
*F3. Fahrenfort, J., Recent Developments in Infrared Reflection Spectroscopy: Attenuated Total Reflection, in *Proceedings X^{th} Colloquium Spectroscopium Internationale*, E. R. Lippincott and M. Margoshes, Eds., Spartan Books, Washington, D.C., 1963, p. 437.
*F4. Fahrenfort, J., and W. M. Visser, On the Determination of Optical Constants in the Infrared by Attenuated Total Reflectance, *Spectrochim. Acta*, **18**, 1103 (1962).
*F5. Fahrenfort, J., Shell Laboratories, Amsterdam, Netherlands (private communication, 1965).
*F6. Fahrenfort, J., and W. M. Visser, Remarks on the Determination of Optical Constants from ATR Measurements, *Spectrochim. Acta*, **21**, 1433 (1965).
F6a. Federov, F. I., and N. S. Petrov, A Special Case of Nonuniform Electromagnetic Waves in Transparent Crystals, *Opt. Spectry.*, **14**, 132 (1963).
F6b. Fellers, R. G., and J. Taylor, Internal Reflections in Dielectric Prisms, *Trans. IEEE*, **MTT-12**, 584 (1964).
*F7. Flournoy, P. A., Attentuated Total Reflection, *J. Opt. Soc. Am.*, **52**, 592A (1962).
*F8. Flournoy, P. A., Applications of Attenuated Total Reflection Spectroscopy to Absolute Intensity Measurements, *J. Chem. Phys.*, **39**, 3156 (1963).
*F9. Flournoy, P. A., and W. J. Schaffers, Attenuated Total Reflection Spectra from Surfaces of Anisotropic Absorbing Films. *Spectrochim. Acta*, **22**, 5 (1966).
*F10. Flournoy, P. A., Attenuated Total Reflection from Oriented Polypropylene Films, *Spectrochim. Acta*, **22**, 15 (1966).
*F10a. Flournoy, P. A., and J. R. Huntsberger, E. I. du Pont de Nemours and Co., Wilmington, Delaware (private communication, 1966).
F11. Försterling, K., and H. Lassen, Kurzwellenausbreitung in der Atmosphäre, *Hochfrequenztech. u. Elektroakustik*, **42**, 158 (1933).
F12. Fragstein, C.v., Zur Seitenversetzung des totalreflektierten Lichtstrahles, *Ann. Physik*, **4**, 271 (1949).

F13. Fragstein, C.v., and C. Schaefer, Zur Strahlversetzung bei Reflexion, *Ann. Physik*, **12**, 84 (1953).

F14. Francis, S. A., and A. H. Ellison, Infrared Spectra of Monolayers on Metal Mirrors, *J. Opt. Soc. Am.*, **49**, 131 (1959).

F15. Franz, W., Einfluss eines elektrischen Feldes auf eine optische Absorptionskante, *Z. Naturforsch.*, **13A**, 484 (1958).

F16. Fraser, R. D. B., The Interpretation of Infrared Dichroism in Fibrous Protein Structures, *J. Chem. Phys.*, **21**, 1511 (1953).

F17. Fraser, R. D. B., Interpretation of Infrared Dichroism in Fibrous Proteins—the 2μ Region, *J. Chem. Phys.*, **24**, 89 (1956).

F18. Friedman, H. H., D. A. Mackay, and H. L. Rosano, Odor Measurement Possibilities Via Energy Changes in Cephalin Monolayers, *Ann. N.Y. Acad. Sci.*, **116**, 602 (1964).

F19. Fröhlich, I., Examination of the Polarisation of the Refracted Beam in Total Reflection, M. *Ind. Academia Math. es Tennerzettud Ertesitöje* (*Budapest*), **35**, 120 (1917).

F20. Fröhlich, P., Neuere Beobachtungen über die Polarisation des bei der Totalreflexion gebrochenen Lichtes, *Ann. Physik*, **63**, 900 (1920).

G1. Gans, R. Fortpflanzung des Lichts durch ein inhomogenes Medium, *Ann. Physik*, **47**, 709 (1915).

G1a. Garbatski, U., and M. Folman, Multilayer Adsorption of Water near Saturation Pressure on Plane Glass Surfaces, *J. Chem. Phys.*, **22**, 2086 (1954).

*G2. Gedeemer, T. J., The Use of ATR Techniques to Evaluate UV Degradation of Plastics, *Appl. Spectry.*, **19**, 141 (1965).

G3. Gee, A. E., and H. D. Polster, A Method for Measuring Extremely Small Non-Uniformities in the Optical Thickness of Evaporated Films, *J. Opt. Soc. Am.*, **39**, 1044 (1949).

*G4. George, R. S., Polarization of the Energy Beam in Perkin-Elmer Infrared Grating Spectrophotometers, *Appl. Spectry.*, **20**, 101 (1966).

G5. Giacomo, P., Les couches réfléchissantes multidiélectriques, appliquées a l'interféromètre de Fabry-Perot. Étude théorique et expérimentale des couches réelles, *Rev. Opt.*, **35**, 442 (1956).

G6. Gibellato, S., Riflessione totale di un'onda elettromagnetica con reflessione metallica dell'onda evanescente, *Nuovo Cimento*, **6**, 344 (1949).

G7. Gibson, A. F., Infra-red and Microwave Modulation using Free Carriers in Semiconductors, *J. Sci. Instr.*, **35**, 273 (1958).

*G8. Gilby, A. C., J. Burr, Jr., and B. Crawford, Jr., Vibrational Intensities. XII. An Optical-Mechanical System from Infrared Attenuated Total Reflection Measurements, *J. Phys. Chem.*, **70**, 1520 (1966).

*G9. Gilby, A. C., J. Burr, Jr., W. Krueger, and B. Crawford, Jr., Vibrational Intensities. XIII. Reduction of Attenuated Total Reflection Data to Optical Constants, *J. Phys. Chem.*, **70**, 1525 (1966).

G10. Giordmaine, J. A., and W. Kaiser, Mode-Selecting Prism Reflectors for Optical Masers, *J. Appl. Phys.*, **35**, 3446 (1964).

G11. Golay, M. J. E., Comparison of Various Infrared Spectrometric Systems, *J. Opt. Soc. Am.*, **46**, 422 (1956).

G12. Goos, F., and H. Hänchen, Über das Eindringen des totalreflektierten Lichtes in das dünnere Medium, *Ann. Physik*, **43**, 383 (1943).

G13. Goos, F., and H. Hänchen, Ein neuer und fundamentaler Versuch zur Totalreflexion, *Ann. Physik,* **1**, 333 (1947).

G14. Goos, F., and H. Lindberg-Hänchen, Neumessung des Strahlversetzungseffektes bei Totalreflexion, *Ann. Physik,* **5**, 251 (1949).

*G15. Gore, R. C., Perkin-Elmer Corporation, Norwalk, Conn. (private communication, 1964).

*G15a. Gottlieb, K., and B. Schrader, Anwendung der ATR-Technik bei der Infrarot-Spektroskopie von Kristallpulvern und Einkristallen, *Z. Anal. Chem.,* **216,** 307 (1966).

*G16. Goulden, J. D. S., and D. J. Manning, Infrared Spectra of Aqueous Solutions by the Attenuated Total Reflectance Technique, *Nature,* **203,** 403 (1964).

G17. Gracheva, T. I., Reflection on Absorbing Solutions Near the Critical Angle, *Opt. i Spektroskopiya,* **2,** 792 (1957).

G18. Grant, G. R., W. D. Gunter, Jr., and E. F. Erickson, High Absolute Photocathode Sensitivity, *Rev. Sci. Instr.,* **36,** 1511 (1965).

G18a. Grant, R. M., Free-Carrier Absorption in Silver Bromide, *J. Opt. Soc. Am.,* **55,** 1457 (1965).

G19. Grant, R. M., Photoelectrically Induced Free-Carrier Absorption and Amplification of Light in Cadmium Sulphide, *Appl. Opt.,* **5,** 333 (1966).

G20. Grechushnikov, B. N., and I. P. Petrov, A Polarizer for the Infrared Region of the Spectrum, *Opt. Spectry,* **14,** 160 (1963).

G21. Greenler, R. G., Infrared Study of Adsorbed Molecules on Metal Surfaces by Reflection Techniques, *J. Chem. Phys.,* **44,** 310 (1966).

G22. Greski, G., FTIR Telephony, *Usp. Fiz. Nauk.,* **12,** 173 (1932).

*G23. Guillemet, C., and P. Aclocque, New Optical Methods for the Determination of the Stresses near Surfaces, *Rev. Franc. Méc.,* **2-3,** 157 (1962).

G24. Gunter, W. D., Jr., E. F. Erickson, and G. R. Grant, Enhancement of Photomultiplier Sensitivity by Total Internal Reflection, *Appl. Opt.,* **4,** 512 (1965).

H1a. Habegger, M. A., J. G. Harris, and J. Lipp, Total Internal Reflection (TIR) Light Deflector, *Appl. Opt.,* **5,** 1403 (1966).

H1. Hall, E. E., The Penetration of Totally Reflected Light into the Rarer Medium, *Phys. Rev.,* **15,** 73 (1902).

H2. Hannah, R. W., An Optical Accessory for Obtaining the Infrared Spectra of Very Thin Films, *Appl. Spectry.,* **17,** 23 (1963).

*H3. Hannah, R. W., and J. L. Dwyer, Infrared Analysis of Suspended Particulates with Millipore Filters and Attenuated Total Reflection, *Anal. Chem.,* **36,** 2341 (1964).

*H4. Hannah, R. W., Perkin-Elmer Corporation, Norwalk, Conn. (private communication, 1966).

*H5. Hansen, W. N., A New Spectrophotometric Technique Using Multiple Attenuated Total Reflection, *Anal. Chem.,* **35,** 765 (1963).

*H6. Hansen, W. N., and J. A. Horton, Spectrometer Cells for Single and Multiple Internal Reflection Studies in Ultraviolet, Visible, Near Infrared and Infrared Spectral Regions, *Anal. Chem.,* **36,** 783 (1964).

*H7. Hansen, W. N., Expanded Formulas for Attenuated Total Reflection and the Derivation of Absorption Rules for Single and Multiple ATR Spectrometer Cells, *Spectrochim. Acta,* **21,** 815 (1965).

*H8. Hansen, W. N., On the Determination of Optical Constants by a Two-Angle Internal Reflection Method, *Spectrochim. Acta,* **21,** 209 (1965).

*H9. Hansen, W. N., Internal Reflection Spectroscopy and the Determination of Optical Constants, *ISA Trans.,* **4,** 263 (1965).

*H10. Hansen, W. N., Variable Angle Reflection Attachment for the Ultraviolet, Visible, and Infrared, *Anal. Chem.,* **37,** 1142 (1965).

*H11. Hansen, W. N., R. A. Osteryoung, and T. Kuwana, Internal Reflection Spectroscopic Observation Of Electrode-Solution Interface, *J. Am. Chem. Soc.,* **88,** 1062 (1966).

*H11a. Hansen, W. N., T. Kuwana, and R. A. Osteryoung, Observation of Electrode-Solution Interface by Means of Internal Reflection Spectrometry, *Anal. Chem.,* **38,** 1810 (1966).

H12. Harrick, N. J., Use of Infrared Absorption in Germanium to Determine Carrier Distributions for Injection and Extraction, *Phys. Rev.,* **103,** 1173 (1956).

H13. Harrick, N. J., Lifetime Measurements of Excess Carriers in Semiconductors, *J. Appl. Phys.,* **27,** 1439 (1956).

H14. Harrick, N. J., Characteristics of Junctions in Germanium, *J. Appl. Phys.,* **29,** 764 (1958).

*H15. Harrick, N. J., Effect of the Metal-Semiconductor Potential on the Semiconductor Surface Barrier Height, *J. Chem. Phys. Solids,* **8,** 106 (1959).

*H16. Harrick, N. J., Reflection of Infrared Radiation from a Germanium-Mercury Interface, *J. Opt. Soc. Am.,* **49,** 376 (1959).

H17. Harrick, N. J., Infrared Polarizer, *J. Opt. Soc. Am.,* **49,** 379 (1959).

*H18. Harrick, N. J., Semiconductor Surface Properties Deduced from Free Carrier Absorption and Reflection of Infrared Radiation, *J. Phys. Chem. Solids,* **14,** 60 (1960).

H19. Harrick, N. J., Semiconductor Type and Local Doping Determined Through the Use of Infrared Radiation, *Solid State Electron.,* **1,** 234 (1960).

*H20. Harrick, N. J., Discussion, December 1959, p. BD-4, following paper presented by R. P. Eischens, Infrared Methods Applied to Surface Phenomena in *Semiconductor Surfaces* (Proc. Second Conf.), Pergamon Press, London, 1960, p. 56.

*H21. Harrick, N. J., Study of Physics and Chemistry of Surfaces from Frustrated Total Internal Reflection, *Phys. Rev. Letters,* **4,** 224 (1960).

*H22. Harrick, N. J., Surface Chemistry from Spectral Analysis of Totally Internally Reflected Radiation, *J. Phys. Chem.,* **64,** 1110 (1960).

*H23. Harrick, N. J., Optical Spectrum of the Semiconductor Surface States from Frustrated Total Internal Reflections, *Phys. Rev.,* **125,** 1165 (1962).

H24. Harrick, N. J., Use of Frustrated Total Internal Reflection to Measure Film Thickness and Surface Reliefs, *J. Appl. Phys.,* **33,** 2774 (1962).

H25. Harrick, N. J., A Continuously Variable Optical Beam Splitter and Intensity Controller, *Appl. Opt.,* **2,** 1203 (1963).

*H26. Harrick, N. J., Total Internal Reflection and Its Application to Surface Studies, *Ann. N. Y. Acad. Sci.,* **101,** 928 (1963).

H27. Harrick, N. J., Fingerprinting via Total Internal Reflection, *Philips Tech. Rev.,* **24,** 271 (1963).

*H28. Harrick, N. J., Multiple Reflection Cells for Internal Reflection Spectrometry, *Anal. Chem.,* **36,** 188 (1964).

H29. Harrick, N. J., Crossed-Plate Infrared Polarizer, *J. Opt. Soc. Am.,* **54,** 1281 (1964).

*H30. Harrick, N. J., Electric Field Strengths at Totally Reflecting Interfaces, *J. Opt. Soc. Am.*, **55**, 851 (1965).

*H31. Harrick, N. J., Variable Angle Attachment for Internal Reflection Spectroscopy, *Anal. Chem.*, **37**, 1445 (1965).

*H32. Harrick, N. J., and N. H. Riederman, Infrared Spectra of Powders by Means of Internal Reflection Spectroscopy, *Spectrochim. Acta*, **21**, 2135 (1965).

*H33. Harrick, N. J., Double-Beam Internal Reflection Spectrometer, *Appl. Opt.*, **4**, 1664 (1965).

*H34. Harrick, N. J., Vertical Double-Pass Multiple Reflection Element for Internal Reflection Spectroscopy, *Appl. Opt.*, **5**, 1 (1966).

*H35. Harrick, N. J., and A. F. Turner, Induced Absorption for Internal Reflection Spectroscopy, *J. Opt. Soc. Am.*, **56**, 553(A) (1966).

*H36. Harrick, N. J., The Rosette—A Unipoint Multiple Internal Reflection Element, *Appl. Opt.*, **5**, 1236 (1966).

*H37. Harrick, N. J., and F. K. du Pré, Effective Thickness of Bulk Materials and of Thin Films for Internal Reflection Spectroscopy, *Appl. Opt.*, **5**, 1739 (1966).

*H38. Harrick, N. J., and J. T. Bloxsom, Study Program to Obtain the Infrared Internal Reflection Spectra of Powdered Rocks. Prepared under NASA Contract #NASw-964 Mod. 1 (1966).

*H38a. Harrick, N. J., A. F. Turner, and F. K. du Pré, Use of Optical Cavity to Enhance Absorption in Internal Reflection Spectroscopy, *Appl. Opt.* (1967).

*H39. Harris, R. L., and G. R. Svoboda, Determination of Alkyd and Monomer-Modified Alkyd Resins by Attenuated Total Reflectance Infrared Spectrometry, *Anal. Chem.*, **34**, 1655 (1962).

H40. Hass, G., Filmed Surfaces for Reflecting Optics, *J. Opt. Soc. Am.*, **45**, 945 (1955).

H41. Hauser, E., Rie, E., Versuche mit einer Flamme besonders hoher Temperatur, *Sitzber. Akad. Wiss., Math.-Naturw. Klasse*, **IIa**, 129 (1920).

*H42. Hermann, T. S., FMIR Infrared Spectroscopy of Coatings on Fibers and Metal Plates, *J. Appl. Polymer Sci.*, **9**, 3953 (1965).

*H43. Hermann, T. S., Identification of Trace Amounts of Organophosphorus Pesticides by Frustrated Multiple Internal Reflectance Spectroscopy, *Appl. Spectry.*, **19**, 10 (1965).

*H44. Hermann, T. S., Sample Preparation of Biological Tissues for Infrared Spectroscopy Using Frustrated Multiple Internal Reflectance, *Anal. Biochem.*, **12**, 406 (1965).

H45. Hett, J. H., Medical Optical Instruments, in *Applied Optical Engineering*, Vol. 5, R. Kingslake, Ed., Academic Press, New York, 1967.

*H46. Hirschfeld, T., Total Reflection Fluorescence (TRF), *Can. Spectry.*, **10**, 128 (1965).

*H47. Hirschfeld, T., Modifications in Photomultipliers with Total Internal Reflection Enhanced Sensitivity, *Appl. Opt.*, **5**, 1337 (1966).

*H48. Hirschfeld, T., Determination of Optical Constants by ATR Measurements, *Spectrochim. Acta*, **22**, 1823 (1966).

*H49. Hirschfeld, T., Attenuated Total Reflection—Applications in the UV-Visible Region, *Can. Spectry.*, **11**, 102 (1966).

*H49a. Hirschfeld, T., High-Sensitivity Attenuated Total-Reflection Spectroscopy, *Appl. Spectry.*, **20**, 336 (1966).

*H49b. Hirschfeld, T., Procedures for Attenuated Total Reflection Study of Extremely Small Samples, *Appl. Opt.* (1967).

*H49c. Hirschfeld, T., A Solution to the Sample Contact Problem in ATR, *Appl. Spectry.* (1967).

*H49d. Hirschfeld, T., The Obtainment of High Sensitivity in ATR, *J. Opt. Soc. Am.*, **56**, 1452(A) (1966).

*H49e. Hirschfeld, T., Reflexión total atenuada, *Rev. Soc. Quim. Mex.*, **7**, 112(A) (1963).

H50. Hora, H., Zur Seitenversetzung bei der Totalreflexion von Materiewellen, *Optik*, **17**, 409 (1960).

*H50a. Horton, J. A., and Hansen, W. N., Relationship of Internal Reflection Measurements to Bulk Optical Properties with a Transmission Comparison, *Anal. Chem.* (1967).

H50b. Humidity and Moisture, Measurement and Control in Science and Industry, in *Principles and Methods of Measuring Humidity in Gases*, Vol. 1, R. E. Ruskin, Ed. (A. Wexler, Editor-in-Chief), Reinhold, New York, 1965.

H51. Hunt, J. M., M. P. Wisherd, and L. C. Bonham, Infrared Absorption Spectra of Minerals and other Inorganic Compounds, *Anal. Chem.*, **22**, 1478 (1950).

H52. Hunt, J. M., and D. S. Turner, Determination of Mineral Constituents of Rocks by Infrared Spectroscopy, *Anal. Chem.*, **25**, 1169 (1953).

H52a. Hunter, W. R., Optical Constants of Aluminum from 300 to 800 Å, *J. Appl. Phys.*, **34**, 1565 (1963).

H52b. Hunter, W. R., Optical Constants of Metals in the Extreme Ultraviolet I. A Modified Critical-Angle Technique for Measuring the Index of Refraction of Metals in the Extreme Ultraviolet, *J. Opt. Soc. Am.*, **54**, 15 (1964).

H53. Huntsberger, J. R., The Locus of Adhesive Failure, *J. Polymer Sci. A*, **1**, 1339 (1963).

I1. Ignatowsky, W. v., Über totale Reflexion, *Ann. Physik*, **37**, 901 (1912).

I2. Ignatowsky, W. v., and E. Oettinger, Experimentelle Untersuchungen zur Totalreflexion, *Ann. Physik*, **37**, 911 (1912).

*I2a. Imanura, R., A. Yamaoka, and K. Aoki. Coated Papers. IV. Analysis of Coated Materials by Infrared Spectrophotometry, *Kami-pa Gikyoshi*, **19**, 33 (1965).

*I3. Ingram, B. M., Polymeric Materials by a New Method of Infrared Spectrophotometry, *Res. Develop. Ind.*, **34**, 18 (1964).

I4. Iogansen, L. V., On the Role of Dimensional Limitations of Total Reflection Resonance Filters, *Opt. Spectry.*, **11**, 292 (1961).

I5. Iogansen, L. V., Totally Reflecting Resonance Filter of Limited Size. I, *Opt. Spectry.*, **12**, 173 (1962).

I6. Iogansen, L. V., Spatially-Limited Total-Internal-Reflection Resonance Filter. II, *Opt. Spectry.*, **13**, 146 (1962).

I7. Iogansen, L. V., A Finite Totally Reflecting Resonance Filter, III, *Opt. Spectry.*, **14**, 67 (1963).

J1. Jacobsen, R. T., Optical Constants of Biaxial Crystals from the Exact Drude Equations, *J. Opt. Soc. Am.*, **54**, 1170 (1964).

J2. Jaffe, J. H., and U. Oppenheim, Infrared Dispersion of Liquids by Critical Angle Refractometry, *J. Opt. Soc. Am.*, **47**, 782 (1957).

J3. Jaffe, J. H., H. Goldring, and U. Oppenheim, Infrared Dispersion of Absorbing Liquids by Critical Angle Refractometry, *J. Opt. Soc. Am.*, **49**, 1199 (1959).

*J3a. Jayme, G., and E. M. Rohmann, Application of the ATR Technique to the China Clay-Casein System, *Papier*, **19**, 497 (1965).

*J3b. Jayme, G., and E. M. Rohmann, Infrared Spectrophotometry in Testing Coated Papers. II, Application of the ATR Technique to the System China Clay Acronal 500 D., *Papier*, **20**, 1 (1966).

*J4. Johnson, R. D., Silver Membrane Filters as a Support for Infrared Analysis by Attenuated Total Reflection, *Anal. Chem.*, **38**, 160 (1966).

J5. Johnson, L. F., and Kahng, D., Piezoelectric Optical-Maser Modulator, *J. Appl. Phys.*, **33**, 3440 (1962).

J6. Jones, A. L., Coupling of Optical Fibers and Scattering in Fibers, *J. Opt. Soc. Am.*, **55**, 261 (1965).

K1. Kahn, A. H., Theory of the Infrared Absorption of Carriers in Ge and Si, *Phys. Rev.*, **97**, 1647 (1955).

K2. Kane, J., and H. Osterberg, Optical Characteristics of Planer Guided Modes, *J. Opt. Soc. Am.*, **54**, 347 (1964).

K3. Kapany, N. S., Fiber Optics. V. Light Leakage Due to Frustrated Total Reflection, *J. Opt. Soc. Am.*, **49**, 770 (1959).

K4. Kapany, N. S., Fiber Optics, *Sci. Am.*, **203**, 72 (1960).

K5. Kapany, N. S., High Resolution Fibre Optics Using Sub-Micron Multiple Fibres, *Nature*, **184**, 881 (1959).

K6. Kapany, N. S., Endoscopes Using Fiber Optics, *Proceedings of the International Congress of Gastroenterology, April, 1960, Amsterdam*, Excerpta Medica Foundation, 1961, p. 577.

K7. Kapany, N. S., and D. F. Capellaro, Fiber Optics. VII. Image Transfer from Lambertian Emitters, *J. Opt. Soc. Am.*, **51**, 23 (1961).

K8. Kapany, N. S., and J. J. Burke, Fiber Optics. IX. Waveguide Effects, *J. Opt. Soc. Am.*, **51**, 1067 (1961).

K9. Kapany, N. S., J. J. Burke, and C. C. Shaw, Fiber Optics. X. Evanescent Boundary Wave Propagation, *J. Opt. Soc. Am.*, **53**, 929 (1963).

K10. Kapany, N. S., Role of Fiber Optics in Ultra-High-Speed Photography, *J. Soc. Motion Picture Television Eng.*, **71**, 75 (1962).

K11. Kapany, N. S., and J. J. Burke, Dielectric Waveguides at Optical Frequencies, *Solid State Res.*, **3**, 35 (1962).

K12. Kapany, N. S., and D. A. Pontarelli, Photorefractometer I. Extension of Sensitivity and Range, *Appl. Opt.*, **2**, 425 (1963).

*K13. Kapany, N. S., and D. A. Pontarelli, Photorefractometer. II. Measurement of N and K, *Appl. Opt.*, **2**, 1043 (1963).

K14. Kard, P. G., Theory of an Improved Interference Light Filter with Total Reflection, *Opt. i Spektroscopiya*, **4**, 643 (1958).

K15. Kard, P. G., Doublet Structure Elimination of The Transmission Band of The Light Filter in Total Reflection, *Opt. Spectry.*, **6**, 244 (1959).

K16. Kossel, D., Interferenzen an Schichten mit einer totalreflektierenden Grenze, *Z. Physik*, **126**, 233 (1949).

*K17. Katlafsky, B., and R. E. Keller, Attenuated Total Reflectance Infrared Analysis of Aqueous Solutions, *Anal. Chem.*, **35**, 1665 (1963).

K18. Kaufman, I., The Band Between Microwave and Infrared Regions, *Proc. Inst. Radio Engr.*, **47**, 381 (1959).

K19. Keldysh, L. V., The Effect of a Strong Electric Field on the Optical Properties of Insulating Crystals, *Soviet Phys. JETP*, **7**, 788 (1958).

K20. Keldyš, L. V., V. S. Vavilov, and K. I. Bricin, The Influence of Strong Electric Field on the Optical Properties of Semiconductors, *Proc. Intern. Conf. Semicond. Phys., Prague, 1960* (Pub. 1961), p. 824.

K21. Keller, W. D., J. H. Spotts, and D. L. Biggs, Infrared Spectra of Some Rock-Forming Minerals, *Am. J. Sci.*, **250**, 453 (1952).

K22. Kobayashi, A., and S. Kawaji, Adsorption and Surface Potential of Semiconductors. I. Photoenhanced Adsorption of Oxygen and Change of Contact Potential of Zinc Sulfide Phosphors with Illumination, *J. Phys. Soc. Japan.*, **10**, 270 (1955)

K22a. Koester, C. J., Laser Action by Enhanced Total Internal Reflection, *IEEE J. Quantum Electronics*, QE-2, 580 (1966).

K23. König, W., Electrochemische Lichttheorie, *Handbuch der Physik*, Vol. 20, Geiger & Scheel, Berlin, 1928, p. 141.

K24. Krüss, H., Die Grenze der Totalreflexion, *Z. Instrumentenk.*, **39**, 73 (1919).

K25. Kruzhilin, Yu. I., An Anisotropic Reflector for Lasers, *Opt. Spectry.*, **20**, 397 (1966).

L1. Laue, M.v., Die Spiegelung und Brechung des Lichtes an der Grenze zweier isotroper Körper, *Handbuch der Experimentalphysik*, **18**, 183 (1928).

L2. Launer, P. J., Regularities in the Infrared Absorption Spectra of Silicate Minerals, *Am. Mineralogist*, **37**, 764 (1952).

L3. Lelyuk, L. G., I. N. Shklyarevskii, and R. G. Yarovaya, Optical Properties of Liquid Hg and Ga in the Visible and Near IR Regions of the Spectrum, *Opt. Spectry.*, **16**, 263 (1964).

L4. Leurgans, P. J., and A. F. Turner, Frustrated Total Reflection Interference Filters, *J. Opt. Soc. Am.*, **37**, 983(A) (1947).

L5. Levitt, R. S., and N. J. Harrick, Internal Reflection at Near-Critical Angles: The Differential Photogoniometer, *J. Opt. Soc. Am.*, **56**, 557(A) (1966).

*L5a. Levitt, R. S., Philips Laboratories, Briarcliff Manor, New York (private communication, 1966).

*L5b. Levitt, R. S., Internal Reflection at Near Critical Angles. II. The Differential Photorefractometer, ISA Conf., October 1966.

L5c. Livingston, W. C., Enhancement of Photocathode Sensitivity by Total Internal Reflection As Applied to An Image Tube, *Appl. Opt.*, **5**, 1335 (1966).

*L6. Loeb, G., U. S. Naval Research Laboratories, Washington, D. C., Infrared Spectra of Surface Films of Poly-γ-Methyl-L-Glutamate (private communication, 1965).

L7. Low, M. J. D., and H. Inoue, Infrared Emission Spectra of Solid Surfaces, *Anal. Chem.*, **36**, 2397 (1964).

L8. Low, M. J. D., Infra-red Emission Spectra of Minerals, *Nature*, **208**, 1089 (1965).

L9. Low, M. J. D., Infrared Emission Spectra of Surfaces—An Interferometric Approach, *J. Catalysis*, **4**, 719 (1965).

L10. Low, M. J. D., The Measurement of Infrared Emission Spectra Using Multiple-Scan Interferometry, *Spectrochim. Acta*, **22**, 369 (1966).

L11. Lucchesi, C. A., Analytic Tools for Coatings research, *Offic. Dig. J. Paint Technol. Eng.*, **35**, 975 (1963).

L12. Lyon, R. J. P., Infrared Analysis—A Neglected Analytical Method for Rocks and Minerals, *Encyclopedia of Earth Science*, Reinhold, New York, 1967.

L13. Lyon, R. J. P., *Minerals in the Infrared—a Critical Bibliography*, Stamford Research Institute (1962).

M1. Maclaurin, R. C., On Newton's Rings Formed by Metallic Reflection, *Proc. Roy. Soc. (London)*, **76A**, 515 (1905).

M2. Maecker, H., Quantitativer Nachweis von Grenzschichtwellen in der Optik, *Ann. Physik*, **4**, 409 (1949).

M3. Maecker, H., Die Grenze der Totalreflexion I. Strahlenoptische Näherung mit der Wolterschen Strahldefinition, *Ann. Physik*, **10**, 115 (1952).

*M4. Malone, C. P., and P. A. Flournoy, Infrared ATR Determination of Alcohols in Aqueous Solution, *Spectrochim. Acta*, **21**, 1361 (1965).

M5. Many, A., N. B. Grover, and Y. Goldstein, *Semiconductor Surfaces*, North-Holland Pub. Co., Amsterdam, and Interscience, New York, 1965.

*M6. Mark, H. B., Jr., and B. S. Pons, An *in situ* Spectrophotometric Method for Observing the Infrared Spectra of Species at the Electrode Surface during Electrolysis, *Anal. Chem.*, **38**, 119 (1966).

M6a. May, K. R., The Cascade Impactor: An Instrument For Sampling Coarse Aerosols, *J. Sci. Instr.*, **22**, 187 (1945).

*M6b. McCall, E. R., S. H. Miles, and R. T. O'Connor, Frustrated Multiple Internal Reflectance Spectroscopy of Chemically Modified Cotton, *Am. Dye Stuff Reporter*, **55**, 31 (1966).

M7. McCarthy, D. E., The Reflection and Transmission of Infrared Materials: I, Spectra from 2–50 Microns, *Appl. Opt.*, **2**, 591 (1963).

M8. McCarthy, D. E., The Reflection and Transmission of Infrared Materials: II, Bibliography, *Appl. Opt.*, **2**, 596 (1963).

M9. McCarthy, D. E., The Reflection and Transmission of Infrared Materials: III, Spectra from 2 Microns to 50 Microns, *Appl. Opt.*, **4**, 317 (1965).

M10. McCarthy, D. E., The Reflection and Transmission of Infrared Materials: IV, Bibliography, *Appl. Opt.*, **4**, 507 (1965).

M11. McCarthy, K. G., S. S. Ballard, and W. L. Wolfe, Transmission and Absorption of Special Crystals and Certain Glasses, in *American Institute of Physics Handbook*, 2nd ed., D. E. Gray, Ed., McGraw-Hill, New York, 1963, Sec. 6, p. 45.

M12. McCutchen, C. W., Refractometer Microscope, *Appl. Opt.*, **1**, 253 (1962).

M13. McCutchen, C. W., Generalized Aperture and the Three-Dimensional Diffraction Image, *J. Opt. Soc. Am.*, **54**, 240 (1964).

M14. McCutchen, C. W., Optical Systems for Observing Surface Topography by Frustrated Total Internal Reflection and by Interference, *Rev. Sci. Instr.*, **35**, 1340 (1964).

*M15. McGowan, R. J., Attenuated Total Reflectance vs Transmission Infrared Spectrometry in the Quantitative Evaluation of Paint Vehicles, *Anal. Chem.*, **35**, 1664 (1963).

*M16. Mellow, D., Hercules Powder, Salt Lake City, Utah (private communication, 1965).

*M16a. Merka, J., Evaluating Attenuated Multiple Internal Reflection (AMIR) for Your Own Analytical Problems, *Can. Spectry.*, **10**, 93 (1965).

M17. Meyer, H. J. G., Infrared Absorption by Conduction Electrons in Ge, *Phys. Rev.*, **112**, 298 (1958).

*M17a. Miller, R. A., and F. J. Campbell, Attenuated Total Reflectance Infrared Spectroscopy as an Analytical Tool, Report of NRL Progress (US NRL), p. 11, May 1964.

M18. Moss, T. S., *Optical Properties of Semiconductors*, Academic Press, New York, 1959.

M19. Mundel, D. F., and R. Zucker, Massachusetts Institute of Technology, Cambridge, Mass. (private communication, 1965).

N1. Nassenstein, H., Totalreflexion an elektrochemischen Grenzschichten, *Z. Naturforsch.*, **17a**, 8 (1962).

N2. Nassenstein, H., Reflexion und Interferenz des Lichtes an elektrochemischen Grenzschichten, *Z. Physik*, **173**, 85 (1963).

N3. Nassenstein, H., Verfahren zur Bestimmung der optischen Konstanten von feinverteilten absorbierenden Feststoffen, *Naturwissenschaften*, **52**, 511 (1965).

N4. Newton, I., *Opticks*, Dover Publications, New York, 1952.

N5. Noether, F., Über die Verteilung des Energiestroms bei der Totalreflexion, *Ann. Physik*, **11**, 141 (1931).

N6. Noyes, G. R., and P. W. Baumeister, Analysis of a Modified Frustrated Total Reflection Filter, *Appl. Opt.*, **6**, 355 (1967).

O1. Osterberg, H., and L. W. Smith, Transmission of Optical Energy Along Surfaces: Part I, Homogeneous Media, *J. Opt. Soc. Am.*, **54**, 1073 (1964).

O2. Osterberg, H., and L. W. Smith, Transmission of Optical Energy Along Surfaces: Part II, Inhomogeneous Media, *J. Opt. Soc. Am.*, **54**, 1078 (1964).

O3. Ott, H., Zur Reflexion von Kugelwellen, *Ann. Physik*, **4**, 432 (1949).

*P1. Parker, F. S., Attenuated Total Reflection Spectra of Glycyl-L-alanine in Aqueous Solutions, *Nature*, **200**, 1093 (1963).

*P1a. Parker, F. S., and R. Ans, Infrared Studies of Human and Other Tissues by the Attenuated Total Reflectance Technique, *Anal. Biochem.*, **18**, 414 (1967).

*P1b. Parker, F. S., and R. Ans, Infrared Spectra of Carbohydrates (700–250 cm^{-1}) Determined by Both Attenuated Total Reflectance and Transmission Techniques, *Appl. Spectry.*, **20**, 384 (1966).

*P2. Parks, G., Stanford University, Stanford, California (private communication, 1964).

P3. Patel, C. K. N., Efficient Phase-Matched Harmonic Generation in Tellurium with a CO_2 Laser at 10.6μ, *Phys. Rev. Letters*, **15**, 1027 (1965).

P4. Patty, R. R., and D. Williams, Further Studies of Pressure-Modulated Infrared Absorption, *J. Opt. Soc. Am.*, **51**, 1351 (1961).

P5. Penrose, L. S., Fingerprints, Palms and Chromosomes, *Nature*, **197**, 933 (1963).

P6. Peters, D. W., Infrared Modulator Using Multiple Internal Reflections and Induced Conductivity, *Proc. IEEE*, **53**, 1148 (1965).

P7. Petrov, N. S., Inhomogeneous Waves in Transparent Uniaxial Crystals, *Opt. Spectry.*, **14**, 54 (1963).

*P8. Pettit, D., and A. R. Carter, Observations on the Use of Infra-red Spectrometry in Leather Analysis, *J. Soc. Leather Trades Chemists*, **48**, 476 (1964).

*P8a. Peyser, P., and R. R. Stromberg, Measurement of the Conformation of Adsorbed Polystyrene by Attenuated Total Reflection in the Ultraviolet, *J. Phys. Chem.* (1967).

P9. Picht, J., Beiträge zur Wellenoptik von Strahlenbündeln endlicher Öffunng und zur Optik bewegter Körper, *Z. Physik*, **58**, 667 (1929).

P10. Picht, J., Beitrag zur Theorie der Totalreflexion I, *Ann. Physik*, **3**, 433 (1929).

P11. Picht, J., Neue Untersuchungen zur Totalreflexion, *Optik*, **12**, 41 (1955).

P12. Picht, J., The Theory of Total Reflection, *Abhandl. Deut. Akad. Wiss. Berlin, Kl. Math. Allgem. Naturwiss.*, **2**, 5 (1955).

P13. Picht, J., Nachschrift zur Arbeit des Herrn v. Schmidt, *Ann. Physik*, **19**, 913 (1934).

P14. Pohl, R. W., *Optik*, Springer, Berlin, 1940.

*P15. Polchlopek, S. E., Attenuated Total Reflectance Effects with Different Prisms, *Appl. Spectry.*, **17**, 112 (1963).

*P16. Polchlopek, S. E., Attenuated Total Reflectance, in *Applied Infrared Spectroscopy*, D. E. Kendall, Ed., Reinhold, New York, 1966, Chap. 15, p. 462.

P17. Politycki, A., and E. Fuchs, Elektronenmikroskopische Untersuchung elektrolytisch erzeugter Siliciumoxydschichten, *Z. Naturforsch.*, **14a**, 271 (1959).

P18. Polster, H. D., Reflection from a Multilayer Filter, *J. Opt. Soc. Am.*, **39**, 1038 (1949).

*P19. Potter, R. F., Analytical Determination of Optical Constants Based on the Polarized Reflectance at a Dielectric-conductor Interface, *J. Opt. Soc. Am.*, **54**, 904 (1964).

*P20. Potter, R. F., Reflectometer for Determining Optical Constants, *Appl. Opt.*, **4**, 53 (1965).

P21. Potts, W. J., Jr., *Chemical Infrared Spectroscopy* (Vol. 1: *Techniques*), Wiley, New York, 1963.

P22. Poynting, J. H., On the Transfer of Energy in the Electromagnetic Field, *Phil. Trans. Roy. Soc. London*, **175**, 343 (1884).

*P23. Puttnam, N. A., Infrared Analysis by Attenuated Total Reflectance, *Proc. Soc. Anal. Chem.*, **2**, 158 (1965).

*P24. Puttnam, N. A., S. Lee, and B. H. Baxter, Application of Attenuated Total Reflectance Spectroscopy to Toilet Articles and Household Products. I. Qualitative Analysis, *J. Soc. Cosmetic Chemists*, **16**, 607 (1965).

*P25. Puttnam, N. A., and B. H. Baxter, Application of Attenuated Total Reflectance Infrared Spectroscopy to Toilet Articles and Household Products, Part II—Quantitative Analysis, *J. Soc. Cosmetic Chemists*, **17**, 9 (1966).

Q1. Quincke, G., Optische Experimental-Untersuchungen. Über das Eindringen des total reflektierten Lichtes in das dünnere Medium, *Ann. Physik*, **127**, 1 (1866).

Q2. Quincke, G., Optische Experimental-Untersuchungen. II. Über die elliptische Polarisation des bei totaler Reflexion eingedrungenen oder zurück-geworfenen Lichtes, *Ann. Physik*, **127**, 199 (1866).

R1. Raker, H. D., and G. R. Valenzuela, A Double-prism Attenuator for Millimeter Waves, *IRE Trans. Microwave Theory Tech.*, **10**, 392 (1962).

R2. Raman, C. V., On the Nature of the Disturbance in the Second Medium in Total Reflexion, *Phil. Mag.*, **50**, 812 (1925).

R3. Raman, C. V., On the Total Reflexion of Light, *Proc. Indian Assoc. Cultivation Sci.*, **9**, 271 and 330 (1926).

R3a. Raman, C. V., Huygens' Principle and the Phenomena of Total Reflexion, *Trans. Opt. Soc. (London)*, **28**, 149 (1926–7).

*R4. Rao, B. V. P., Pennsylvania State University, University Park, Pa. (private communication, 1965).

R5. Rao, C. N. R., *Chemical Applications of Infrared Spectroscopy*, Academic Press, New York, 1963.

R5a. Rassow, J., Über ein neues Verfahren zur Bestimmung optischer Parameter an dunnen streuenden und inhomogenen Schichten im Bereich der Totalreflexion, *Optik*, **22**, 527 (1965).

*R6. Rawlins, T. G. R., Attenuated Total Reflection Spectroscopy, *Can. Spectry.*, **9**, 12 (1963).

*R7. Rawlins, T. G. R., Measurement of the Resistivity of Epitaxial Vapor Grown Films of Silicon by an Infrared Technique, *J. Electrochem. Soc.*, **111**, 810 (1964).

*R8. Reed, A. H., Western Reserve University, Cleveland, Ohio (private communication, 1965).

*R9. Reichert, K-H., Anwendung der ATR-Methode zur infrarotspektrospischen Untersuchung von Mehrschicht-Anstrichfilmen, *Farbe lacke*, **72**, 13 (1966).

R10. Renard, R. H., Total Reflection: A New Evaluation of the Goos-Hänchen Shift, *J. Opt. Soc. Am.*, **54**, 1190 (1964).

R10a. Rhein, W. J., Demonstration of Penetration of Potential Barriers, *Am. J. Phys.*, **31**, 808 (1963).

*R11. Robinson, F. P., and S. N. Vinogradov, Infrared Attenuated Total Reflection Spectra of Aqueous Solutions of Some Amino Acids, *Appl. Spectry.*, **18**, 62 (1964).

R12. Roblin, M. L., Étude de méthodes de réfractométrie utilisant le pouvoir réflecteur, *Rev. Opt.*, **44**, 341 (1965).

R13. Roblin, M. L., Étude de méthodes de réfractométrie utilisant le pouvoir réflecteur, *Rev. Opt.*, **44**, 410 (1965).

R14. Rogers, G. L., Total Internal Reflexion and Huygens' Construction: The Immersion Grating, *Nature*, **160**, 25 (1947).

R15. Rose, H., and A. Wiegrefe, Versuche über die Sichtbarmachung von Lichtströmungen durch die Einfallsebene im isotropen Medium bei Totalreflexion, *Ann. Physik*, **50**, 281 (1916).

R17. Rostagni, A., Über die bei der Totalreflexion im zweiten Medium strömende Energie, *Ann. Physik*, **12**, 1011 (1932).

R16. Rostagni, A., Le Manifestazioni Luminose Nel Secondo Mezzo Nella Riflessione Totale, *Nuovo Cimento*, **4**, 81 (1927).

R18. Rostagni, A., Su la Riflessione Totale, *Nuovo Cimento*, **4**, 218 (1927).

*S1. Samoggia, G., A. Nucciotti, and G. Chiarotti, Optical Detection of Surface State in Ge, *Phys. Rev.*, **144**, 749 (1966).

S1a. Sandford, B. P., Measurement of the Optical Constants of Thin Dielectric Films by Means of Frustrated Total Reflection, *J. Opt. Soc. Am.*, **48**, 482 (1958).

S1b. Sawyer, R. A., *Experimental Spectroscopy*, Dover Publications, New York, 1963.

S1c. Scandone, F., and G. Leone, Studio della trasmissione e riflessione in lamine sottili di indice inferiore all'unità, *Nuovo Cimento*, **1**, 325 (1943).

S2. Schafer, C., Über eine modifizierte Reststrahlmethode für das sichtbare und ultraviolette Spektralgebiet, *Z. Physik*, **75**, 687 (1932).

S3. Schaefer, C., and G. Gross, Untersuchungen über die Totalreflexion, *Ann. Physik*, **32**, 648 (1910).

S4. Schaefer, C., and R. Pich, Ein Beitrag zur Theorie der Totalreflexion, *Ann. Physik*, **30**, 245 (1937).

S5. Schaefer, C., and C. v. Fragstein, Zur Theorie der Reflexion und Brechung, *Ann. Physik*, **6**, 39 (1949).

*S6. Schatz, P. H., and J. S. Plaskett, On the Robinson and Price (Kramers-Kronig) Method of Interpreting Reflection Data Taken through a Transparent Window, *J. Chem. Phys.*, **38**, 612 (1963).

S6a. Schilling, H., Die Strahlversetzung bei der Reflexion linear oder elliptisch polarisierter ebener Wellen an der Trennebene zwischen absorbierenden Medien, *Ann. Physik*, **16**, 122 (1965).

S6b. Schineller, E. R., Variable Optical Double Prism Attenuator with Multi-wavelength Spacing, Polytech. Inst. of Brooklyn, *Microwave Res. Inst. Symp. Ser.*, **14**, 517 (1964).

S7. Schmaltz, G., *Technische Oberflächenkunde*, J. Springer, Berlin, 1936.

S8. Schmidt, O.v., Über die Totalreflexion in der Akustik und Optik. (Auf Grund experimenteller Ergebnisse der Springseismik), *Ann. Physik*, **19**, 891 (1934).

S9. Schmidt, P. F., and W. Michel, Anodic Formation of Oxide Films on Silicon, *J. Electrochem. Soc.*, **104**, 230 (1957).

S10. Schulz, L. G., Experimental Studies of the Optical Properties of Liquid Hg and Ga in the Wavelength Range of 0.23 μ to 13 μ, *J. Opt. Soc. Am.*, **47**, 64 (1957).

S10a. Schulz, L. G., and F. R. Tangherlini, Optical Constants of Ag, Au, Cu and Al. II. The Index of Refraction *n*, *J. Opt. Soc. Am.*, **44**, 362 (1954).

S11. Schuster, A., On the Total Reflexion of Light, *Proc. Roy. Soc. (London)*, **107A**, 15 (1925).

*S11a. Schwab, O., Infrarotspektrometrische Analyse von Papierverdelungsmittelen *Papier*, **19**, 115 (1965).

S12. Sélényi, P., Sur l'existence et l'observation des ondes lumineuses sphériques inhomogènes, *Compt. Rend.*, **157**, 1408 (1913).

S13. Seraphin, B. O., and D. A. Orton, Field Effect Light Modulation in Ge, *J. Appl. Phys.*, **34**, 1743 (1963).

S14. Seraphin, B. O., Optical Field Effect in Silicon, *Phys. Rev.*, **140**, A1716 (1965).

S15. Seraphin, B. O., Electroreflectance in GaAs, *Proc. Phys. Soc.*, **87**, 239 (1966).

S16. Shaklee, K. L., F. H. Pollak, and M. Cardona, Electroreflectance at a Semiconductor–Electrolyte Interface, *Phys. Rev. Letters*, **15**, 883 (1965).

*S17. Sharpe, L. H., Observation of Molecular Interactions in Oriented Monolayers by Infrared Spectroscopy Involving Total Internal Reflection, *Proc. Chem. Soc.*, **1961**, 461.

*S18. Sharpe, L. H., New Infrared Spectroscopic Technique, *Bell Lab. Record*, **40**, 62 (1962).

*S19. Sherman, B., Infrared Spectroscopy by Attenuated Total Reflection, *Appl. Spectry.*, **18**, 7 (1964).

S20. Shklyarevskii, I. N., V. P. Kostyuk, L. G. Lelyuk, and R. G. Yarovaya, On the Magnitude and Sign of the Phase Difference $\Delta = \delta_p - \delta_s$ Resulting from TIR, *Opt. Spectry.*, **18**, 476 (1965).

S21. Shockley, W., and G. L. Pearson, Modulation of Conductance of Thin Films of Semiconductors by Surface Charges, *Phys. Rev.*, **74**, 232 (1948).

S21a. Shurcliff, W. A., *Polarized Light*, Harvard Univ. Press, Cambridge, Mass., 1962.

S22. Simon, I., Spectroscopy in Infrared by Reflection and Its Use for Highly Absorbing Substances, *J. Opt. Soc. Am.*, **41**, 336 (1951).

S23. Simon, I., and H. O. McMahon, Study of the Structure of Quartz, Cristobalite and Vitreous Silica by Reflection in Infrared, *J. Chem. Phys.*, **21**, 23 (1953).

S24. Sliker, T. R., and J. M. Jost, Linear Electro-Optic Effect and Refractive Indices of Cubic ZnTe, *J. Opt. Soc. Am.*, **56**, 130 (1966).

S25. Sloane, H. J., T. Johns, W. F. Ulrich, and W. J. Cadman, Infrared Examination of Micro Samples—Application of a Specular Reflectance System, *Appl. Spectry.*, **4**, 130 (1965).

S26. Spitzer, W. G., and H. Y. Fan, Determination of Optical Constants and Carrier Effective Mass of Semiconductors, *Phys. Rev.*, **106**, 882 (1957).

S27. Spitzer, W. G., F. A. Trumbore, and R. A. Logan, Properties of Heavily Doped *n*-type Ge, *J. Appl. Phys.*, **32**, 1822 (1961).

S28. Spitzer, W. G., and D. A. Kleinman, Infrared Lattice Bands of Quartz, *Phys. Rev.*, **121**, 1324 (1961).

S29. Stasiw, O., Messungen des bei der Totalreflexion in das zweite Mittel eindringenden Lichtes, *Ann. Physik*, **3**, 209 (1929).

S30. Steele, E. L., W. C. Davis, and R. L. Treuthart, A Laser Output Coupler Using Frustrated Total Internal Reflection, *Appl. Opt.*, **5**, 5 (1966).

S31. Stern, F., Transmission of Isotropic Radiation Across an Interface Between Two Dielectrics, *Appl. Opt.*, **3**, 111 (1964).

S31a. Stewart, R. D., and D. S. Erley, Detection of Volatile Organic Compounds and Toxic Gases in Humans by Rapid Infrared Techniques, in *Progress in Chemical Toxicology,* Vol. 2, A. Stolman, Ed., Academic Press, New York, 1965.

S32. Stokes, G. G., On the Formation of the Central Spot of Newton's Rings Beyond the Critical Angle, *Trans. Cambridge Phil. Soc.*, **8**, 642 (1849).

S33. Sullivan, M. V., The Simultaneous Polishing of Both Faces of Germanium Slices, *Electrochem. Tech.*, **5**, 33 (1967).

T1. Taylor, A. M., and A. M. Glover, Studies in Refractive Index. I and II, *J. Opt. Soc. Am.*, **23**, 206 (1933).

T2. Taylor, A. M., and D. A. Durfee, Studies in Refractive Index. III, *J. Opt. Soc. Am.*, **23**, 263 (1933).

T3. Taylor, A. M., and A. King, Studies in Refractive Index. Part IV, *J. Opt. Soc. Am.*, **23**, 308 (1933).

T4. Turbadar, T., Complete Absorption of Plane Polarized Light by Thin Metallic Films, *Opt. Acta,* **11**, 207 (1964).

T5. Turner, A. F., Some Current Developments in Multilayer Optical Films, *J. Phys. Radium,* **11**, 444 (1950).

T6. Turner, A. F., Frustrated Total Reflection Interference Filter, U. S. Pat. 2,601,806 (July 1, 1952).

T7. Turner, A. F., and P. H. Berning, Induced Absorption in Thin Films, *J. Opt. Soc. Am.*, **45**, 408(A) (1955).

*T8. Turner, A. F., Bausch & Lomb, Rochester, New York (private communication, 1966).

*T9. Tweet, A. G., G. L. Gaines, Jr., and J. W. D. Bellamy, Angular Dependence of Fluorescence from Chlorophyll *a* in Monolayers, *J. Chem. Phys.*, **41**, 1008 (1964).

U1. Ujhelyi, G. K., and S. T. Ribeiro, An Electro-Optical Light Intensity Modulator, *Proc. IEEE,* **52**, 845 (1964).

U2. Usiglio, G., Sulla Rifrazione di uni Onda Elettromagnetica con Particolare Riguardo al Caso di Riflessione Totale, *Nuovo Cimento,* **13**, 180 (1936).

V1. Vafiady, V. G., Production of Short Light Flashes by Interrupted TIR, *Opt. Spectry.*, **14**, 377 (1963).

V2. Vašíček, A., *Optics of Thin Films,* North-Holland Pub. Co., Amsterdam, and Interscience, New York, 1960.

V3. Vašíček, A., *Tables for the Determination of the Optical Constants from the Intensities of Reflected Light,* Vol. 40, Czech. Acad. Sci., 1964, p. 113.

V4. Vincent-Geisse, J., M. Queyrel, and J. Lecomte, Méthode par réflexion pour la détermination des constantes optiques dans l'infrarouge de solides très absorbants, *Compt. Rend.*, **247**, 1330 (1958).

V5. Vincent-Geisse, J., Utilisation des couches minces a la détermination des constantes optiques de cristaux absorbants dans l'infrarouge, *J. Phys. Radium,* **25**, 291 (1964).

V6. Vincent-Geisse, J., and J. Dayet, Réflexion et transmission a la surface d'un milieu absorbant. Application a l'étude critique de la méthode du refractomètre d'Abbe pour la détermination des indices de réfraction, *J. Phys. Radium,* **26**, 66 (1965).

*V7. Vincent-Geisee, J., Réflexion totale attenuée, *Méthodes Phys. Analyse* (GAMS), No. 3–4, 108 (1965).

V8. Voigt, W., Zur Theorie der Beugung ebener inhomogener Wellen an einem geradlinig begrenzten unendlichen und absolut schwarzen Schirm, *Nachr. Akad. Wiss. Goettingen,* **3**, 1 (1899).

V9. Voigt, W., Über die Schwingungen im zweiten Medium bei totaler Reflexion, *Ann. Physik,* **34**, 797 (1911).

V10. Voigt, W., Zwei Antworten, *Ann. Physik,* **36**, 866 (1911).

*W1. Weintraub, S., Clean Surfaces and Surface Phenomena in Semiconductors, *Nature,* **199**, 238 (1963).

W2. Weltner, W. W., Jr., and D. McLeod, Spectroscopy of Carbon Vapor Condensed in Rare Gas Matrices at 4° and 20°K, *J. Chem. Phys.*, **40**, 1305 (1964).

W3. Weltner, W. W., Jr., and D. McLeod, Spectroscopy of TaO and TaO_2 in Neon and Argon Matrices at 4° and 20°K, *J. Chem. Phys.*, **42**, 882 (1965).

*W4. Wendlandt, W. W., and H. G. Hecht, *Reflectance Spectroscopy,* Interscience, New York, 1966.

W5. Wiegrefe, A., Neue Lichtströmungen bei Totalreflexion. Beiträge zur Kenntnis des Poyntingschen Satzes, *Ann. Physik,* **45**, 465 (1914).

W6. Wiegrefe, A., Neue Lichtströmungen bei Totalreflexion. Beiträge zur Kenntnis des Poyntingschen Vektors (2. Mitteilung), *Ann. Physik,* **50**, 277 (1916).

W7. Wiener, O., Stehende Lichtwellen und die Schwingungsrichtung polarisierten Lichtes, *Ann. Physik,* **40**, 203 (1890).

*W8. Wilhite, R. N., and R. F. Ellis, The Infrared Determination of Nitrate Ion in Aqueous Solutions by Attenuated Total Reflection, *Appl. Spectry.*, **17**, 168 (1963).

*W9. Wilks, P. A., Jr., Wilks Scientific Corp., Norwalk, Conn. (private communication, 1966).

*W9a. Wilks, P. A., Jr., and T. Hirschfeld, Internal Reflection Spectroscopy, *Applied Spectroscopy Reviews*, E. G. Brame, Ed., Marcel Dekker, New York, 1967.

W10. Williams, R., Electric Field Induced Light Absorption in CdS, *Phys. Rev.*, **117**, 1487 (1960).

W11. Wolfe, W. L., S. S. Ballard, and K. A. McCarthy, Refractive Index of Special Crystals and Certain Glasses, in *American Institute of Physics Handbook,* 2nd ed., D. E. Gray, Ed., McGraw-Hill, New York, 1963, Sec. 6, p. 11.

W12. Wood, R. W., *Physical Optics,* 3rd ed., Macmillan, New York, 1934.

W13. Wood, R. W., Über die Einschliessung von Strahlung durch Totalreflexion, *Physik. Z.*, **14**, 270 (1913).

*Y1a. Yamada, H., and K. Suzuki, Attenuated Total Reflection Spectra of Naphthalene Single Crystal, *Spectrochim. Acta* (1967).

Y1. Young, T. R., Frustrated Total Reflection—Its Application to Proximity Problems in Metrology, *J. Opt. Soc. Am.*, **51**, 1038 (1961).

Y2. Young, T. R., and B. D. Rothrock, Theory of Frustrated Total Reflection Involving Metallic Surfaces, *J. Res. Natl. Bur. Std.*, **67A**, 115 (1963).

Z1. Zernicke, F., Latest Wave in Physical Optics, *J. Opt. Soc. Am.*, **47**, 466 (1957).

*Z2. Zolotarev, V. M., and L. D. Kislovskii, On the Choice of the Optimum Conditions for the Production of Spectra by the Frustrated Total Internal Reflection Method, *Opt. Spectry.*, **19**, 346 (1965).

*Z3. Zolotarev, V. M., and L. D. Kislovskii, On the Possibilities of Studying Band Contours in Frustrated Total Internal Reflection Spectrophotometry, *Opt. Spectry.*, **19**, 446 (1965).

*Z4. Zolotarev, V. M., and L. D. Kislovskii, An Attachment for IKS-14 Spectrophotometer for Obtaining Spectra of Liquid and Solid Samples by the Total Internal Reflection Method, *Pribory i. Tekhn. Eksperim.*, **5**, 175 (1964).

Subject Index*

* **Boldface** page numbers refer to detailed discussion of subject; *italic* page numbers refer to tables or illustrations.